L

Jane Legget was born and grew up in Scotland. She graduated from the University of Durham and read Ethnology at Oxford University before taking a Master's degree at the State University of New York. A compulsive visitor to places of historic interest, she has worked in museums in Essex and Leicestershire, and is currently Keeper of Leicestershire History. Jane Legget lives in the Midlands.

LOCAL HEROINES

A Women's History Gazetteer
of
England, Scotland and Wales

JANE LEGGET

LONDON

PANDORA

BOSTON   SYDNEY   WELLINGTON

First published in Great Britain by Pandora Press, an imprint
of the trade division of Unwin Hyman Limited, in 1988

Unwin Hyman Limited
15–17 Broadwick Street
London W1V 1FP

Allen & Unwin Inc.,
8 Winchester Place, Winchester
Mass. 01890

Allen & Unwin Australia Pty Ltd
8 Napier Street, North Sydney, NSW 2060, Australia

Allen & Unwin New Zealand Pty Ltd with the
Port Nicholson Press
60 Cambridge Terrace, Wellington, New Zealand

British Library Cataloguing in Publication Data
Legget, Jane
    Local heroines: a women's history gazetteer of
    England, Scotland and Wales.
    1. Women—Great Britain—Biography
    I. Title
    920.72'0941   C73320

ISBN 0–86358–037–8 (c)
       0–86358–193–5 (p)

Printed and bound in Great Britain at The Bath Press, Avon

'AND GREET A KINDRED SPIRIT HOVERING NEAR'

Epitaph to **Lady Anna Millar** inscribed on her memorial in Bath Abbey and composed by **Anna Seward**, 1781.

Contents

Acknowledgments

There are many people who have helped in the preparation of this in so many ways. Their enthusiasm has been a constant source of encouragement. I should especially like to thank Judith Mills and her mother Dorothy Mills, Rory O'Brien, Debra Mancoff, Steve Wood, Andrew Chisholm, Gail Green, John Faure, Roger Bettess, Dee and Dick High, Lyn Marks, Paul and Marie-Suzon Stenhouse, the Lady Saye and Sele, Vera and Gerry Russell, Beth Hill, Nora King, Lee Jolliffe, all of whom have generously shared their hospitality, map-reading skills, local knowledge and moral support during the project. A special 'thank you' is due to Helen Bass and Dr Betty Bass who have, in the spirit of heroines, come to the rescue with the title *Local Heroines*. I must also thank all the members of my family who found themselves unavoidably but willingly drawn into the project, and whose continuing interest in its progress has spurred me on: my parents Wilma and Robin Legget, my sisters Catherine Legget and Sheila Legget Evans, my brother Robert Legget, my sister-in-law Shelagh Legget and my brother-in-law Richard Evans. The late Thurston M. Moore helped me in the initial stages with his reassuring confidence in the Gazetteer's possibilities.

I should also like to thank all the librarians, incumbents, proprietors and local historians who have answered my many queries, granted me access to books and records, shown me round their homes, churches, chapels, communities and institutions with such knowledge, enthusiasm and generosity. David Doughan of the Fawcett Library has been forthcoming with many helpful comments and suggestions. In the course of the research I have met so very many marvellous people who have extended a warm welcome and generously shared their time and local insights, which has made the work a special pleasure.

Philippa Brewster, Candida Lacey, Helen Mott, Helen Wythers and their colleagues at Pandora Press deserve to have a purple plaque of their own. They have certainly earned a place in my gallery of local heroines and I should like to record my thanks for their sisterly encouragement and gentleness with a novice and their warm exhortations throughout this lengthy project.

My lasting debt of gratitude is to Douglas Russell, without whom this work could never have been undertaken. His endless patience, his computing skills which brought me into the twentieth century, his tolerance and understanding, his faith in the Gazetteer and his willingness to share our lives with so many remarkable women for so long have made this book as much his as anyone's.

Illustrations

xi

Introduction

This book is a reaction to all those guidebooks featuring too many men and few, if any, women. The overwhelming presence of famous men – kings, politicians, lawyers, generals, local dignitaries, and proud citizens, often eminently forgettable – and the virtual absence of women deemed worthy of mention is yet another example of how women have been excluded from public history. As a compulsive seeker-out of historic places to visit and reader of local guidebooks, I have found this increasingly irritating. We know that women must have shared in shaping their communities, be it London or Losslemouth, but this is not apparent from reading the average town guide or list of worthies. Indeed there is a marked tendency to latch onto a casual link with a male figure of national standing at the expense of a local woman whose actions may have made a more substantial contribution to the locality or regon. It is the aim of this book to change the focus of visitors seeking the haunts of significant figures, and if I am guilty of erring in the other direction, by highlighting tenuous associations with women whose achievements deserve our attentions, I am heartily unrepentant.

There is a special indefinable feeling when you stand where a favourite heroine has stood; where you can admire a view, the same view that she has seen and enjoyed, albeit possibly changed beyond recognition. Equally the birthplace or burial place of someone whose past achievements may have shaped a nation's history, delighted thousands of readers, influenced the lives of succeeding generations, can be extraordinarily moving. Someone's former home, a studio, place of work or place of worship can inspire and energise a visitor years later, particularly so when that 'someone' is a woman. That, at least, has been my experience.

Many sites with such associations with great personalities have become almost obligatory destinations for tourists and travellers in Britain, but how many of these are associated with the lives and achievements of women? Apart from Jane Austen's home at Chawton in Hampshire and the Brontë sisters' Haworth Parsonage, there are few places which readily spring to mind. Yet we know of many women whose place in history has been acknowledged in other ways, and current research into women's history is uncovering more whose achievements are being reassessed and revalued. Tourism is becoming an increasingly important industry throughout Britain and many apparently unlikely places are actively seeking to attract visitors. Even industrial areas, generally regarded as unattractive to tourists, are competing with the established beauty spots, stately homes, picturesque villages and architectural gems. It is surprising that so many towns and villages continue to neglect or undervalue their past associations with significant women.

There is a long tradition of tourism playing on the lives of important individuals, be they sovereigns, saints, statesmen or literary figures, to attract visitors to a place. Chaucer's account in his *Canterbury Tales* [*c.* 1387] of the pilgrims travelling to the tomb of Thomas à Becket in Canterbury is testimony to the fact that women as well as men took part in such journeys. It would be difficult to list the number of places where King Charles I is said to have hidden to avoid his captors or where other kings have stayed overnight. It would be equally difficult to account for all the hostelries which have capitalised on this link, however hypothetical, in their promotion and advertising over the centuries. Certainly many English hotels, inns and public houses boast in their publicity that 'Queen Elizabeth I slept here', whilst Scottish establishments claim that 'Mary Queen of Scots slept here'. The connection with royalty [if it was good enough for a sovereign, it is good enough for you] is valued as much as the connection with these two women as historically significant individuals in their own right. Besides, it is rarely explained that the sovereign often embarked on royal progresses throughout the realm, in order to hold court in different places, administer justice locally, interview landowners and aristocrats in their own domain, assess their loyalty to the Crown, their power and wealth, and therefore was bound to stay overnight in all sorts of accommodation *en route*.

For some time I had been keeping an index of local associations with better-known women, and gradually I took steps to explore these and to seek out others. The search continues to be rewarding and fun, but the way has often proved frustrating and obscured. Sometimes, I knew only of a general association of an individual with a particular place; referring to published biographies has not always been helpful for this specific task but has always yielded more information and insights into the women. Biographers have developed their own interests in their subjects, and the published works may deal more with relationships, character, writings and achievements, rather than dwelling on the precise localities where their subjects lived and worked. Autobiographies may be more informative about places and often offer a wealth of detail, but inevitably rarely extend to cover place of death or burial. Clearly published biography only serves as a source of information for those women about whom enough material is known to have survived to attract an author or researcher. Brief references have been found in biographical dictionaries, and these have proved useful starting points for many searches. Local histories have also proved useful, but generally these titles are readily available only in libraries in the immediate vicinity. Some communities can boast a published local women's history guide [e.g., Cambridge and Sheffield] or a women's history trail [e.g., Manchester] but these are few and far between. These are, however, both informative and entertaining publications, often modestly produced. Doubtless more will appear as women's history groups, adult education classes and individuals publish their findings in accessible form.

The phrase 'hidden from history' has justly been used to describe the way in which traditional historians have treated the lives of both ordinary and, dishearteningly, exceptional women. However, academic historians have recently turned their attention to the study of women's experience in earlier centuries, both collective experience of groups or classes of women and of individual women whose lifestories, 're-excavated', can now intrigue and inspire us. This is an encouraging trend, and many informal women's history groups and dedicated amateur local historians are matching the discoveries of their academic colleagues by their own researches. Using local informants and recording memories of oral histories, many women are finding their pursuit of local history rewarding not only for themselves but in giving recognition to the achievements of older members of their community, recording experiences from personal accounts which shed new light on events, described from the standpoint of people who lived through them as participants or close observers, and sharing them with a wider and very appreciative audience. Some of this work is being published in local journals, in small booklets, as well as professionally produced books, reaching a variety of audiences, often very localised.

Other media are also focusing on women's experience. Women's lives and creative works increasingly provide the subject matter and content for films, radio and television documentaries and theatrical performances. Exhibitions of women's art are now shown in traditional as well as more adventurous art galleries. Since 1984 Women, Heritage and Museums [WHAM], a group of curators and users of museums and art galleries, has been working to make their collections more relevant and more accessible to those interested in women's contribution to the past and present, and to promote the positive display of women's history and creative heritage. However, there are many local landmarks which remain overlooked or unacknowledged. Local pride in a native or former resident in a community often takes the form of a statue in the town centre, a memorial in the local church or a 'blue plaque' or other marker on a building. The majority of people thus recognised are male. The decision to make a permanent, formal recognition of such associations has usually rested with the city or town 'fathers', with the initiative taken by a historical society, a civic trust, proud descendants or other appreciation society. Planning permission, granted by local authorities, is required now for the erection of any commemorative sign or similar monument. Local authorities have included women as local councillors since 1907. The time is surely ripe for approaching town and city 'mothers' and other councillors about public recognition for local women. Where a local authority has formally adopted an equal opportunities policy, there should be many receptive members on the planning committee.

Pressing for the rescue of historic landmarks is not a new cause for women. Octavia Hill was one of the three founders of the National Trust for the Places of Historic Interest and Natural Beauty in 1895, and that body continues to rely on its women members for its base support. In the United States of America, Ann Pamela Cunningham initiated and directed the nationwide campaign to save George Washington's home at Mount Vernon in Virginia as long ago as 1853. The success of this way of organising women across that continent, at a time when communications were slow by today's standards, demonstrated to the leaders of the American Women's Rights Movement that it was possible to mobilise support among women for issues that mattered to them. Following that example, the Women's Rights Movement was represented in all the US territories. It should be much easier to find support locally for more modest projects seeking tangible recognition of women's past and present achievements. One example of a current campaign is the Pankhurst Appeal, which is restoring the Pankhurst home in Manchester as both a local landmark and a resource centre for the study of various campaigns on women's issues, including the 'Votes for Women' struggle in which the Pankhursts played leading roles.

The women who feature in this Gazetteer represent the wide range of activities and achievements of women in England, Scotland and Wales since the first century AD. It is inevitably selective, and the choice has been a personal one. I have tried to cover the whole period, but the survival of individual women in the historical record, especially for the early centuries, is sporadic. In the later period, more fascinating women are coming to light as more biographies appear in print. The decision to include living women only when there are sites closely associated with them that are readily accessible to the general public was taken out of respect for those individuals. There is also a second and very encouraging reason: there are now thousands of women living lives which are creative, demanding, productive, and leading their chosen fields. We can already learn about their achievements through other media, although this time we must ensure that their exemplary achievements stay in the public consciousness. We can gain so much from their experience.

Many of the sites mentioned in the book are in their own way architectural monuments. In the case of many buildings featured in the Gazetteer, it is often only the exterior that can be seen. The owners and occupiers deserve that their privacy be respected. It is also unavoidable that the majority of women featured here came from relatively privileged backgrounds. These were the ones who had access to the books, the education, the financial independence or the social connections which enabled them to attain their goals or lead their exceptional lives. Thus there are many stately homes, castles, rectories and vicarages, and other substantial properties, which may have been maintained or preserved on account of their architectural merit or links with powerful families, and where the association with a significant woman has been incidental to its survival today. Many women have played influential roles as mothers, sisters, daughters or wives of key figures in local, national or international history, and some of these feature in the Gazetteer. In general, though, I have tried to focus on women who are noteworthy for achievements in their own right. In the case of royalty, I have concentrated on women who ruled as sovereign rather than as Queen Consort, but where they, by design or circumstance, found themselves in pivotal positions in political struggles or dynastic successions, affecting the course of a nation's history, it seemed important and appropriate to include them. I am also aware that working-class and black women are under-represented. I hope that as more work is done to highlight the contribution of the many deserving women currently missing from this book, readers will draw the author's and publishers' attention to this for inclusion in the next edition. We recognise that this book is just a start and hope that it will prove to be a growing project, with the help of women from all corners of Britain and visitors from abroad. If the present work puts the women mentioned here on the cultural map of Britain and prompts the recognition of them and other wonderful women in their localities, it will have taken the direction I intended. At the end of her history of *The Suffragette Movement* [1931] Sylvia Pankhurst referred to the continuing need to work to extend the widest opportunities to all women; her words can equally be applied to the task of gaining public recognition for past achievements of women as a source of reassurance and inspiration to present and future generations of women: 'Great is the work which remains to be accomplished!'

My constant companion on so many of my expeditions has been Celia Fiennes, the late seventeenth-century compulsive traveller whose journals are published as *The Illustrated Journeys of Celia Fiennes c. 1682–1712*, C. Morris [ed.], Macdonald, London, 1982. Her desire to see her country sent her on her 'Great Journeys', a course she thoroughly recommended:

> If all persons, both Ladies, much more Gentlemen, would spend some of their time in Journeys to visit their native Land, and be curious to inform themselves and make observations of the pleasant prospects, good buildings, different produces and manufactures of each place, with the variety of sports and recreations they are adept to, would be a souveraign remedy to cure or preserve from these epidemick diseases of vapours, should I add Laziness?

She concludes:

> With a hearty wish and recommendation to all, but especially my own Sex, the study of those things which tend to improve the mind and makes our Lives pleasant and comfortable as well as proffitable in all the Stages and Stations of our Lives, and render Suffering and Age supportable and death less formidable and a future State more happy.

In our very different times, such remarkable results cannot be guaranteed, but for those who wish to follow in the fooootsteps of some splendid characters, I hope that the way will be easier, and that this work will have put these women on the map.

How to use this book

The information in this book is presented in three ways:

[i] **The Maps**
[ii] **The Gazetteer**
[iii] **The Biographical Index**

THE MAPS

The island of Britain has been divided into maps for the purpose of indicating the rough location of the places entered in the Gazetteer. For precise locations, readers should always refer to larger scale maps, using the maps here only to make outline plans for routes, or to locate the general area of a place. The only places named and marked on the maps are those which feature in the Gazetteer. The boundaries of the administrative counties and regions are also shown. There are separate maps covering Central London, Kensington and Chelsea and the Greater London area. These show the boundaries of the Boroughs, the local administrative territories.

THE GAZETTEER

The Gazetteer of places associated with significant women and events is organised alphabetically by the name of the city, town, village or nearest sizeable community or local landmark. The placename is given first, followed by the administrative county [for England and Wales] or region [for Scotland]. London entries are arranged by Boroughs in alphabetical order. A map reference follows, and the places can then be located by reference to the maps. Each gazetteer entry names individuals or events associated with the place mentioned, including, where traced, location and brief description of relevant buildings, monuments, gravemarkers, plaques, etc., and some information about the women concerned and the nature of the association. These will vary widely in the amount of detail given. Where a reference is made to a literary work, only the date of the initial publication is given, as some works have appeared in several editions. Occasionally it has been possible to refer to current publications which relate specifically to that locality.

Many of the buildings mentioned are open to the public on a regular basis. These are indicated by ★; those maintained by the National Trust are marked ★[NT], and those by the National Trust for Scotland ★[NTS]. As the seasons and hours of opening vary from year to year, readers are advised to check the current arrangements for public openings with local tourist information offices. For the purposes of tourism Britain's summer appears to be defined as lasting from Easter weekend until late September and many seasonal openings fall within this period. Most churches and chapels are accessible but local arrangements are generally indicated by a sign outside the building or in the porch. Incumbents and churchwardens are always pleased to welcome interested visitors, but if a special journey is to be made it is worthwhile to write in advance to avoid disappointments. Sundays may be the best days for places of Christian worship, but visitors will be expected to respect the worship during services and sacred occasions of all religious faiths.

Other buildings or sites may be in private hands, and the owners' right to privacy should be respected at all times. Most properties featured here can be seen from public highways or footpaths. Institutional attitudes will vary but the response of most administrators has been encouraging and welcoming.

If you are planning a trip to a particular part of the country and want to find out whether there are any special associations in that region with interesting women from our past, you should refer directly to the Gazetteer of placenames, if you have already determined your destination. Alternatively you may be making a visit to a broader area or planning a route. In this case, refer to the map section first, where the maps also indicate the county boundaries. Guided by the places marked on the map, you can then look up entries in the Gazetteer to discover which places will hold most interest for you.

THE BIOGRAPHICAL INDEX

The biographical index is organised alphabetically by surname, the main entry generally under the name by which the woman is generally best known. Cross-references are given to other names – maiden names, married names, pen-names, nicknames – as necessary. Entries are not intended to be brief biographies; rather they are a guide to the sphere of achievement or interest, dates of active life of the woman named, together, where known, with a source of reference for further information. In general these are biographies or autobiographies and, as far as possible, more recent or readily accessible publications. The index then refers the reader to the Gazetteer entries which feature the woman concerned.

If you are interested in a particular woman and wish to find out where she lived, was educated, worked, wrote, died or was buried or commemorated, this is the starting point for you.

Entries on queens generally appear under their first name, e.g., **Anne**, **Elizabeth I**, **Philippa of Hainault** etc., unless they are regularly referred to with a surname, e.g., **Boleyn, Anne**; **Howard, Catherine**. Many of the women in this book had titles. These may have been awarded to a woman in recognition of her achievements, e.g., **Dame Ethel Smyth**; **Baroness Young**. Other women by virtue of the circumstances into which they were born or married [often both], may inherit or acquire titles, e.g., **Lady Mary Wortley Montagu**; **Georgiana Cavendish**, Duchess of Devonshire. Where these titles continue to serve as part of their identity, these are generally included both in the Biographical Index and the Gazetteer.

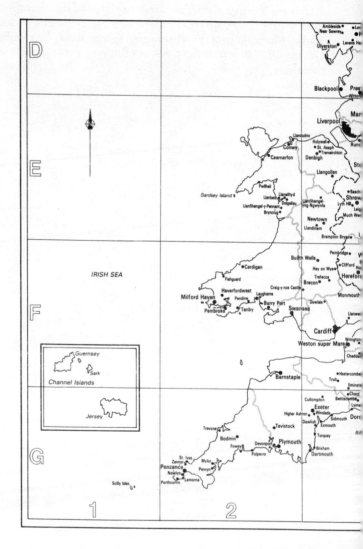

1. Southern Britain (England and Wales)

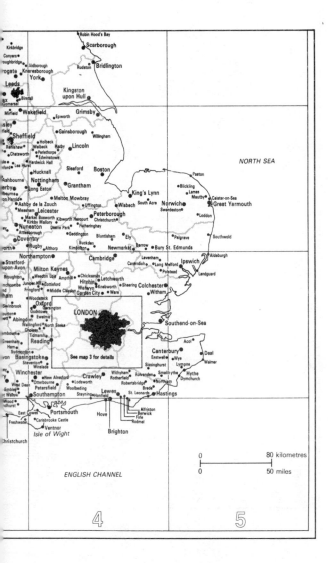

Kirkbridge
Conyers
roughbridge
rogate Knaresborough Aldborough
York
Leeds Birstall
ax
omersal
Mirfield Wakefield
sley Epworth
field
Sheffield Holbeck
Renishaw Welbeck Haxby
Chatsworth Perlethorpe
le Hardwick Hall
nford Las Hurst
Ashbourne Hucknall
erby Nottingham
bourne Long Eaton
on Harold Ashby de la Zouch Melton Mowbray
Masham Leicester Uffington
Market Bosworth Kibworth Harcourt
Kirkby Mallory Christchurch
Nuneaton Deene Park Fotheringhay
Attleborough Geddington Bluntisham
Coventry Buckden
orth Rugby Althorp Kimbolton
Northampton
Stratford-
upon-Avon Milton Keynes
Broughton Weedon Lois Ampthill Chicksands
nchcombe Juniper Hill Cottisford Letchworth
nd Fringford Middle Claydon Hitchin
ham Welwyn Knebworth
Woodstock Garden City Ware
Swinbrook Oxford Carsington
oulton Godstow
ett Abingdon Ewelme
Wallingford North Stoke
ambourn Cholsey
Greenham Tidmarsh
Ham Sydmonton
avon Basingstoke Steventon
Winslade
ry Winchester
West Dean New Alresford Crawley
Otterbourne Lodsworth
Embley Petersfield Woolbeding
nt Walton Lewes
Southampton Steyning
Wood
dhurst
East Cowes Portsmouth Hove
Freshwater Carisbrooke Castle
Ventnor Brighton
Isle of Wight
Christchurch

Robin Hood's Bay
Scarborough
Rudston Bridlington
Kingston
upon Hull
Grimsby
Gainsborough Willingham
Lincoln
Sleaford Boston
Grantham
King's Lynn
Wisbech South Acre Norwich
Peterborough Swardeston
Christchurch Loddon
Ely
Palgrave
Barrow Bury St. Edmunds
Newmarket
Cambridge Lavenham
Cavendish Long Melford Ipswich
Polstead
Sheering Colchester
Witham
LONDON
Southend-on-Sea
Canterbury
Eastwell Wye Deal
Sissinghurst Lympne Walmer
Withyham Rolvenden Smallhythe Hythe
Rotherfield Northiam Dymchurch
Robertsbridge
Brede
Honfield St. Leonards Hastings
Alfriston
Berwick
Firle
Rodmel

Paston
Blickling
Lamas
Maurtby Caistor-on-Sea
Great Yarmouth

Southwold

Aldeburgh
Landguard
Acol

NORTH SEA

See map 3 for details

0 ———————— 80 kilometres
0 ———————— 50 miles

ENGLISH CHANNEL

4   5

XXV

2. Northern Britain (northern England and Scotland)

xxvi

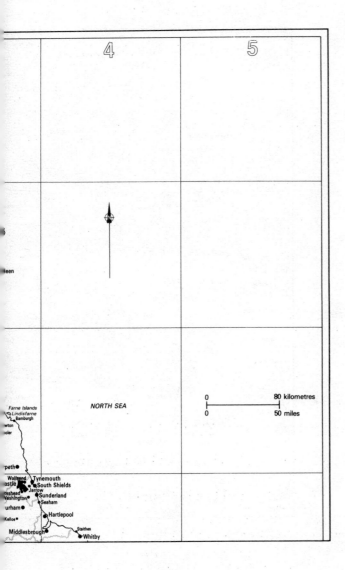

4

5

een

Farne Islands
Lindisfarne
Bamburgh
wton
oler

peth

Wallsend Tynemouth
astle South Shields
esshead Jarrow
Washington Sunderland
urham Seaham
Kelloe Hartlepool

Middlesbrough Staithes
Whitby

NORTH SEA

0   80 kilometres
0   50 miles

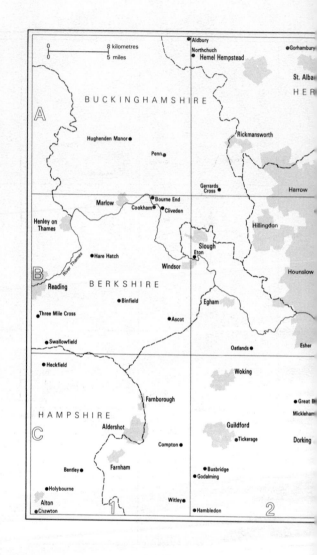

3. London and the Home Counties

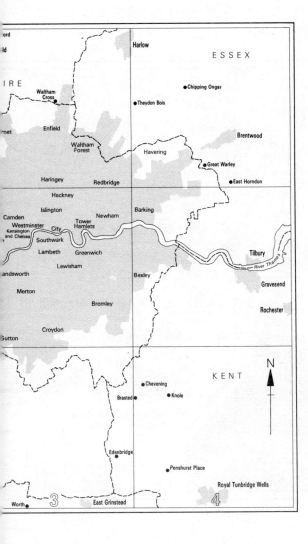

ord
ld
IRE
net

Waltham
Cross
Enfield
Waltham
Forest
Haringey
Hackney
Islington
Camden
Westminster
City
Kensington
and Chelsea
Southwark
Lambeth
Greenwich
Lewisham
andsworth
Merton
Croydon
Sutton

Harlow

ESSEX

●Chipping Ongar

●Theydon Bois

Brentwood

Havering

●Great Warley

Redbridge
●East Horndon

Newham
Tower
Hamlets
Barking

Bexley

Bromley

Tilbury

River Thames

Gravesend

Rochester

KENT

N

●Chevening
Brasted●
●Knole

Edenbridge

●Penshurst Place

Royal Tunbridge Wells

Worth●
③
East Grinstead
④

xxix

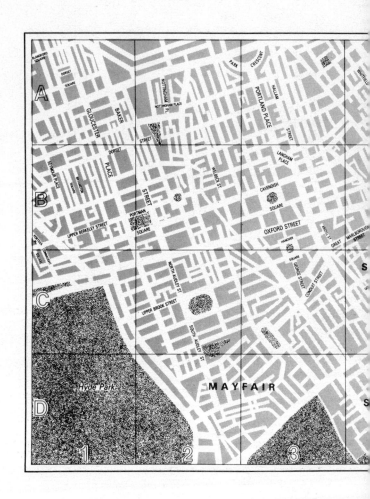

4. Central London

xxx

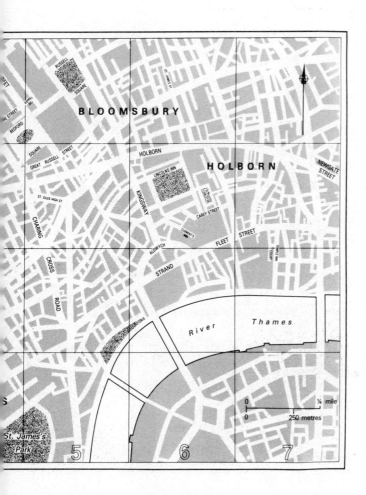

BLOOMSBURY

HOLBORN

River Thames

St. James's Park

5

6

7

0 ¼ mile
0 250 metres

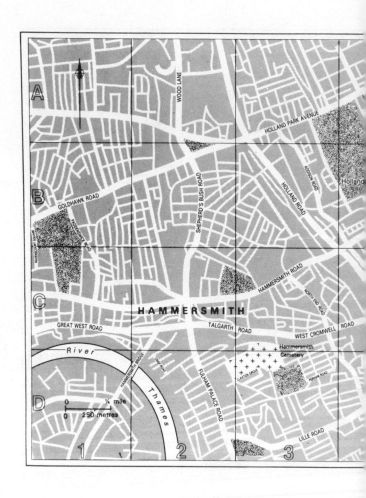

5. Kensington and Chelsea area

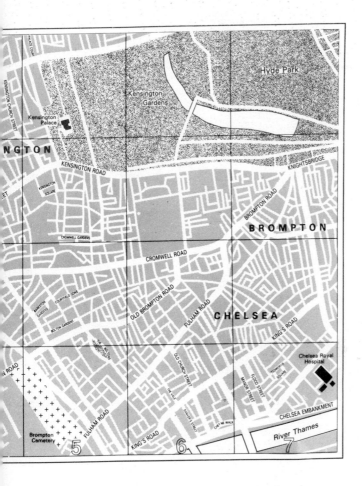

ENGLAND, SCOTLAND AND WALES

excluding London

A A

ABERDEEN, Grampian [see Map 2, B3]   Aberdeen was possibly the birthplace in *c.* 1712 of **Elizabeth Blackwell**, whose achievement as the author and illustrator of *A Curious Herbal* [1737] was undertaken out of necessity, when the husband with whom she eloped from Scotland fell into debt. What is certain is that **Mary Slessor**, the missionary who worked in West Africa, was born in the 'granite city' in 1848; the Rosemount viaduct now covers the site of her childhood home. A plaque on the United Presbyterian Church in Belmont Street records that she worshipped here before the family moved to Dundee when she was eleven years old. She received some of her scant education at the Sunday school run by the Church.

In many ways **Christian Watt**'s association with the city is the most remarkable. Born in 1833 into a nearby fishing community, she led a hard life preparing and selling the fishing catch, losing members of her family at sea. In 1879 she became an in-patient at Cornhill, Aberdeen's hospital for the mentally ill, which was to be her home until her death in 1923. In 1883 she began to write, almost obsessively, chronicling the lives of her people, friends and family, the local responses to national and international events, such as the Crimean, Boer and Great Wars. Her papers survive as unique testimony to a sane life, acutely and compassionately observing and documenting the northern experience over nearly a century.

ABINGDON, Oxfordshire [see Map 1, F4]   In 1873 Abingdon was the birthplace of **Dorothy Richardson**, whose early school days were spent here before her education was continued in Germany. Hers was a stressful youth and early adulthood, as both her parents demanded her attention. There were constant financial worries and consequent depression. However, after her mother's death in 1895, she was able to pursue her own career and lifestyle. She eventually became a writer, her major work being the thirteen-volume *Pilgrimage* [1915-67]. She wrote most perceptively from a woman's point of view, evolving a new style known since as stream of consciousness writing.

In 1936 RAF Abingdon was the scene of the start of a pioneering flight. The aviator **Beryl Markham** took off from the military airfield in a small plane, a Vega Gull, to cross the Atlantic flying 'west with the night'. She arrived in Nova Scotia twenty-one hours and twenty-five minutes later, the first person to cross the Atlantic from east to west taking off from England. It was a record-breaking flight which almost ended in disaster. The

3

experience led to her writing a moving autobiography, set mainly in Africa, which describes her early flying and a very tenacious will to lead her own life. She gave it the title *West with the Night* [1942]. An independent woman of many talents, she was Kenya's leading racehorse trainer and a professional bush pilot. At the time of this flight she was thirty-four and already accomplished in both these fields.

ACOL, Kent [see Map 1, F5]   Cleve Court on the Minster road in Acol, on the Isle of Thanet, was rented by **Baroness Orczy** and her husband 1908-9. She had already published *The Scarlet Pimpernel* [1905] and she followed up its success with further popular fictional works about the same central character. They had three Hungarian horses brought to Britain from her native Hungary. These were harnessed three abreast to a trap in which she and her husband used to ride round here.

ALDBOROUGH, North Yorkshire [see Map 1, D3]   The archaeological remains of the Roman settlement of Isurium Brigantium★ can be visited. The presence of the site testifies to the importance which the Romans placed on the area. It was the territory of the Brigantes, the tribe led by **Cartimandua**. At first the Romans supported her against her husband and rival Venutius, from AD 69, but, eventually defeated in 71, she submitted to Roman rule.

ALDBURY, Hertfordshire [see Map 3, A1]   **Mrs Humphrey Ward** lived at Great Stocks, a large brick country house now a country club on Stock Road to the north-east of the village. She held house parties and some of her Anti-Suffrage campaigning was planned at the house; her time was divided between here and London. Although she worked all her life to improve the lot of women, she did not believe in votes for women. In many ways a traditionalist, she felt that women could contribute more to improve society through the upbringing which they gave their children and the example set in the home. A local murder was incorporated in her novel *Marcella* [1894]. She died in 1920 in London, where she had been involved in social work and settlements, but was buried in the churchyard at Aldbury. Her grave lies to the north-west of the church; it is of marble and stone and commemorates her literary work with the image of a book.

ALDEBURGH, Suffolk [see Map 1, F5]   Two campaigning sisters, **Elizabeth Garrett Anderson** and the younger **Millicent Garrett Fawcett**, who was born in the town in 1847, were raised in this coastal town. Their father was a local merchant whose means enabled them to receive a good education. Both were active supporters of women's rights, Elizabeth becoming the first woman to qualify as a doctor in Britain, and Millicent as a leader of the women's suffrage movement. Elizabeth retired here, and her husband became involved in local politics. When he died in office as mayor she was asked to take on his duties. This she accepted and later was elected to a further term in her own right, thus becoming the first woman to be elected to this office in England. She died here in 1917 and was buried in the local churchyard.

1 Marianne North's grave in Alderley, Gloucestershire

ALDERLEY, Gloucestershire [see Map 1, F3] **Marianne North**, the botanical artist, retired here after a life of travelling and painting. She died here in 1890 and was buried on the southside of the churchyard. Her gravestone records her death but the inscription tells more about her father, a Member of Parliament, than it does about her even though she was a botanical artist of exceptional skill who travelled unaccompanied to remote parts of the world to record plant life. Her drawings are displayed in a special gallery at the Royal Botanical Gardens at Kew in London.

ALDERSHOT, Hampshire [see Map 3, C1] The town of Aldershot has long associations with the British Army. **Juliana Horatia Ewing**, author of many well-loved books such as *Lob-lie-by-the Fire* [1873] and *Jackanapes* [1873] for children, lived in Aldershot for seven years as an army wife, after accompanying her husband on a tour of duty in Canada in the 1870s. She enjoyed her writing, and many of her stories were written here. **Violette Szabo** married her French army officer husband here after she joined the Land Army in the First World War. The Museum of the Queen Alexandra's Royal Army Nursing Corps★ records the dedicated service of this women's service in war and peace time. It is in the Royal Pavilion, Farnborough Road.

ALFRISTON, Sussex [see Map 1, G4] In 1895 **Octavia Hill**, the social reformer, was also a founder of the preservation society, the National Trust for Places of Historic Interest and Natural Beauty. Her energies were mainly devoted to housing improvement in the capital city, but she appreciated the benefits of fresh air and the countryside. She was originally concerned that beautiful rural areas should be acquired and accessible to all. The desire to conserve, for future generations, buildings of historic and architectural interest soon followed and in 1896 she was involved in the acquisition by the Trust of the Old Clergy House ☆[NT] on the village green, its first property. It is quite a modest building compared with many owned by the Trust, but an important milestone in the development of the heritage preservation movement in Britain.

ALTHAM, Lancashire [see Map 1, D3]   **Lydia Becker**, one of the first women's suffragists, lived in Altham from 1837 when she was ten until 1865. She may have found the village too isolated from the intellectual and political society of Manchester which she found so stimulating. It was in Manchester in 1868 where she first made her mark with a speech in favour of women having the right to vote.

ALTHORP, Northamptonshire [see Map 1, E4]   Although Althorp Hall★ attracts visitors because it is the childhood home of Lady Diana Spencer, who became Princess of Wales in 1981, another interesting former resident was her ancestor **Georgiana Spencer**, later Georgiana Cavendish, Duchess of Devonshire. Born in 1757, she was brought up partly here and partly abroad, where she accompanied her parents on their visits to Europe. It was on one of these in 1773 that she met her future husband, the fifth Duke of Devonshire. Then she began her life at the centre of British political and social life. As a charming hostess with openly Whig sympathies, she had considerable influence on contemporary politics.

ALTON, Hampshire [see Map 3, C1]   In 1867 Alton was the scene of a tragic and brutal murder the young victim of which, **Fanny Adams**, is buried in the churchyard, where an ornate cross marks her grave. Her murderer, a legal clerk, was quickly apprehended, tried and hung. A small display about the infamous trial can be seen in the Curtis Museum★ in the High Street. Poor Fanny's name is much invoked now but her sad story is probably only remembered here. Sailors in the Royal Navy gave the unfortunate nickname 'Sweet Fanny Adams' to the canned mutton which was regularly served to them as rations. This new feature of the naval diet was introduced in the same year as the murder hit the headlines and some wag made the association between the meat cut up for canning and the child's dismembered body. The phrase 'Sweet Fanny Adams' has altered in significance over the years and now means 'nothing at all', hardly an appropriate epithet to be applied to such a horrific end to an innocent eight year old.

AMBLESIDE, Cumbria [see Map 1, D3]   **Harriet Martineau** spent her later years here at the Knoll, the house she had built here in 1845 on the west side of the Rydal Road, just up from Haven Cottage. By the time she died here in 1876 she had made a living for herself by writing and journalism for nearly fifty years, despite recurring deafness. Her novel *Deerbrook* had been published in 1839: here she wrote her autobiography and *A Complete Guide to the Lakes* [1855]. The house is well preserved. Although she died at the Knoll she was buried in Birmingham beside her mother. She became acquainted with **Dorothy Wordsworth** who lived with her brother,

William, and his family nearby at Rydal Mount. This was to be Dorothy's home from 1813 till her death in 1855. She kept detailed journals, many of which were the source of inspiration for her brother's poetry. She wrote some verse herself, but mainly devoted herself to encouraging and supporting William and his art.

Anne Jemima Clough started a school in Ambleside with her mother in 1852. Among their pupils was the future **Mrs Humphrey Ward**, then called by her maiden name Mary Arnold. This was further valuable experience in teaching for Anne Clough, whose career laid the foundation of women's university education. She served from its inception in 1866 on the North of England Council for Promoting the Higher Education of Women, later serving as first principal of Newnham College, one of the first women's colleges at Cambridge. In adult life Mrs Humphrey Ward shared her aim of establishing higher education for women.

AMPTHILL PARK, Bedfordshire [see Map 1, F4]   Before her divorce from Henry VIII was finalised in 1533, **Catherine of Aragon** had been detained in the castle in Ampthill, which at the time stood in the Great Park. The park is now a public recreation facility at the north of the town, but there is no obvious sign of the castle. However, on a gentle hill near the war memorial stands a stone cross. Its inscription recalls the life of the ill-treated queen: Ampthill is described as 'the mournful refuge of an injured queen'. Her refusal to break with her devout Roman Catholic tradition and permit a divorce led the king to break away from the old religion and set himself up as the head of the independent Church of England. About one mile further north beyond the park, some ruins remain of Houghton House★, the last home of **Mary Sidney**, Countess of Pembroke. She had it built with designs by the fashionable architect of the day, Inigo Jones, in 1615. She was altogether more fortunate than Queen Catherine. She was talented, wealthy and well connected, moving easily in literary circles and hosting writers at several of her homes.

ANCRUM, Borders [see Map 2, C3]   In 1545 the Battle of Ancrum was won by the Scots, thanks to the courageous fighting of **Lilliard**, a Scottish military heroine. Her parents and lover were killed during a raid by the English; she tried to get revenge by taking up arms herself. She managed to kill the leader of the English forces, but lost her own life. This was one of the last of the Scottish victories in the Border struggles. The site on Ancrum Moor is now called Lilliard's Edge.

APPLEBY, Westmorland, Cumbria [see Map 2, D3]   That inveterate builder, **Lady Anne Clifford** had the castle at Appleby restored and refortified in 1653. The country was still in turmoil as a result of the English Civil War. Appleby was originally the county town of Westmorland, and as such had strategic importance. It dominates the main thoroughfare, the Boroughgate. Lady Anne also established the almshouses called St Anne's Hospital in 1651 and carried out restoration of two churches: St Michael's in

Bondgate and St Lawrence's, where she was buried in 1676 beside her mother. Throughout her eighty-seven years she had asserted herself exactly according to her motto which can be read on the crosses at both ends of the Boroughgate: 'Retain your loyalty, preserve your rights.'

ARDVERIKIE, Grampian [see Map 2, B2]   **Queen Victoria** spent her first long holiday in Scotland at Ardverikie, the large highland mansion on the south shore of Loch Ness, in the summer of 1847. It can best be seen from the main road on the opposite shore. It is easy to understand why she fell in love with the Highlands, although throughout her stay the weather was wet and misty. She entertained thoughts of buying the house but it was not really large enough for all her entourage. In the end she bought Balmoral in Royal Deeside.

ASCOT, Berkshire [see Map 3, B1]   It was **Queen Anne** who, in 1711, introduced the horse-racing for which Ascot still has an international reputation. The date on the national racing calendar known as Ladies' Day, when traditionally women attending the races wear striking clothes, is also a red-letter day in the diaries of fashion designers. Both female and male designers aim to attract attention to their novel designs.

ASHBOURNE, Derbyshire [see Map 1, E3]   This market town in Derbyshire was the birthplace in the nineteenth century of two women of achievement. **Catherine Booth**, born in 1829 as Catherine Mumford, had a strict and somewhat stifling religious upbringing here, until her family moved to London when she was fifteen. She was always driven by a sense of Christian mission, and after associating with various non-conformist churches, founded the Salvation Army with her husband in 1877. **Eleanor Jourdain**, born here in 1863, made her contribution in the field of women's education, eventually becoming vice-principal of St Hugh's, a women's college at Oxford.

ASHBY DE LA ZOUCH, Leicestershire [see Map 1, E3]   **Mary Queen of Scots** was imprisoned in Ashby Castle★ in 1568 and 1569, in the charge of the Earl of Hastings. This was one of the first strongholds in which she spent her seventeen years in the power of her cousin the English queen, Elizabeth. The Hastings family, which dominated the town's history, was very much part of the establishment. However, in the eighteenth century **Selina Hastings**, Countess of Huntingdon, broke the mould and upset her husband's family by adopting the cause of religious reformists. Raised in the Church of England, she became aware of the need for reforms within the established Church. In 1738, ten years after her marriage, she was encouraged by her sister-in-law to help some Evangelicals. She supported the Methodists who were attempting to change the church from within, and in 1746 took a house, Ashby Place [no longer standing], in the town, leaving Donnington Hall, her husband's grand country seat. She was an heiress in her own right, and her husband's death left her with a considerable fortune which she spent in fostering Methodism in Britain and abroad. She was free to involve herself fully in her social and religious work. As a peeress she was able to appoint chaplains and found chapels, although after 1768 these were required to be registered as dissenting places of worship under the Toleration Act. The network of chapels and safe houses which had her patronage were collectively known as 'the Countess of Huntingdon's Connection'.

Despite her long and close association with non-conformism, her body is buried in St Helen's Parish Church, in the family vault. She had died in London in 1791. The brass plaque on the floor refers to her daughter, one of her four children all of whom she outlived. The Methodist church was the beneficiary of her will.

ASTLEY, Warwickshire [see Map 1, E3]   Astley Castle was one of the childhood homes of the ill-fated **Lady Jane Grey**. Her family were well established in court circles and ambitions for further power were pursued through Lady Jane being the granddaughter of Henry VIII's sister Mary. Her family had this teenager proclaimed sovereign on the death of Edward VI in 1553. Her reign lasted nine days, and eventually she suffered imprisonment and execution, along with her family.

ATTLEBOROUGH, Warwickshire [see Map 1, E3]   Now virtually a suburb of Nuneaton, Attleborough was a separate village when **George Eliot**, then Mary Anne Evans, was sent to a boarding school here in 1824. She was only five years old, so it must have been a great comfort to have her older sister Chrissey as a fellow pupil. She boarded here until 1828 when she went further afield to Coventry.

AUCHENGIBBERT, Dumfries and Galloway [see Map 2, C2]   The religious leader, **Elspeth Buchan**, disappointed her Buchanite followers by dying in 1791. They had believed her to be the woman mentioned in the Book of Revelation. Many believers had expected her to live for ever; at the very least they were confident of her resurrection. It was said that her body was eventually buried here in secret, but by then most of the Buchanites had dispersed.

AYR, Strathclyde [see Map 2, C2]   In 1897, as a seventeen year old, **Mary Macarthur** started her first job, as a clerk in her father's drapery shop here. By 1901 she was leading the Ayr branch of the Shop Assistants' Union, having been convinced of the value of trade unions by a speech from John Turner. This was the start of a lifelong commitment to improving the position of working people, especially women. The following year she had become president of the union's Scottish council, and in 1903 her appointment as secretary of the Women's Trade Union League took her to London and the start of her full-time involvement with trade unionism.

B B

BALMORAL, near Ballater, Grampian [see Map 2, B3] **Queen Victoria** first rented Balmoral Castle in 1848; she returned each summer until she bought the estate in 1853. She then had it rebuilt in the 'Scottish baronial' style, and thereafter spent as much time as possible here in 'this dear Paradise'. After the death of her husband Prince Albert in 1861, she withdrew from public life. During this period of extended mourning she became reliant on a local member of the estate staff, John Brown, whose opinions she valued. This relationship became the subject of speculation, and many felt that his influence on the Queen was unduly strong. However, there is no doubt that he was a devoted, if possessive, servant to Queen Victoria. Her own accounts of her life in Scotland can be read in *Leaves from a Journal of our Life in the Highlands 1848-1861* [1868]. Balmoral Castle continues to be the summer home of the British royal family, and the gardens are open to the public when the family is not in residence.

BAMBURGH, Northumberland [see Map 2, C3] In 1815 **Grace Darling** was born in Bamburgh in her grandfather's modest cottage, now adjacent to the Grace Darling Museum★ on Radcliffe Road. She spent most of her life on the Farne Islands, where the courageous deeds which led to her fame took place. She was the heroine of a dramatic sea rescue in 1838. The museum, which is run by the Royal National Lifeboat Institution, records her life and the appreciation of her many contemporary admirers. Exhibits include medals, clothing, biographies, her boat and other mementos of Grace and her family.

Sadly, her last months were also passed in Bamburgh: she developed tuberculosis in 1841 and was brought to the mainland, where despite the attention of the best doctors, provided by anxious friends, she died at her sister's house in 1842. Formerly the old Post Office at 9 Front Street, overlooking the green, it is now a sweet shop, and a plaque on the wall records Grace's death here. She is buried with members of her family in the churchyard opposite the museum. A Victorian gothic monument was erected in 1893 to replace the original memorial.

BARDEN TOWER, North Yorkshire [see Map 1, D3] In the seventeenth century, the northern landowner and Dowager Countess of Pembroke, **Lady Anne Clifford**, restored several of her castles, including that at Barden Tower. The Cliffords were a powerful northern family, whose ancestors accompanied William the Conqueror to England from Normandy in 1066. Originally they were rewarded for their service with estates at Clifford in Herefordshire, but by the fourteenth century had properties in Westmorland and Craven. Born in 1590, Lady Anne was the last of the line, and full of fighting spirit. She disputed her brother's claims to the family inheritance on their father's death in 1605, and spent the rest of her life first acquiring and then restoring the vast estates which she deemed to be hers by right. She married two rich husbands, whose positions enabled her to pursue her claims. By the period of the English Civil War she had reclaimed all her northern estates, and she immediately set to work to restore them. Damaged in the Civil War, Barden Tower was one of the six castles which she had repaired and refortified by her death in 1676.

BARDSEY ISLAND, Gwynedd [see Map 1, E2]   The painter and writer **Brenda Chamberlain** lived in virtual seclusion on the island from 1947-61. Its Welsh name Ynys Enlli means 'Island of the Tides', and it has long been a place of pilgrimage. She loved Wales and also lived at Pwllheli.

BARKING   See **LONDON BOROUGH OF BARKING**.

BARNES   See **LONDON BOROUGH OF RICHMOND**.

BARNSLEY, South Yorkshire [see Map 1, E3]   An obelisk on a hill in the grounds of Wentworth Castle, now the Trades Union Congress's Northern College on the west of the town, records the life and achievements of **Lady Mary Wortley Montagu**, 1689-1762. This remarkable and independent woman, born Lady Mary Pierrepont, spent her early married life in Yorkshire, after defying her parents and eloping with Edward Wortley Montagu. She accompanied him to Turkey in 1716, having already published articles and poetry. This was to be the first of many foreign travels later described in her *Turkish Letters* [1763]. Wentworth Castle is a Baroque mansion rather than a fortified stronghold; two crumbling towers on the site of the prehistoric camp being all that remain of a fashionable folly. The house was built by one branch of the Wentworth family. It should not be confused with the palatial house at Wentworth Park to the south of Barnsley, near Rotherham, built by a rival member of the same family. Wentworth Castle is signposted from Barnsley as 'Wentworth Education Centre'. **Queen Anne**, who ruled the whole realm of Great Britain and Ireland and united the Scottish and English parliaments by the Act of Union in 1707, is also commemorated at Wentworth Castle by a monument. The south suite of state rooms was built in anticipation of a royal visit, but Queen Anne died in 1714 before the building was completed. The ceiling decoration of the Great Hall, a scene showing the Awakening of Aurora, is possibly the work of the painter **Angelica Kauffmann**. Lady Wentworth, as her patron, was responsible for bringing the Swiss painter to London where she established a career for herself as a professional artist.

BARNSTAPLE, Devon [see Map 1, F2]   Arlington Court☆ [NT], ten miles to the north of Barnstaple, houses the costume and decorative arts collection of **Rosalie Chichester**. Many great collections were brought together by women; this one, which is highly regarded by dress historians, is of interest because of the continuous association with one family over several generations. Miss Chichester was born here in 1865 and died here in 1949. She tended the house, its contents, gardens and estate with care and devotion, leaving it for the benefit of future generations. Her ashes are buried beneath a neoclassical urn by the lake, but the whole complex is the finest memorial to her work and generosity.

BARROW, Suffolk [see Map 1, E4]   The artist **Mary Beale** was born into a clerical family at the rectory here in 1633. Her maiden name was Mary Cradock. She married in the village in 1652, and soon settled in London, but it is thought that she had already begun drawing and painting while living in Suffolk. She is considered to be the first British-born professional woman artist. She specialised in portraits, and over 160 are known to have been painted by her; other surviving works may also exist, possibly attributed to other artists.

BASCHURCH, Shropshire [see Map 1, E3]   **Agnes Hunt**, who was born in this community in 1866, pioneered the care of crippled children, by setting up a small home for them here in 1900. As a child, a bone disease had left her very lame. She had overcome this physical disability herself to train and practise as a nurse, and it was the aim of her experiment to stretch rather than coddle her patients. Her ideas have profoundly influenced developments in this field of health care and education.

BASINGSTOKE, Hampshire [see Map 1, F4]   **Harriet Stanton Blatch**, daughter of American Women's Rights campaigner Elizabeth Cady Stanton, spent the first twenty years of her marriage in Basingstoke. She had married an Englishman, William Blatch, in 1882. Their home was The Mount in Bounty Road; the building now standing on the site is more recent and serves as the Conservative Club. Harriet was a frequent guest of the Pankhursts in London, and she often hosted the Pankhurst daughters at The Mount. She was an active supporter of women's suffrage, and took over leadership of the American campaign on her mother's death in 1902. In 1907 she founded the Women's Political Union and drew more American working women into their Women's Rights Movement. She remained involved in many aspects of the Movement until her death in 1940.

BASS ROCK   See **NORTH BERWICK**.

BATH, Avon [see Map 1, F3]   Bath is an attractive city with a history of long- and short-stay visitors, many of whom were women. The health-giving properties of its hot springs made it a social centre for the wealthier classes in the eighteenth and nineteenth centuries, but **Celia Fiennes** was unimpressed by the baths on her visit in *c.* 1687: 'The baths in my opinion makes the town unpleasant, the aire thick and hot by their steem, and by its own situation so low, encompassed about with high hills and woods.' Today it is an elegant place to visit. Plaques on buildings record the lodgings and homes of many well-known names. However, there is scope for more; indeed a women's history guide to the city is just waiting to be written. The Feminist Archive at the University of Bath is a new project which will become a valuable resource for researches into women's history. Its special aim is to record for the future the history of the Women's Liberation Movement. It is based at the University of Bath, on the east of the city, on Claverton Down. It is best to make an appointment.

Jane Austen is probably the woman whose association with Bath is best known and best acknowledged there. Her first visit was in 1790. There are several buildings where she is known to have stayed. In 1800 when her father decided that the family should move here from Steventon, Jane is said to have fainted with shock. However, she later enjoyed life here very much indeed. They arrived here in the summer of 1801, living first at 1 The Paragon, where they had rooms on the top floor, moving in June to 4 Sydney Place, where a bronze plaque records her stay. It was in this house that *Lady Susan* [1925] and *The Watsons* [1927] were written. In 1804, their next home was at 27 Green Park Buildings, a terraced town house with verandas overlooking the green park by the old railway station. Her father died at the end of 1804, and she, together with her mother and her dear sister Cassandra, moved to less expensive lodgings in Gay Street – 14 then 25 – and in 1806 to Trim Street. Her six main novels are considered to be classics of English literature. The first novel to be published was *Sense and Sensibility* [1811], written thirteen years earlier. Much of the action in her novels *Persuasion* [1818] and *Northanger Abbey* [1818] is set in Bath and these give a well-observed picture of the concerns and pressures of women of her class; certainly places such as the Assembly Rooms★ and the Pump Room★, which can be visited, have changed little since her day.

Fanny Burney came to Bath with **Hester Thrale** in 1780, staying with the Thrales at 14 South Parade, a town house at the end of the terrace, now called Amelia House and marked with a plaque, overlooking the river. She came back after her marriage and ten years in France. As Madame d'Arblay, she took up residence first in 1814 in River Street, which was convenient for the Assembly Rooms, moving to 23 Great Stanhope Street from 1815 until she was widowed in 1818. The rest of her life was mainly spent in London but she is buried in Bath with General d'Arblay and their son in the graveyard of St Swithin's Church on the corner of London Street and Walcott Street. Their gravestone stands alone in the grassed area on the north side of the church. Her lively diaries describe many of the characters she encountered here and elsewhere in her full social life. These and her letters are now less known than when Jane Austen admired them; *Evelina* [1788] was an immediate success, followed by *Cecilia* [1792] and *Camilla* [1796].

Catherine Macaulay, the historian, came to live in the city in 1774. She was then a widow of forty-three. For a time she lived at 2 Alfred Street, but

2   Belvedere House in Bath, Avon, where Harriet and Sophia Lee ran their school for young ladies

the plaque on the house only mentions Thomas Lawrence's stay there. In 1778 her marriage to a much younger man astounded her friends and she moved away to start what proved to be a very happy new life.

Mrs Ann Radcliffe, later the author of gothic novels such as *The Mysteries of Udolpho* [1794], grew up in Bath, leaving for London after her marriage in St Michael's Church here. As Ann Ward she attended Belvedere House, the school run by **Sophia** and **Harriet Lee** in the Belvedere. It was started on the proceeds from Sophia's book *A Chapter of Accidents* [1785] and other writings, and she was helped by Harriet and another sister, Anne. In 1803 they gave up teaching here and settled in Bristol.

Mary Wollstonecraft, a key figure in eighteenth-century feminism, first supported herself in 1778 in Bath with a job as a lady's companion, which must have been rather limiting for a woman of her abilities. She stayed barely two years. Her daughter, **Mary Shelley**, was here briefly in 1816 at 4 Roman Pavement and 6 Queens Square [this was bombed in the Second World War and has been replaced by a hotel], already living with the poet Percy Bysshe Shelley, but not yet having married him. It was on their extended visit to the Continent the next year that she wrote *Frankenstein, or the Modern Prometheus* [1818]. Another literary figure who spent time in Bath was **Mary Martha Sherwood**; she is known to have stayed with her mother and sister in South Parade in 1801. Like Jane Austen, she too became

3   Caroline Herschel's house at 19 New King Street, Bath, Avon

a writer whose novels were later regarded as classics, but her readership was mainly younger. Her moral tale *The History of the Fairchild Family* [1818], 1842 and 1847] is the best known.

The social life of Bath attracted several theatrical groups. One of the better known actresses is **Sarah Siddons**, whose stay at 33 The Paragon is commemorated with a plaque on the building now named Siddons House. She appeared often in the area from 1777-81, gaining a fine reputation for her tragic roles. From 1782 her career was well-established on the London stage. **Lola Montez** also frequently entertained audiences here, with her Spanish dancing. She cultivated an aura of exoticism which enabled her to lead an unconventional life. From 1847 she was an influential figure in the Bavarian court, having entranced King Ludwig with her performances.

Caroline Herschel's scientific achievements receive minimal recognition at her former home at 19 New King Street★. The house is opened to the public as a shrine to her brother William, the astronomer to whom she was more than just the housekeeper suggested by the displays inside. She had first come to Bath in 1772 to train as a singer and care for William who was already established in England. No doubt she did indeed spend time in the kitchen and in 'Caroline's garden', but her astronomical work went beyond taking notes for William. Her own observations included the first sightings of eight comets and fourteen nebulae. Together they built telescopes and wrote accounts of their sightings, reporting to the Royal Astronomical Society, of which she became a fellow in 1828. William's death in 1822 ended a half century of scientific partnership, and she returned to Hanover.

Selina Hastings established one of her chapels here, now the Trinity United Reform Church in Vineyards, in 1765. Her own house next door bears a plaque declaring the 'Huntingdon Connection' – it is a castellated gothic building called Chapel House. The building has been restored and is now the headquarters of the Bath Architectural Heritage Trust★. She had spent a considerable amount of time here since her husband's death in 1746. She deplored the lifestyle set as an example for all by the leader of Bath's social fashions, Beau Nash, and introduced the sobriety of Methodism through her patronage and protection of non-conformist preachers. It was her hope that the Methodists would reform the Church of England, but eventually they became a separate community of churches.

Another sort of non-conformism which could be encountered in Bath was that of the 'Blue Stocking Circle' who met at **Mrs Elizabeth Montagu**'s house in the magnificent Royal Circus. Number 16, right in the centre, is now a hotel, but it was here that the 'Queen of the Blue Stockings', as she was known, presided during the Bath season over intellectual discussions on wide-ranging topics. Started in London, these were enjoyable evenings where good conversation was the only requirement. The formality of black silk stocking for male evening dress was dispensed with, and the daytime wear of blue woollen stockings was encouraged. They were social occasions, hosted by intelligent and accomplished women, and men were welcomed as well as women.

Hannah More spent much of her long life in the Bath and Bristol area. A plaque at 76 Great Pulteney Street records her staying there between 1792 and 1802. She was always busy pursuing her various causes, writing clearly on her views of the Christian church and morals, making plans for her schools, writing plays and poetry. Her output includes the tragedy *Fatal Falsehood* [1779], the novel *Coelebs in Search of a Wife* [1809] and *Thoughts on the Importance of the Manners of the Great* [1788]. With her talents and ideas she was an ideal contributor to the Blue Stockings' gatherings. Hannah More was a later entrant to the Circle, whose original members met in London and included **Mrs Thrale** and **Mrs Carter**.

Mrs Thrale returned to Bath after her first husband's death in 1781. In 1783 she stayed in Russell Street, and the next year she married Gabriel Piozzi at St James Church [demolished] and together they left for Italy. Widowed again in 1809, she returned to live at 14 Gay Street from 1814-20, noted by a plaque. She always had plenty of visitors and a full life, and hosted Blue Stocking evenings here as well as in London. Her intellect and friendship were valued by Samuel Johnson; she later published *Anecdotes of the Late Samuel Johnson* [1786], though they had parted company on her second marriage. The expense incurred in keeping up with Bath society obliged her to escape the distractions of the spa town. Her eightieth birthday was celebrated by a ball attended by six hundred guests. One of the places to which she moved to save money was Penzance, in 1820.

Women whom she would have known who also visited Bath include **Elizabeth Carter**, the scholar, and **Anna Seward**, the poet, who wrote the epitaph on the memorial in the Abbey to **Lady Millar** of Batheaston. The memorial is on the wall at the east end of the Abbey beside the altar. Lady Millar encouraged literary talent, including Anna Seward, and held literary parties on Thursdays during 'the season' at her home Bath Easton Villa. The villa stands on a hill to the north of the city, now 172 Bailbrook Lane, the Vedanta Movement's property. The gardens contain a folly, a small round temple where guests often joined in her word-games.

Batheaston also boasts a campaign centre for women's suffrage activity. Eagle House [subject of a tribute *A Nest of Suffragettes in Somerset*, B.M. Willmott Dobbie, the Batheaston Society, Bath, 1979] was the home of the Blathwayt family, supporters of the cause. From 1906 many well-known suffragettes and suffragists were regular visitors: **Annie Kenney**, organiser for the West of England, the **Pankhursts**, **Mrs Pethick-Lawrence**, **Millicent Garrett Fawcett** and sympathisers from overseas. It became almost a resort for them, where restorative fresh country air and good company were a source of strength to endure further action and consequent imprisonment. Many key figures in the movement planted trees which the Blathwayt family tended, labelling each with the planter's name. Sadly 'Annie's Arboretum', as it was called, has been built over but Eagle House survives.

4   Lady Anna Millar's temple, now at 172 Bailbrook Lane, Bath, Avon

There were many other notable women associated with Bath as residents or visitors: the artist **Lady Diana Beauclerk**; the diarist **Dorothy Wordsworth**; the children's author **Juliana Horatia Ewing**, who died here in 1885; the sailors' friend **Agnes Weston**, who grew up here; **Madame Sarah Grand**, who held the office of mayor here six times, living at 7 Sion Hill Place, to name a few. Sarah Grand had already made a name for herself as a novelist before her political involvement in the suffrage campaign. The Museum of Costume★ in the Assembly Rooms shows the collection of one of the first serious dress historians, **Doris Langley Moore**, who has also written biographies, and deserves attention. Dress is one aspect of women's material history that has received considerable coverage in museums and galleries, but inevitably its strengths are the clothes of more privileged members of society.

BENBECULA, Highlands and Islands [see Map 2, B1] In 1746 the Scottish heroine **Flora MacDonald** helped Charles Edward Stuart to escape after the defeat at Culloden. He was known as the Young Pretender, and he had hoped to reinstate the Stuarts to the British crown, by relying on the support of the Scottish people. Flora risked her own life by taking him over to Skye from here, disguised as her maid Betty.

BENTLEY, Hampshire [see Map 3, C1] The country home of **Olave Baden-Powell**, organiser of the Girl Guide movement, and her husband, whom she had married in 1912. Pax Hill, is now a community centre.

BERWICK, Sussex [see Map 1, G4] The Church of St Michael and All Angels was decorated during the Second World War with a series of striking mural paintings by **Vanessa Bell**, her lover Duncan Grant and members of her family. They depict traditional scenes from the Bible, and though extensive are not overwhelming. The figures in their rich colours were modelled by local people and their friends and family, and many are shown in contemporary dress, and include churchmen, servicemen in uniform and lay people.

BETTISCOMBE, Dorset [see Map 1, G3] **Dorothy Wordsworth** came to live in this area with her brother in 1795. An admirer had made Racedown Lodge, a fine redbrick three-storeyed house overlooking Bettiscombe to the south, available to them. This was their first chance to share each other's lives, something that they had long wanted to do. They were here for two happy years, making Racedown Lodge their home in the glorious Dorset countryside.

BEWDLEY, West Midlands [see Map 1, E3] Tickenhall Manor was the birthplace and one childhood home of **Mary Sidney**, later Countess of Pembroke. Born in 1561, she also spent much of her youth at Penshurst Place in Sussex. Her aristocratic connections enabled her in later life to support and encourage struggling writers, such as Nicholas Breton and Samuel Daniel.

BINFIELD, Berkshire [see Map 3, B1] **Catherine Macaulay**, the historian, is buried here. She moved to Berkshire after her second marriage to William Graham. There is a memorial in marble to her on the south wall in All Saints' Church, beside the south porch; fittingly it shows the owl, the symbol of wisdom. The church is at the north end of the village. By the time she died, in 1791, her literary output had attracted much attention but it was her eight-volume *History of England* [1763–83] which was most admired.

BIRMINGHAM, West Midlands [see Map 1, E3]   Radical women seem to have been attracted to Birmingham, which developed as a centre for non-conformism and socially conscious business families. **Harriet Martineau** was brought up as a Unitarian but when she died in 1876 she had specifically asked to be buried without rites. She is buried beside her mother in the cemetery at Keys Hill, just north of the present city centre. The American suffragist **Alice Paul** came here first from America in 1907. She was twenty-two and had come primarily to study at Birmingham's university, before moving to work for various causes in London, including the women's suffrage movement. The City Art Gallery attracted the attention of the militant suffragettes: **Bertha Ryland** slashed George Romney's painting 'Master Thornhill' with a chopper concealed under her coat in 1914. Such activities were common in London, less so in the provinces, but Birmingham post boxes were blown up and the Carnegie Library was also severely damaged by fire. In 1918 **Christabel Pankhurst** stood as parliamentary candidate for the Smethwick constituency. This was the first time that women were eligible to vote and stand for election to the House of Commons. There were sixteeen women candidates throughout Britain. Christabel, unfortunately, was not successful.

The Cause had been only one field in which Birmingham women worked. Pioneering women's associations against slavery were established in Birmingham in 1825, and there was an active settlement doing social work before the First World War.

The city had some good art schools; the ever practical business community recognised early the value of good design and formal training. Among artists who studied here were **Helen Allingham**, the water-colourist, who spent five years at the School of Design from 1862, and **Margaret Gere**, who studied under her brother at the School of Art and specialised in figure and flower painting. The family of **Edith Holden**, the artist-diarist, lived in several villages, now all incorporated in the metropolitan area of the city. These included Moseley, where she was born at Holly Green, Church Road, in 1871, and King's Norton. Her family were typical Birmingham radicals of the middle class. She and her sisters attended the Birmingham Municipal Art School. She excelled at studies of nature, many of which have become familiar on stationery, bed linen and tableware. It is disappointing that her present reputation as the creator of *The Country Diary of an Edwardian Lady* [1977] can bring her no direct benefit, while others have thrived on her gentle artistic output.

Edith Holden would have known the Birmingham Botanical Gardens★ in Edgbaston. The gardens and glasshouses were designed by the Loudons. **Jane Webb**, who married John Loudon in 1830, was a local writer. She embarked on garden design after her marriage, collaborating on many London parks and writing gardening books. When she was widowed in 1843 she returned to writing, mainly instructional works for genteel women.

The Spare Rib Diary for 1983 contained a Women's History walking tour of the city, pointing out landmarks in the local past.

BIRSTALL, West Yorkshire [see Map 1, D3] **Charlotte Brontë**'s friend, Ellen Nussey, lived at the Rydings. Charlotte had met her when they were at school together and their friendship was important to them both. Oakwell Hall★, on Nutter Lane in the country park, was the model for Fieldhead in Charlotte's book, *Shirley* [1849]; it was the home of the heroine, heiress Shirley Keeldar. The Rydings became Thornfield Hall in *Jane Eyre* [1847]. Ellen, who herself became Caroline Helston in *Shirley* was buried in the churchyard. The church also appears in *Shirley*, as Briarfield Church.

BLACK BOURTON, Oxfordshire [see Map 1, F3] **Maria Edgeworth**, the prolific novelist, was born here in 1768 at the Old Hall, which formerly stood near the church. She was the eldest of her father's twenty-two children, and much of her life was devoted to bringing up her siblings. Eventually the family settled in Ireland, and it was there that she wrote and set many of her works. She became the first regional historical novelist; later Sir Walter Scott used the same style of writing for his novels set in Scotland.

BLAGDON, Avon [see Map 1, F3] Probably the village is best known for 'the Blagdon Controversy' which focused on **Hannah More** and the school which she started here in 1795, in Church Street. The building is now a private residence called Hannah More House. Most of her moral tales were written as teaching material for her pupils. They proved so popular that a Religious Tract Society was formed to make them more widely available. Some appeared together in *Cheap Repositary Tracts* [1795-8]. Both the local squirearchy and clergy saw disadvantages in the labouring classes receiving any education and they concocted 'The Controversy' at the turn of the century, claiming that Dissenters were meeting in the school. As it was not a registered meeting place for Dissenters, Hannah was forced to take her teaching elsewhere.

BLICKLING, Norfolk [see Map 1, E5] Blickling Hall★ [NT] is a Jacobean house built on the site of **Anne Boleyn**'s childhood home, before she had attracted the attentions of Henry VIII. Her reign as Henry's second queen was short-lived. When she failed to produce a male heir, she fell from favour and was eventually beheaded in 1536. She did in fact provide England with a better legacy, her daughter the future Queen Elizabeth whose long reign was one of the most impressive in English history.

BLUNTISHAM, Cambridgeshire [see Map 1, E4]   Bluntisham House, the former rectory, was the family home of the novelist **Dorothy Sayers**. A large Georgian house of the local yellow brick, it stands on the main road from Earith. Dorothy was very involved in the life of the church, where her father served as rector. She knew the surrounding Fenlands well and used them as the setting for her novel *The Nine Tailors* [1934]. Her association with the old rectory, 1897-1917, is marked by a plaque beside the front door.

BODMIN, Cornwall [see Map 1, G2]   The writer **Daphne du Maurier** based her popular novel about smuggling *Jamaica Inn* [1936] on the Jamaica Inn which stands in comparative isolation on Bodmin Moor. Her non-fiction work *Vanishing Cornwall* [1967] is testimony to her love of the Cornish landscape.

BOROUGHBRIDGE, Yorkshire [see Map 1, D3]   In 1831 the traveller **Isabella Bird** was born in Boroughbridge Hall, which stands at the north end of the High Street, behind the war memorial. It now serves as offices. Hers was a genteel church family, an unlikely background for the woman who later travelled alone in the Rocky Mountains, Japan, Korea, the Sandwich Islands and Hawaii, often in rough country where European women had seldom, if ever, been seen. Her published accounts make lively reading.

BORTHWICK CASTLE, Lothian [see Map 2, C3]   The fifteenth-century castle near Gorebridge has changed little since **Mary Queen of Scots**, whose life was so often in jeopardy, escaped her enemies in 1567, disguised as a boy, with her third husband. She had been blockaded here once more. It was her last year of freedom before her cousin and rival Elizabeth I incarcerated her for seventeen years in England.

BOSBURY, Hereford and Worcestershire [see Map 1, F3]   The writer 'Edna Lyall' was buried in the graveyard, under a granite monument near the church porch. The inscription records her death in 1903 under her proper name **Ada Ellen Bayly**. Her pen-name is a partial anagram of her full name. Her best known works are *Donovan* [1882] and *We Two* [1884]. Her sympathies with the campaigns for greater opportunities for women and for Irish Home Rule are evident in her writing.

BOSTON, Lincolnshire [see Map 1, E4]   It is easy to forget that Boston was once a busy port; its position now is far inland. In the seventeenth century it was a boarding point for early colonists for North America, and gave its name to the thriving city in Massachusetts. **Anne Bradstreet** is thought to have embarked here for the New World in 1630. By then she was eighteen years old and already married. She is claimed as the first American poet. When her poems were published in 1650 without her knowledge, their author was described as 'the tenth muse, lately sprung up in America'. **Anne Hutchinson**, who left from Boston four years later, was already in her forties, was actively involved in the religious life of the colony, but became a controversial figure through her unorthodox views, for which she paid with her life in 1643. It is thought that before their voyage the early colonists prayed in the beautiful church, known as Boston Stump. They are commemorated inside.

Jean Ingelow, Lincolnshire's regional poet, was born in Boston in 1820. She celebrated local life and landscape in her works. Her *Poems* were published in 1863. There is a collection of memorabilia on display in the Banqueting Hall of the Guildhall★, South Street.

BOTHWELL, Strathclyde [see Map 2, C2]   The manse is thought to have been the birthplace in 1762 of **Joanna Baillie**, whose father was the local minister. Although she spent most of her adult life in England, she continually turned to her native country as a source of inspiration for her many plays, novels and poetry. She would have known the ruins of the castle, once the largest in Scotland. It was the seat of **Mary Queen of Scots**' third husband; it was blown up by Scots who feared Bothwell's ambitions. Mary was continually on the move, either with her court or on the run from her enemies, and she spent little time here.

BOURNE END, Buckinghamshire [see Map 3, B1]   Fieldhead, now an old people's home, stands off a cul-de-sac called Fieldhead Gardens, near the station in Bourne End. It is a Tudor revival style building in which the sisters **Rosamund Lehmann**, the writer, and **Beatrix Lehmann**, the actress, were born and grew up at the beginning of the present century. It was the setting for their brother John's book *The Whispering Gallery*.

BOURNEMOUTH, Dorset [see Map 1, G3]   For two significant women this was to be the final resting place. **Mary Shelley** and her mother, **Mary Wollstonecraft**, whom she never knew, lie together beneath a prominent white tombstone on the hill in the north-east of St Peter's Churchyard. The grave also contains the heart of the poet, her husband, and the body of her father, the writer William Godwin. Mary Shelley had her parents' remains removed from their original burial place in Old St Pancras churchyard in London in 1851. They were both writers whose lives broke the traditional mould; the older Mary concentrated on politics, and the younger on novels.

Radclyffe Hall, author of the controversial novel of lesbian love, *The Well of Loneliness* [1928], was born at Surrey Lawn, Westcliffe, in 1880. Hers was a conservatively respectable family, from whom she gained independence at twenty-one. Another native, **Elizabeth Scott** the architect, received her schooling in Bournemouth before the First World War. The town still has a reputation as a fine place for convalescence but it did not live up to it in 1886 for **Olive Schreiner**, whose months here were plagued by ill health. She was a South African feminist and novelist who managed to find a British publisher for *The Story of an African Farm* [1883] under her pen-name, 'Ralph Iron'. She returned to South Africa in 1889. **Lillie Langtry**, however, managed to enjoy the air here with the Prince of Wales at a house which is now Langtry Manor Hotel, 26 Derby Road in the East Cliff district. Originally called the Red House, it was built in 1877 as a present for Lillie. It retains many furnishings of the period, and the associations with the actress are very much a feature of the hotel today.

BRADFORD ON AVON, Avon [see Map 1, F3]   **E.H. Young** came here from London in 1940 and spent her last years in this delightful small town not far from Bath. She died here in 1949 after a successful career as a novelist. Many of her works were set in nearby Bristol; they include *Miss Mole* [1930], *The Vicar's Daughter* [1928] and *William* [1925]. Her last novel, *Chatton Square*, published in 1947, was written in Bradford on Avon.

BRAMPTON, Cumbria [see Map 2, D3]   In the 1920s **Winifred Nicolson** lived at Bankhead Farm here with her fellow artist, and later husband, Ben Nicolson. Once they had separated in 1932 she took their three children to Paris, but she returned in 1938, afterwards making Bankhead her permanent home. The house is near Hadrian's Wall and there is Roman masonry in the farm buildings. She had long known the area, having often visited her grandfather, the ninth Earl of Carlisle, whose home was nearby at Naworth Castle. He too was an artist and encouraged Winifred's endeavours. Winifred adored Cumbria and the fells. She painted wild and garden flowers and had a fascination for rainbows, which the wet Cumbrian skies offered frequently in so many different forms. Born in 1893, she was still a practising artist well into her eighties, regularly going on painting trips to the Hebrides and Greece. She died in 1981.

BRAMPTON BRYAN, Hereford and Worcestershire [see Map 1, E3] **Lady Brilliana Harley**, heroine of the English Civil War, bravely defended Brampton Bryan, her married home, in the uncertain times she lived through. Castles and grand country homes were frequently targets for Royalist and Parliamentarian attacks. Lady Brilliana resisted a siege, and her home survived relatively intact.

BRASTED, Kent [see Map 3, C4]   **Octavia Hill** saved Toy's Hill, near Brasted, for the National Trust. She knew the area well as her sister lived at Chart Brow, where Octavia had a well dug for the use of the local people. In 1981 the National Trust bought a wood here which was named the Octavia Hill Woodland in her memory✳[NT]. She was one of the Trust's founders in 1895; her life of philanthropy, which ended in 1912, was dedicated to the poor of London, whose quality of life she tried to enrich.

BRECON, Powys [see Map 1, F3]   The actress **Sarah Siddons** is said to have been born at the Shoulder of Mutton Inn in 1755, into an acting family, the Kembles, who travelled throughout the Welsh border country entertaining with a variety of acts. The town can claim an association with a later star of the stage – **Adelina Patti**, the Italian singer, married in the Roman Catholic church in Glamorgan Street in 1898. By this time she had already been living in Wales for twenty years and had been adopted by the Welsh people as one of their own.

BREDE, Sussex [see Map 1, F4]   The artist and journalist **Clare Sheridan** first saw Brede Place, a fine mansion dating from the fourteenth century, in 1895, although her family did not live there permanently until they had restored it a few years later. It was to be her base in a life of travel, art and journalism until 1947. A war widow with two children to support after 1915, she took up portraiture in clay and sculpture, and began a successful career as an artist. Her second, more controversial, profession as a writer led her around the world interviewing statesmen of all political persuasions, North American Indians and literary figures, many of whom sat for her as models. When she died in 1970, she was buried in the churchyard at Brede. There are examples of her work inside the church, including a Madonna and Child carved from a single tree from the grounds of Brede Place.

BREDON'S NORTON, Hereford and Worcestershire [see Map 1, F3] The first woman to stand for the presidency of the United States of America, in 1872, **Victoria Woodhull** was a very determined individual. Her career included lecturing on spiritualism and free love, publishing a journal with her sister Tennessee Claflin *Woodhull and Claflin's Weekly*, partnering her sister again as the first women stockbrokers and always fighting for equal rights for women. She was less in the public eye after she moved to Britain, eventually marrying an Englishman, John Biddulph Martin, and settling here in a comfortable country house. She maintained an active interest in women's rights, editing *The Humanitarian* in the 1890s and supporting the suffrage movement. By the time she died in 1927, she was a well liked local personality.

BRENTWOOD, Essex [see Map 3, A4]   The graveyard of the Roman Catholic cathedral, St Helen's, is the last resting place of **Ellen Willmott**. She was a botanist, gardener and musician, who died in 1934. Her grave is hard to spot, only its border being marked by kerb stones on which her name is recorded. It is right up against the wall of the Roman Catholic Social Centre. As a well-respected gardener, she would appreciate any care and planting which her own and other graves could receive.

BRIDLINGTON, Humberside [see Map 1, D4]   The trophies awarded to the pioneer aviator **Amy Johnson** together with her Pilot's Log Book can be seen at Sewerby Hall★, the clifftop mansion which has been open to the public as a museum and gallery since she was asked to perform the opening ceremony in 1936. She grew up in nearby Kingston upon Hull. When she disappeared in 1941, it was presumed that the plane she was delivering had crashed into the Thames estuary. Her parents wanted to have her memorabilia displayed locally.

BRIGHTON, Sussex [see Map 1, G4]   In the eighteenth century the health-giving properties of sea-bathing brought many fashionable visitors

5   Norton Park, Bredon's Norton, Hereford and Worcestershire, home of
Victoria Woodhull

to Brighthelmstone as it was then called, especially once the Prince Regent
decided to build himself an elaborate summer home in the town. Its
development as a centre for Society in the last half of the century brought
much business to **Martha Gunn**. Known as the 'Bathing Woman of
Brighton', and as 'Queen of the Dippers', she supervised the people who
took women bathers into the water for the 'sea-water cure' in the bathing
machines, from her base at 36 East Street, identified with a plaque and now
an Italian restaurant, Al Forno. The sea must have done her health some
good, too, as she lived until 1815, her eighty-eighth year, which was quite
an achievement at that time. Her gravestone in the churchyard of
St Nicholas' stands to the south-east of the church, surrounded by railings.
The inscription describes her as 'peculiarly distinguished as a bather'.
Nearby, also protected by railings, is the grave of another long-lived local
heroine, **Phoebe Hassall**. Reputedly 108 years old when she died in 1821,
Phoebe Hassall made a name for herself by her military service. Her exploits
with the Fifth Foot [Royal Northumberland Fusiliers] are recorded on the
tombstone, including wounds received at Fourtenay, and other service in
Europe.

St Nicholas was where some of the visitors worshipped during their stays here. The social life of Brighton attracted **Hester Thrale**, her husband and their friends **Fanny Burney** and Dr Samuel Johnson from 1765. In the 1770s they stayed at the house which the Thrales had built for themselves at the south end of West Street, on the east side, and a plaque now marks where it used to stand. They went to the Assembly Rooms, where they danced and enjoyed themselves. Episodes from these days were noted by both women in their diaries, both later published and now valued for their comments on social life of those times. They attended services at St Nicholas'. Other regular visitors to Brighton included the artist **Lady Diana Beauclerk** and the philanthropist **Lady Byron**. The children's author, **Mary Sewell**, brought her invalid daughter, the better known **Anna Sewell**, to the south coast for more serious health reasons. Anna's sole work was the enduring classic *Black Beauty* [1877].

The established church did not hold complete sway in the town at this time. **Selina Hastings**, Countess of Huntingdon, founded and supported a dissenting chapel here. Selling her jewellery for £698, she had it built in 1761 in the grounds of her private house in North Street [demolished in the 1960s]; it was the first of the 'Huntingdon Connection' chapels. **Mrs Fitzherbert** contributed substantially to the building of St John the Baptist Roman Catholic Church in Bristol Street. Founded in 1835 it was only the third Catholic church to be built in England since Henry VIII created the Church of England in 1534. Mrs Fitzherbert's remains are buried in a vault under the floor in the centre of the aisle, marked by a lozenge-shaped flagstone. She died in 1837. Her step-daughter had a monument to her put up on the south wall. It shows Mrs Fitzherbert with three wedding rings on her finger. Her last years were spent at 55 Old Steine [now the YMCA], on the corner of Steine Lane. Her third marriage, though denied by the Prince Regent, was recognised by the Catholic church. She had refused to become his mistress, and the marriage had been concealed by the Prince to avoid offending his subjects. It broke her heart when he married, for political reasons, Caroline of Brunswick.

Brighton's social life attracted the richest woman in Europe, **Harriot Mellon**, later Duchess of St Albans. She was an actress whose marriage to the elderly banker Thomas Coutts shocked his family but brought him great happiness at the end of his life. As an immensely wealthy widow, she married the Duke of St Albans and lived in grand style at 131 Kings Road, a seafront house on the corner of Regency Square. The mansion which was the centre of Brighton society from 1830-7 is now called St Albans and houses the Regency Fish Restaurant. Her niece and heiress **Angela Burdett-Coutts** inherited not only her money but also her generosity. Between them they spent their money in much charitable work. Angela latterly took a whole floor for several months each year at the Royal York Hotel.

The sea air may also have been an attraction to those who set up schools in the Brighton area. There were over one hundred schools for young ladies in the town by 1830, but the educational standards were very mixed. The novelist **Ada Ellen Bayly**, who wrote as **Edna Lyall**, was a native of Brighton born in 1857 and received private schooling here. **Frances Power Cobbe** boarded at a school at 32 Brunswick Terrace for two years after being privately educated. She later worked in Mary Carpenter's ragged schools in Bristol, a contrast to her own experience. The socialist **Eleanor Marx** taught at a school here in 1872, after her parents' disapproval of her involvement with a French Communard called Lissagaray. **Nancy Spain**, the broadcaster, was one of several important women who attended Roedean School, a large private school of red brick east of the town looking out to sea. Founded in 1885, it was one of the progressive institutions offering education for girls at that time. It was founded by the three Lawrence sisters, whose pupils included their five younger sisters, who themselves later taught in the school.

Millicent Garrett Fawcett certainly supported her husband in his work as Member of Parliament for Brighton. He was a radical and his loss of sight was not allowed to hinder his political activity. Millicent was inevitably deeply involved in his work, and developed her own political convictions, later leading the campaign for Votes for Women. Another significant woman in the political sphere had her first job as a fourteen-year-old apprentice shop assistant in a draper's business in Weston Road in 1887. This was **Margaret Bondfield**, whose career direction led through trade union involvement to holding a parliamentary seat as a Labour member, and ultimately becoming, in 1929, the first woman in the Cabinet, as Minister of Labour.

More recently, the fine actress **Flora Robson** spent her last years in Brighton's Dyke Road, maintaining contact with the theatrical world through a lively interest in local acting groups. When she died here in 1984, aged eighty-two, her stage and television career had spanned more than sixty years.

BRISTOL, Avon [see Map 1, F3] Eighteenth-century Bristol took on some of the flavour of Bath, not merely in its architecture but also its social life. Entertainment could be found in the theatrical performances where **Sarah Siddons** [especially 1777-81] and her friend **Elizabeth Inchbald** attracted a following at the Theatre Royal. Elizabeth had made her debut as Cordelia on its stage in 1772, when she was eighteen. She later had a second career as a novelist and playwright. Another actress, **Mary Robinson**, later known as Perdita, the role she played in *The Winter's Tale*, in which the Prince of Wales first saw her, grew up in Minster House [long demolished]. She had been a pupil at **Hannah More**'s school here in Trinity Street, College Green. Hannah was one of five sisters born in the house near the church facing the park in the Fishponds area of north-east Bristol. It was with some of her sisters that she set up the Trinity Street school. The success of this first venture enabled them to take on specially built premises at 43 Park Street [where there is a plaque] in 1762. 1774 took her to London, but she returned to the West Country later. Her last years [1828-33] were spent in Clifton at Windsor Terrace, considered to be a good neighbourhood which acquired a reputation as a health resort.

This particular aspect of Bath attracted several other women to the area. The novelist **Maria Edgeworth** accompanied her sick brother here in 1791; the family lodged at Princes Buildings. She was in Clifton again in 1799. **Sophia** and **Harriet Lee** retired here in 1803; abandoning the running of their school in Bath. Their last works were written here, and they both died here, Sophia in 1824 and the more robust Harriet in 1851, but St Andrews, the church on Clifton Hill where they were buried, no longer stands. The success of Sophia's play *A Chapter of Accidents* [1780] was matched by Harriet's *Canterbury Tales* [1798]. They collaborated on further work after the move to Bristol. It was in 10 Sion Terrace that the elderly **Hester Thrale** spent a few months before her death there in 1821. She had also been an *habituée* of Bath and would have known the Lee sisters there.

Education of girls seems to have been both practised and much discussed in Bristol. In addition to the sisters Lee and More, **Mary Carpenter** became involved in this work. She was herself educated at her father's school here, but in 1829 started her own school for girls with her mother. She realised that schooling should be available to working-class children as well and opened a 'ragged school' in 1846 in the Lewin's Mead district. She began to publish her ideas, exploring less punitive teaching and closer personal relationships between the teacher and the taught. She extended these ideas to what are now known as young offenders, opening a new style of reformatory for boys in the Kingswood area in 1852 and for girls in the Red Lodge, Park Row, two years later. **Lady Byron** wholeheartedly supported her ideas and bought the Red Lodge for her. Mary worked tirelessly for women's education at all levels, publishing widely on this and other much needed social changes, and her campaigning took her abroad to spread the message and to learn from other systems. She died in 1877 and was buried in Arno's Vale Cemetery. She is commemorated by a plaque in Bristol Cathedral.

Frances Power Cobbe, who was a native of Bristol born in 1822 and rather more privileged than most of Mary's pupils, came to work with Mary Carpenter and her own work as campaigner for women's suffrage, social reforms and anti-vivisectionism was greatly influenced by Mary's example. **Emmeline Pethick-Lawrence** was another Bristol-born campaigner for women's votes and better social conditions. She was born Emmeline Pethick in 1867, and when she married, her husband Frederick Lawrence took on her name, not uncommon practice in progressive circles at this time. The Pethick-Lawrences' partnership was a keystone of the Women's Social and Political Union until 1912. Emmeline Pethick-Lawrence continued as an active feminist until her death in 1954.

Elizabeth Blackwell, the medical pioneer, was born in the Counterslip area in 1821. It is her achievements as a doctor that are now best known. However, after a childhood at 1 Wilson Street in St Paul's, following what appears to be a Bristol tradition, she, too, ran a school for four years but this was in Kentucky, where her family had emigrated in 1832 after the collapse of her father's sugar business. Independent-minded women who spent time here during much-travelled lives include **Fanny Trollope**, who was born in 1780 in Stapleton, then a separate village; she stayed at 7 Caledonia Place, Clifton, in 1843. By then her career as a writer, begun out of financial necessity in her fifties, was already established. Her initial bestsellers were travel books, but she also produced some very popular novels. More recently the artist **Paule Vézelay**'s family home was here; she was born in Clifton in 1892 as Margery Watson-Williams, but during her formative years in France she adopted the name Paule Vézelay. She returned here from Paris during the Second World War to care for her parents. She continued to paint and some of her work, recording the bombed city, is held by the City Art Gallery.

Others who spent time in the city include the journalist **Harriet Martineau**, briefly at school here in the 1810s; the author of *Our Village* [1832] **Mary Russell Mitford** who visited in the 1840s; and **Clara Butt**, who lived here from her birth in 1873 until she pursued her singing training in London when she was sixteen years old. In 1892 **Amelia Blandford Edwards**, novelist, traveller and sponsor of Egyptian archaeological studies, was buried in the graveyard of Henbury Parish Church. She has a most appropriate monument, an obelisk with a stone version of the ancient Egyptian symbol of life, the ankh, on the ground in front of it. The memorial stands beside the wall of the church.

Bristol also features as the setting for works by women writers: some of **Maria Edgeworth**'s stories for children and ten novels by **E.H. Young**, including *Miss Mole* [1930], were set here. Bristol certainly has much to offer anyone seeking out women from the past.

BRIXHAM, Devon [see Map 1, G3] **Flora Thompson**, whose books are set in the South Midlands, wrote her last two, *Candleford Green* [1943] and *Still Glides the Stream* [1948], while she was living here from 1940, at Lauriston, New Road, Higher Brixham. It was here that she died in 1947.

BROCKHAM, Surrey [see Map 3, C2] **Octavia Hill**, who died in 1912, was buried on the hillside beside her sister Miranda, overlooking a favourite view. She had selflessly worked for improved social and housing conditions for London's poor, aiming to enhance their experience of life. She valued the countryside, convinced that sharing access to it would be beneficial to all.

BROMLEY See **LONDON BOROUGH OF BROMLEY**.

BRORA, Highland Region [see Map 2, A2] **Jane Gordon**, Countess of Sutherland, was a remarkable woman, able to use the assets at her disposal to establish some industries in her husband's territory in the late sixteenth and early seventeenth centuries. She established the mining of coal at Brora, an industry which continues to the present, and it is thought that this was the first underground coalmine in Britain. She also set up a salt works here.

BROUGH, Cumbria [see Map 2, D3] On the hill stands the ruins of Brough Castle★. **Lady Anne Clifford** was proud of her inheritance and restored the castle in the seventeenth century. It has since fallen into disrepair, but is now in the care of the government. It was one of six seats in her northern estates which suffered damage during the Civil War. Her power derived from the wealth she gained through her two marriages, and from her own inheritance which she was determined to secure despite her brother's claims. She gained many titles during her life; one of which she was especially proud was that of 'High Sheriffesse by inheritance of the Counttie of Westmorland'.

BROUGHAM, Cumbria [see Map 2, D3] Brougham Castle★ is another which was largely repaired by **Lady Anne Clifford**. She finished work on it in 1660, but visited it regularly throughout her remaining years. Her death here at the age of eighty-seven in 1676 brought an end to the extensive building programme which she had initiated. She had fought through the courts for her inheritance of the large Clifford estates in Westmorland and Craven, and once she acquired them she energetically set about repairing first her six castles, most of which had suffered structural damage during the English Civil War.

BROUGHTON, Oxfordshire [see Map 1, F3] Broughton Castle★, a glorious moated mansion to the west of Banbury, is still owned by the same family as when **Celia Fiennes** knew it, although it is now in a better state of repair. As she wrote, 'Broughton is an ancient Seate of the Lord Viscount Say and Seale; its an old house moted round and a parke and gardens, but are much left decay and ruine.' She would certainly appreciate the care given to it by her descendants. Celia Fiennes travelled extensively in England in the late seventeenth and early eighteenth century. She wrote about the places she visited, her impressions, the scenery, the comforts and discomforts of transport and accommodation. Celia was the granddaughter of the first Viscount Saye and Sele, who played a leading role in the English Civil War, on the side of the Roundheads. The original manuscripts in which she described her 'Great Journeys' are still held by the family at Broughton Castle, where she had been a regular visitor, especially after her brother took over the estate.

BROUGHTON, Staffordshire [see Map 1, E3] **Rhoda Broughton**, author of *Belinda* [1883], *Mrs Bligh* [1892], *Lavinia* [1902] and other novels, spent her childhood at Broughton House. She had the traditional upbringing of a clergy daughter.

BRYNCRUG, Gwynedd [see Map 1, E2] When **Mary Jones** died in 1872, she was buried in the chapel burial ground. A Welsh speaker, she had avidly studied the Bible since she was sixteen. Her perseverance to acquire a copy of the Bible indirectly led Thomas Charles of Bala to found the British and

Foreign Bible Society. He had given her his copy when, after six years of saving money and a hard walk in barefeet, she was unable to obtain one in Bala.

BUCKDEN, Cambridgeshire [see Map 1, E4]   The ruins of the Bishops of Lincoln's Palace★ here are all that remain of what was effectively a prison for the unhappy **Catherine of Aragon**. After Henry VIII had divorced her, she was kept here by the Bishop of Lincoln on the king's orders from 1533-4. She had a staff of English and Spanish servants who remained devoted to her. The ruins are behind the Anglican parish church, and they incorporate a modern Roman Catholic church and activities centre. Buckden Palace had other royal visitors: **Margaret Beaufort** in 1501 and Henry VIII's fifth wife **Catherine Howard** with the king in 1541.

BUCKLAND, Gloucestershire [see Map 1, F3]   The sympathetic corres-pondent, **Mrs Delaney**, came to live at the Manor here in 1715, aged fifteen, when the family were under suspicion of Jacobite Cause. She was still only a teenager when she left, on her marriage to Alexander Pendarves in 1718. This, Mary Granville's first marriage, was not her choice, and it proved to be an unhappy union. Mary's family found themselves in changed circumstances when the death of Queen Anne brought the Hanoverian succession, not the re-establishment of the Stuarts on which her father's career had depended. The family was obliged to move to the quiet backwater of Buckland Manor, now a well-appointed country house hotel. Mr Pendarves was a prosperous gentleman with property in Cornwall, considered by Mary'a aunt a good prospect for a husband. Mary's misery in Cornwall ended in widowhood after six years, but she was no better off financially as there was no will in her favour. She, however, was happy to be free again.

BUILTH WELLS, Brecon [see Map 1, F3]   This Welsh spa resort gained a fashionable reputation when **Lady Hester Stanhope** brought her uncle William Pitt to take the waters in the early years of the nineteenth century. She made a home at Glan Irfon, but left Britain for the Middle East in 1810, never to return. The novelist **Hilda Vaughan** was later born here, in 1892. Her first novel *Battle to the Weak* [1925] was set nearby. Other works also have a Welsh setting: *Her Father's House* [1930] and *The Soldier and the Gentleman* [1932].

BURNTISLAND, Fife [see Map 2, C3]   **Mary Somerville** grew up in a small house which has been restored in Somerville Square, becoming interested in the study of mathematics here at the age of fifteen, after a fairly free childhood. Her marriage to a sea captain in 1804 left her widowed after three years. She continued her studies alone, later receiving support in her endeavours from her second husband. She progressed further when they moved to London in 1816.

BURRY PORT, Dyfed [see Map 1, F2]   In 1928 the American aviator **Amelia Earhart** landed after over twenty hours as logkeeper on a flight from Newfoundland. This made her the first woman to cross the Atlantic Ocean in an aeroplane. In 1932 she made the first solo transatlantic flight by a woman, flying from west to east.

BURY ST EDMUNDS, Suffolk [see Map 1, E4]   **Elizabeth Inchbald** and **Mary Robinson** were natives of this area and near-contemporaries. Elizabeth was born at Standingfield in 1753, and Mary Robinson in Bury five years later. They both began their careers as actresses, later supporting themselves by writing novels. Elizabeth was probably the more successful, her second career progressing so well that she was soon able to give up the stage. Her best known novels were *A Simple Story* [1791] and *Nature and Art* [1796]. Curiously it is the performance of one of her plays, *Lovers' Vows* [1798], in the action of Jane Austen's *Mansfield Park* [1814], that has earned it a permanent place in English literature. Mary, briefly a royal mistress, died in desperate circumstances after harsh later years. Her works, mainly novels such as *The Widow* [1794] and *Walsingham* [1798], are seldom read today.

The novelist **Marie Louise de le Ramee**, known as **Ouida**, also died in poverty after a career as a popular writer. She was born in 1839 in Bury St Edmunds and later moved to France, her father's native land. She spent much of her life on the continent, but all her forty-three novels were written in English. She died in Italy in 1908.

BUSBRIDGE, near Godalming, Surrey [see Map 3, C2]   **Gertrude Jekyll** is buried at the Church of St John the Baptist in Busbridge. Her career as a garden designer and writer continues to influence British gardeners. Her fruitful partnership with the architect Edwin Lutyens created some most enchanting properties. Some can be visited in many parts of Britain such as Hambledon and Ilminster, and also in Ireland and France. Her last years were spent at Munstead Wood, *not* open to the public, where she died in 1932. Her gravestone to the east of the church was designed by Lutyens and describes her simply as 'Artist, Gardener, Craftswoman'.

C c

CAERNARFON, Gwynedd [see Map 1, E2]   The present castle, still an impressive fortress, was begun by Edward I. His adored wife **Eleanor of Castile** is commemorated in the naming of the east gate after her. She gave birth to her fourth son here in 1284.

CAISTOR, Norfolk [see Map 1, E5]   **Margaret Paston** came to live at Caistor Castle, which had been acquired by her husband's family in 1459 on the death of Sir John Falstaf. It was from here that she wrote many of the *Paston Letters* [selections first published in 1787], to her husband while he was in London. She took sole responsibility for running their estates, successfully despite the attempts of others who disputed her husband's claims to them and tried to take advantage of his absence. She succeeded in thwarting their attempts. Her letters remain important documentary evidence of household and estate management of the day. The fifteenth-century castle still stands, though in ruins. In 1751, **Sarah Martin** was born in Caistor. In her day she was as well known as Elizabeth Fry for her prison visiting. Her work was more local, however, and she concentrated her efforts in nearby Great Yarmouth.

CAMBRIDGE, Cambridgeshire [see Map 1, F4]   This old university city has a long history as a major European centre of learning. Although it was a long time before women were accepted as students, they played their part in the life of the University. **Marie de Saint Pole**, the wealthy and religious widow of the Earl of Pembroke, founded Pembroke College in *c*. 1342; Clare College benefited from the generosity of her friend, another rich widow, **Elizabeth de Burgh** of Clare, taking its new name in 1346. The founders and benefactresses of Queens' College were **Margaret of Anjou** [1448] and **Elizabeth Woodville** [1465]. The woman whose patronage of educational establishments went further than founding colleges was **Margaret Beaufort**. Responsible for setting up both Christ's College in 1505 and St John's in 1508, she took an active interest in academic life. Her own studies included medicine, and she lectured in theology at Cambridge, funding a professorship, the Lady Margaret Chair of Divinity, in 1502, and writing books on the subject herself. The foundation of Sidney Sussex College in 1589 was made possible through the will of **Lady Frances Sidney**, widow of the Earl of Sussex, who had herself been left a substantial fortune. She had gained a reputation as a learned woman, who recognised the value of university studies.

It was in the nineteenth century that the attempts to allow women students began in earnest. **Emily Davies** long cherished the idea of a women's college and brought five of her own students, whom she had been preparing for Cambridge examinations in Hitchin, to Cambridge in 1873. She was helped in this by **Barbara Bodichon**, **Bessie Rayner Parkes** and others. These students included **Louisa Lumsden**, whose examination success was finally rewarded with the Master of Arts degree in Classics from the University when fifty-five years later, in 1928, she attended the first graduation for women. Emily Davies had been determined that her students should follow the same courses as the men, and she managed to set up a more formal college at Girton on the north edge of the city in 1874, becoming its Mistress. She is commemorated in the college chapel. The college is hung with paintings of artists and pioneers of women's rights.

A different approach to higher education for women was pursued by **Anne Jemima Clough**. In 1871 she had five students of her own at 74 Regent Street [the building now houses a restaurant], where she supervised their studies. Her aim was that her students should become better teachers, rather than that they should obtain degrees. University staff, sympathetic to the idea of women in academic life, helped her but there was no formal link with the University system. Her group moved to Merton Hall, Northampton Street, as she took on more students, then in 1875 Newnham College was founded in Sidgwick Avenue as 'Newnham Hall', with her as principal, after a fund-raising effort. It gained college status in 1880. The original building complex is a Victorian redbrick ideal of a women's scholarly community; the later extension for the college built by the architect **Elizabeth Whitworth Scott** is in a contrasting but harmonious style. Emily Davies and Miss Clough clashed in their ideas about women students at Cambridge; the Newnham women continuing to sit separate examinations for several years. Miss Clough died in Cambridge in 1892 and is buried in Grantchester, a village to the south-west.

The third women's college was New Hall, founded in 1954, and from small beginnings soon grew to match the other women's colleges in status and size. It has its buildings in Huntingdon Road. More recently Lucy Cavendish College was established in 1965 as a graduate society. Situated off Lady Margaret Road it now gives women an opportunity to start their studies at a later stage in their lives rather than straight after their schooldays, as well as serving graduate women. **Lucy Cavendish**, after whom it is named, was a philanthropist and social reformer who campaigned tirelessly from the 1800s onwards for women's educational needs and for oppressed minorities abroad. She died in 1926.

The majority of the colleges now have both women and men as students and academic staff, but men continue to outnumber women. Most of the colleges can be visited but at restricted times.

Since these educational opportunities were opened to female students, several Cambridge women have made their mark in many spheres of activity. Past students of Newnham include **F. M. Mayor**, the novelist; her friend, the pacifist **Mary Sheepshanks**; **Philippa Garrett Fawcett**, who attained the top mathematics success in 1890, though not given a degree [the university, initially moderately welcoming to women, would not grant them full degrees until 1948]; philosopher and novelist **Iris Murdoch**, who undertook postgraduate research here; classicist **Jane Harrison** who later held a fellowship here; **Sylvia Plath** the American poet; and **Dora Russell** who obtained first-class results and then accepted a fellowship in modern languages. **Margaret Llewelyn Davies**, early secretary of the Women's Co-operative Guild, **Helena Swanwick**, the journalist and pacifist and **Rosamund Lehmann**, the writer, are among the better known Girton women. **Wendy Savage**, the gynaecologist, is a more recent graduate from Girton. Many have followed, their education here taking them into new fields for women. **Dorothy Crowfoot Hodgkin**, who received her doctorate from Cambridge University, was later awarded the Nobel Prize for Chemistry and a Fellowship of the Royal Society.

The University has tended to dominate life in Cambridge, and many women grew up greatly influenced by it, yet were not officially part of it. **Elizabeth Montagu**, the Blue Stocking, was brought up here by her grandmother, whose second husband was the Universty Librarian. **Millicent Garrett Fawcett**, the leading suffragist, was married to the professor of economics here in 1867, and her daughter Philippa was born a year later. The Fawcett home in Brookside was a meeting place for feminists and Newnham students, as Millicent actively supported Anne Jemima Clough's work. In October 1928 Virginia Woolf gave two influential lectures at Newnham and Girton on writing, entitled 'Women and Fiction', later published as *A Room of One's Own* [1929]. She stressed that financial independence and her own space were essential for a woman writer. The novelist **Rose Macaulay** was raised in a local academic family: her father lectured in English at the University.

An earlier visitor to the university town was **Mary Lamb**. A plaque on 11 King's Parade records her stay here with her brother Charles. She shared his regret that he had not been a student here. **Mary Kingsley** resented the fact that her brother was able to study at the University, but that she was not. However, she acquired her own, broad education from her father's library and his intellectual friends. Mary Kingsley lived from 1882 at 7 Mortimer Road where her family had moved for her brother's sake. When her parents died ten years later, leaving her financially independent, she set sail for Africa where she studied the wildlife and took a serious interest in anthropology. Her accounts of her expeditions were published in *Travels in West Africa* [1897], and make wonderful reading.

A Woman's Guide to Cambridge by Sue Oosthuizen, Woody Press, Cambridge, 1983 is an informative booklet, presenting five guided walks in the city, which focus on the lives of many local women whose history is generally ignored by the inhabitants of the city, and therefore not drawn to the attention of visitors.

CANFORD, Dorset [see Map 1, G3]   In 1895 **Lady Charlotte Guest** died at her son's home here, Canford Manor, now a public school for boys and is buried beneath a red granite gravestone in the south of the churchyard. By this time she was Lady Charlotte Schreiber, having married a second time later in life. It was the end of a very full life, one active in widely differing areas: industry, business, Welsh literature, and art collecting. *The Mabinogion*, a collection of medieval Welsh tales, was published in 1838 by Lady Charlotte, who had made a study of the language and culture of the country into which she had married. The manor, now much altered, is thought to have been the birthplace of **Ela**, the thirteenth-century saint generally linked with Wiltshire.

CANTERBURY, Kent [see Map 1, F5]   **Bertha**, French wife of the Saxon king Aethelbert, had made it a condition of her marriage to him in AD 596 that she could worship in the Christian manner. She therefore founded St Martin's Church outside the old town walls and encouraged the spread of Christianity through her protection and support of the missionary Augustine. On her death *c.* 612, she was buried in St Martin's porch, in the Church of St Peter and St Paul.

Over a thousand years later **Anne Finch**, the poet, lived and wrote here. As Countess of Winchilsea and a former Maid of Honour to Mary of Modena, James II's queen, she was well connected with ready access to court circles. Her poetry was published as *Miscellany Poems on Several Occasions* [1713]. **Celia Fiennes** visited Anne Finch in 1697: 'To Canterbury most thro' Lanes we come by my Lord Winchilseas House gardens and parck, the house is an old building'. The Winchilseas' home was called The Moat and stood on the east of the city, on the route from Littlebourne. Celia was impressed by Canterbury: 'It's a noble Citty, the gates are high tho' but narrow, the streetes are most of them large and long and the buildings handsome, very neat but not very lofty, most are of brickwork; its a flourishing town. . . . There is fine walks and seates and places for musick to make it acceptable and commodious to the Company; there is a large Market house and a town Hall over it in the town, but the Cathedrall is the finest sight there, the carving of stone is very fine on the outside, as also within.' The cathedral has long been an attraction for visitors, as Chaucer's *Canterbury Tales* [*c.* 1387] bear witness.

CARDIFF, South Glamorgan [see Map 1, F3]   The city was granted the status of Capital City of Wales only in the reign of the present Queen. The National Museum of Wales★, Cathays Park, has works by the Welsh artist **Gwen John**. A major bequest was the art collection of **Margaret** and **Gwendolin Davies**. Their French Impressionist paintings are especially prized. These sisters were among the first British collectors to recognise the strength of the Impressionist style.

CARDIGAN, Dyfed [see Map 1, F2]   In 1648, when she was sixteen, **Katherine Philips** married an older Welshman, and from then on lived

6 Joan Eardley's first studio: The Watch House in Catterline, Grampian

partly at The Priory, next to the church here, and partly in London. The former Benedictine Priory became the meeting place for her Society of Friendship, whose members all called themselves by romantic names, and wrote poetry and translations for each other. Katherine was the 'Matchless Orinda' and the 'Lucasia' to whom many of her works were addressed was **Anne Owen**.

CARISBROOKE, Isle of Wight [see Map 1, G4] **Dorothy Osborne** saved her brother from the Roundheads here in 1648. He foolishly revealed his Royalist feelings by scratching an appropriate quotation on the window of the inn in which he and Dorothy were spending a night before leaving for France. At the time the place was crawling with Roundheads because Charles I was imprisoned in Carisbrooke Castle★. Needless to say, they were called before the Cromwellian authorities in the castle, but Dorothy pluckily took the blame and they were allowed to continue their journey to France. Whilst on their journey into exile she met William Temple, her future husband. She was then twenty-one years old. The letters they exchanged during their six-year engagement are an affectionate and literary record of a troubled period in British history.

CASTERTON, Cumbria [see Map 1, D3] **Dorothea Beale** taught at the girls' school here before taking up her best-known post at Cheltenham Ladies' College. Casterton Girls' School is the successor to the school attended by the Brontës at Cowan Bridge and had been set up to educate the daughters of clergymen.

CATTERLINE, Grampian [see Map 2, B3] The Scottish artist, **Joan Eardley**, first visited this clifftop fishing village near Stonehaven in 1950, and immediately fell in love with it. She bought and restored the cottage known as The Watch House in an isolated situation to the north of the village. This exposure to the elements gave her a very different outlook from her Glasgow scene. In 1956 she moved into number one, at the southern end of the row of stone cottages, keeping it on as a studio when she came to live later at number eighteen. The subjects of her paintings were the ever-changing sea, and local children on the shore. She died after a long illness, and her ashes were scattered on the beach.

CAVENDISH, Suffolk [see Map 1, F4]   The Sue Ryder Foundation which has supported many homes for the care of the sick and disabled has its headquarters here. The Foundation's Museum★ traces the history of the work started by **Sue Ryder**, Baroness Ryder of Warsaw in Poland and Cavendish in Suffolk, who continues to lead the Foundation.

CHARD, Somerset [see Map 1, G3]   **Margaret Bondfield**, who was brought up in the neighbourhood, taught as a pupil-teacher at the High Street school in Chard, before her involvement with trade unions set her on the road to becoming the first woman Cabinet Minister in Britain. The cottage in which she was born in 1873 stands unmarked in Chaffcombe Road.

CHATSWORTH, Derbyshire [see Map 1, E3]   Chatsworth, the magnificent country house★, replaces one of the many homes of **Bess of Hardwick**, later **Elizabeth Talbot**, Countess of Shrewsbury. In 1547 this powerful woman married her second husband, Sir William Cavendish, and through him acquired huge mineral-rich estates which she managed skilfully, dealing in coal, lead and timber most profitably. She came here to live after leaving her fourth husband, the Earl of Shrewsbury. **Mary Queen of Scots** was held prisoner here on behalf of Elizabeth I, and the garden building now known as Queen Mary's Bower derives its name from her period here. There are also rooms inside the house nominally associated with her, but almost certainly built much later.

When the Cavendishes were created Dukes of Devonshire the present house was built. In 1774 **Georgiana Cavendish** became mistress of the house by marrying the fifth Duke. She was extremely influential in the Whig party, and played as full a part in politics as was possible for a woman at that time. She was also beautiful, and many of the best artists of the day painted her portrait; examples can be seen in the house. She was at the centre of a lively set of intellectuals. There are many reminders of her in the house and grounds.

CHAWTON, Hampshire [see Map 3, C1]   **Jane Austen**, her mother and her sister Cassandra settled in Chawton Cottage in 1809. This Georgian redbrick building hs been little altered and today is generally known as Jane Austen's House★. It is opened to the public by the Jane Austen Memorial Trust. The house has great charm, much of its character retained, including the squeaking door which served Jane as an advance warning of someone's

7   Hannah More Cottage, Lower North Street, Cheddar, Somerset

approach. Her novels were furtively written, though she later acknowledged their success, albeit with modesty. Her writing was a sign that she
was happier at Chawton than she had been at Southampton where she had
written little apart from letters. In Chawton she was in her element.
Surrounded by her family, she was again creative: the final versions of her
six novels, now so well known as classics of English literature, were
produced here. These are: *Sense and Sensibility* [1811], *Pride and Prejudice*
[1813], *Mansfield Park* [1814], *Emma* [1816], *Northanger Abbey* [1818] and
Persuasion [1818]. *Mansfield Park, Emma* and *Persuasion* are known to have
been entirely written here. The others were earlier works revised and re-
titled before eventual publication.

Jane was a good correspondent, keeping in touch with distant family and
friends. She was especially close to her sister Cassandra and whenever one
of them was away from home they would describe their hosts' homes,
acquaintances and relations and all the domestic detail with keen observation and understated wit. Some of these letters survive and give insights
into the interests, amusements and, to a lesser extent, emotions of one of
Britain's best-loved writers.

The house includes early editions of her books, as well as pictures, clothing, pieces of furniture and many treasured objects which together put the visitor in tune with Jane's life at 'our Chawton home'. The house stands on the corner of the main road, and is well signposted. The church, which Jane attended, held an important place in their restricted but by no means restricting social life. A walk round the village will show that sufficient remains untouched to give substance to the quiet country life which Jane now so enjoyed.

CHEDDAR, Somerset [see Map 1, F3] At the suggestion of the abolitionist William Wilberforce **Hannah More** opened a school in 1788 for those who were unable to read. She moved into the whitewashed building in Lower North Street now called Hannah More Cottage, most recently functioning as a meeting place for Red Cross Groups. Local farmers did not take kindly to the idea of their labourers being educated: they foresaw all sorts of trouble, and made life difficult for Hannah. She left for Blagdon in 1795.

CHELTENHAM, Gloucestershire [see Map 1, F3] The town is probably best known for its Ladies' College. Now an exclusive girls' school, it played a significant part in the development of serious academic education for girls. **Dorothea Beale** was principal from 1858 until 1904 and established it as a pioneering institution. One of her early staff was **Louisa Lumsden**, who drew on the experience when asked to set up a similar institution in Scotland. One former pupil among many who achieved academic success was **Jane Harrison**, the classical scholar and anthropologist. Others became novelists: **Margaret Kennedy**, **May Sinclair**, **Phyllis Bentley** and **Anne Puddicombe**, who wrote under the pen-name **Allen Raine**. The architect **Elizabeth Whitworth Scott** worked in Cheltenham in her professional capacity. The Ladies' College has splendid carvings, statues and memorials, showing women of achievement to inspire the pupils. Among these is **Josephine Butler**, the campaigner for many social reforms affecting women who lived in Cheltenham from 1857 to 1866.

CHEVENING, Kent [see Map 3, C4] **Lady Hester Stanhope**, the traveller in the Middle East, was brought up in the village, in privileged circumstances. This was in marked contrast to the poverty in which she spent her later years in the Lebanon. She was the niece of the Prime Minister William Pitt the Younger, and acted as his escort during his later years of office [1783-1801]. After his death she was financially independent. She began to travel on the Continent, and eventually settled in the Middle East, where she led an eccentric life in a crumbling Christian ruin.

CHICKSANDS, Bedfordshire [see Map 1, F4] **Dorothy Osborne** may have been born here. Certainly the now ruined priory was her childhood home. She carried on some of her correspondence with her future husband, whom she married in 1654, from here. The letters describe the lifestyle and everyday concerns of an upper-class woman in a period of uncertainty. The priory now stands in the middle of an RAF base.

8 Castle House, Chipping Ongar, Essex, the home of Jane and Ann Taylor

CHIPPING ONGAR, Essex [see Map 3, A4] The Taylor family which produced much work for young people moved to Castle House in 1811. The house is now a farm, standing behind the church. The overgrown mound of the early castle stands beyond it. **Ann** and **Jane Taylor** wrote stories, nursery rhymes and hymns, including *Original Poems for Infant Minds* [1804]. 'Twinkle, twinkle, little star' is their best known composition. Their father was a Nonconformist minister, and the family lies buried in the floor of the Unitarian Chapel, hidden from the main road by a building on which a plaque records David Livingstone's brief visit before leaving for Africa. More significance appears to be attached to this short stay than to the longer term residence of the Taylor family.

CHOLSEY, Oxfordshire [see Map 1, F4] When the prolific writer of detective fiction **Agatha Christie** died in 1976, her works were almost as widely available as the Bible and the works of Shakespeare. She had fully earned the epithet the 'Queen of Crime'. Her large carved grave stands in Cholsey Churchyard.

CHRISTCHURCH, Cambridgeshire [see Map 1, E4] The redbrick Victorian rectory next to the village church on Upwell Fen was the home of **Dorothy Sayers'** family from 1917. The action in one of her best known books, *The Nine Tailors* [1934], is set in this area, and the seat of her aristocratic detective, Lord Peter Wimsey is sited in the Fen. The old rectory is now a boys' home.

9   Agatha Christie's grave in the
churchyard at Cholsey, Oxfordshire

CHRISTCHURCH, Dorset [see Map 1, G3]   In 1818 **Louisa Marchioness of Waterford**, the Victorian artist, was born as Louisa Stuart in Highcliffe Castle, a splendid mansion in the gothic style, now under threat from building development. Although more generally associated with Ford, in Northumberland, she is remembered locally by a window in St Mark's Church.

CLIFFORD, Hereford and Worcestershire [see Map 1, F3]   The twelfth-century romantic figure **Rosamund de Clifford** is thought to have been born in the castle here. Her beauty attracted the attention of Henry II and it is said that his jealous wife had her poisoned. The castle, now a ruin, was built by the ancestors of the seventeenth-century castle builder, **Lady Anne Clifford**.

CLIVEDEN, Buckinghamshire [see Map 3, B1]   The magnificent house☆ [NT] overlooking the Thames was built for the husband of **Barbara Villiers**, who led a notorious life as mistress of Charles II. When she lost the king's attentions she found consolation elsewhere. It was not only in the seventeenth century that residents of Cliveden were at the forefront of British politics. **Nancy Astor** held court here: her 'Cliveden Set' included the foremost political figures of the inter-war years. As Britain's first woman to hold a seat in the House of Commons, her own career was closely followed by the press. When she died in 1964, her ashes were buried in the charming Octagon Temple beside her husband. The grounds are open to the public but part of the house has recently been turned into a luxury country house hotel.

A description of Cliveden in Nancy Astor's time is given in *Cliveden and the Astor Household Between the Wars* by Geoffrey Tyack, published by Geoffrey Tyack, 1982. An alternative view comes from Rosina Harrison's

Rose: my life in service, published in 1975 by Cassell, London. Rosina Harrison was on the staff of the house.

COCKERMOUTH, Cumbria [see Map 2, D3]   **Dorothy Wordsworth**, the diarist, was born here in 1771, at Wordsworth House☆[NT], Main Street. The death of her mother in 1778 led to the family being split up and she was sent to Halifax to live with relatives.

COLCHESTER, Essex [see Map 1, F4]   One of the most devastating events in the history of this ancient town was inspired by a woman: in AD 55 **Boudicca** [formerly known as Boadicea] led an attack on the major Roman colony, then called Colonia Claudia by the Romans or Camulodunum, its native name, which completely destroyed the town, ruined the temple [at the time the largest Roman temple outside Rome], and thoroughly demoralised the Roman army. The Romans had not fully appreciated the strength of feeling of one of the conquered British tribes. The Iceni were not prepared to have their traditional system of government overturned by the demands of Rome. The refusal to be subjugated to Roman rule, which would ignore the rights to succession of Boudicca and her descendants, brought together a formidable insurrection, and Colchester suffered for this. The Norman castle which houses the Colchester and Essex Museum★ was built on the foundations of the Roman temple and its original extent can still be appreciated.

Once Roman rule was established more firmly, **Helena**, who later became a popular saint, is supposed to have been born here, probably *c*. AD 250, according to tradition. Most of what is known of her life is apocryphal. Reputedly her effect on the Roman Empire was ultimately greater than Boudicca's: Helena was converted to Christianity in AD 312, persuading her son, Constantine the Great, who had by then been Emperor for twenty years, to adopt her new religion. Christianity then became the official religion of the vast area under Roman domination, and its impact on European civilisation was clearly far-reaching. There are many churches in Britain dedicated to her: one of the earliest must be St Helena's, on the corner of St Helen's Lane and Maidenburgh Street, Colchester, sadly no longer in use as a church. No matter how much or little of this can be accounted for by historians, Colchester is proud to claim Helena as a daughter.

In the same part of the town, the so-called Dutch Quarter, a plaque on 11 and 12 Stockwell Street commemorates the building as the childhood home from 1796 of **Ann** and **Jane Taylor**. While resident here they published a number of nursery rhymes and children's books. These include *Original Poems for Infant Minds* [1804], *Rhymes for the Nursery* [1806] and *Hymns for Infant Minds* [1810]. The plaque recalls their most popular nursery rhyme 'Twinkle, twinkle, little star'. The family moved to Chipping Ongar in 1811.

COMPTON, Surrey [see Map 3, C1]   The artist, designer and architect,

Mary Watts, ran a craft school and a business venture called Terracotta Arts in Compton at the end of the nineteenth century. Heavily involved in the Arts and Crafts Movement, she specialised in designing terracotta tiles and panels for architectural use. A fine example of her work can be seen on the Watts Mortuary Chapel in Compton cemetery, which she designed in 1896 and where she was buried in 1938.

CONWY, Gwynned [see Map 1, E2]   Well sited and well fortified, Conwy Castle★ perches above the river. According to tradition the first sweetpeas in Britain were grown by **Eleanor of Castile** on the Queen's Terrace here: a gentle achievement during turbulent times.

COOKHAM, Berkshire [see Map 3, B1]   **Emilia Lanier**, herself a poet, is thought by some to have been the 'Dark Lady' of Shakespeare's sonnets. She came from Cookham, a place where passions seem often to have run high. **Hilda Carline** came here to live with her husband and fellow-artist Stanley Spencer. Theirs was an unconventional relationship. They lived at Lindworth, off Cookham High Street, but separated when her mental health declined. She died in 1950, and was buried in Cookham cemetery. She is commemorated on her husband's white square tombstone beside the path in the churchyard. Two other artists lived and worked in Cookham, and found their lives closely involved with the Spencers: it was with Dorothy Hepworth that the painter **Patricia Preece** shared Moor Cottage, now a residence for retired people, a redbrick house at the end of the High Street looking over Cookham Moor. They continued to live here together even after Patricia's marriage, as the second wife, to Spencer.

CORFE CASTLE, Dorset [see Map 1, G3]   The castle itself is now an impressive ruin, having been blown up by the Parliamentarians after its surrender in 1646. It had been the home of Royalist supporters, and during her husband's absence in support of the King, **Mary, Lady Bankes** resolved to defend the castle against the Roundheads. A long siege in 1643 eventually ended in her favour, Lady Bankes having inflicted considerable losses on the attackers and herself demonstrating great courage and resourcefulness. However, a further siege begun in 1645 was not easy to withstand and Lady Bankes had to abandon her home. It was then destroyed by her opponents, who first allowed her to leave. She lived on elsewhere in Dorset until 1661.

Earlier a Welsh heroine **Maud de Valerie** died here as prisoner of King John, against whose oppressive regime she had rebelled. Earlier still **Elfrida**, widow of Edgar the Saxon king, had her stepson, King Edward the Martyr, murdered in the castle in 978. Her husband had died in 975 and his heir was his son by his first wife. Elfrida was ambitious for Ethelred, her own son, then just in his teens, to have the throne of Wessex, and this led her to arrange the murder. After she saw Ethelred crowned she left him to rule himself.

Three hundred years later the village was the last home of the New

Zealand artist, **Frances Hodgkins**. She lived a solitary life here from 1939-47, working in a converted chapel on West Street, in straitened circumstances. Her mental health gradually deteriorated, reaching a crisis here, before she spent her last weeks in an institution in Dorchester.

COTTISFORD, Northamptonshire [see Map 1, F4]   The school which **Flora Thompson** attended as a child and which features in her trilogy *Larkrise to Candleford* [1945] stands much altered as a private home at the village crossroads, on a triangular island. Born Flora Timms, she left school at the age of fourteen to take up employment in a village post office.

COULSTON, Wiltshire [see Map 1, F3]   **Mrs Delaney**, then Mary Granville, was born in the village in 1700, but her family soon moved to London, where she spent most of her childhood. Her middle age and widowhood were her happiest years, and also very productive. She wrote letters and devised a new artform involving painted cut paper.

COVENTRY, West Midlands [see Map 1, E3]   Although **Lady Godiva**'s ride through the town is well known, the supposed reason for it is often forgotten. She is said to have challenged her husband's cripplingly heavy taxation of the local people, having seen how they suffered. She agreed to ride naked through the streets, provided that he would lift the tax. The people supported her efforts on their behalf by closing their shutters and keeping away from the streets. According to the legend, the only person who watched was blinded as punishment from heaven and known thereafter as Peeping Tom. Godiva's challenge was honoured, but it was not the only act of generosity which she initiated. She held lands and property in her own right and was the benefactress and founder of some religious institutions, including a Benedictine convent here in *c.* 1043. Indeed the town's name is said to derive from Conventre, meaning convent town. Godiva is commemorated in the city centre by a bronze statue. A display in the Herbert Museum and Art Gallery★, Jordan Well, tells more about her life and the ways in which the image of Godiva has developed over the years.

The town also featured in the lives of some other unconventional women. **Hannah Snell** joined the army as a foot soldier here in *c.* 1744 as 'James Gray' at the time of the Jacobite rebellion, the start of a career in the forces which took her overseas, especially to India. **George Eliot** went to a Baptist school here at Nant Glyn, now 29 Warwick Row, from 1832-35. It is thought that her first attempts at writing fiction were written at this school. Six years later she and her father moved to a large semi-detached house, Bird Grove, on Foleshill Road. When she lived there it stood in quite a rural setting, far back from the road. Now the area has been developed by terraced housing and some shops, but the association is recognised in the naming of George Eliot Road. Mary Anne Evans, as she then was, became involved in a circle of non-conformist, radical thinkers and her views were well-respected. She began to produce works for publication, first a translation from German, Strauss's *Life of Jesus* [1846] and then essays, reviews and other articles. Her published novels, which include *Adam Bede* [1858], *The Mill on the Floss* [1860] and *Silas Marner* [1861], established her as a sensitive writer in her own lifetime. After her father's death, she was gaining a reputation as a writer, and left Coventry in 1849 for London. Around this time, 1847, **Ellen Terry** was born in Smith Street into an acting family. It was inevitable that she should travel widely in her childhood and equally inevitable that she herself would go onto the stage.

Angela Brazil, writer of many books for girls, died here in 1947. She had moved into a house called The Quadrant with her brother, a doctor. She became very involved in the life of the city, especially the cathedral, and was much respected. Her titles, such as *A Fourth Form Friendship* [1909], *The Nicest Girl in the School* [1909], *Ruth of St. Ronan's* [1927] and *The School on the Loch* [1946], popularised a new genre of schoolgirl fiction which remains a favourite today with younger readers.

COWAN BRIDGE, Lancashire [see Map 1, D3] **Charlotte** and **Emily Brontë** attended the Clergy Daughters' School in 1824-5, as a plaque on the end of the row of stone cottages at the north end of the town's main road recalls. The experience was grim, and when their two older sisters caught typhoid there and died, Charlotte and Emily returned to continue their education at home in Haworth.

CRADLEY HEATH, near Halesowen, West Midlands [see Map 1, E3] This was the scene of the 1910 Cradley Heath Chainmakers' Strike, in which the Scottish trade union activist **Mary Macarthur** and Lancashire suffrage worker **Selina Cooper** were involved. The types of work which women did at the chainmaking forges can be appreciated by seeing demonstrations of forging at Avoncroft Museum of Buildings★, Bromsgrove, and the Black Country Museum★ at Dudley, West Midlands. This strike was a milestone as a demonstration of women's power in the workforce, and is still emotive today. Women had been earning only one old penny per hour, but through their action they won an improved wage.

CRAIGENPUTTOCK, Dumfries and Galloway [see Map 2, D2] **Jane Welsh Carlyle** inherited Moorland Farm, in Dunscore Glen, in 1828. She moved here with her husband, and she was happy living on the farm. However, after six years in the solid but remote farmhouse, he was anxious for more company and they left for London in 1832.

CRAIG-Y-NOS, West Glamorgan [see Map 1, F3] **Dame Adelina Patti**, the Italian singer, retired to the splendid gothic villa on the hillside overlooking the Swansea valley. She first visited the site on a picnic and reputedly was so overwhelmed by the beauty of the surroundings that she sang out loud in sheer delight. She bought the estate for £8,000 in 1878. It includes a small concert theatre, modelled on Drury Lane Theatre, London, and it was in her own theatre that she made her first recording for His Master's Voice in 1905. Until recently it was a hospital but its future is under threat. The Welsh people loved Adelina Patti, and made her welcome in their country. She died here in 1919 and was widely mourned.

CRAWLEY, Surrey [see Map 1, F4]   The Franciscan monastery church-yard is the final resting place of the ashes of **Catherine Walters**, whose lifestyle might not have met the approval of the monks but they sympathised with her wish to be buried as a Roman Catholic. An Irish Liverpudlian, she died in 1920 after a merry life in London as a courtesan.

CROMFORD, Derbyshire [see Map 1, E3]   **Alison Uttley** was born on a farm near Cromford in 1884. Her country childhood instilled in her an enduring love of nature, and the desire to study science. Her keen observation is demonstrated in her writing. She wrote for both adults and children, but is probably best known for her character Little Grey Rabbit who features in several of her books.

CULLODEN, Grampian [see Map 2, B2]   The decisive battle of Culloden put an end to the ambitions of the Stuart pretenders to the British throne in 1746. A Visitor Centre☆[SNT] interprets the action, and the site serves as a memorial to the many slain. At least two women were fighting on the winning side: **Hannah Snell** and **Mary Ralphson**, 'Trooper Mary', who served with her husband in the 3rd Dragoon Guards.

CULLOMPTON, Devon [see Map 1, G3]   **E.M. Delafield** settled in Devon, writing forty books, of which the best known is probably *Diaries of a Provincial Lady* [1931], which pokes fun at the small concerns of middle-class women living in the country. She died in Cullompton in 1943.

D D

DARLEY DALE, Derbyshire [see Map 1, E3]   **Richmal Crompton**, the author of the popular series of children's books, the *Just William* tales, lived here. The first *Just William* appeared in 1922. She had attended St Elphin's School as a girl at the turn of the century, and later taught there.

DARTMOUTH, Devon [see Map 1, G3]   **Flora Thompson** began writing the books based on her early life on the Oxfordshire-Northampton-shire border after settling in the south-west in 1928. The first was *Lark Rise* [1939], followed by *Over to Candleford* [1941] and then *Candleford Green* [1943]. Her home was at The Outlook, 126 Above Town, just above the church up steep narrow streets. Although she moved further east in 1940, she was buried in Dartmouth's Long Cross Cemetery on her death seven years later.

DEAL, Kent [see Map 1, F5]   The fact that **Elizabeth Carter** was born here in 1717 is recognised by the siting of a plaque on Elizabeth Carter House, South Street. This was the home in which she gained a good education from both her father and her own efforts to teach herself. She was a most accomplished woman, with wide-ranging knowledge and interests, proficient in several languages. In 1758 the publication of her fine translation of the thoughts of the Stoic philosopher Epicetus from the Greek drew her to the attention of the Blue Stockings, especially Mrs Montagu, and other contemporary intellectuals. The ensuing income enabled her to buy property elsewhere in the town. She set up home with her father, who was now retired from his curacy, but her intellectual life continued to be stimulating. They spent the winters in London, and enjoyed Deal the rest of the year. She was a splendid correspondent, and also produced poetry. Her letters give a full account of eighteenth-century life in the town.

DEENE PARK, Northamptonshire [see Map 1, E4]   Once a somewhat irregular relationship with Lord Cardigan had gained respectability through marriage in 1858, **Adeline Horsey de Horsey** settled happily in the stately home, Deene Park★, as Countess of Cardigan; this idyll was short-lived as she was widowed in 1868. She lived on to a good age, having meantime married again and acquired another title, Countess de Lancastre. She was buried with her first husband in St Peter's Church, Deene. The elaborate effigy which she had designed shows her dressed in her Countess's robes lying beside Lord Cardigan and gazing adoringly at him.

DENBIGH, Clwyd [see Map 1, E3]   The **Ladies of Llangollen [Eleanor Butler** and **Sarah Ponsonby**] eloped from Ireland in 1776, intending to set up home together in a cottage in England. However, their first base on mainland Britain was at Denbigh, and their exploratory travels from here led them to their future home at Llangollen. **Mrs Thrale**, herself a native of North Wales, frequently travelled in the country. In 1794 she wrote 'I shall be loth to leave Denbigh – 'tis such an admirable Thinking-Place.' In 1840 **Rhoda Broughton**, whose novels later brought her notoriety, was born near Denbigh and she always had a love of North Wales.

DERBY, Derbyshire [see Map 1, E3]   Derby was already a town of some importance in the tenth century. An attractive target for the Viking invaders, it was saved by **Aethelflaed**, Lady of the Mercians, in 917. As Queen of Mercia, she used her good grasp of tactics and strategy to defend her people and territory.

A blind martyr to the Protestant religion, **Joan Waste**, was burned at the stake in the town in 1556. The spot at which she died is marked in the road. Despite the handicap of being blind from birth and her humble origins, she had studied and memorised the Bible. She was a victim of Mary I's attempts to restore the Roman Catholic faith in England. Over two centuries later, in happier circumstances, **Maria Edgeworth** attended a boarding school in the town from 1775 until 1780, but its site is not known. She returned to her father's large family and used what she had learned in bringing up and teaching her many younger sisters and brothers. Two much more local figures are buried in Derby. **Elizabeth Talbot**, better known as Bess of Hardwick, who died in 1608, her ninetieth year, is commemorated by a magnificent monument in All Saints, Derby's Cathedral. One of her successors as mistress of Chatsworth, **Georgiana Cavendish**, the Whig activist, was buried in the family vault of the Dukes of Devonshire in St Stephen's Church, Derby, in 1806.

A more recent notable daughter of Derby was **Constance Spry** who through her teaching, writings and example, elevated flower arranging and fine cooking to the status of art. She was born in a redbrick terrace house at 58 Warner Street in 1886, and her childhood was spent in the town until her family moved away when she was eight years of age.

DEVONPORT, Devon [see Map 1, G2]   This coastal town on the Tamar estuary with its long association with the British navy was chosen by the religious philanthropist **Agnes Weston** as the site of her first 'Sailors' Rest' home, founded in 1876. She worked tirelessly on behalf of the seamen, trying to provide support for those in difficult circumstances. Christian example was her guiding principle. Her work was duly appreciated and when she died in 1918, she received a burial with full naval honours, a rare event where women are concerned. Her grave monument in Weston Mill Cemetery is surmounted by an angel looking heavenwards and an anchor adorns the inscription where she is described as 'the Sailor's Friend'.

DOLGELLAU, Gwynned [see Map 1, E2]   The passionate social reformer, **Frances Power Cobbe**, moved to Dolgellau in 1884. By then she
was sixty-two years old. A pioneering feminist and suffragist, all her life she
was involved in humanitarian causes, especially women's, and she
continued to campaign against animal vivisection in retirement. When she
died in 1904, she was buried with her close companion, the sculptress Mary
Lloyd, in Llanelltyd churchyard. Prominent lesbians, they had shared a
home at Hengwrt. Frances Power Cobbe's published works covered
subjects ranging from moral issues to travel literature: titles include *Cities of
the Past* [1864], *Darwinism in Morals* [1872] and *The Duties of Woman* [1881].

DORCHESTER, Dorset [see Map 1, G3]   The last desperate weeks of the
life of **Frances Hodgkins**, the New Zealand artist, were passed in the
nearby Harrison Mental Institution. She died there in 1947. The archives of
poet **Valentine Ackland** and novelist and poet **Sylvia Townsend Warner**
are deposited at the Dorset County Museum★ and can be consulted by
appointment. Having left the London literary scene in the early 1930s, after
the success of Sylvia's first novel *Lolly Willowes* [1926], they moved to
Dorset where they stayed together for the rest of their lives. In addition to
their writing of prose, fiction and poetry, they became actively involved in
the Dorset Communist Party.

DORKING, Surrey [see Map 3, C2]   **Marie Stopes**, campaigner for birth
control, could escape some of the pressures of her stressful controversial life
at Norbury Park, her eighteenth-century country home. She entertained
many intellectual friends here, and it was here that she died of cancer in
1958. In the early nineteenth century, the house was also known to **Jane
Austen** who stayed with relatives in nearby Great Bookham and set her
unfinished novel *The Watsons* in Dorking.

DORNOCH, Sutherland [see Map 2, B2]   The cathedral houses the tombs
of the Earls and Dukes of Sutherland, and it is thought that **Jane Gordon**,
Countess of Sutherland, was buried here. Jane died in 1628 after making an
important contribution to the economic life of the county. A successor,
Millicent Duchess of Sutherland, is commemorated in the window
which she designed herself. Traditional values and superstitions had a tight
hold in Sutherland, and the last witch was burned in Dornoch as late as
1722.

DOWLAIS, Mid-Glamorgan [see Map 1, F3]   Dowlais Ironworks were
run by **Lady Charlotte Guest** after her first marriage in 1883 to Josiah
Guest, the proprietor. His business interests kept him in London so much
that effectively she was the works manager. Under her management several
novel iron-working techniques were introduced. Her home was Dowlais
House, and here she also made time to bring up ten children, to learn
Welsh, to translate into English *The Mabinogion* [completed in 1838], a cycle
of Welsh mythology and traditional tales, and to support her employees and
the wider community. Her husband's death in 1852 left her in sole charge of

the ironworks, and she succeeded in riding various industrial relations storms with humanity and dignity. She withdrew from the works on her second marriage in 1858, when she became Lady Charlotte Schreiber.

DUMFRIES, Dumfries and Galloway [see Map 2, D3]   The oldest bridge crossing the River Nith which divides the town is known as Dervoguilla's Bridge. **Dervoguilla, Lady of Galloway**, was a thirteenth-century benefactor whose foundations included abbeys, almshouses and colleges. The stone bridge, now of six arches instead of its original nine, does not date from her time but is certainly on the site of the wooden one which she had built.

DUNBAR, Lothian [see Map 2, C3]   The ruined Castle★ stands above the harbour as testimony to an indomitable woman, **Agnes Dunbar**, Countess of March and Dunbar. Herself the granddaughter of the Scottish hero-king, Robert the Bruce, she showed her own fighting spirit in 1338, defending the castle against a siege and blockade led by the Earls of Salisbury and Arundel. Her husband was fighting the English elsewhere, and, undeterred, Black Agnes, as she was also known, held out against the force sent by Edward II, so successfully that the siege was abandoned. It was a less than glorious setting for **Mary Queen of Scots** in 1567. It was one of the many strongholds in which she sought refuge before she was forced to abdicate in favour of her infant son.

DUNDEE, Tayside [see Map 2, C3]   Dundee is probably known far and wide for its marmalade and the cake which bears its name. **Mrs Keiller's** famous recipe was invented here in 1797, starting a flourishing industry in jams and conserves, and its fame abroad probably travelled on the routes served by the trade in jute from this port. The outspoken abolitionist and utopian social reformer, **Fanny Wright**, was born in the town in 1795, but she was soon orphaned and taken away to be brought up by relatives in London. **Mary Shelley**, also motherless, lived here as a teenager with a local family. Her foster parents would have been surprised to learn that they had nurtured the author of the famous science fiction *Frankenstein, or the Modern Prometheus* [1818].

Dundee was certainly the home town from the age of eleven of the missionary **Mary Slessor**, whose departure for the Calabar coast of West Africa in 1876 marked the start of nearly forty years devoted service to the native peoples. She had worked part-time at Baxter Brothers' Dens Works, Crescent Street [now demolished and new buildings erected], as a linen-weaver, becoming a full-time worker at fourteen. Her spare time was fully accounted for, educating herself by reading the Bible, the writings of Carlyle and Emerson, and much more, and teaching children at Sunday Schools and evening schools. A plaque at 6 Queen Street marks the site of the [long gone] Mission where she first became involved in Christian social work. She is remembered elsewhere in the town, notably in the Albert Museum★, which displays items associated with her life both in Scotland and West Africa.

DUNFERMLINE, Fife [see Map 2, C3]   **St Margaret**, Queen of Scotland, had fled to Scotland from England when her brother, Edgar Aethling, had unsuccessfully tried to claim the English throne in 1066. She married the Scots King Malcolm Canmore in a small church near the royal castle of which only Malcolm Canmore's Tower in Pittencrieff Park remains, and was crowned Queen in 1070. Devoutly religious, she established the first Benedictine abbey in Scotland. She was also responsible for building the now ruined 'new' Royal Palace★. On her death in 1093 she was buried in the great Abbey Church of the Holy Trinity here, one of her foundations. During the Reformation the bodies of herself and her husband were taken to Spain for safety by the Roman Catholic Philip II, to the Scots College at Douai, a seminary for Roman Catholic ordinands. She was canonised in 1250 and a chapel in the Church was dedicated to her the same year. The site of her shrine is marked by a white stone slab in the ruins at the east end of the Church. In 1401 another popular Queen of Scotland, **Annabella Drummond**, was buried in the Abbey Church.

Anne Halkett was an exceptionally well-educated woman who was able to benefit from her own scholarship by supporting herself in uncertain times. Widowed in 1676, she taught at her home, the Commendatory House in Maygate, thus making a living. A sixteenth-century building, it now forms part of Abbot House. She too is buried in the Abbey Church, in the Halkett family plot in the nave, having died in 1699.

DUNKELD, Tayside [see Map 2, B3]   Although she is more usually associated with the Lake District, **Beatrix Potter** was greatly influenced by her childhood summers spent in the country round Dunkeld. Dalguise, a country house [now the Dalguise Centre, owned by the Boys' Brigade] north of Dunkeld on the west bank of the Tay, was rented annually for the summer months – May to October – from when she was five until she was sixteen. She was able to get very close to nature, becoming familiar with the habits of local wildlife and plants, much of which appear later in her children's books in her well-observed illustrations. She did come back to the area in her twenties, and an illustrated letter which tells the story of her most famous children's book, *The Tale of Peter Rabbit* [1900], was written at Eastwood, where she spent the summer of 1893. She did not shape it into its published form until 1897. More about her times here can be learned from *Beatrix Potter in Scotland* by Deborah Rolland, Frederick Warne, London, 1981.

DUNNOTTAR, Grampian [see Map 2, B3]   The spectacular ruins of Dunnottar Castle★, perched perilously on the side of fearsome cliffs, immediately impress the visitor as presenting a stiff challenge to potential attackers. Cromwell's troops besieged it for eight months in 1650, when it was the last stronghold to hold out against the Parliamentarians. The Earl Marischal of Scotland was not only defending the castle but also the Honours of Scotland – the Crown, Sceptre and Sword which signify the authority of the Scottish sovereign. **Christian Fletcher**, the wife of the

10   Dunnottar Castle, Dunnottar, Grampian

local minister, was able to gain access to the castle occasionally, despite the state of siege, and managed to smuggle out the Honours undetected. She took them to the church at Old Kinneff for safety, and her heroism and patriotism could only safely be recognised much later once Charles II was restored to the throne.

DURHAM, County Durham [see Map 2, D3]   This northern cathedral city includes within its present boundaries on the west side the site of the Battle of Neville's Cross. In 1346 the Scots took the opportunity to attack the English while most of the English King Edward III's forces were engaged in France. It was his queen, **Philippa of Hainault**, who managed to raise an army of 12,000 to defeat the Scots at this northern battleground. In 1792 at Elemore Hall in Durham city, **Lady Byron** was born as Anna Isabella Millbanke into a prosperous local family.

DYMCHURCH, Kent [see Map 1, F5]   **Edith Nesbit** retired to Dymchurch, an area she had loved as a child on holiday. She had brightened the lives of many children with her own stories, *The Five Children and It* [1902] and *The Railway Children* [1906].

E E

EAST COWES, Isle of Wight [see Map 1, G4]   **Queen Victoria** had Osborne House★ built here overlooking Osborne Bay in the Italianate style in 1845-6 at her own expense and it was to become her favourite residence, where she and Prince Albert spent many happy times with their family. It was here that she died in 1901, aged eighty-two, the longest reigning British sovereign. The State Apartments, which can be visited, include many items directly associated with the Queen.

EAST GRINSTEAD, Sussex [see Map 3, C3]   The Danish ballet dancer, **Adeline Genee**, opened a theatre here named after her in 1967. She had made her home in Britain since her marriage in 1910.

EAST HORNDON, Essex [see Map 3, A4]   It is said that the heart of **Anne Boleyn** was recovered from the Tower of London after her execution there in 1536 and buried in All Saints Church, East Horndon. The church, now rarely used for worship, sits on a ridge overlooking the busy A127 route from London to Southend. Two of her family's properties were in Essex at Rochford and Chelmsford.

EAST KILBRIDE, Strathclyde [see Map 2, C2]   Flora MacDonald was not the only woman to help Bonnie Prince Charlie and later suffer for it. **Jean Cameron** of Glen Dessary also supported him in 1745 and was consequently persecuted. Her grave is in the churchyard in the street named after her birthplace.

EASTWELL, Kent [see Map 1, F4]   **Anne Finch**, Countess of Winchelsea, is said to have died at Eastwell Park in 1720. This aristocratic poet earned the admiration and friendship of her literary contemporaries Alexander Pope, Jonathan Swift and John Gay. Several of her works appeared in *Miscellany Poems on Several Occasions* [1713], the best known being her long poem *The Spleen*. It was well-received on its publication in 1709.

EAST WELLOW, Hampshire [see Map 1, F3]   The Church of St Margaret of Antioch on the hill in this hamlet contains a monument and some photographs associated with **Florence Nightingale**. She and her sister, Parthenope Verney, are buried in the family vault in the churchyard on the south of the church. The vault is marked by a gothic-style monument and is well tended, generally with flowers on it. The family home was nearby at Embley Park.

ECCLESFIELD, South Yorkshire [see Map 1, E3] **Juliana Horatia Ewing**, whose works for children are still occasionally read and were in her time widely enjoyed by younger readers, was born at the vicarage in Ecclesfield in 1841. *Melchior's Dream* [1862] and *The Land of the Lost Toys* [1869] are among Mrs Ewing's books. Her mother **Margaret Gatty**, whose home this was to be for thirty-three years, was also a very popular children's author. She edited *Aunt Judy's Magazine* and most of her daughter's writing first appeared in its pages. Mrs Gatty died in 1873 and is buried in the churchyard here. Both are commemorated on tablets inside the church, and books by them are displayed on a bookcase there. The tablet dedicated to Margaret Gatty was subscribed to by her devoted younger readers.

EDENBRIDGE, Kent [see Map 3, C3] Hever Castle★ is substantially the same as it was in the days of **Anne Boleyn**, one of whose childhood homes it was. This was the scene of her courtship by Henry VIII, before becoming his second wife in 1533 and the mother of Elizabeth I, a course which eventually took her to Tower Hill and execution. Visitors can see a room thought to have been hers. There is also an Anne of Cleves' Room. As part of Henry's divorce settlement in 1540, **Anne of Cleves**, the fourth wife, became mistress of Hever, and she was to spend much of the rest of her life here privately, but enjoying some privileges with the status of the 'King's sister'.

In the twentieth century, Kent continues to hold many attractions. **Emma Cons**, whose work in London to improve social conditions has probably received less recognition than her achievements in theatre management, died in nearby Hever village in 1912, and her ashes were scattered there.

EDINBURGH, Lothian [see Map 2, C3] The Castle★ on the volcanic rock dominates the city skyline – it has always been central to the history of Scotland's capital. Within its citadel stands the oldest building in Edinburgh, the small very simple chapel of **St Margaret**, Malcolm Canmore's queen. This was built for her own worship and her example was to root Scots Christianity more firmly in the Roman Catholic tradition which she had brought with her from Hungary. It was said that the Black Rood, an ebony cross which contained a piece of the True Cross, came to Scotland with her. The Palace of Holyrood★ at the east end of the Royal Mile stands beside the ruined abbey of the Holy Rood, the Black Rood itself having disappeared after the Reformation. Holyrood featured strongly in the life of the Catholic **Mary Queen of Scots**, at a time when the Protestant following of John Knox was gaining influence in Scotland. The murder, in 1566, of her Italian favourite Riccio, a Roman Catholic, in the Palace was a forceful reminder of this. Her audience chamber, bedroom and supper room can be seen. She also spent time in Edinburgh Castle, where her son, James VI of Scotland and James I of England, was born in 1566 in a tiny bedroom; the unpopular prospect of a Catholic heir led to his being lowered from the castle fastnesses in a basket, so that he might be spared in the event of her capture.

There were other royal Marys whose lives touched the city's history. **Mary of Gueldres**, wife of James II of Scotland, founded a hospital. She ruled as Regent for her son from 1460 until her death three years later. She was buried in Trinity College Church, her own foundation, but it was demolished in the last century. Her remains were re-interred in the Royal vaults in Holyrood. **Mary de Guise**, mother of Mary Queen of Scots, reigned briefly as Regent for her young daughter. It was she who arranged for Mary to be educated at the French court, preparatory to Mary's first marriage to the Dauphin. She died in 1560, the year after Mary had become Queen of France. Mary was first widowed in 1560, and came to Scotland to claim her Scottish throne. Her attempt to reinstate the supremacy of Catholicism was her undoing.

One of those who spoke out most forcefully against episcopal rule in the Church of Scotland in later years was a local woman **Janet ['Jennie'] Geddes**. She was so angered by a preacher in the High Kirk of St Giles, halfway up the High Street, that she hurled a stool at him in the pulpit, denouncing him. That was on 23 July 1637, when, as it says on the brass plaque on the floor between two pillars of the arcading in the south aisle, she 'struck the first blow in the Great Struggle for freedom of conscience which, after a conflict of half a century ended in the establishment of religious liberty.' She has since then been regarded as a Scottish folk heroine. In 1676 the youthful **Lady Grizel Baillie**, then Grizel Hume, pleaded successfully for the life of her father who was a prisoner in the city for his political associations. She too is regarded as a Scottish heroine.

Strong-minded women always played their part in the life of the capital. **Alison Rutherford** arrived here in 1731 and set up a literary salon in the Parisian style, entertaining writers, artists, thinkers and political figures of the 'Scottish Enlightenment', when Edinburgh considered itself the intellectual capital of Europe, the Athens of the North. She gave her support to women and wrote poetry both serious and satirical; she left sketches of many key Edinburgh figures of the day.

A more romantic character in Scots history, **Flora MacDonald**, was sent to school in the city from her native Skye. The school operated in Old Stamp Office Close, off the Royal Mile. The Scots have a slightly better record than the English in valuing education for their daughters, but the academic standards varied greatly. In 1818 **Jane Welsh Carlyle** attended Miss Hall's Finishing School in Leith Walk, but she was too much of an intellectual to have derived much real benefit from it. She did live in the city briefly after her marriage to Thomas Carlyle. Their first home together was at 21 Comely Bank, a modest terraced town house where they stayed for two years from 1826.

The capital has numbered among its former residents several women who have written about rural life in Scotland. **Elizabeth Hamilton**, best known for her novel *The Cottages of Glenburnie* [1808], was living in west Edinburgh when she wrote it. **Elizabeth Grant** was born at 6 Charlotte

Square in 1797. Her love of the Scottish Highlands, where she spent her happiest years, were recalled in her *Memoirs of a Highland Lady*, published posthumously in 1898. She shares her surname with another writer from the north, **Mrs Anne Grant**. Less fortunate than Elizabeth, the widowed Mrs Grant was obliged to depend on her pen in order to bring up her eight children. In addition to poems and letters, she published an account of her girlhood in Albany, New York, which is still a key source for social history of colonial North America. She had been encouraged to publish by **Jane Duchess of Gordon**, herself a daughter of Edinburgh, born in 1748. Towards the end of her life Mrs Grant resided in Edinburgh, dying there in 1838. She was buried in the churchyard of St Cuthbert's, at the west end of Princes Street, below the castle. Writing about her travels abroad was also the métier of **Isabella Bird**. She was one of those women who appeared to suffer from the languishing weaknesses which were expected of Victorian ladies. She seems to have turned this to her advantage, making it the necessity for travelling to the Rocky Mountains, Japan and Honolulu. Her letters home make thrilling reading and her daring adventures more than compensated for spending time convalescing on a sofa at her home in 3 Castle Terrace. When she died in 1904 she was buried on the west coast island of Mull.

Isabella Bird's contemporary **Margaret Oliphant** was obliged to use her pen to support not only her own family, on the death of her husband, but also her brother's. A prolific writer, her preferred products were novels, such as *Passages in the Life of Mrs Maitland of Sunnyside* [1849] and *Miss Marjoribanks* [1866]. She was born outside Edinburgh in 1828, and, although most of her life was spent in England, she never forgot her home country. She is commemorated on the south wall of St Giles High Kirk. The bronze, incorporating a bust of her, was erected that 'we may remember her genius and power as novelist, biographer, essayist and historian.' The Tron Church, nearby, was attended by an earlier novelist, **Mary Brunton**. She moved to the city in 1803 when her husband became minister at this church as well as holding a chair in Oriental Languages at the University. Her life was steeped in the Christian values of her day, and she decided to keep herself busy by writing an illuminating novel. *Self Control* was published in 1811, followed by *Discipline* [1815] and *Emmeline* [1819]. The first two received a good response, and were enjoyed by Jane Austen. Her death in childbirth in 1818 cut short a promising literary career. She is buried in the Canongate Churchyard, at the bottom end of the High Street, described on the gravestone as 'Mary Balfour, authoress of *Self Control*', and as wife of the Reverend Alexander Brunton.

Catherine Sinclair wrote for a very different readership. She was born in the city in 1800 and spent much of her life here. She shared a home with her sisters at 133 George Street. She wrote the first books for children that were aimed purely at entertaining them. This was a marked departure from the moral tales and school textbooks which were then accepted as suitable for young readers. *Holiday House* published in 1839 was her best known work. She was also a benefactor to the city, founding boys' clubs, shelters for cabmen, the city's first public fountain and subsidised meals for the needy at special kitchens. At the west end of Queen Street a monument in the style of the Eleanor Crosses records her deeds.

Edinburgh University has a well-deserved reputation as a centre for the study of medicine, and although it was a long time before women could officially qualify as doctors there, some significant women have worked in this field here. Before age was considered as a criterion for entry to medical studies **James Miranda Barry** matriculated as a medical student at the age of ten, as a 'boy'. Graduating at twelve, she continued her studies in London and went on to hold high rank in the army medical service. Throughout her life she dressed and acted as a man, and her true gender was only discovered on her death. **Sophia Jex-Blake** and four other women started to study medicine at the University in 1869 but were prevented from graduating by the hostile male students and university authorities. Nonetheless she started a medical practice in Grove Street in 1878 and, after a spell in London, where she disagreed with Elizabeth Garrett Anderson, she started her own Medical School for Women at her dispensary in 1885. She was able to close it in 1894 when, shortly afterwards, women were at last admitted to the university medical school and she retired to her native Sussex. Her small hospital for women, which had started with five beds, expanded to meet the growing demand. She had lived with her friend Miss du Pré at Bruntsfield Lodge, in the south of the city, and when she moved south in 1899, the Lodge became the new hospital. Still known as Bruntsfield Hospital, the fine tradition of medical care continues. A plaque on the north wall of the High Kirk of St Giles commemorates Sophia Jex-Blake 'by whose energy, courage, self-sacrifice and perseverance the science of medicine and the art of healing were opened to women in Scotland.'

One of her first students at her Edinburgh medical school was **Elsie Inglis**. As a young woman she showed herself to be independent-minded: a pupil at Charlotte Square School for Girls, she canvassed all the Square's residents and obtained their agreement to the girls being allowed to play games in the gardens in the Square. Sophia Jex-Blake's teaching methods did not suit her so she moved west to Glasgow. After qualifying there as a doctor she returned and set up the first maternity centre in Scotland, run by two women. It is now the Elsie Inglis Hospital, in Springfield, at the back of Holyrood Palace. She made her home at 8 Walker Street, identified by a discreet inscription. She became involved with the Scottish Suffrage struggle, acting as secretary of the Scottish Federation of the National Union of Women's Suffrage Societies, and supported the women's war effort. She organised the Scottish Women's Hospitals in 1914, supported by the NUWSS, and led her teams to Serbia, France, Belgium, Corsica and Russia, in their distinctive hodden grey uniform. Her wartime experience in Serbia was not without its dangers and suffering. She died of dysentery on her way home in 1917. Crowds of women attended her funeral in the High Kirk of St Giles, and accompanied her coffin, wheeled on a gun carriage, to the Dean Cemetery where she was buried in the north section. The first woman to graduate officially as MD from Edinburgh University was **Mrs Chalmers-Watson** who went on to lead women in the First World War as most senior officer in the Women's Army Auxiliary Corps in 1916. In 1920 she was a founder-member of the board of the feminist periodical *Time and Tide* in London with Lady Rhonda and other women directors.

There were others from here who played important roles in the struggles for women's rights. **Emily Faithfull** had read about the existence of women printers in the fifteenth century, and in 1857 she decided to set up a women's printing press in Edinburgh for general printing. It was valuable experience for her when she moved to London in 1859 as secretary of the Society for Promoting Women's Employment and founder of the Victoria Press. **Chrystal Macmillan**, a daughter of the city, born in 1871, was an early woman law graduate of the University. She was an active suffragist who was instrumental in founding the Women's International League for Peace and Freedom in 1915. She later served as secretary of the International Woman Suffrage Alliance for ten years from 1913. **Marie Stopes**, whose work for women was in the then controversial area of contraception, was a native of the city and attended St George's School for Girls before continuing her education in London and becoming an academic. **Rebecca West** came here at the age of ten with her widowed mother and became a pupil at George Watson's Ladies' College in George Square, leaving it to become a journalist, a calling which gave her the opportunity to spread her emancipated ideas. She took her name from a character she had portrayed in Ibsen's play *Rosmersholm* in her brief career as an actress. Her own independent stance and lifestyle reflected that of Ibsen's creation.

The city has also seen its women achieving success in the arts. **Ethel Walker**, the artist, was a daughter of Scotland's capital, born here in 1861, though she studied and worked mainly south of the border. **Anne Redpath** came to the Edinburgh College of Art as a student in 1913, finishing her postgraduate studies in 1918. She won scholarships to paint abroad, living and travelling in Europe until the unsettled situation there brought her home in 1934. She moved to 16 Mayfield Gardens in 1949, and to her last home, 7 London Street, three years later. She died in Edinburgh in 1965. A scholar whose life's work was to study and preserve the cultural heritage and history of the Scots people was **Isobel Grant**. A native of the capital, this distinguished historian spent much of her working life in the Highlands and islands but she died in the city, where she had been associated with the University's School of Scottish Studies.

There are others who continue to pursue their work: **Thea Musgrave** the composer is now an American citizen, but her student days were spent at Edinburgh University, where she had originally intended to study medicine. It was also the Alma Mater of **Jennie Lee**, a recent Labour Minister of Education and founder of the Open University, which has provided many women of all ages with the chance to study at university level.

EDWINSTOWE, Nottinghamshire [see Map 1, E4]   The parish church in this village on the edge of Sherwood Forest is claimed in folk legend as the place where **Maid Marion** married Robin Hood, but Runnymede and Wakefield make rival claims. However, Marion's very existence is in doubt.

EGHAM, Surrey [see Map 3, B2]   The actress **Mary Robinson** came to live here after she had been neglected as his mistress by George IV. She tried to make a living by her pen and published a handful of novels, but they were too liberal to be well received. She died a pauper at Englefield Cottage, Englefield Green, in 1800. A more optimistic venture here was the founding of Royal Holloway College, established in 1886 for the higher education of women. It later became a college of London University, though currently its future is under threat.

ELY, Cambridgeshire [see Map 1, E4]   The Northumbrian Queen **Etheldreda** became a nun despite her husband's wishes. When he tried to persuade her to change her mind and leave the convent at Coldingham she chose to make her way to her native East Anglia, establishing a church and a double monastery which was for both nuns and monks on the Isle of Ely *c*. AD 673. The lands had come into her possession as part of her first marriage settlement. Her sister Sexburga who latterly also lived at the monastery took over at her death in 679. Etheldreda had worked with the nuns caring for the poor and practising medicine. She had been simply buried, at her request, but later her sister wished to honour her by reburying her and erecting a worthy shrine. Although Etheldreda's foundation was razed to the ground by Danish invaders, the site eventually became Ely Cathedral, the marvellous medieval architectural gem which can be seen from miles around, raised up in the flat fenlands. Her shrine, which stood in front of the High Altar, became the object of many pilgrimages and was attributed miraculous powers. It was destroyed in the Dissolution of the Monasteries. Since then a chapel has been dedicated to her at the east end of the cathedral; it also serves as a war memorial. The story of Etheldreda's eventful life is depicted in the carved capitols of the eight pillars supporting the Octagon, fashioned in the fourteenth century.

EMBLEY, Hampshire [see Map 1, F3]   Embley Park, the home of **Florence Nightingale**'s family, stands surrounded by lovely parkland. It is now a boys' boarding school which has meant that fire-escapes and additional classrooms have been added to the building, but the outlook and grounds enjoyed by the family can still be appreciated.

EMERY WOOD, Hampshire [see Map 1, G3]   Annesley House, Bank, is a large brick house in the New Forest, behind the Royal Oak public house. The prolific writer **Mary Braddon** lived here. Her novels *Lady Audley's Secret* [1862] and *Aurora Floyd* [1863] were sensational. Her own life was not without its unorthodoxies. She lived with her publisher, bearing him five children; they were able to marry in 1874 on the death of his wife, who had long been confined in an asylum.

11   Florence Nightingale's family home at Embley Park, Hampshire

EPPING   See **LONDON BOROUGH OF WALTHAM FOREST**.

EPSOM, Surrey [see Map 3, C3]   The health-giving Epsom Salts are still used in baths today, but in the eighteenth century the Woman Bonesetter of Epsom, **Sarah Mapp**, had gained wide recognition for her orthopaedic skills. Healthy diets and clean homes were the subject of **Isabella Beeton**'s famous cookery book. As Isabella Mayson, she lived here at her stepfather's home, before her marriage to Samuel Beeton, journalist and publishing entrepreneur. She was familiar with the local horseracing scene through her father's position as Clerk of the Course.

Epsom Downs is the site of the famous racecourse. Indeed at one time there was a race for the Mrs Mapp Plate. However, one of the most affecting moments in the struggle for votes for women took place on the racecourse. In 1913 on Derby Day [the first Wednesday in June], the suffragette **Emily Wilding Davison** threw herself, shouting 'Votes for Women', at the King's horse at Tattenham Corner. She died in Epsom Cottage Hospital as a result, and her supporters were outraged that many racegoers were more concerned at the fate of the horse. Her epitaph at Morpeth, 'Deeds not words', sums up her dedication to the cause for which she sacrificed her life. It was another five years before her aim was, at least, partially achieved.

EPWORTH, Humberside [see Map 1, E4]   **Susanna Wesley** was mother of nineteen children, all of whom she educated herself at the Old Rectory★. She taught both girls and boys in what became more or less the local school, as neighbouring children also came to her teaching sessions. Both sexes received the same education, and she taught there six hours a day for twenty years. Altogether she is believed to have had 200 pupils. The original rectory was burned down in 1709 but another was built on the site. She wrote religious textbooks for her classes, and even held religious services for them, thus offending the [male] clergy. Indeed there was little local sympathy with her views, and her family suffered great hostility. It has been said that 'Methodism was founded in her home', as John Wesley was, of course, one of her children. A feature has been made of 'Susanna's kitchen', where the unofficial services were held, and the adjacent room where her school operated. There was a strict timetable: nine till noon, and two till five in the afternoon. The family had to give up the rectory when Susanna's husband, the rector Samuel Wesley, died in 1735.

ESHER, Surrey [see Map 3, B2]   Claremont, the Palladian house built for Clive of India, became the home of the very popular **Princess Charlotte**, after her marriage to Prince Leopold of Saxe-Coburg in 1816. Her stay here was sadly very brief as she died in childbirth the next year, depriving George IV of his heiress. It was the first royal confinement attended by a physician rather than the usual midwives. Later another royal Princess who was in direct line for the throne of Britain spent much of her childhood here. **Queen Victoria** enjoyed the gardens✷[NT] which were designed by the eighteenth-century landscape architects Vanbrugh, Kent and Brown. The house is now a school.

The adjacent estate, Moore Place, was one of the principal homes of **Lady Byron** from 1841 until the death of her daughter, **Ada Lovelace**. Ada had moved here with her three children including the future **Anne Blunt**, and their grandmother wished to be nearby.

ETON, Berkshire [see Map 3, B2]   **Anne Halkett**, the Royalist supporter, was brought up in Eton, where her father was Provost of Eton and tutor to Charles I. No doubt she acquired some of her thorough academic education as a result of her links with the boys' college, but almost certainly indirectly. **Mrs Oliphant** moved to Eton in 1866. She was now a widow with three sons to support. She was able to finance their education at Eton through her writing – novels, essays and biographies. She was buried locally when she died in 1897.

EWELME, Oxfordshire [see Map 1, F4]   Henry VIII once had a palace sited in this attractive village. All that remains of it is the present Manor House, below the church. It is now a much altered farmhouse but it does incorporate in its fabric part of a wing of the palace where **Catherine Howard** spent her honeymoon in 1540, as his fifth queen.

EXETER, Devon [see Map 1, G3]   Killerton, a country house✷[NT] to the north of the city, houses the important collection of the dress historian **Paulise de Bush**. Costume is one of the few forms of women's material culture to be adequately represented in museums and galleries, and this collection is no exception. **Mrs Sophia Acland**, founder and first secretary of the Women's Co-operative Guild, died in 1935 and her ashes were laid in Columbjohn Chapel, near Killerton, with those of her husband, Henry

12   A la Ronde, designed by Jane and Mary Parminter, in Exmouth, Devon

Acland, who was equally involved in the Labour movement. The educational and penal reformer **Mary Carpenter** was born in the city itself in 1807, living here for her first ten years. Then her family settled in Bristol, the city with which she is always associated. **Mary Anne Evans**, whose later marriage to the Victorian Prime Minister made her **Mrs Disraeli**, was a native of Exeter, having been born here in 1792.

EXMOUTH, Devon [see Map 1, G3]   Exmouth, like several other towns on the south coast, attracted visitors through the supposed benefits of seaside air and sea bathing. The high terrace overlooking the bay is named the Beacon. At number 19 a plaque records that **Lady Byron** and her daughter **Ada Lovelace** stayed in the house in 1828. Nearer the town centre at number 6, Lady Nelson, the neglected wife of the British admiral, lived and died. It is now called Nelson House. She is buried in the churchyard of St Margaret and St Andrew's at Littleham, a village on the north edge of the town.

One of the most extraordinary buildings in Britain is A la Ronde★. Built on Summer Lane on a site overlooking the town from the north, it is sixteen-sided, having an octagonal centre. It was designed in 1795 by two cousins, **Jane** and **Mary Parminter**, who lived in its odd-shaped rooms furnishing it with many unusual objects of craftwork in a variety of materials and creating a shell gallery high in the roof. They had toured continental Europe, which gave them an opportunity to study architectural styles *in situ*. Further up the hill stands Point in View★, their little church, where they are both buried, by the altar. This pair of intriguing characters also had designed and built almshouses for four single women and six orphaned children who were to be converted from Judaism and brought up as Christians.

EYAM, Derbyshire [see Map 1, E3] The rectory in this small Peak District village was the birthplace and first home of **Anna Seward**. In 1747, when she was seven years old, the family left for Lichfield, the city with which she is associated as the 'Swan of Lichfield', having acquired a national reputation for her poetry.

F F

FARNBOROUGH, Surrey [see Map 3, C1]   The exiled **Empress Eugénie** lived at Farnborough Hill from 1882 until her death in 1920, her ninety-fifth year. She wanted to build a mausoleum for her husband, inspired by the one erected by Queen Victoria at Frogmore, Windsor. Nearby she built St Michael's Abbey where she settled some French monks. She had the bodies of her husband, Napoleon III, and their son moved here when it was completed in 1888. She herself was buried in the crypt with them. She had died in Madrid, and her funeral here filled the abbey with all the key European figures of the day, paying their last respects to a woman whose long life was affected by the major political upheavals of almost a century.

FARNE ISLANDS, Northumberland [see Map 2, C3]   These islands☆ [NT] off the Northumbrian coast are well known as a haven for birdlife and can be visited in the summer by boats operated by the National Trust. They are also the sites of lighthouses which served to guide ships away from hazardous rocks. **Grace Darling** helped her father to keep the lights lit. The whole family was involved but only he was paid. Although born on the mainland in 1815, she lived from babyhood till the age of eleven on Brownsman Island in a cottage with her family; they tended a small garden here and kept some livestock. In 1826 they moved to Longstone, the farthest island, to look after the lighthouse there, the Brownsman Light having been closed down. They did continue to go to Brownsman as their animals still grazed there. It was from Longstone in September 1838 that she courageously ferried the boat in atrocious weather and sea conditions to save lives from the wreck of *Forfarshire*. She was honoured by the nation for her brave actions. There is a memorial to her in St Cuthbert's Chapel on Inner Farne which can be visited.

FARNHAM, Surrey [see Map 3, C1]   **Dorothy Osborne** came to live at Moor Park [now a Christian adult education college], Moor Park Lane, in 1680 when her husband's diplomatic service had ended, leaving them free to settle together in England. Sir William Temple had named it after the Moor Park in Hertfordshire where they had honeymooned in 1654. Clearly they maintained romantic memories from their long courtship in the Civil War period. Dorothy is remembered for the letters which she wrote to him during that time.

FIRLE, Sussex [see Map 1, F4]   The Bloomsbury Group seemed to take its social life to the country in these parts. **Virginia Woolf** came across a farmhouse, Charleston★, near Firle in 1916 and decided it was ideal for her sister **Vanessa Bell** who was looking for a rural retreat. It became her principal home in 1939 and she lived there until her death. Frequent guests included artists, writers, conscientious objectors and, of course, Virginia who would walk over from the Monk's House at Rodmell. Vanessa decorated the house with fellow-artist Duncan Grant, and there are works by both of them and their contemporaries in the large studio and throughout the house. Virginia rehearsed her play *Freshwater* in the studio. The house, its contents, its unique decorative scheme and the gardens are being lovingly preserved by the Charleston Trust, which is maintaining it as the 'very lovely, very solid and simple' home which Vanessa loved. Although her life here was not altogether happy – her relationship with Duncan Grant had its difficulties and her son Julian, to whom she was very close, was killed in the Spanish Civil War – she nurtured an extraordinary household which pulsated with creativity and emotion. She died at Charleston in 1961 and is buried in Firle. Her grave in the churchyard of St Peter's is marked simply with a grey headstone. It stands to the north side of the church near the boundary wall, beside that of Duncan Grant.

FISHGUARD, Dyfed [see Map 1, F2]   Fishguard gives scarce tribute to a local heroine whose intelligent action may well have saved Britain from invasion by the French. In 1797 **Jemima Nicholas** is said to have frightened off the French force with a small group of women. Dressed in the traditional tall black Welsh hats and red skirts, they proceeded to march round the hill on Carresgwasted Point, to the east of Fishguard and within sight of the French who assumed that they were soldiers preparing to defend the Welsh shores. She was reputedly a strong character, a cobbler by trade, who also took several French prisoners by brandishing a pitchfork. Her gravestone in St Mary's churchyard is her only memorial in the town today.

FORD, Northumberland [see Map 2, C3]   **Louisa Marchioness of Waterford** moved into Ford Castle, now a study centre belonging to the local education authority, in 1859 after her husband's death. She devoted herself to improving the quality of life of those living on the estate and nearby. Among other philanthropic works, the Old Schoolhouse, now called Lady Waterford Hall★ in particular stands out. She had it built for the children and, being herself an energetic amateur painter, she covered the walls with murals illustrating scenes from the Bible. They are painted in watercolour on cartridge paper, and the whole project lasted twenty-one years. Her models were all chosen from the community round about. There is now a newer school building but the Old Schoolhouse has been kept as a memorial to her generosity. A display of her sketches and other memorabilia can be seen inside. *The Lady Waterford Hall and its Murals* by Michael Joicey, published by the Trustees in 1983, gives a full account and description.

      She died in 1891 at the castle, which she had also remodelled. She had earned the love and respect of all the local people, and was widely mourned. She was buried in the local churchyard, nearby. Her monument, decorated with a celtic cross and angels, bears a quotation from Dante: 'For certain he has seen all perfection who among other ladies hath seen her; she walked with humbleness for her array seeming a creature sent from heaven to stay.'

FORT AUGUSTUS, Grampian [see Map 2, B2]   **Mrs Anne Grant** moved to the fort here when her father's posting in colonial New York came to an end in 1770. He was barrack master, and her future husband whom she met here was chaplain to the barracks. Nothing remains of the military fortifications which would have formed a vital link in the defences of the Crown in keeping the peace in the aftermath of the support for the Stuart Pretenders to the British throne: it stood at the end of Loch Ness, commanding views up and down the valley. A boys' school now stands on the fort's site.

FOTHERINGHAY, Northamptonshire [see Map 1, E4]   **Mary Queen of Scots**' last days were spent as a prisoner at the Castle★, now a ruin. She had been brought there as a prisoner in September 1586, accused of plotting against **Elizabeth I**. By this time she had already been in Elizabeth's power for sixteen years. A trial was held in the Great Hall in October, hardly a fair trial under the circumstances. It continued in London where a verdict of guilty was reached and a sentence of death given the following month. She was executed in the Great Hall in February 1587 after all appeals had failed, Elizabeth I having then ended any threat from her Scottish rival conclusively.

FOWEY, Cornwall [see Map 1, G2]   The children's illustrator and writer, **Mable Lucie Atwell**, lived here from 1948 until her death in 1962. Her terraced house, 3 Finbarras, is built high in the hillside port, overlooking the estuary and harbour.

FRESHWATER, Isle of Wight [see Map 1, G3]   The photographer, **Julia Margaret Cameron**, moved to the island in 1860. It was here that she took many of her famous portrait photographs, now regarded as masterpieces of the then new art form. She was forty-eight when one of her daughters gave her a camera, and she demonstrated that it could be a responsive tool for the artist. Her house, Dimbola, is now divided into two homes, one of which retains the name Dimbola. Julia Margaret Cameron had her studio in a garden building, no longer standing. Her visitors and sitters included **Ellen Terry** and Lord Tennyson, and her works can be seen at the National Portrait Gallery in London.

FRINGFORD, Oxfordshire [see Map 1, F4]   **Flora Thompson** came to work at the post office on the large village green here at the age of fourteen. She stayed for six years, until her marriage in 1896. The village is the Candleford of her trilogy *Lark Rise to Candleford* [1945], and it gives a clear, unsentimental account of country life at the turn of the century. She married a postmaster and moved with him to the south coast.

FROME, Somerset [see Map 1, F3] **Christina Rossetti** tried to run a school here in 1851, in order to make a living when her father was obliged to retire through illness. Her own health was not strong, and she returned to London after barely two years. The school in Brunswick Terrace, now 31 to 33 Fromefield, on the old road leading to Bath, was not a success. Several local women ran schools in the same building before and after Christina Rossetti, but none were long-lived.

G G

GAINSBOROUGH, Lincolnshire [see Map 1, E4] **Sybil Thorndike**, the actress, was born in this bustling market town in 1882, but her father's career in the Church of England soon took her family to Rochester. **George Eliot** had visited it in 1859, while seeking a riverside setting for her novel *The Mill on the Floss* [1859].

GALASHIELS, Borders [see Map 2, C3] This woollen town was the birthplace in 1895 of one of the foremost Scottish artists of the twentieth century, **Anne Redpath**. Her father designed fabrics for local tweedmills, so there was already artistic talent in her family.

GARSINGTON, Oxfordshire [see Map 1, F4] The Manor, a charming medieval house in the village overlooking Oxford, was once regarded with a great deal of suspicion. **Lady Ottoline Morrell** held house parties there when she was away from London and her guests included writers, artists, known pacifists and conscientious objectors. Among those she entertained here were **Virginia Woolf**, **Katherine Mansfield** and **Dora Carrington**. She and her husband Philip made the Manor their country home from 1915-28. This delightful village also attracted the American painter, **Ethel Sands**, who lived here until she settled in London in 1920. She trained in France and kept up a house there but eventually became a British citizen.

GARTMORE, Central [see Map 2, C2] Gartmore House, by the Lake of Menteith, was the home from 1885 of **Gabriela de la Balmondière**, a poet who deliberately obscured her origins as a Yorkshire surgeon's daughter. The details of the life of this intriguing character are only now coming to light. She seems to have run away from home to become an actress and it may be at this point that she adopted the name Gabriela; her family now disowned her. Herself a poet, she married Robert Cunninghame Graham in 1878. Her husband was raised in Argentina but his adult life as writer, politician and traveller was spent mainly in Europe. Gartmore was a family estate which he had inherited. Together they rode from San Antonio in Texas to Mexico City and back in 1880; later they were both involved in politics in Britain, as radical socialists. The Gartmore estate had to be sold in 1900. She died in 1906 in Spain where she was gathering material for a book. She had already published a full biography of St Teresa of Avila as well as poetry. Her story has still to be told in full.

GASK, Tayside [see Map 2, C3] In Gask House, in the heart of the

Scottish countryside, the writer of some of the best-loved ballads, **Lady Nairne**, was born in 1766. She was born in the Old House, now a romantic ruin, and a corner turret is said to be where she wrote such songs as 'Caller Herrin', 'Charlie is my darling' and 'Will ye no' come back again?'. She married in 1806, but returned to her childhood home as a widow. She died here in 1845 and is buried in the chapel south of the Old House. There is a simple monument, a cross, commemorating her, to the west of the chapel on a slope overlooking her beloved Strathearn. *Lays of Strathearn* [1846] was the title given to the collection of her writings published posthumously. Only then was her identity as a poet revealed.

GATESHEAD, Tyne and Wear [see Map 2, D3]   **Emily Davies**, founder of one of the first women's colleges, had moved to Gateshead as a school girl from the south coast in 1840 when her father, a clergyman, took a living here. She started the Durham and Northumberland branch of the Society for Promoting the Employment of Women in 1859, and her involvement in seeking improvements for women took her to London, and further activity, two years later. One woman who was a beneficiary of these efforts was the novelist **E. H. Young**. Born in Northumberland in 1880, she was educated at Gateshead High School. **Catherine Bramwell Booth** was a near contemporary of Emily Davies. She was guided in all her work by a firm religious conviction. She preached her first sermon in Gateshead; clearly it was well received for she stuck to her chosen work, and eventually founded the Salvation Army in London with her husband, William Booth.

GAWSWORTH, Cheshire [see Map 1, E3]   Gawsworth Hall★, to the south of Macclesfield on the Congleton road, is a sixteenth-century house with the black and white half-timbering which is often associated with buildings of this period in the north-west. It is said to be the birthplace, in *c*. 1578, and home of **Mary Fitton**. She became a Maid of Honour of Queen Elizabeth I, and it was thought that she may have been the 'Dark Lady' who inspired the *Sonnets* of Shakespeare [1609]. In the adjacent church, St James', a fine monument to her father is adorned with mourning figures of her, her mother, her sister and two brothers.

GEDDINGTON, Northamptonshire [see Map 1, E4]   In the centre of this ironstone village stands one of the surviving Eleanor Crosses. When **Eleanor of Castile** died in 1290 her body was brought to London by her grieving husband, Edward I, for burial. At each point where a night was spent along the route of this last journey, the King had a stone cross erected. This one is now in the care of the government and the visitor to Geddington cannot fail to see it. It has a triangular plan and has three statues of the queen in its niches.

GERRARDS CROSS, Buckinghamshire [see Map 3, A2]   The character actress, **Margaret Rutherford**, passed her last years in Gerrards Cross. She is remembered for the role of Madame Arcati in Noël Coward's play *Blithe Spirit*, but she also played a wide range of classical parts. She remains familiar from her screen appearances as Miss Marples, Agatha Christie's marvellous detective, and many cameo roles played in old age. When she died in 1972, aged eighty, she was buried in the extension to the parish churchyard behind St James' Church. Her pink granite grave stands in a circular layout under a large conifer. It is shared with her husband Stringer Davis, and bears on the kerb the words 'A Blithe Spirit'.

GLAMIS, Tayside [see Map 2, B3]   The Angus Folk Museum⋆[NTS], Kirk Wynd, Glamis, proudly shows the collection established by **Lady Maitland**. It illustrates the life of country people in the Angus region; much of this kind of material would have been lost but for the foresight of Lady Maitland who fully appreciated the value of the old ways and traditions. The nearby Glamis Castle is the childhood home of **Queen Elizabeth, the Queen Mother**, who was born at St Paul's Waldenbury in 1900.

GLASGOW, Strathclyde [see Map 2, C2]   Scotland's industrial capital has had its fair share of strong and very individual women, some whose lives have been shaped by the local industry. **Joanna Baillie**, however, probably had little contact with that side of life in the city. The daughter of a minister in a nearby town, she was sent as a ten-year-old to school in the city in 1772. Two years later, when her father was appointed as theology professor at the University, the family accompanied him, living in university accommodation. She obviously benefited greatly from this educational upbringing, ultimately supporting her family on the proceeds of her writings when she moved to London in 1778 on her father's death. The University was also where, towards the end of the nineteenth century, **Elsie Inglis** took herself to study medicine in 1889, having found Sophia Jex-Blake's Edinburgh teaching system unsatisfactory. She was able to qualify as a doctor, and also gained the right to pursue the study of surgery on an equal footing with the male students. She then pursued her career in London, before returning to Edinburgh to set up her own hospital and play a central role in the struggle for women's votes.

Elsie Inglis' involvement with the women's movement differed in its origins from that of native Glaswegian, **Mary Macarthur**. She was born in the city in 1880 and attended Glasgow High School. On leaving school she started shop work and began a career of supporting women through the unions. When Glasgow hosted the Trades Union Congress in 1875, Londoner **Emma Paterson** became the first woman to attend as full delegate at a national meeting of the TUC. There was also strong local support for the Suffragettes, and the People's Palace⋆, the museum of Glasgow's history, houses the collections of the Scottish Suffragette Fellowship, moving testimony to women's struggle for the right to vote. The Scottish activity of the Women's Social and Political Union had its headquarters at 141 Bath Street, and the Women's Freedom League had local premises at 302 Sauchiehall Street and in George's Road.

Glasgow has also had its artists. **Margaret Macdonald Mackintosh**, whose husband Charles Rennie Mackintosh is better known, was an artist and designer in her own right, and highly original. She excelled in stained-glass design. The Hill House★, in Helensburgh, was as much a product of her work as his. **Jessie King**, the illustrator, trained at Glasgow School of Art, where she later taught book decoration, and practised as an artist here and in Paris. She had been born in Bearsden, now a fashionable suburb, in 1876. **Joan Eardley**, another graduate of the art school, found models among the children on the streets of the Townhead district, now altered by slum clearance schemes. She had a studio at 204 St James's Road, Townhead, in 1952, and taught part-time at the art school.

Glaswegians have a reputation, well deserved, for a great sense of humour. **Nellie Wallace** seems to have inherited her fair share when she was born in the city in 1870, into a theatrical family. She was a stalwart music-hall comic who spent almost all her life on the stage, sharing her jokes with audiences throughout Britain.

The National Trust for Scotland has recently opened to the public a home which is in notable contrast to the stately country houses which attract many visitors by their grandeur, scale and associations. The Tenement House☆[NTS], 145 Buccleugh Street, Garnethill, north of Charing Cross, is very modest and more typical of the lifestyles of recent Glaswegians. It is almost a time capsule of the early part of this century. Its last tenant **Agnes Toward** would be more than surprised at the wish to preserve intact her tiny flat. She lived here from 1911, and it was her home until her death in 1975, though she spent her last years in hospital. All her possessions and papers have been preserved, and the flat evokes her busy life, working hard as a typist to support herself and her widowed mother, yet having time for some recreation.

GLOUCESTER, Gloucestershire [see Map 1, F3] Two women with similar names are associated with Gloucester. **Beatrice Webb**, whose name before her marriage was Beatrice Potter, was born in 1858 and brought up at Standish House, near Gloucester. Her family had sufficient means to give her a good education with governesses at home, where she mixed with many liberal intellectual friends of her parents. She herself was able to become involved in charitable work, an acceptable occupation for a young lady who would not be required to earn a living. It opened her eyes to the conditions of the less fortunate majority and clearly influenced her life's direction. She joined the Fabians, published reports on social conditions and founded the London School of Economics.

Beatrix Potter, who did write under this name, having produced most of her children's books before her marriage to William Heelis, set one of her better-known stories in a narrow lane near the cathedral. She was staying with a cousin near the city at Harescombe Grange, when she heard a story about a tailor who was helped by some fairy workers. She wrote her version, *The Tailor of Gloucester* [1902], about mice, and set it in 9 College Court★, which is now a book and gift shop specialising in merchandise depicting the characters she created.

The actress **Vesta Tilley**, whose speciality was male impersonation, spent much of her early life travelling. Her father was a theatre manager; it is said that while he was employed in Gloucester she made her stage debut, at the age of three.

A millennium earlier, **Aethelflaed**, the Lady of the Mercians, who had won back for the Saxon English much of the territory annexed by the Danes, was buried in Gloucester. No definite site is known. She had died in Tamworth in 918.

GODALMING, Surrey [see Map 3, C2]   South of Godalming at Hambledon is Vann★, a Tudor and William and Mary house whose real joy is the watergarden designed by **Gertrude Jekyll**. Her family had moved to Surrey when she was five, and she lived in the county for most of her life, creating garden schemes for many clients in the county, latterly in partnership with architect Edwin Lutyens. Another Gertrude, **Gertrude Tuckwell**, is associated with the area, although her contribution was in a very different field. She was an active trade unionist whose life's mission was to pursue rights for working women. She served as secretary of the women's Trades Union Congress League from 1893 until 1903. Her retirement was spent at Little Woodends, Wormley, where she died aged ninety in 1951.

GODSTOWE, Oxfordshire [see Map 1, F4]   The ruins of Godstowe Nunnery★, which can be reached on foot from Oxford, became almost a point of pilgrimage for Ruskin and his friends who looked back to the

13   9 College Court, Gloucester: the setting of Beatrix Potter's *The Tailor of Gloucester*

romantic Middle Ages in their artistic pursuits. The main attraction was the tomb of **Rosamund de Clifford**, long thought to have been buried there in the choir of the chapel. '**The Fair Rosamund**' had been mistress to Henry II, first of the Plantagenets. She is said to have done much to help the nuns, but, despite that, a bishop objected, on moral grounds, to her body receiving burial here. The nunnery fell into disrepair at the Dissolution of all monastic houses in the 1530s.

GOLSPIE, Highland [see Map 2, A2]   The seat of the wealthy Dukes of Sutherland is Dunrobin Castle★, to the south of Golspie. It has claims to being the oldest continuously inhabited building in Scotland. **Jane Gordon**, Countess of Sutherland, almost certainly lived there in the early seventeenth century. Her abiding local contribution was economic. She established the coalmines in Brora to the north. Her successor, **Millicent Duchess of Sutherland**, is buried in the graveyard next to the Castle. Her remains were brought from France where she died in 1955. She had spent much of her life trying to repair the social and economic devastation of Sutherland inflicted by her husband's ancestors in the eighteenth and early nineteenth centuries: many highlanders, crofters and fisherfolk were forced to emigrate in poverty to North America and elsewhere. She supported local schools, founded Sutherland Technical School and a self-help scheme, the Highland Home Industries. From the 1930s she lived mainly in France, and it is appropriate that a Cross of Lorraine marks her final resting place, with the French motto '*Vers Dieu sans peur*' [Fearlessly towards God].

GOMERSAL, West Yorkshire [see Map 1, D3]   **Charlotte Brontë** spent many happy weekends at the Red House★, a seventeenth–century redbrick building, in Oxford Road, now a museum. Her school friends Martha and Mary Taylor often invited her to stay. She had become acquainted with them as classmates when she attended Roehead School at Mirfield near Dewsbury from 1831-2, and became very close to the family, continuing to visit until 1840. The Taylors appear as the Yorkes and their home as Briarmains in Charlotte's novel *Shirley* [1849], set in a Yorkshire woollen mill community suffering from economic distress as a combined result of war and new technology. The Spen Valley provided the background for the action.

GORDON, Borders [see Map 2, C3]   The splendid Georgian mansion, Mellerstain★, has a magnificent situation, looking out onto the Scottish border country. Designed by the family of Scottish architects, the Adams, it was the marital home, for nearly fifty years, of **Lady Grizel Baillie**. She presided over William Adam's work, the first two wings begun in 1725. Her *Household Book*, which itemises her accounts and gives details of her household management, is an important source for Scottish social history and part of the original can be seen inside the house. There are also portraits and other material associated with her life. She died here in 1746, and is buried in the mausoleum, where a marble monument recalls her deeds. As a girl she saved her Covenanter father, Sir Patrick Hume, during Scotland's troubled times, and entered Scottish history as an example of courageous patriotism. She had enabled him to survive concealment from the supporters of Charles I. She later wrote songs, many of which are still sung today.

GORHAMBURY, Hertfordshire [see Map 3, A2]   The ruined sixteenth-century house in Gorhambury Park★ is all that remains of the home of **Anne Bacon**, the scholarly mother of Francis Bacon, a future statesman and philosopher, who was greatly influenced by his mother's Puritan thinking. She hosted many significant figures of her day, including **Elizabeth I** and her political advisers. A high value was placed on Anne's opinions. There is a portrait and a carved wooden bust of her on show inside the present house. In the portrait, painted when she was fifty-one, she holds a copy of her translation of Bishop Jewel's *Apologia Pro Ecclesia Anglicana* [1564], a highly-praised rendition into English from the Latin. She died in 1610, having lived here from her marriage in 1557.

GRANTHAM, Lincolnshire [see Map 1, E4]   It would be impossible not to mention Grantham in this Gazetteer, despite attempts to limit entries to women whose achievements live on after their own lives have ended. Grantham's famous daughter is **Margaret Thatcher**, the first woman Prime Minister of Great Britain and Northern Ireland. She was born and grew up in the premises of her parents' grocery shop, on the corner of North Parade. The shop, formerly Roberts', is now a restaurant, appropriately called The Premier, and inside the door a reconstruction of a typical grocery counter of the 1930s and 1940s has been recreated, with authentic packages, advertising and sales display units, including Roberts' own products. It has become quite a tourist attraction in the area, but its future is uncertain. She attended Kesteven and Grantham Girls' Grammar School, serving as head girl in her last year. Her teachers clearly discerned some leadership qualities at that stage.

GRASMERE, Cumbria [see Map 2, D3]   **Dorothy Wordsworth** and her brother William moved here in 1799 to Dove Cottage★. It was their first home in the Lake District, the area with which they are so closely associated. Dorothy began her *Grasmere Journals* here in May 1800. These journals were very descriptive, and were of enormous help to William. Her accounts were often the source of inspiration for subjects and sometimes even the actual words and phrases in his poetry. Her entry for 15 April 1802 inspired William's poem about the daffodils, 'I Wandered Lonely as a Cloud'. She continued to live there with him after his marriage to her friend Mary Hutchinson, and seems to have been very settled there. Close by Dove Cottage is the small Wordsworth Museum which, though concentrating on her brother, tells more about their life here.

As the household grew in size with the arrival of children, the cottage became too small and they all found more spacious accommodation at Allen

Bank, to the north-west of Grasmere, in Easedale. Here they lived for three years from 1808. They had one further home in Grasmere before moving in 1813 to near Ambleside. She kept up her journals most of her life, enduring periods of illness and stress and recording the visits of literary friends and their own travels. However, Grasmere continued to be important to them and they are all buried in the churchyard of St Oswald's, Dorothy having died in 1855.

GRAVESEND, Kent [see Map 3, B4]   Gravesend proved to be the final earthly destination of **Pocahontas**, daughter of Powhatan, an Indian leader. As a girl in Virginia, she saved the lives of early colonists by intervening with her father on their behalf. She later accompanied her English husband, John Rolfe, to Britain in 1616, where she had proved a popular visitor. Gravesend was to have been the point of departure for her return to her native America in 1617 but she succumbed to illness here. She had become a Christian and so is buried in St George's Church here.

GREAT BOOKHAM, Surrey [see Map 3, C2]   After her marriage to the exiled Frenchman, General d'Arblay in 1793, **Fanny Burney** lived here for four years on the corner of East Street at the Hermitage, now much altered. She worked hard on her novel *Camilla, or a Picture of Youth* [1796], the proceeds from which enabled her to build a home here, which she called Camilla Cottage. It no longer stands, but Camilla Close carries the name. **Jane Austen** much admired this work, and herself set part of *Emma* [1816] in this area. She was on several occasions a guest at the vicarage, where her godfather was the vicar. The village may be the 'Highbury' of this novel. Certainly the picnic, which is a turning point in the action, is set on Box Hill, two miles to the south.

GREAT NORTON, Cheshire [see Map 1, E3]   **Emma Hamilton** is said to have been born here in 1765 in very modest circumstances. Her father was a blacksmith and, following a common course open to country girls at the time, she left home as a teenager to go into service.

GREAT WARLEY, Essex [see Map 3, A4]   A meadow adjacent to the Thatchers' Arms public house in the village was once part of the gardens of Warley Place. Warley Place was the home of **Ellen Willmott**, who made an important contribution to both botany and horticulture, honoured both by the scientific body, the Linnaean Society, and by having several roses named after her. The meadow is now a nature reserve managed by the Essex Naturalists' Trust.

GREAT YARMOUTH, Norfolk [see Map 1, E5]   This old fishing port and holiday resort has several seventeenth-century houses still preserved. In one, now called Sewell House, in Church Plain, next to the Fishermen's Hospital, **Anna Sewell** was born in 1820. Both she and her mother **Mary Sewell** wrote works for young people, though today it is probably Anna's *Black Beauty* [1877] which is still most read and loved. Mary's contemporary, **Sarah Martin**, began her own campaign for prison reform by visiting the prison in Great Yarmouth and working to improve the lives of the inmates. A window in the splendid parish church of St Nicholas commemorates her good work.

GREENHAM COMMON, Berkshire [see Map 1, F3]   The Women's Peace Camp at Greenham Common airbase has survived the hostility of the establishment, the media and many local people. Since the first women set up the camp in December 1981, it has become a symbol of the strength of women, of their determination to express their horror of nuclear weaponry in a peaceful manner and of the values which women put on the safety of the world for future generations. Women visit for a few hours or days, weeks or months, giving support to the campers whose lives are constantly interrupted by eviction orders, verbal and physical abuse and threats. As an example of a peaceful demonstration, they have set an international example and are a moving testimony to the strength and determination of women in adversity. They welcome and encourage support of all kinds. *Greenham Common: Women at the Wire*, edited by Barbara Harford and Sarah Hopkins, and published by the Women's Press, London, 1984, is an affecting tribute to their persistence, spirit and power.

GRIMSBY, Humberside [see Map 1, E4]   **Anne Askew**, whom Henry VIII later martyred even though she was a Protestant, was born in Grimsby *c.* 1521.

GUERNSEY, Channel Islands [see Map 1, F1]   **Elsie Henderson**, artist and etcher, grew up on the island, attending the Girls' College, before training as an artist in London. She worked in Paris until the First World War, when she returned home. She married the French Consul in 1928, settling permanently on the island at La Falaise. She remained on Guernsey during the German Occupation of the Second World War, keeping diaries which describe the hardships endured by the islanders. She died aged eighty-seven, in 1967, painting to the end of her life.

GUILDFORD, Surrey [see Map 3, C2]   One of the few museums devoted to aspects of women's history is in Guildford. This is the Museum of the Women's Royal Army Corps★, Queen Elizabeth Park, which records the contribution of this women's service. **Mrs Chalmers-Watson**, who was also a doctor and later a publisher, was appointed in 1916 to lead the newly-formed Women's Army Auxiliary Corps. In this task she was aided by her cousin, **Louisa Garrett Anderson**, and Louisa's friend, **Flora Murray**, and **Helen Gwynne-Thomas**. Together they set up a structure which organised support for the military in Britain and France. The motto of the Corps is 'Suaviter in modo; fortiter in re' [Gentle in manner; strong in action]. *The Women's Royal Army Corps*, S. Bidwell, Leo Cooper, London, 1977 is an account of its history. Another museum here, Guildford Museum★, Castle Arch, houses the collections of Surrey country life material made by **Gertrude Jekyll**, and her gardening boots, made famous through being the subject of a painting by Sir William Nicolson, held by the Tate Gallery in London. Gertrude Jekyll had loved Surrey since her childhood at Bramley Park in the south-west of the county. She herself settled in the area to work on her garden designs which influence British domestic gardens to the present day. Many of her commissions for country houses can be visited and these are referred to in her entry in the biographical index. In addition to the Guildford Museum a Jekyll Museum has been proposed and a trust has already been set up.

The local theatre, the Arnaud Theatre, honours the name of **Yvonne Arnaud**. This French-born actress made a successful career in Britain on stage, in films and on the radio. Her endearing French accent, combined with great stage presence and technique, made her a comedy star in the middle years of this century. She was born in Bordeaux in 1892 and died in England in 1958.

One local stately home of an earlier period, Clandon Park☆[NT], can be visited to the north near West Clandon. It has been exquisitely furnished with the decorative arts collection of **Mrs Gubbay**. She made a magnificent collection of porcelain and furniture at her home in Hertfordshire, and left it to the National Trust on her death in 1968. Displayed in its present appropriate setting, it is testament to her discerning eye and her sensitive approach to these fine examples of craftsmanship. She has rightly been described as 'one of the great connoisseur-collectors of her generation'.

Also nearby, at Stoke-juxta-Guildford, the prolific writer **Charlotte Smith** was buried in the parish churchyard in 1806. She wrote both prose and poetry. *Emmeline* [1788] and *The Manor House* [1793] were among her more popular works.

H H

HADDINGTON, Lothian [see Map 2, C3]   **Agnes Sampson**, a leading defendant in one of Scotland's most famous witch trials, was a lay-healer and wise woman from Haddington, having been implicated in a plot against the Scottish King James VI. She was interrogated by the King himself. Although the events leading to her trial in 1592 were fully reported, her residence in Haddington cannot be traced to any particular building. A nearby stately home, Lennoxlove★, is associated with **Frances Stuart**, Duchess of Lennox and Richmond. Renowned for her good looks, she became the model for the figure Britannia which featured on penny and halfpenny copper coinage until the introduction of decimal currency in 1971. She was nicknamed 'La Belle Stuart' and was prominent in court society. Her marriage saved her from the attentions of the philandering King Charles. She died childless in 1702, leaving her estate to a cousin's heir. She had chosen the name Lennoxlove for the house, previously called Lethington. There are portraits, a casket and other items relating to her life on view inside the house.

Two miles to the south, the manse at Bolton was the first marital home of **Mary Brunton**. In 1798, Mary Balfour, an Orcadian by birth, married Alexander Brunton, a scholarly minister. She learned much from him during their six years in the parish, but it was only after their move to Edinburgh that she began to write. *Self Control* [1811], a novel admired by Jane Austen, was her successful first attempt.

The woman most celebrated by Haddington is **Jane Welsh Carlyle**. Jane was born at the house in Lodge Street, now known as Jane Carlyle's House★, in 1801, and this was the family home until her marriage. The rooms have been furnished with items typical of the period, and some of her belongings are displayed together with pictures of her contemporaries. Her father was the local doctor and valued education for women. She was sent to the school in St Ann's Street, acquiring a classical education there and finishing as *dux* [best student] of the school. Her reputation as a fine intelligent young woman gained her the name the 'Belle of Haddington', and her admirers included Edward Irving, who had earlier taught her at school. It was, however, Thomas Carlyle who became her husband, and he courted her here where they first met in 1821. Most of their married life was spent in London, but she had wished to be buried in her father's grave. This was arranged and her grave is marked in the floor of the restored choir of St Mary's Church, the epitaph having been written by Thomas. A booklet

14   Plaque to Jane Welsh Carlyle in St Mary's Church, Haddington, Lothian

From Threshold to Rooftree: the Haddington Home of Jane Welsh Carlyle, published by the Pentland Press, gives a picture of her life in the town and includes, as a walking tour, the route of her favourite evening stroll.

HAGLEY, Hereford and Worcester [see Map 1, E3]   In 1841 **Lady Lucy Cavendish** was born as Lady Lucy Lyttleton at the solid but stately home Hagley★. Her family was well placed in the influential circles. She was able to use her connections to advantage in the numerous causes which she supported: women's education, the Irish, persecuted Christians in Armenia and local charities and institutions.

HALIFAX, W. Yorkshire [see Map 1, D3]   **Dorothy Wordsworth** was brought to Halifax to live with relatives from 1778 when her mother died. She was here for nearly ten years, longing to be with her brother all that time. **Emily Brontë** taught at a school at Law Hill here from 1837–8, but she was never really happy away from Haworth. A writer more closely associated with Halifax is **Phyllis Bentley**, born in the town in 1894. The area provided the setting for many of her novels, including *Carr* [1929], *Inheritance* [1932] and *A Modern Tragedy* [1934]. She was a dedicated student of the Brontë sisters and published writings on them. She was also involved in the management of the Brontë Parsonage at Haworth.

HAM, Wiltshire [see Map 1, F3]   The artist **Dora Carrington** came here from Tidmarsh with her lover Lytton Strachey, in 1924. They lived at Hamspray House, where she nursed him when he was dying of cancer. His death in 1932 was more than she could bear, and she shot herself two weeks later. Her ashes are buried under some laurels in the garden.

HAMBLEDON, Surrey [see Map 3, C2]   The watergarden at Vann✲[NT] is enchanting. It is the work of the premier garden designer, **Gertrude Jekyll**, and is maintained beautifully by the National Trust's team of gardeners. The house is partly Tudor and partly William and Mary, but it is the watergarden which is the real joy. Gertrude Jekyll's family had moved to Surrey when she was five and she lived in the county for most of her life, creating garden schemes for many clients in the county, latterly in partnership with the architect Edwin Lutyens.

HARBY, Nottinghamshire [see Map 1, E4]   It was here that Edward I lost his beloved wife **Eleanor of Castile**, who died in 1290. He wished her to be buried in London, and arranged that all the points along the route of the cortege where her body rested should be marked by stone monuments, now described as Eleanor Crosses. Examples remain at Geddington, Northampton and Waltham Cross.

HARDWICK, Derbyshire [see Map 1, E3]   **Elizabeth Talbot**, more familiar perhaps as Bess of Hardwick, could probably look out of the windows of Hardwick Hall and rightly say that 'all she surveyed' was hers. This rich, powerful and much married woman acquired large mineral-rich estates in Derbyshire and had Hardwick Hall✲[NT], then called Hardwick New Hall, built beside her former home Hardwick Old Hall★, even now a substantial ruin. In fact she supervised the building of both in her lifetime, eventually replacing her own childhood home. Her new mansion is a rare survival, in that it has been little altered since her building works were completed in 1597, and many of the early contents remain there, in the rooms in which they are known to have been placed: inventories from 1601 are extant, as are some of the account books, both invaluable as sources for study of the period.

No one can fail to be impressed by the New Hall. Bess wanted the widest possible recognition of her status and wealth: the roof line and towers all bear her initials ES [Elizabeth of Shrewsbury] in silhouettes of stone for all to see. Inside her coat of arms is a constant motif of the decorative scheme. It is little wonder that Elizabeth I saw a rival in this strong and ambitious woman. Bess's encouragement of a match between one of her daughters and a Stuart who could conceivably claim the Scots and English thrones resulted in the birth of **Arabella Stuart** in 1575. Bess became her granddaughter's guardian when the parents died, and fostered ambitions for Arabella as a future queen, while bringing her up here.

Bess's last marriage, to the Earl of Shrewsbury in 1568, has been described, quite appropriately, as a merger of two major companies. Both partners controlled assets and resources on a large scale. Two such strong and powerful characters were bound to come to blows, and eventually they led separate lives, but remained married to each other. The energetic Bess died in 1608, by then a widow for eighteen years. Her heirs later included three of the most significant Dukedoms, Devonshire, Newcastle and Portland, in the British aristocracy.

HARE HATCH, Berkshire [see Map 3, B1]   **Maria Edgeworth** grew up at Hare Hatch Grange, now Biggs Antiques, on the main street [A4]. This is a large redbrick house of three storeys and several additional wings, clearly necessary to house adequately the twenty-one other children of her father's four marriages. However, the family moved permanently to Edgeworthstown in Ireland, and it was there that she produced most of her published work. She helped to bring up all her siblings, before establishing herself as a major nineteenth-century writer. Her novels, such as *Castle Rackrent* [1800], an immediate success, followed by *Belinda* [1801], so admired by Catherine in Jane Austen's *Northanger Abbey*, were interspersed with works for young readers. She had enough experience with children to write *The Parent's Assistant* [1796-1800] and *Moral Tales* [1801], and, with her father, *Practical Education* [1798].

HARROGATE, N. Yorkshire [see Map 1, D3]   This northern spa town had the usual reputation of benefiting health. However, its effect on **Elizabeth, Hamilton** was far from salutary. In 1816 this Scottish author was travelling south from Edinburgh precisely for the good of her health when she stopped here *en route*. She had become ill on the journey, and unfortunately died in Harrogate. She lies buried in Christ Church, High Harrogate, where there is a memorial to her on the wall of the north aisle. *The Cottagers of Glenburnie* [1808] was her best novel.

In 1928 **Agatha Christie** suddenly turned up without explanation at a hotel in Harrogate ten days after 'disappearing'. This was one particular mystery that the author of numerous detective stories chose never to resolve satisfactorily for her readers. She was at this time very unhappy, her first marriage having failed, but by 1930 she was again married, this time to the archaeologist Max Mallowan; it proved to be a lasting relationship. Although she wrote *An Autobiography* in 1977, she made no allusion at all to the incident in Harrogate which had made headlines in 1928.

HARTLEPOOL, Cleveland [see Map 2, D4]   During the period of flourishing Anglo-Saxon culture in the North-East of England, one of the most significant women of the day, **Hilda**, was Abbess of the double monastery for nuns and monks here, appointed to head the house by St Aidan. She led the community for ten years, moving to Whitby in c. 657.

HASTINGS, Sussex [see Map 1, F4]   This coastal town seems to have had its share of artistic, literary and medical characters, especially since fresh sea air was considered conducive to good health. **Marianne North** was born here in 1830, growing up here until she was of an age to accompany her father, a local Member of Parliament, on travels on the Continent and to the Middle East. She had begun drawing and studying plants at the local botanical gardens. Following her father's death in 1869, she returned to make her home base in Hastings. However, travelling was by now a way of life for her. She maintained households here and in London, though most of her remaining years were spent in distant countries, making her beautiful and precise delineations of plants, many of which were to be the first recorded accurate representations for scientific purposes. Several plants now bear her name. Also involved in the artistic scene at the end of the last century was **Anna Mathilda Whistler**, who is best known as the subject of the painting by her son James McNeill Whistler and given by him the title 'Arrangement in Black and Grey' [1872]; at once popularised as a sentimental image of a beloved aged parent, it is now more commonly known as 'Whistler's Mother', and is in the French national collection at the Louvre in Paris. She lived at 43 St Mary's Terrace, where a plaque records her residence from 1876 until her death in 1881. She was buried in the town.

A more recent inhabitant active in the art world, but also a journalist and traveller, was **Clare Sheridan**, generally associated with Brede. Her contemporary and near neighbour, **Sheila Kaye-Smith**, was born in 1887 in Hastings. She is regarded as Sussex's own regional novelist, *Joanna Godden* [1921] being her most enduring title.

Hastings' other literary residents include two women from the colonies. **Olive Schreiner**, the South African writer and feminist, had come to Britain in 1811 in pursuit of a publisher for her first book, *The Story of an African Farm* [1883]. The English climate did not suit her and hoping for milder weather she spent the colder months in Hastings from 1882-7, returning to Africa in 1889. She died in 1920 after a later visit to Britain; her wish to be buried in her native country was honoured. In the twentieth century **Henry Handel Richardson**, the Australian writer, spent most of her adult life in London. Her husband had died by the time she moved into Green Ridges [now called Atlantis] in the 1930s. She lived in this house in Tilekiln Lane, an unmetalled road off Fairlight Road, on the east of Hastings, until her death in 1946. Her semi-autobiographical novel *The Getting of Wisdom* [1910] describes her youth in Australia, contrasting the freedom of bush life with the confining attitudes of a city boarding school.

A writer whose early life was spent on Tyneside and whose works are generally associated with the north-east is **Catherine Cookson**. However, at the age of twenty-three she bought a house called the Hirst at 81 St Helen's Park Road in Hastings and began a life that was in striking contrast to that she had previously known. She first came to Hastings in 1929 to manage the Workhouse Laundry. She married one of her lodgers and stayed on in Hastings for forty years. Still a prolific and popular author she has long since returned to Northumberland, but her unsentimental autobiography, *Our Kate* [1969], surprised her readers with its honesty.

Two pioneering women whose example enabled women to join men in the established medical profession also have links with Hastings. **Elizabeth Blackwell**, the first woman to graduate as a doctor from a university medical school, obtained her qualification in the United States, but she was

British and eventually practised in London, becoming the first female doctor on the British Medical Register, later Professor of Gynaecology at the Royal Free Hospital. She came to live at The Rock House, at the top of the steep hill called Exmouth Place, in 1897, and, as a marker on the building states, died there in 1910. The accompanying quotation from Robert Browning's *Asolando*, 'One who never turned her back but marched straight forward', is a fine tribute to this persistent and courageous woman.
Sophia Jex-Blake, who also received her first medical training in the United States before pursuing studies in Scotland, Ireland and London, was a native of Hastings, having been born here in rather privileged circumstances in 1840. After her eventful life she finally retired to the south of England, dying in 1912.

HATFIELD, Hertfordshire [see Map 3, A3]   The principal attraction at Hatfield is Hatfield House★, built for William Cecil, minister of Elizabeth I. However, immediately to the west of the main Hatfield House stands the remaining wing of the Hatfield Palace★ [now the scene of period banquets], where **Mary I** and **Elizabeth I** passed much of their childhood. Indeed Elizabeth spent much of Mary's reign confined here. However, in 1558 news reached her here of Mary's death and her own consequent succession to the English throne. Supposedly she was sitting under an oak tree when the news was brought to her, and the remains of the tree are displayed in the gift shop. It was to be a great reign, showing that a woman could govern as well as, if not better than, recent male sovereigns. There are many objects inside Hatfield House associated with Elizabeth I, but most outstanding are two superb paintings in the Marble Hall. These are the Rainbow Portrait and the Ermine Portrait, which depict the magnificently dressed queen with appropriate symbols of her status.

   Lady Caroline Lamb, herself a novelist and writer, is possibly mainly known for her relationship with Lord Byron, judged scandalous by the standards of her contemporaries. The short-lived affair did not bring her much happiness, and a chance sighting of his funeral cortege in 1824 drastically affected her state of mind. She died four years later and is buried in a vault in Old Hatfield Church, dedicated to St Etheldreda, which stands near the main entrance to Hatfield House. There is a commemorative plaque on the wall by the pulpit, but it mentions her husband, the politician Lord Melbourne. She had turned to literature and her first novel *Glenarvon* [1816] owed its success in part to the parallels with her love-affair with the poet.

HATHERSAGE, Derbyshire [see Map 1, E3]   **Charlotte Brontë** visited her friend Ellen Nussey in Hathersage in the Peak District, where Ellen's brother had the living. Charlotte may have taken the surname of the heroine in *Jane Eyre* [1847] from memorials in the church here.

HAUXWELL, North Yorkshire [see Map 1, D3]   The future nurse, **Sister Dora of Walsall**, was born at Hauxwell Rectory, south of Richmond, and grew up here as Dorothy Pattison, in a church family. She left home in 1861, aged twenty-nine, to begin an independent and useful life in nursing.

HAVERFORDWEST, Dyfed [see Map 1, F2]   **Gwen John**, the artist, was born at 7 Victoria Place, now Lloyds Bank, in 1876. This was the family home until they moved in 1884 to Tenby.

HAWES, North Yorkshire [see Map 1, D3]   In Wensleydale the Upper Dales Folk Museum★ in Station Yard contains the significant collection of material relating to everyday life in the Yorkshire Dales, made by **Joan Ingilby** and **Marie Hartley**. They were concerned that the changes to farming and social life were not being recorded, and determined that the old ways should not be lost to future Dalesfolk. The lives of women are given equal treatment with those of men; many country tasks were tackled by both sexes.

HAWICK, Borders region [see Map 2, C3]   **Isobel Baillie**, the singer, was born here in 1895, but spent most of her upbringing in England. However, she never forgot that she was a Scot. Born the same year, but in a neighbouring wool town, was **Anne Redpath**, who attended Hawick High School, where her career in art was encouraged by her art teacher here, on condition that she would qualify as a teacher of art herself. This she duly did, later inspiring students at the School of Art in Edinburgh.

HAWORTH, West Yorkshire [see Map 1, D3]   Haworth is closely associated with the literary family, the **Brontës**. The Georgian Parsonage★ was the home of the sisters **Charlotte**, **Emily** and **Anne**, and their brother Bramwell, all of whom were writers and all of whom had tragically short lives. Their father had come into the living of Haworth in 1820, but was widowed the following year. His sister joined the household until 1842 to help with his six children, the eldest two later dying of tuberculosis due to poor conditions at their boarding school. Although they all at various times were elsewhere being educated or themselves in teaching posts, it was at the Parsonage that they spent most of their lives and produced their surviving works. They all began to write as children. In the comparatively isolated village they found their own entertainment in creating fantasy worlds for their brother's toy soldiers. They all wrote stories in miniature books and journals, basing their characters in two imaginary realms, Angria and Gondal. Some of these youthful products can be seen in the house, along with memorabilia and furnishings which capture the atmosphere of this intensely close family of genius.

    Charlotte Brontë was the eldest daughter to reach adulthood, the most prolific and the longest living. The first published work of the sisters was entitled *Poems by Currer, Ellis and Acton Bell* [1846]. Each woman used a pseudonym, hers being Currer Bell. The disappointing response to this work was followed by publishers' initial rejections of *The Professor* [1857]. This novel took its subject from Charlotte's time in Brussels which in 1842 was supposed to prepare her for opening a school with Emily at the

Parsonage, a scheme which foundered through lack of demand. Her next book, her best known, *Jane Eyre* [1847], met with an overwhelming response, encouraging her sisters to put their own novels into the hands of now eager publishers. She continued to write, but she was not able to share these successes with her sisters: *Shirley* [1849] and *Villette* [1853]. She eventually married Mr Nicholls, her father's assistant, in 1854, but died the next year while pregnant.

Emily Brontë was two years younger, and had attended the same boarding school as her two eldest sisters and Charlotte. She was very much a 'home bird', her short periods away being utterly miserable, even in the company of one of her sisters. After Charlotte's success with *Jane Eyre*, she was greatly encouraged, and dropped her pen-name Ellis Bell to publish *Wuthering Heights* [1847]. She had set it in the Yorkshire moors, where the elemental passions mirrored the rugged landscape. The initial reception was mixed, and she did not live to see its later appreciation, dying at the end of 1848 of consumption.

Anne Brontë, the youngest sister, received the least schooling though she herself, like her sisters, tried to earn a living as a governess. She, too, had written poems, drama and prose at the Parsonage from an early age, and she was the Acton Bell of their 1846 poetry collection. It was under this name that her first novel, *Agnes Gray* [1847], was published. She also was encouraged by the response to *Jane Eyre*, and in her own name, *The Tenant of Wildfell Hall* was published in 1848, and well received. Never healthy herself, she was devastated by the deaths in that year of first their brother Bramwell and later Emily. She died in 1849 when Charlotte had taken her to the coast in the hope of improving her condition.

The Brontë Parsonage Museum★ has been open to the public as a research centre and historic home since 1927, but much of the material on show was already held by the Brontë Society before the end of the last century. An archive of Brontë papers and furniture, personal items and other memorabilia together create the atmosphere which brings this remarkable family within reach of the visitor. **Mrs Gaskell**, later Charlotte's biographer, had visited her here and walked on the moors which so influenced their lives and works. Several publications on sale give further details of their lives but their own works give many insights to their thoughts and concerns. The Yorkshire novelist **Phyllis Bentley**, who also wrote *The Brontës and their World* [1969], was a member of the management committee. *The Illustrated Brontës of Haworth*, Bryan Wilks, Collins, London, 1986, also describes their lives here.

St Michael's Church where their father officiated has been rebuilt but still contains the family vault where Charlotte and Emily are buried. It has been marked with a brass plaque on the floor, and usually has fresh flowers beside it. The memorial chapel built on the site of the family pew used by the Brontës is a later tribute. There is a marble monument to the whole family. Charlotte was married here on 15 June 1854, and the marriage certificate can be seen.

HAY-ON-WYE, Powys [see Map 1, F3]   The Welsh border country is crowned at strategic points by fortified strongholds. One such castle dominates Hay-on-Wye; it is the successor to that built by **Maud de Valerie**. She had stood up to the tyranny of King John, but later paid dearly for this. She was taken prisoner and held in Corfe Castle, Dorset, where she died.

HEADLEY, Surrey [see Map 3, C2]   In 1835 **Emily Faithfull** was born at the rectory; her father had the living here. Active early as a feminist, she later founded the Victoria Press in London, employing only women compositors.

HEBDEN BRIDGE, West Yorkshire [see Map 1, D3]   This industrial community thrived when the textile mills were in full production. **Anne Loughlin**, who had a long and distinguished career in trade unionism, led the Clothing Workers Strike in 1916. The government could ill-afford to ignore it and the consequences in wartime, so it proved an effective action. Local women became involved early in the Labour Movement. The first branch of the Women's Co-operative Guild was established in Hebden Bridge on 17 September 1885, only months after **Sophia Acland** was appointed secretary of this new national network. Its motto was 'Of the whole heart cometh hope', and its aim was 'Caring and Sharing'.

HECKFIELD, Hampshire [see Map 3, C1]   **Fanny Trollope**, whose literary career was launched, through necessity, in her fifties, spent her childhood and youth in this village where her father was the vicar. When, in 1803, her brother obtained a job in London, Fanny saw her chance to taste city life; she and her sister accompanied their brother, ostensibly to keep house for him.

HEMEL HEMPSTEAD, Hertfordshire [see Map 3, A2]   After a life spent campaigning for women's and children's rights, the social worker and feminist **Maria Rye** retired here with her sister in 1895. She had founded organisations to aid emigrant women and children. She died here eight years later, and is buried in the churchyard.

HENFIELD, Sussex [see Map 1, F4]   The feminist actress and author **Elizabeth Robins** had a double success as a writer: the play *Votes for Women* [1907] and the novel *The Convert* [1907]. It enabled her to buy Backsettown Farm here. Following the example set earlier by Barbara Bodichon at Robertsbridge, she encouraged women involved in the struggle for votes to enjoy this retreat and renew their energies for the Cause.

HENLEY ON THAMES, Oxfordshire [see Map 3, B1]   The major bridge across the Thames in Henley has some fine heads carved on it and dates from the eighteenth century. The heads are the work of the sculptor **Anne Damer**, who sculpted them in 1785. They represent Isis and Thames, and follow an ancient tradition of heads protecting springs and bridges.

HEPTONSTALL, West Yorkshire [see Map 1, D3] The poet **Sylvia Plath** committed suicide in 1963. She is buried in the extension to the graveyard by the ruined Thomas à Becket Memorial Church and its Victorian successor. Although an American by birth, she had married the British poet Ted Hughes, who came from these parts, and is named on her grave as Sylvia Plath Hughes. A yellow rose is struggling valiantly on the unkempt grave, rendering even more poignant the inscription:

> 'Even amidst fierce flames
> The Golden Lotus can be planted'.

HEREFORD, Hereford and Worcestershire [see Map 1, F3] **Nell Gwyn** is said to have been born in this cathedral city in 1650, but the house in Pipe Street was demolished last century. There is a plaque in Gwynne Street claiming her for Hereford. It is not known how much time she spent here, but the almshouses are supposed to have inspired her to persuade Charles II to set up the Royal Hospital in Chelsea for pensioned soldiers.

HESTERCOMBE, Somerset [see Map 1, F3] The beautiful gardens at Hestercombe★, near Taunton, show **Gertrude Jekyll**'s feel for combining stonework into her plantings as an integral part of her garden designs. It is an enchanting place to visit. It is one of the more remarkable products of her partnership with the architect Edwin Lutyens. It has all the best features of a classic Jekyll–Lutyens endeavour: watergardens, pergola, orangery, rose garden, parterre, with glorious views and vistas of exceptional plantings. The 1903 design has been restored by the Somerset County Fire Department which uses the house as its headquarters.

HEXHAM, Northumberland [see Map 2, D3] The abbey which dominates this northern market town replaces an earlier foundation of the Saxon saint **Etheldreda**. Her second husband was a Northumbrian prince, who found difficulty coping with his wife's strong religious commitment. Eventually he bowed to the inevitable and she became a nun, first in the north, and latterly at Ely.

HIGHER ASHTON, Devon [see Map 1, G3] In 1685, as Mary Lee, **Lady Mary Chudleigh** came to Higher Ashton as reluctant wife of Sir George Chudleigh. Their marriage was not happy, and Mary spent much time analysing the status of women. She wrote various accounts of her views, the first being published as *The Ladies' Defence* in 1701. She died here in 1701, probably at Barton Place, and was buried in the church, but there is no memorial.

HINDON, Wiltshire [see Map 1, F3] It is thought that in the eighteenth century **Mrs Sarah Mapp** was born here. Certainly her father practised in the village as a bonesetter, and she followed his trade, acquiring something of a reputation for success later in Epsom.

HITCHIN, Hertfordshire [see Map 1, F4] In 1869 **Emily Davies** opened her 'college' with five women students, including **Louisa Lumsden** and

15   Benslow House in Hitchin, Hertfordshire; the forerunner to Girton College, Cambridge

Constance Maynard, at Benslow House. She had made a private arrangement whereby her students would be prepared for the Cambridge University examinations. The house on Benslow Rise, off Benslow Lane, is now the Benslow Nursing Home, and a notice at the front gate reminds visitors of its brief use as the forerunner of Girton College, Cambridge. The group moved to Cambridge in 1873.

   Annie Kenney was an equally forthright activist for women's rights and opportunities. A militant suffragette and friend of the Pankhursts, her early years were certainly lively. Latterly she led a quiet life in Hertfordshire dying in Hitchin in 1953 at the age of seventy-four.

HOLBECK, Nottinghamshire [see Map 1, E4]   The pacifist **Lady Ottoline Morrell** was brought up at Welbeck Abbey, home of the Cavendish-Bentincks, Dukes of Portland. She was well connected, and mixed in the aristocratic intellectual circles, herself hosting many significant women at Garsington in Oxfordshire as well as her London home. When she died in 1938, she was buried at Holbeck Church, beside her husband. Her grave lies to the east of the pleasing small church, in the romanesque style, and she is commemorated by a bronze plaque inside on the south wall.

HOLYBOURNE, Hampshire [see Map 3, C1]   In 1865 **Mrs Gaskell** bought The Lawns as a surprise gift for her husband. Sadly she died in the drawing-room before they had fully settled in. At the time she was still at work on *Wives and Daughters* [1866]. The house, which does have rolling lawns, stands back from the High Street, and serves as a home for the elderly.

HOLYWELL, Clywd [see Map 1, E3]   In 1490 **Lady Margaret Beaufort** helped to establish the Chapel of St Winifride, now also known as the Beaufort Chapel. It was built at the site of the well said to have sprung when **Winifride**'s head was cut off. She was fleeing the unwanted attentions of a Welsh prince. She had already decided to devote herself to the church as a nun, and was running there to seek sanctuary, when the prince slashed at her with his sword and sliced off her head. St Beuno, her uncle, picked it up and reconnected it with her body and she lived on here in charge of a small group of nuns. When she died in *c.* 650 her remains were taken to Shrewsbury.

HOPE END, Hereford and Worcestershire [see Map 1, F3]   The family of **Elizabeth Barrett Browning** lived at Hope End, and she grew up here, the eldest of eight brothers and four sisters, always regarding it as home. The house was a Moorish fancy, but has been remodelled quite traditionally. However, traces of the exotic architecture remain in the stables and carriage entrance where there are slim minarets and Islamic symbols, such as crescent moons, in stone. The family's prosperity was founded on estates in the West Indies, but their fortunes fluctuated. The house is now a country house hotel.

HOVE, Sussex [see Map 1, G4]   **Ivy Compton-Burnett** lived at 20 The Drive, a double-fronted four-storey building, now occupied as flats. The Drive is a wide boulevard leading down to the seafront promenade. Ivy belonged to a very large family, her father having several children from his two marriages. It was her home from 1892, when she was eight, until she moved permanently to London in 1919 to share a flat with her lifelong companion, Margaret Jourdain. The Compton-Burnett children were taught at home initially, and although Ivy studied from 1902 until 1907 in London, she came home to educate the younger children once she had graduated.

HUCKNALL, Nottinghamshire [see Map 1, E4]   **Ada Lovelace**, only legitimate child of Lord Byron the poet, was never permitted to meet her father, who died when she was still a child. However, she had cherished a wish to be buried with him. She died at an early age of cancer, and her body was placed with his in the Byron family vault of the Church of St Mary Magdalen at Hucknall in 1852. The Church houses a generous number of tributes to her father. A single memorial in the gothic style, on the north wall of the chancel, records her life. It was probably put up by her mother **Lady Byron**. The vault lies beneath the choir stalls on the north side. Until quite recently Hucknall was known as Hucknall Torkard.

HUGHENDEN, Buckinghamshire [see Map 3, A1]   Hughenden Manor ☆[NT] is open to the public as Benjamin Disraeli's home. However, it was his wife **Mary Anne Disraeli** who made her mark on it, decorating the house in the gothic taste, which the Victorians loved, and laying out the gardens. From the moment that they moved in, in 1848, she started to make changes, but her plans always depended on the current financial situation. Although the National Trust has published *Mary Anne's Receipts and Household Hints* [1981], she was much more than a housekeeper. Her opinions were actively sought and valued, and she was greatly respected. In 1868 she became Viscountess Beaconsfield in her own right, when her husband asked that her contribution be acknowledged. She died in 1872 and is buried in St Michael's churchyard up against the east end of the church.

HYTHE, Kent [see Map 1, F5] **Elizabeth Bowen**, the novelist and writer of fine short stories, retired here. Her last home was in Church Hill. She died here in 1973 but was buried in her native Ireland at Bowen's Court, the ancestral home. *The House in Paris* [1935], *The Death of the Heart* [1938] and *The Heat of the Day* [1949] are among her outstanding works.

I i

ILMINSTER, Somerset [see Map 1, F3] **Gertrude Jekyll** designed the complex flower gardens of Barrington Court☆[NT], at Barrington, just north of Ilminster, in 1917. Her first commission was undertaken in 1880 and her last in 1932, the year in which she died – her ninetieth.

INCHMAHOLME, Central [see Map 2, C2] This island in the middle of the Lake of Menteith is the site of a ruined thirteenth-century priory. It was the retreat to which the young **Mary Queen of Scots** was taken in 1547 after the English had won the Battle of Pinkie. Shortly afterwards she was sent to France to be brought up at the French Court. The island can be visited by boat from Port of Menteith, and the ruins include the little garden named Queen Mary's Bower. The body of the poet and adventurer **Gabriela de la Balmondière** was brought back from Spain for burial on the island. She died of tuberculosis in 1906 while undertaking research for a book. The details of her unconventional life are only now being uncovered.

INVERNESS, Grampian [see Map 2, B2] **Rachel** and **Margaret McMillan**, known for their social work in London, were both raised in Inverness. They were born in New York in 1859 and 1860 respectively, but their mother brought them back to Scotland in 1865 when their father died. They attended Inverness High School, and eventually themselves became involved in education and welfare work in the English capital.

IONA, Strathclyde [see Map 2, C1] The island earned its place in history as the landing place in Scotland of St Columba, who brought with him from Ireland the Celtic version of Christianity. **St Margaret**, Queen of Scotland, is said to have refounded a monastery here and built St Oran's Chapel in 1080. She had been responsible for establishing the Roman Catholic form of Christianity in Scotland. Later there was a Benedictine nunnery here. The island provided the first home for **Isobel Grant**'s Highland Folk Life collection in 1935, until she moved it ten years later to Kingussie. It started as a small personally funded project housed in a redundant United Reformed Church and was established through one woman's clear commitment to the preservation of traditional Scots culture which she saw was in danger of disappearing unrecorded.

IPSWICH, Suffolk [see Map 1, F5] **Clara Reeve** was a Suffolk novelist. She was born in Ipswich in 1729, her father being curate of St Nicholas Church. When he died in 1755, Clara moved away but returned here in her last years. She was buried in 1793, having written several gothic novels, notably *The Champion of Virtue: a Gothic Story* [1777], later re-titled *The Old English Baron*, and critical works. An eighteenth-century Australian pioneer, **Margaret Catchpole**, went into service with a family of brewers, the Cobbolds, in this East Anglian port. She was born in 1762 into a poor country family, possibly at nearby Nacton. She was a young woman of spirit who broke out of Ipswich gaol after imprisonment following a horsetheft. She had pursued her lover to London on a horse stolen from her employer. The next time she was caught she was transported to Australia. She eventually ran a small business there and practised as a midwife. Her life story, greatly embellished, was published by the Suffolk writer Richard Cobbold. In the nineteenth century the poet **Jean Ingelow**, who is commonly associated with her native Lincolnshire, moved here in the 1830s as a teenager with her family. By then Lincolnshire had already made its strong impression on her and was to be the inspiration for many of her poems.

IRVINE, Strathclyde [see Map 2, C2] The town celebrates in its Marymass Week each August the visit to Irvine of **Mary Queen of Scots**, in 1563. She stayed in Seagate Castle, now a ruin. In the eighteenth century, **Elspeth Buchan** followed the doctrines of the Presbyterian minister Hugh White. Originally from north-east Scotland, she had married a Church of Scotland minister, but by 1782 she had separated from him. Influenced by White, she was then regarded as the woman who could save the world, becoming the centre of a millenarian cult. She and her own followers were regarded with the utmost suspicion by the townspeople, and the Buchanites were banished from Irvine in 1784. Known as Mother Buchan or Lucky Buchan, she led her followers to New Cample in Dumfries-shire, but they were soon moved on again.

ISLAY, Strathclyde [see Map 2, C1] **Kate Sheppard** was born on the island in 1848. She emigrated to New Zealand in the late 1860s where she was an active campaigner for the rights of women. She pursued dress reform, improved status for married women and women's suffrage. New Zealand women were granted the vote in 1893, many years ahead of their northern sisters. She continued to fight for the right for women to stand for the New Zealand parliament, a battle eventually won in 1919. She did not confine herself to the campaign in New Zealand but was active internationally, visiting Europe on several occasions.

J J

JARROW, Tyne and Wear [see Map 2, D3]   The Jarrow March of 1936, when local unemployed marched to London to publicise the plight of the jobless in the capital, was wholeheartedly supported by their Member of Parliament, **Ellen Wilkinson**. Red Ellen, as she was known, was the first woman Labour MP. Jarrow was her second seat, from 1935. She had been active in the Labour and Co-operative movements all her life and identified closely with her constituents. She helped to lead the march, which is still regarded as one of the most potent symbols of British labour history. It is commemorated by a plaque on the wall outside Jarrow's town hall. Ellen Wilkinson was made Minister for Education in 1947. She described the devastating unemployment in *The Town that was Murdered* [1939].

Jarrow was also the home town of the novelist **Catherine Cookson**, whose moving autobiography *Our Kate* [1969] describes her upbringing during hard times in the north-east. The local tourist board currently promotes the area as 'Catherine Cookson Country', with the co-operation of the author. This must be a rare honour for a living writer. The places associated with her include the site at 5 Leam Street, where she was born in 1906, her childhood home at 10 William Black Street and the Roman Catholic Church of St Peter and St Paul which she attended. There are two leaflets associated with her life here, *The Catherine Cookson Trail* and *A Drive through Catherine Cookson Country*. The novelist continues to be concerned about the plight of the area, and her support includes funding for medical research at the nearby university at Newcastle upon Tyne.

JEDBURGH, Borders [see Map 2, C3]   One of the sites of this Scottish border town is Mary Queen of Scots House★. **Mary Queen of Scots** stayed here in 1566 during an important Royal Progress through her kingdom. Ostensibly to administer justice in local court cases, her visit aimed to gather support for the crown in the strategically-important Border region. In this it was to some extent successful, but she also suffered ill-health during her stay. The sixteenth-century house can be visited and it contains, among other items, a letter in the Queen's handwriting.

Mary Somerville, the mathematician, was born at the old manse here in 1780. Her uncle was then the minister. At that time the parish church was in the Abbey site, but it is now ruined. She was soon taken north to Burntisland where she spent her childhood.

JERSEY, Channel Islands [see Map 1, G1]   **Delarivier Manley** may have

94

16 'Catherine Cookson Country':
Jarrow, Tyne and Wear

been born here in 1663. Certainly hers was a Royalist family; although another version claims she was born at sea between Jersey and Guernsey. Her father, Sir Roger Manley, later became governor, as a reward for his support of the Stuart cause. When he died in 1687 Delarivier was obliged to marry a cousin; unknown to her he was already married. He soon deserted her and she appeared to have been well rid of him. It certainly gave her an experience of men which was not one they could be proud of. She then began to lead a life which was unconventional for women of her time, moving to England where she travelled and made a living as a writer. Her *The New Atlantis* [1709] described the activities of her contemporaries, and for those who could not immediately identify them from her characters she provided a key at the end. Another novel *The Adventures of Rivella* [1714] draws on her own life, itself quite exciting, for its story. The controversy about the circumstances of her birth somehow seems appropriate.

Better known for her association with the island is **Lillie Langtry**, the 'Jersey Lily'. She was born here as Emilie Charlotte le Breton in 1853, her father being Dean of Jersey and Rector of St Saviour's. The Old Rectory still stands near the church at St Saviour's. With six brothers, she had a wild childhood, enjoying life to the full, free from the constraints usually imposed on girls of her class. After her marriage in 1874 to Edward Langtry, she spent much of her life in England, where she soon grew close to the Prince of Wales, and abroad, when her career as an actress took her to North America. However, she never forgot that she was a Jerseywoman. She was strikingly good-looking, and became widely known by her nickname after Millais, the Pre-Raphaelite artist and fellow-native of Jersey,

17 'Lark Rise': Flora Thompson's cottage in Juniper Hill, Oxfordshire

painted her portrait holding a lily. He gave it the title 'A Jersey Lily' and it attracted a great deal of admiration when it was exhibited in London. She had a cottage at Beaumont but retired to Monaco in 1919, and, after her death there in 1929, her body was buried in St Saviour's churchyard. Her grave has a bust of her in marble on a granite plinth. There is also a memorial tablet to her inside the granite church. She left several items: portraits, clocks and other memorabilia to the *Société Jersiaise*. These are on display in the Jersey Museum★ in St Helier together with other mementoes of her life.

Elinor Glyn was another daughter of Jersey, born on the island in 1864. Her life was as glamorous as that of Lillie Langtry, but in a different field. She began to write romantic novels after her marriage had taken her to mainland Britain. *Three Weeks* [1907] became a sensational bestseller, its exotic story of passion in a Venetian setting was an instant success. She later wrote film scripts in Hollywood for silent films, some based on her own novels.

JUNIPER HILL, Oxfordshire [see Map 1, F4]   The tiny cottage where **Flora Thompson** was born in 1876 and spent all of her childhood is at the end of an untarmacked track on the edge of the village. It is now called Lark Rise and looks out over the fields towards Cottisford, where she attended school. The thatched roof has been replaced with slate, but otherwise is little changed. There is a plaque on the wall which recalls its former resident, whose book *Lark Rise to Candleford* [1945] gives a detailed account of life in the village at the end of the nineteenth century.

K k

KELLOE, Durham [see Map 2, D3] Nothing remains of Coxhoe Hall, where the poet **Elizabeth Barrett Browning** was born in 1806, but she is remembered in the church at Kelloe. She lived here until she was three, her family then moving to Hope End in Hereford and Worcestershire.

KELMSCOTT, Oxfordshire [see Map 1, F3] Kelmscott Manor was leased by the Morris family in 1878. It is generally associated with William Morris but **Jane Morris**, his wife, and **May Morris**, their younger daughter, in fact spent more time here and were more closely involved with this small farming community. Jane Burden was already a popular model for the pre-Raphaelite artists before her marriage to Morris in 1859, and she had striking good looks. She developed into a fine embroideress and designed some distinctive pieces of her own, although much of her output was of designs for William Morris and Co. When she died in 1914 she was buried in Kelmscott churchyard under the gravestone which she had commissioned from the architect Philip Webb on her husband's death in 1895. May was also a significant embroiderer and she made a career out of her art. However, she was also a socialist and her concern for a better society found local expression in her activities in the village of Kelmscott. She provided the village hall, supported the school, initiated the Women's Institute and organised welfare, food and practical advice during the First World War and its aftermath. She died in 1938 and was greatly mourned. In addition to the village hall, many other more modest buildings have survived through her aid to their tenants. This includes two cottages which she had built by Ernest Gimson as a memorial to her mother.

KENDAL, Cumbria [see Map 1, D3] Little is known of the early life of **Catherine Parr**, last wife of Henry VIII, but it is thought that she was born at Kendal Castle in 1512. Certainly her family was from here. The castle now stands in ruins on a hill above the town.

KENILWORTH, Warwickshire [see Map 1, E3] The town's best-known feature is probably Kenilworth Castle★, where **Elizabeth I** stayed during some of her Royal Progresses through her realm. At that time it was the seat of Robert Dudley, Earl of Essex, an ambitious nobleman who enjoyed the Queen's friendship and respect. During her 1575 visit a special masque was performed for her entertainment, and this is the subject of the exhibition in one of the roofed areas of the largely ruined castle. **Edith Cooper** was a

18   Kenilworth Castle, Warwickshire

native of the town who wrote poetry and plays together with her aunt **Katherine Bradley** under the joint pseudonym Michael Field. She was born in the town in 1862. Their preferred literary form was the verse drama: *Callirhoe* [1884] and *Canute the Great* [1887].

Ann Radcliffe visited Kenilworth in 1802 and was impressed by the remains of the castle. They inspired her last novel *Gaston de Blondeville* [1883], which was published posthumously, Mrs Radcliffe having died in 1823. She had made the gothic novel her speciality. Gaunt, ruined castles beaten by howling winds were typical settings for these tales of the macabre with a touch of the supernatural, an atmosphere of horror. *The Mysteries of Udolpho* [1794] was the outstanding example from her works, thoroughly disapproved of by Jane Austen, whose *Northanger Abbey* [1818] mocks the heroine Catherine for reading too many of Ann Radcliffe's works and getting carried away by them.

KIBWORTH HARCOURT, Leicestershire [see Map 1, E4]   The writer **Anna Barbauld** was born Anna Laetitia Aiken in 1743 in this rural community, where her father was a Nonconformist minister. She was educated in Warrington where her family later moved. Her literary career encompassed poetry, stories for children [*Evenings at Home* [1792-6] published with her brother John Aiken], editions of literary correspondence and other works. She belonged to a tradition of radical dissenters, influenced by her upbringing in an academic congregationalist family.

KILMUIR, Isle of Skye, Highland [see Map 2, B1]   The Highland heroine, **Flora MacDonald**, is buried in the cemetery at Kilmuir, at the north end of the Isle of Skye. After the episode in which she helped the Young Pretender [Charles Edward Stuart] to escape his captors in 1746, her life continued to be eventful. She was briefly imprisoned in the Tower of London. She and her husband lived in the American colonies for some years, before returning to Scotland. She died a much respected lady in Edinburgh in 1790 but wished her final resting place to be on Skye. Her grave is marked with a granite Celtic cross.

KILMUN, Strathclyde [see Map 2, C2]   **Elizabeth Blackwell**, the pioneering woman doctor, is buried in St Munn's Auld Kirkyard. Her medical training and experience was gained abroad, mainly in the United States, at a time when no British medical school was accepting women. By her efforts medical training both in Britain and America was opened to women, at great personal cost to her. Towards the end of her life she had spent many happy summers here on the shores of the Holy Loch. A white stone monument with a Celtic cross design marks her grave. She died in Hastings in 1910.

KIMBOLTON, Cambridgeshire [see Map 1, E4]   Kimbolton Castle★ was the last prison of **Catherine of Aragon**. After the divorce from Henry VIII, she was effectively under house arrest, and her later life was quite miserable. The castle, which stands in the centre of the village, has been much altered, and from the outside appears to be a splendid stately home. It is now a school, but the architectural features of several periods have been preserved. The room in which Catherine is said to have died in 1536 now serves as the headmaster's study.

KINCRAIG, Grampian [see Map 2, B2]   **Jane Duchess of Gordon** was a beautiful woman whose portrait was painted by many artists of her day. Recruits into the regiment, the Gordon Highlanders, are said to have been persuaded to accept the King's shilling with a kiss from her. At a time of unrest, she had felt she must contribute to the nation's security by thus helping her husband to raise a regiment. She is buried on her husband's Kinrara estate, near Kincraig. A small pyramid was erected over her tomb, now surrounded by rhododendrons, near the River Spey. She had died in London in 1812 and the funeral cortege took several days to reach Kinrara. The hearse was drawn by six black Belgian horses, and mourners along the route paid their last respects. She was a well-loved patroness, and she had supported the local writer **Anne Grant** with her first published work *Letters from the Mountains* [1803].

KING'S LYNN, Norfolk [see Map 1, E4]   Regard for the women writers born in this East Anglian port is lacking in the town's promotion for tourism. **Margery Kempe** was born here in 1373; her father, John Burnham, was a leading citizen and later mayor of the town. She married another respected burgess, John Kempe, who was less than supportive when his wife began to have strange religious experiences. He found her bursts of religious fervour embarrassing, and was more than happy for her to take a vow of chastity in 1413 and visit several holy people and places in England. She eventually went to the Holy Land, a remarkable achievement for an illiterate woman on her own. On her return she dictated her life story, which was written down between 1431 and 1436, and is now known as *The Boke of Margery Kempe*. Not only is it the first book on a secular theme in English by a woman, it is the first English autobiography. Margery would have known the parish church of St Margaret, which has the distinctive feature of two west towers.

It was at St Margaret's that **Fanny Burney**'s father was the organist. She was born in 1752 in one of the buildings near the church. The family moved to London in 1760, but maintained links with King's Lynn. Fanny began writing at the age of ten, often while on holiday at her step-mother's home, The Dower House, also by the church here. The habit of writing was then with her for the rest of her life – she kept diaries for seventy-two years.

KINGSBURGH, Isle of Skye, Highland [see Map 2, B1]   At great personal risk, **Flora MacDonald** brought Bonnie Prince Charlie to a kinsman's home here, where he remained in hiding for two months after the defeat of his supporters at Culloden in 1746. Eventually he saw that his cause was lost and left for his exile on the continent later that year.

KINGSTON UPON HULL, Humberside [see Map 1, D4]   Hull's best known daughters are **Stevie Smith**, born here in 1902, and **Amy Johnson**, the aviator, born two years later. Stevie Smith then spent most of her life in London, having moved away at the age of five. Her quirky style in verse and prose remains popular. Her *Novel on Yellow Paper* [1936] and her poetry, especially *Not Waving But Drowning* [1957], continue to have a following. Amy's birthplace, 154 St George's Road, was a modest terraced house. Her childhood was spent in Hull, where she was a pupil at Boulevard Secondary School [later this became Kingston High School]. She continued her education at Sheffield University but returned home on graduating. At this time she had no ambitions to fly. Although she had work she found it hard to settle in Hull and left for the capital in 1927. Her former school has a collection of her books, and in the main shopping area there is a statue commemorating her life and achievements.

KINGSTON UPON THAMES   See **LONDON BOROUGH OF KINGSTON**.

KINGUSSIE, Grampian [see Map 2, B2]   The Highland Folk Museum★ is testimony to the love and concern for Scottish life of the respected economic historian, **Isobel Grant**. In the 1930s Dr Grant recognised that many aspects of country life were changing rapidly, many disappearing unrecorded, and their value unrecognised. She was unable to stand back while the traditions and material culture of generations were lost and she began to collect items which had been in everyday use in the small highland and island communities. She opened her museum first on Iona but moved it in 1944 to its present permanent home. Am Fasgadh, as it is called in Gaelic, shows the tasks involved in making a living from the harsh environment and the ways in which the people entertained themselves when time allowed. The Highland Folk Museum is a fine memorial to the life's work of a woman determined that the heritage and traditions of her homeland should have a future.

KINMOUNT, Dumfries and Galloway [see Map 2, D3]   The adventurous **Lady Florence Dixie** is buried in the family mausoleum at Kinmount. Her aristocratic family, the Marquises of Queensberry, owned large estates in south-west Scotland. She had been a journalist, breaking new ground with her intelligent coverage of the Boer War, 1880-1, as the first woman war correspondent. She also travelled widely and very independently. She died in 1905, having spent her last years in Glen Stuart, campaigning against bloodsports.

KIRKBRIDGE, Yorkshire [see Map 1, D3]   The sisters **Mary** and **Agnes Berry** were born in this village in 1763 and 1764 respectively. Their family was not able to provide them with much education. However, they eventually made a tour of France and Italy, on which they learned a great deal, and they made a favourable impression on Horace Walpole who took them into his circle in London.

KIRKBY LONSDALE, Cumbria [see Map 1, D3]   **Margaret Llewelyn Davies**, founder secretary of the Women's Co-operative Guild from 1883 until 1915, spent most of her adult life at the vicarage in Kirkby Lonsdale, travelling to Manchester and elsewhere for meetings and campaigns.

KIRKBY MALLORY, Leicestershire [see Map 1, E3]   Kirkby Mallory Hall was the home of **Lady Byron**, after her separation from the poet. Their daughter was born in 1815, shortly after their six months of marriage came to an end. **Ada Lovelace**, the only legitimate child of the poet, was brought up by her mother here, and never met her father. The hall was demolished in the 1930s, but the stables and outbuildings remain, incorporated in the Mallory Park motor-racing track. In the local churchyard to the north-east of the church is a gothic-style monument to Ada erected by her mother, who outlived her. Ada's body was buried at her request at Hucknall beside her father.

Ada had been encouraged in her youth to study mathematics, a subject which interested her mother greatly. Indeed Byron called his wife the Mathematical Medusa and Princess of the Parallelograms. Indeed Lady Byron had a long and active interest in education and she sponsored schools for the tenants of her family estates here. Ada had died in 1852 of cancer, her energies and resources spent in supporting the research of Charles Babbage.

19 Memorial to Ada Augusta King, Countess of Lovelace, erected by her mother Lady Byron in the churchyard at Kirkby Mallory, Leicestershire

His difference engine is generally credited as the forerunner of the computer, while Ada's contribution as sounding board for many of his ideas and her own mathematical research had, until recently, little recognition. However, the exact extent of her contribution is being reassessed and may prove to be of a different order. A computer language devised in 1977 bears the name ADA: however, it is doubtful that she would have approved its use by the US navy. Ada brought up three children, including **Anne Blunt** the Arabist and traveller, who also spent time here with her grandmother. Lady Byron was able to support her own progressive and philanthropic projects through her situation as a wealthy aristocrat. Among these were **Mary Carpenter**'s school in Bristol and the abolition of slavery. Other friends included **Barbara Bodichon**, the women's rights campaigner.

KIRKCALDY, Fife [see Map 2, C3] The infant prodigy, **Marjory Fleming**, was born at 130 High Street in 1803. During her short life she kept a journal which was published in 1858. She is said to have played as a child in Raith Park, now maintained as a public park. She died in her ninth year in 1811 and was buried in the graveyard of Abbotshall Kirk, where a statue portrays her writing her diary. Kirkcaldy Museum★ displays some of her belongings. It also houses material relating to **Mary Somerville**, who lived in nearby Burntisland.

A writer whose childhood was also spent here was **Anna Buchan**. She was born *c.* 1880 in the manse at Pathhead, and enjoyed a comparatively carefree youth with her brothers, including the writer and diplomat John Buchan. A description of their time here can be found in *Unforgettable, Unforgotten* [1948], published under her *nom de plume* O. Douglas. The family moved to Glasgow in the 1880s.

KIRKCUDBRIGHT, Dumfries and Galloway [see Map 2, D2] **Dorothy Sayers** set one of her better known books in Kirkcudbright. The story of *Five Red Herrings* [1934] revolves round a murder in an artists' colony here. It is solved by her fictional detective Lord Peter Wimsey, and the Dorothy L. Sayers Historical and Literary Society has published a tour by car of sites which feature in the book. Dorothy herself stayed at 14a High Street, a small cottage. The Scottish artist **Jessie King** also lived in the High Street. Here she made her book illustrations and her batik work, which gave this medium the status of art. The white house is marked by a mosaic over the doorway; it records her sharing her home with her husband and fellow-artist E. A. Taylor. Jessie had grown up in the town; her father had been the minister of New Kirkcudbright Church. She died in the town in 1949.

KIRKNEWTON, Northumberland [see Map 2, C3] **Josephine Butler**, the persistent campaigner for women's rights against the intolerable Contagious Diseases Prevention Acts, was buried in the graveyard of

20 Jessie Marion King's home at 44 High Street, Kirkcudbright, Dumfries and Galloway

St Gregory's Church. These acts, passed in 1864, 1866 and 1869, were an attempt to control the spread of venereal diseases in naval ports and garrison towns and regulate prostitution. They led to women being supervised by the police and subjected to painful and humiliating examinations. Josephine Butler, who had earlier become aware of the plight of prostitutes in Oxford, took on the task of opposing the acts and the double standards of those who supported them. She drew a following from all classes and her campaign became a by-election issue. It was a distressing and draining experience for her, but her Christian faith sustained her throughout the sixteen years from her founding of the Ladies National Association for Repeal until the repeal of the acts in 1886. In addition to her main campaign she was founder-president of the North of England Council for Promoting Higher Education of Women from 1867 until 1873; and latterly supported the Women's Suffrage Movement. Her unostentatious flat tombstone, bearing a simple cross, is beside the tower at the west end of the church. The Church of England recognises her Christian efforts by celebrating December 30 as Josephine Butler Day.

KNARESBOROUGH, Yorkshire [see Map 1, D3]   The sixteenth century was a dangerous period in which to claim to have powers of foretelling the future. However, **Mother Shipton**, who was a native of this Yorkshire market town, did just that, and despite being accused of witchcraft, she escaped the usual fate and lived to seventy-three – a very good age in those days. She is said to have been born in the cave in the riverside park in *c.* 1488. Both Mother Shipton's Cave★ and the associated Dropping Well can be visited. Mother Shipton's prophecies were published and she has been regarded as a Nostradamus character, whose predictions may well interpret major events in more recent history. In 1697 **Celia Fiennes**, an expert on spas, was impressed with the petrifying qualities of the Dropping Well, already a tourist attraction: 'The whole rock is continually dropping with water besides the showering from the top which ever runns, and this is called the dropping well; there is an arbour and the Company used to come and eat a Supper there in an evening, to have the pleaseing prospect, and the murmuring shower to divert their eare; in a good space of tyme it will harden Ribon like stone or any thing else.'

KNEBWORTH, Hertfordshire [see Map 1, F4]   The magnificent Kneb-worth House was the family home of **Lady Constance Lytton**, the suffragette. She was born in Vienna in 1869 and her early years were mostly spent overseas. In adulthood, as an unmarried daughter, she was expected to live at home and become involved in parish work. However, in 1908 she broke with that tradition and became a suffragette. She was imprisoned several times, and eventually had to retire from active campaigning due to a heart condition which was aggravated by her prison experiences. She exposed the double standards of the treatment given to women prisoners of different classes in *Prisons and Prisoners: Some Personal Experiences by Constance Lytton and Jane Warton* [1914]. Taking the name of Jane Warton during her internment in a Liverpool gaol, she was treated very roughly, in stark contrast to her imprisonment as Lady Constance Lytton. The original manuscript, which is displayed in the house, was written with her left hand at Homewood, the house built for her and her mother in Knebworth village. When she died in 1923 her ashes were placed in the family mausoleum in a casket bearing a palm leaf of purple, green and white, the suffragette colours. There is an inscription on it which reads: 'Endowed with a celestial sense of humour, boundless sympathy and rare musical talent, she devoted the latter years of her life to the political enfranchisement of women and sacrificed her health and talents in helping to bring victory to this cause.' Emmeline Pethwick-Lawrence added her tribute: 'Dearest comrade, you live always in the hearts of those who love you and you live forever in the future race which inherits the new freedom you gave your life to win.' The mausoleum stands in a secluded group of trees near the church.

Gertrude Jekyll designed the quincuncial layout of the herb garden beside Knebworth House in *c.* 1908 and she may have helped her design partner, Edwin Lutyens, with other parts of the garden. Although they worked together on several stately homes, the majority of Gertrude Jekyll's plantings were drawn up for more modest homes, especially in her beloved Surrey.

KNOLE, Kent [see Map 3, C4]   The magnificent country house Knole✶ [NT], near Sevenoaks, was the family home of **Vita Sackville-West**. She was born here in 1892, and wrote its history *Knole and the Sackvilles* [1923]. She started writing at an early age, producing several complete plays and novels before her marriage. She adored Knole and was vexed at the laws of inheritance which prevented her from inheriting it herself because of her sex. It was one of the largest private homes in England, and had been given to her ancestors by their royal cousin **Queen Elizabeth I**. The building dates from the fifteenth century with some later additions. Vita left it to marry Harold Nicolson in 1913 and accompany him abroad on his diplomatic postings. Vita used it as the background to her own novel, *The Edwardians* [1930], where it is called Chevron. **Virginia Woolf** set her own work *Orlando* [1928] here, using Vita as the model for the central character. Theirs had been, for a while, a very close relationship. Virginia felt that her book was so much a part of Knole that she bequeathed the manuscript to the house, and it can now be seen displayed in the Great Hall.

KNUTSFORD, Cheshire [see Map 1, E3]   This north country market town was the model for **Mrs Gaskell**'s novel *Cranford* [1853]. Mrs Gaskell, then Elizabeth Stevenson, was brought here in 1811, the year after her birth in London. Her mother had died and she was brought up here at Heath House, now Heathwaite House, Gaskell Avenue, overlooking a public park known as Knutsford Heath. A plaque records that this solid redbrick house was to be her home until her marriage in 1832 to the Reverend William Gaskell. She had been brought up as a Nonconformist, attending the United Reform Chapel in Brook Street, near the station. It was here that she married; her body is buried in the north-east corner of the graveyard, beside her husband. The grave is marked with a cross. The life of the Chapel is described in her book *Ruth* [1853]. The nearby stately home, Tatton Park✲[NT], is thought to appear in *Wives and Daughters* [not finished at her death in 1865, but published later] as Cumnor Towers.

Helena Swanwick moved to Knutsford in 1900, but she kept closely in touch with Manchester society. She regularly attended women's suffrage meetings and reported on them for the National Union of Women's Suffrage Societies. She moved to London in 1911, where she continued to edit the *Common Cause*, the NUWSS's weekly newspaper. She maintained her involvement in the campaign for women's enfranchisement, but on the outbreak of war in 1914 she devoted all her energies towards pacificism. She was a strong supporter of the League of Nations which she saw as the key to a long term peace.

L L

LAGGAN BRIDGE, Grampian [see Map 2, B2] **Mrs Anne Grant** came to live at Laggan Bridge after her marriage in 1779 to James Grant. In addition to holding the chaplaincy to the barracks at Fort Augustus he was minister of the church here. Their home was the former manse, a solid stone house, now a farm called Gardie, up a farm track. It stands on the north side of the valley, looking south across the glen. Mrs Grant is said to have sat writing under a tree in the garden; however, she did not seriously pursue this means of making a living until her husband's death in 1801. She was left with eight children, and turned to writing in order to support them. In particular she wished to ensure for one son a career in the East India Company. Her first work was a collection of poems published through the patronage of Jane, Duchess of Gordon, in 1803. The same year saw the publication of her *Letters from the Mountains* [1803] which are three volumes of anecdotes about life in these parts. Her most significant work today is her *Memoirs of an American Lady* [1808] in which she recalled her youth in Albany, New York. It is still a prime source for the social history of colonial life in upstate New York, an area strongly influenced by its Dutch settlers. The church around which her life centred for so long has a certain austere charm, and in the graveyard stands a gravestone which she had put up for her husband, intending that she should herself ultimately be buried here also. However, she is buried in Edinburgh, where she died in 1838.

LAMAS, Norfolk [see Map 1, E5] The former Quaker burial ground here contains the graves of **Anna Sewell**, who died in 1878, and her mother, **Mary Sewell**, who outlived her by six years; they both wrote books for children. It was at nearby Buxton that Anna had learned to love horses, a love which inspired her *Black Beauty* [1877], now a children's classic. This, her only book, of which more than thirty million copies have been printed, has been translated into all the main European and Asian languages. The story of a mistreated horse inspired charities to organise against cruelty to animals. At the time of writing there is a move to sell the burial ground, and a local campaign is trying to save it.

LAMBOURN, Oxfordshire [see Map 1, F3] Ashdown House☆[NT], to the north of Lambourn, is the seventeenth-century house built by Lord Craven for **Elizabeth of Bohemia**, known as the 'Winter Queen'. Her unhappy life might have found welcome tranquillity in this pleasant setting of period gardens, box hedges and parterres, but she died of the Plague in

1662 before seeing it. William, the first Earl of Craven, had been her most loyal supporter during her years of exile, and on her death she bequeathed to him many of her possessions and papers, some of which are on display in the house. Her importance lies in her dynastic connections: herself the sister of Charles I, her twelfth child Sophia was the mother of George I.

LAMORNA, Cornwall [see Map 1, G2] In the inter-war period this attractive cove near Newlyn became the focus for an artists' colony. Among those who came here to paint were **Gluck, Laura Knight** and **Dod Shaw**. Laura Knight was fortunate in having the patronage of the local squire, Colonel Paynter. She had rented a cottage on the hill in 1910 before the colonel built a studio for her. She lived at Oakhill, which was converted from cottages, from 1912 until making her base in London in 1919. Her picture 'Daughters of the Sun' [1910] was painted here, showing girls on the shore; it gained her the interest of the art establishment. She had first been attracted to the area by seeing the work of the Newlyn School at an exhibition while she was a student.

LANARK, Lanarkshire [see Map 2, C2] **Jennie Lee** had already been involved in the Labour Movement for some years before becoming, at twenty-four, the youngest Member of Parliament of her day, sitting as an Independent Labour member for North Lanark. She lost the seat two years later but continued working for the Labour Party, ultimately becoming Minister of Education.

LANDGUARD, Suffolk [see Map 1, F5] The fort here was where **Delarivier Manley** grew up. Her father's career in military administration brought the family to the fort in 1680, where he served as governor until he died in 1687. On his death, Delarivier Manley was obliged to marry her guardian, who was also her cousin. It turned out that he was already married, so she set off to lead her own unconventional life, living by her writing. She edited a Tory periodical, *The Examiner*, from 1711-16. Her anti-Whig feelings were evident earlier in *The New Atalantis* [1709]; those unable to identify in the text the political figures whom she pilloried were able to look them up in the Key which she published at the same time. Her own life provided many episodes for her novel, *The Adventures of Rivella* [1714].

LAUGHARNE, Dyfed [see Map 1, F2] The educational pioneer **Bridget Vaughan** is associated with Derlys Court, through her marriage to John Vaughan. As Bridget Bevan, she used her own wealth and position to found charitable schools in several communities in the former county of Montgomeryshire in the early eighteenth century. She also supported itinerant teachers, being the principal patron of the Welsh Circulating Schools. These were founded in 1731 by Griffith Jones. The teachers spent the winter months in different communities teaching basic mathematics and the reading of the Bible in Welsh.

LAVENHAM, Suffolk [see Map 1, F4]   The children's writers, **Ann** and **Jane Taylor**, moved to Lavenham from London in 1786. They lived in Shilling Street, first at The Cooke's House, now Shilling Grange, where they wrote the popular nursery rhyme 'Twinkle, twinkle, little star', published in 1806, moving later to Arundel House, further along the street. In the Guildhall☆[NT], there is on display a collection of memorabilia relating to the Taylor family. This is a beautiful and historic Suffolk town, with a superb church. Jane and Ann would recognise much of it today, as care has been taken to preserve its character. The family moved to Colchester in 1796.

LEA HURST, Derbyshire [see Map 1, E3]   This was the country estate of **Florence Nightingale**'s family. The future nursing pioneer grew up here and stayed here regularly in the summer months, after her parents acquired Embley Park in Hampshire. She had been born in 1820 in Italy, and her parents gave her the name of her birthplace, Florence.

LEEDS, Yorkshire [see Map 1, D3]   The prosperity of Leeds was based on the woollen trade and the textile and clothing industries. A Victorian respect for education and culture led to the establishment of several significant institutions. In 1867 the inaugural meeting of the North of England Council for Promoting the Higher Education of Women was held here by **Anne Jemima Clough**, **Josephine Butler** and other concerned women. **Adelaide Neilson** was born in Leeds in 1846. Her given name was Elizabeth Ann Brown but she took on the stage name of 'Adelaide Neilson' in London in 1865 and then embarked on her international career. The artist **Barbara Hepworth** received her art school training here in the 1920s, with the help of a scholarship. A contemporary of hers, **Kathleen Lonsdale**, had lived in the city for three years after her marriage to Thomas Lonsdale in 1927. A scientist and pacifist, she became in 1945 one of the first women honoured by Fellowship of the Royal Society, in recognition of her original research into the structure of crystals, partly carried out at Leeds University. The University recognised the far-ranging work for women's higher education undertaken by **Lady Lucy Cavendish** with the award of an honorary degree in 1904.

Inevitably such an intensively industrial city would produce its own union activists. Leeds can claim one of the finest in **Dame Anne Loughlin**, born here in 1894. She worked in the garment industry as a teenager, and immediately became a local union representative. From then on, her commitment to the unions and, especially, working women was total. She became in 1943 President of the Trades Union Congress, the first woman to take that leadership position. Her experience and dedication could hardly differ more from that of **Adeline Horsey de Horsey**, whose energies were applied to acquiring titled husbands and being at the centre of high society. Always well connected, she spent part of her childhood locally, where

Kirkstall Abbey★, now Leeds' museum of social history, was one of her family's properties.

Most local people had more practical concerns, and were prepared to strive to meet local needs, often taking radical action, a tradition which continues. This may have been the reason for **Marie Stopes** opening one of her first controversial birth control clinics in the city.

LEICESTER, Leicestershire [see Map 1, E4]   Leicester's importance as a Roman town has been confirmed by the archaeological record. **Dame Kathleen Kenyon**'s excavations in Jericho added significantly to the chronology of the ancient history of the Middle East. However, the result of one of her earliest digs can be more readily seen in the Jewry Wall Museum★, adjacent to the Roman bath-house site in the centre of the modern city of Leicester. Leicester maintained its economic and strategic significance after the withdrawal of Rome. **Aethelflaeda**, ruler of the Mercians, preserved the town from the Danes in 918, having fought them off in other centres of her Midlands domain. She died the same year, having ensured her brother's succession to an unthreatened kingdom, south of the Humber. She is honoured locally by a statue, but it has been taken down for restoration.

Another local woman who achieved an equally powerful position was the ill-fated **Lady Jane Grey**. Her claims to the English throne were founded on her being a niece of Henry VIII, and she became a pawn in the succession game. In 1553, on the death of Edward VI, she was put forward as queen by her politically ambitious father, the Marquis of Dorset, and his friends. Her family home was Bradgate House, now an attractive ruin in the centre of Bradgate Park★, to the north-west of Leicester. The park is a popular recreation area for the city, and the unspoilt grounds include a deer park. Local tradition holds that Lady Jane was married, reluctantly, in All Saints Church in Newton Linford, the nearest village. Her husband was Guildford Dudley, the younger son of the Duke of Northumberland. The Duke supported Jane's father's plans and saw a means of benefittingly politically himself through this union. **Elizabeth Talbot**, better known as Bess of Hardwick, married the second of her four husbands in the chapel of Bradgate House in 1547.

Mary Linwood, an artist now little known outside Leicestershire, earned a national reputation in her own day. She developed a means of producing pictures in wool which from a distance looked like paintings. Using her 'needle-painting technique' she copied many works of art popular in her day, by, for instance, Gainsborough and Stubbs. She was honoured with exhibitions in London, a distinction for a woman artist in any medium at that time. The county museum service has a collection of her works, examples of which can be seen in Newarke Houses Museum★, The Newarke, and in Belgrave Hall★, Thurmaston Road. Works of art in textiles can only be shown for limited periods and so these works are changed from time to time. Although born in Birmingham in 1755, her family moved to Leicester while she was still an infant. Her home in Belgrave Gate no longer stands. Her main source of income was the boarding house for young ladies which she kept here. She died in 1845, in her ninetieth year, and was buried in St Margaret's Church. Her achievements are acknowledged on the wall-mounted memorial where she is described as a person 'whose genius has shed a light on her age, her country and her sex, and whose works are a splendid monument of art and perseverance'. However, this recognition was short-lived. At her death a collection of over one hundred needle paintings was offered to the nation but the British Museum turned it down.

Margaret MacDonald accompanied her husband, Ramsay MacDonald, to Leicester where he was the local Member of Parliament from 1906 for twelve years. She was active in social work all her life; the care of children was one of her particular concerns; in the entrance hall of the Leicester Museum and Art Gallery★ on New Walk, a plaster model of the bronze statue erected in her memory in London commemorates her compassion and energy. There is also a children's ward named after her in the Leicester Royal Infirmary. In 1906 she presided over one of the early national meetings of the Women's Labour League which was held in Leicester. **Emmeline Pethwick-Lawrence** encouraged local suffragettes during the period when her husband, himself a loyal and active feminist, represented the constituency in Westminster.

LEIGHTON, Shropshire [see Map 1, E3]   The Lodgehouse at Leighton was the birthplace of the writer, **Mary Webb**, in 1881. The nearby Wrekin was the backdrop of several of her novels set in this countryside; it haunted her all her days. She was the author of *Gone to Earth* [1917] and *Precious Bane* [1924], two of her regional novels.

LEMSFORD, Hertfordshire [see Map 3, A3]   The solid stately home Brocket Hall was home and refuge for **Lady Caroline Lamb**, especially after her separation from Lord Melbourne. Her fleeting relationship with Lord Byron is a familiar story, but her own success as a novelist is virtually forgotten. They were written before her mental decline of 1824, the first, *Glenarvon* [1816], being thinly disguised criticism of the poet.

LETCHWORTH, Hertfordshire [see Map 1, F4]   The suffragist and trade unionist **Annie Kenney** moved to Letchworth with her husband James Taylor in 1921. She had earned retirement here after a fully committed life of activism. It was here that she wrote *Memoirs of a Militant* [1924], chronicling her long involvement with the Pankhursts in the Women's Social and Political Union. She died in 1951. During the Second World War the town was considered safe enough by **Virginia Woolf** who had her Hogarth Press Publishing venture moved here, which had been bombed in London in 1940. The press continues to publish but is now part of a larger publishing house.

LEVENS HALL, Cumbria [see Map 1, D3]   This historic house near Kendal was where **Mrs Humphrey Ward** spent the winter of 1896-7. She used Levens Hall★ as a model for Bannisdale in her novel *Helbeck of Bannisdale* [1898], which was written during her time here.

LEWES, Sussex [see Map 1, F4]   The town now runs a museum of local history at Anne of Cleves' House★, on the High Street, Southover. It was not in fact **Anne of Cleves'** home, but one of the several properties settled on her as part of the surprisingly amicable divorce settlement with Henry VIII in 1540.

In the nearby hamlet of Beddingham, stands Asham House, the first Sussex home of **Virginia Woolf**. Virginia and Leonard Woolf lived here from 1912 until the lease ran out in 1919, mainly at weekends and holiday times. Many of their Bloomsbury friends visited them here. The title piece in Virginia's collection of short stories *A Haunted House* [1943], published posthumously, is set here. By 1919, the Woolfs were totally addicted to the South Downs, and after a long search, they found and bought Monk's House at Rodmell, their country home for the rest of their lives.

LICHFIELD, Staffordshire [see Map 1, E3]   Lichfield's 'Ladies of the Vale' are, in fact, the three spires of the Cathedral. However, the building does have some significance for those seeking out associations with women's history. In 1754 the Bishop's Palace here became the home of **Anna Seward**, the poet. Her father had been appointed canon of Lichfield Cathedral. She held literary salons here, becoming known as the 'Swan of Lichfield'. Her 'blue boudoir' overlooked the Cathedral. She wrote of her view:

> Ah lovely Lichfield! that so long has shone
> In blended charms, peculiarly thine own;
> Stately yet rural; through thy choral day,
> Though shady, cheerful and though quiet, gay.

Her friends included the actress **Sarah Siddons**, Erasmus Darwin, whose *Memoirs* [1804] she wrote, Samuel Johnson, and Sir Walter Scott, who published a collection of her poetry in 1810. She lived at the palace until her death in 1809, and there is a memorial to her in the Cathedral near the west door. Also commemorated here is **Lady Mary Wortley Montagu**, traveller, letter writer and vaccination pioneer, who died in 1762.

LINCOLN, Lincolnshire [see Map 1, E4]   **Matilda**, daughter of Henry I, claimed the English throne in 1135, her brother, William the Aethling, having died at sea in 1126. Henry's nobles had recognised her as heiress in Henry's lifetime, but in 1135 supported a male candidate, Stephen of Blois, a grandson of William the Conqueror. Matilda was a strong-minded woman, who had already had a taste of power during her eleven-year marriage to the Emperor of Hungary. After returning to England when widowed, she had married a second time, to Geoffrey of Anjou in 1129.

Her half-brother, Robert of Gloucester, helped her to pursue her claim, invading England and capturing Stephen in 1141. She won a decisive victory at Lincoln in 1141, but her sovereignty was to be short-lived.

The glory of Lincoln is its cathedral, which dominates the skyline of the city. There was a tradition that the heart of **Eleanor of Castile**, who had died just across the border in Nottinghamshire at Harby in 1290, was buried here. Her formal burial place is Westminster Abbey. In the Minster Yard **Elizabeth Penrose** died in 1837. She had written several works of history for young people, writing as **Mrs Markham**. The most popular were those of England and France. Five Minster Yard was where a liberal thinker, **Ada Ellen Bayly**, who also used a pen-name, lived with her sister until 1884. In this house, as **Edna Lyall**, she wrote *Donovan* [1882] and *We Two* [1884]. An earlier worshipper in the cathedral, **Anne Askew**, was considered too extreme in her Protestant orthodoxy, and was eventually taken from here to London where in 1546 she was martyred.

LINDISFARNE, Northumberland [see Map 2, C3] The garden of Lindisfarne Castle☆[NT] has recently been restored to the plantings of **Gertrude Jekyll**. This premier garden designer began a fruitful professional partnership with the architect Edwin Lutyens, who worked on the castle itself and on the layout of the garden. Her plan for the former walled kitchen garden was drawn up in 1911; it is now a delightful haven on this windswept island. It is worth remembering to check the tide-timetable since the access to Lindisfarne by the causeway is covered by the incoming tide and the island is quite cut off.

LINLITHGOW, Central [see Map 2, C3] It was in Linlithgow Palace★ that **Mary Queen of Scots** was born in 1542. The ruins are impressive. Mary Stuart was the only child of James V and **Mary de Guise**. The reaction of her father to the news that a daughter had been born was disheartening. By then he knew that he was on his deathbed. Referring to the Stuart dynasty, he supposedly lamented: 'It cam' wi' a lass and it'll gang wi' a lass.' The Stuarts had come to the throne of Scotland through the female line, and their successive hold of that throne had not been without problems. It did not bode well for the Stuarts that this latest sovereign should be both a woman ruler and a minor, and the dying king rightly foresaw troubled times for the realm. Mary became queen at eight days old. Mary de Guise, who now became queen-dowager, did not become Regent until much later. It was natural that she should look towards her native France when building alliances for her daughter's reign, though Scotland ultimately suffered. The young Mary was sent to the French court from childhood, to be educated in royal circles in a firmly Catholic country and to cement the 'Auld Alliance'.

LIVERPOOL, Merseyside [see Map 1, E3] The spirited vitality, generous nature and good humour of Liverpudlians became well known in Britain through a television series *The Liver Birds*. This situation comedy chronicled the lives of two young women from different backgrounds sharing a flat in the early 1970s. The roles were portrayed by actresses Nerys Hughes and Polly James, who showed that there was much more to Liverpool than the Beatles pop group and that women were, and continue to be, the strength and essential spark of the community. The 'Liver birds' from which the series took its names are the two statues of mythological birds which surmount the Liver Insurance building which dominates the port skyline and acts as a landmark for sea traffic as well as a symbol of the importance of the port.

Felicia Hemans was a literary daughter of this major sea-faring city. There is unfortunately no longer a plaque on 118 Duke Street where she was born as Felicia Dorothea Browne in 1793. Now sadly neglected, this was her home until the Browne family moved to Wales in 1800. She returned to the town of her birth in 1827, having been abandoned by her husband. She had been supporting her five sons since 1818; although she had been writing poetry from an early age it now became imperative to get it published. Fortunately *The Forest Sanctuary* [1826] had been a great success. One or two works were produced each year until her death in Dublin in 1835. She had moved to Ireland from her house on the north side of Wavertree High Street [no longer standing] in 1831.

Two other writers spent time here. **Mrs Oliphant** had come here as a girl when her father's work as a customs official required him to leave Edinburgh. She wrote her first book *Passages in the Life of Mrs Maitland of Sunnyside* [1849] while living here. The American author of the anti-slavery novel *Uncle Tom's Cabin* [1852] **Harriet Beecher Stowe** made three trips to Britain. The first was in 1853 when she stayed at Dingle Bank, which she found delightful. She found support in Britain for her views on the appalling slave conditions in the southern United States.

The busy port was the focus of the city's commercial life, and transport to and from the colonies of settlers and visitors as well as goods meant that thousands of women passed through. In 1850 the singer **Jenny Lind** sailed to New York for her North American debut. In 1869 **Maria Rye** took fifty orphan girls to a new life in Canada [with the permission of their relatives] as part of her mission to improve the lot of children. In 1893, **Mary Kingsley** the explorer and anthropologist sailed to West Africa on her expedition to collect new species of freshwater fish.

Liverpool was also the scene of key struggles for women's rights. **Anne Jemima Clough** put her energies into the campaign for women's education. She was born into a prosperous cotton family here in 1820, growing up in the cotton-growing state of South Carolina. On her return from America to Liverpool when she was sixteen, she taught at a school here for five years from 1841, eventually opening her own with her mother in Ambleside in 1852. With **Josephine Butler** she set up the North of England Council for the Promotion of Higher Education of Women in 1867. She was one of those responsible for the admisson of women to Cambridge University. A plaque on Miss Clough's birthplace at 9 Rodney

Street records her as first principal of Newnham College. Josephine Butler concentrated her energies into striving for the repeal of the degrading Contagious Diseases Prevention Acts. She met with great hostility from the establishment, but persisted, exposing the double standards prevalent in Victorian morality. She and Anne Jemima Clough are two of the women represented in the stained glass windows of Liverpool's Anglican Cathedral. The windows are hard to find on the stairs leading down to the Lady Chapel and at the west end of that chapel. Repeating the motto 'Bear ye one another's burdens', the windows commemorate among others **Grace Darling**, **Susannah Wesley**, **Christina Rossetti** and **Mother Julian of Norwich**.

The fight for women's votes was **Lady Constance Lytton**'s cause. She was nearly forty when she became a militant suffragette, and was convinced that, as an aristocrat, she had received privileged treatment in Holloway and premature release on health grounds. In 1911 she was arrested in Liverpool for stoning the Governor's residence at Walton Gaol. When she was then imprisoned there, she described herself as 'Jane Warton, seamstress', and later published an account of her contrasting incarcerations: *Prisons and Prisoners: Some Personal Experiences by Constance Lytton and Jane Warton* [1914]. Her spells inside permanently damaged her health. The prison, three miles north of the city centre, is still in use.

In 1872 **Eleanor Rathbone**, a leading feminist and social reformer, was born into a local family with a tradition of philanthropy and the means to support it. She became involved in social work as soon as she could and in 1909 was elected a city councillor for the Granby ward in order to promote local improvements. The first woman on Liverpool Council, she served for twenty-six years. She took her ideas to Parliament, as an Independent Member for the Combined English Universities in 1929, holding the seat until 1946. Her lasting achievement was the introduction of family allowances paid to the mother; she was the architect of this scheme to ensure that mothers had some financial independence in caring for their families. Her concern for the condition of women was not confined to those in Britain. It extended to women in Britain's African colonies and also the Middle East. Her companion throughout her active life was Elizabeth Macadam with whom she shared homes both here and in London. Eleanor's contemporary, the pacifist **Mary Sheepshanks**, was born into a stiflingly religious household in Anfield in 1872. Her father was an Anglican minister who imposed a joyless regime on his many children. Mary left home to study at Cambridge, where she thrived on the social and intellectual freedom she had long craved.

Liverpool's best known political daughter is **Bessie Braddock**. 'Battling Bessie', as she was dubbed by the press, earned the great affection and respect through her involvement in the Labour Party. Born in 1899 into a family of Labour Party activists and trade unionists, she was a city councillor from 1930 until 1961 and as a Member of Parliament she represented the Exchange constituency from 1945 until 1969. In 1970 she was the first woman to be granted the Freedom of the City, and she died, much lamented, later that year. Latterly she lived in Zigzag Road in the West Derby district.

Catherine Walters' life was in complete contrast to the lives of these women. She was born in Liverpool in 1839, but made her way into London society through her own efforts. Of Irish parentage, she worked briefly at a public house called the Black Jack Tavern, before leaving for the capital at the age of seventeen. She is known now as the 'last Victorian Courtesan', and by all accounts she was a fun-loving extrovert with an attractive personality, well able to hold her own in any social situation. Moving in London society, she would certainly have known the great actress **Mrs Patrick Campbell**, whose career began in Liverpool. 'Mrs Pat's' debut in 1888 arose out of a necessity: she had two children to provide for, in her husband's absence abroad. It was the start of a memorable stage career.

LLANBEDR, Gwynedd [see Map 1, E2] **Angela Brazil**'s success as a writer of popular schoolgirl adventure fiction enabled her to enjoy the Welsh countryside. Her sister was a district nurse in this corner of Wales and Angela eventually bought a cottage here. The contrast with industrial Coventry where she lived with her brother would have been refreshing.

LLANDINAM, Powys [see Map 1, E3] The sisters **Gwendoline** and **Margaret Davies** were born here, in 1882 and 1884 respectively. They grew up in a cultured and prosperous home, and, when they eventually inherited a considerable sum, they used it to develop the arts at Newtown for the people of Wales.

LLANDUDNO, Gwynedd [see Map 1, E2] This seaside town on the north coast of Wales was the site of the holiday home of the Liddell family. **Alice Liddell**, the model for Lewis Carroll's *Alice in Wonderland* [1865], enjoyed summers away from Oxford here at Pen Morfa [the English translation is 'beachy head'], on the West Shore, now incorporated in the Gogarth Abbey Hotel. Carroll composed part of the story during a stay with the Liddells in 1862, and told it to Alice. A statue of the White Rabbit, one of the first characters in the story, marks this association.

LLANFIHANGEL-Y-PENNANT, Gwynedd [see Map 1, E2] **Mary Jones**, born here in very modest circumstances in 1784, saved up for a Welsh Bible, a task that took her six years. The daughter of a weaver, she walked barefoot the twenty-five miles over the hills to Bala to buy the Bible in 1800. This dedication so impressed Thomas Charles that he established the British and Foreign Bible Society to make Bibles readily available to all who wanted them. The ruined cottage Tyn-y-dol, is now her memorial.

LLANFIHANGEL YNG NGWYNFA, Powys [see Map 1, E3] **Ann Griffiths**, a farmer's daughter, spent all her life at Dolwar Fach Farm, two miles to the south of the village. In 1797 she joined the Methodists and used her poetic gifts to express her new faith. Dolwar Fach became registered as a place of worship for dissenting congregations and remained her home after her marriage in 1804. Her hymns were all in Welsh, but, as she herself could not write, they were put down in writing for her by a literate farm servant, Ruth Evans. Her most famous hymn is 'Wele sefytt rhwng y myrtwydd'. It is sung to the tune 'Cwm Rhondda', familiar to English-speakers as 'Bread of Heaven'. She died after childbirth in 1805, and was buried in the village.

LLANGOLLEN, Clwyd [see Map 1, E3]   In the eighteenth century the **Ladies of Llangollen** attracted many visitors, not all welcome. The Ladies, **Lady Eleanor Butler** and the **Honourable Sarah Ponsonby**, came to live at Plas Newydd★, a black and white gothicised house, in 1780. They were both members of Irish aristocratic families, Eleanor's being Roman Catholic, and Sarah's being Protestant. They shocked their kinsfolk by determining to spend their lives together. All steps were taken to prevent them from achieving the idyll to which they aspired. However, they managed to elope together, leaving for Britain in 1778.

They travelled a little in Wales before finding Plas Newydd where they settled for the rest of their days. They lived on a modest but uncertain income, gradually turning the plain Welsh house which they rented into a gothic cottage, a style then much in vogue. They did eventually acquire the property. They kept diaries and were inveterate letter writers; many of their papers survive. An account of their long lives here can be found in Elizabeth Mavor's book *The Ladies of Llangollen* [1984], which draws fully on the archives. Their devoted maid Mary Caryll lived with them through their ups and downs. Indeed it was Mary's own good management which enabled her to buy Plas Newydd and bequeath it to the Ladies. They erected a stone triangular monument to Mary Caryll in St Collen's churchyard when she died. They are themselves buried under the same monument.

Their lifestyle was much admired. For two women to live so closely in such companionship for fifty years was indeed unusual. The ten-year difference in their ages was of no significance to them. Their visitors included **Hannah More** with one of her sisters, Harriet Bowdler, and other leading figures of their day, most of whom brought gifts which can be seen in the house. Llangollen was on the main route between London and Holyhead and on to Ireland, so it was convenient for callers.

Lady Martin, the actress **Helen Faucit**, whose home was three miles away at Bryntisilio, latterly lived next to Llanttsilio Church and was buried there after her death in 1898. She had retired from her stage career in 1865. She is commemorated in the chapel on the north side of the choir of the church.

LLANWERN, Gwent [see Map 1, F3]   When **Lady Rhondda** died in 1958, her ashes were scattered here in her native Wales, but the family home was demolished in the early 1950s. She had actively sought to improve the status of women and encouraged debate through the journal *Time and Tide* which she founded in 1920. Towards the end of her life its reputation declined but it achieved the major aim of full enfranchisement for women in 1928.

LOCHGELLY, Fife [see Map 2, C3]   This mining community was the native town of **Jennie Lee**. She was born in 1904 and won a scholarship to Edinburgh University from the local school. Through her father, a miner, she became involved in the Labour Movement at an early age.

LOCH LEVEN, Tayside [see Map 2, C3]   **Mary Queen of Scots**, was imprisoned in the fifteenth-century fortress here in 1567. She was a prisoner in Loch Leven Castle★ for nearly a year, before she was able to escape. It was here that she abdicated as queen, handing over the crown to her two-year-old son with the Earl of Moray as Regent. Mary made several attempts to leave the island. The story of her successful attempt is well known. William Douglas, a youth who had been appointed to attend her, dropped his napkin over the keys which lay beside the Laird's place at table. He was able to free the queen, whom he then rowed to the shore where her supporters rallied round.

LODDEN, Norfolk [see Map 1, E5]   **Ann Charlotte Bartholomew** was born here in 1800. However, she spent most of her life in London. Norfolk has recognised her as a native artist and some of her work can be seen in the collections of the Norfolk Museums Service in Norwich.

LODSWORTH, Sussex [see Map 1, F4]   When the economist **Barbara Ward** was created a life peer in 1976 in recognition of her achievements, she took the title Baroness Jackson of Lodsworth.

LONDON   See pages 205-91.

LONG EATON, Derbyshire [see Map 1, E3]   The artist **Laura Knight** was born here in 1877, but she spent most of her childhood in Nottingham.

LONG MELFORD, Suffolk [see Map 1, F4]   A frequent visitor to this charming town was **Beatrix Potter**. She used to stay with her relations at Melford Hall★[NT], the redbrick Elizabethan house with a gatehouse and turrets. One of the rooms which can be viewed is the bedroom where she used to stay. A much loved soft toy on show was the model for Jemima Puddleduck, one of her popular children's characters.

LONG SLEDDALE, Cumbria [see Map 1, D3]   **Mrs Humphrey Ward** used this valley to the north of Kendal as Long Whindale, the background for some of the action in her novel *Robert Elsmore* [1888]. It was a part of the country which she loved dearly.

LOSSIEMOUTH, Grampian [see Map 2, B3]   In 1911 **Margaret MacDonald** died tragically young, aged only forty-one. She was cremated in London but her ashes were buried in the churchyard at Spynie, to the south of Lossiemouth. She had been a tireless worker for the welfare of women and their children, and a founder member of the Women's Labour

21   The Philpot Museum in Lyme
Regis, Dorset

League. Ramsay MacDonald, her husband, by whom she had six children,
later became Britain's first Labour Prime Minister.

LUDLOW, Shropshire [see Map 1, E3]   The imposing Ludlow Castle★ has
royal connections. **Catherine of Aragon** lived here during her brief first
marriage to Henry VII's heir Prince Arthur. After his death in 1502, and a
great deal of diplomatic wrangling, it was agreed that she should marry
Arthur's younger brother, the future Henry VIII. This wedding eventually
took place in 1509. When Henry tired of her as his queen, he tried to get a
divorce on the grounds that his marriage to Catherine was not legal because
she had previously been his brother's wife. Before the eventual divorce,
Catherine brought up her daughter **Mary Tudor**, later queen herself, here
as well as at other royal homes. Later **Mary Sidney**, poet and patron, born
in 1561, spent much of her childhood in this castle as well as at Penshurst
Place.

LYME REGIS, Dorset [see Map 1, G3]   This lovely town on the south
coast of England has many attractions, not least its associations with some
significant women. The best known association must be that of **Jane
Austen**. She was a visitor to the town in 1803 and 1804, and a plaque in
Broad Street marks Pyne House where she is thought to have taken

lodgings. She later included Lyme in her novel *Persuasion* [1818] in which the character Louisa Musgrove caused a stir by falling off the Cobb [the harbour breakwater], down the primitive stairway known locally as Grannie's Steps. The Cobb also features prominently in the work by John Fowles, *The French Lieutenant's Woman* [1969], whose central male character was attracted to the town by its geology. Fossils had been found here for centuries, but **Mary Anning**, a local carpenter's daughter, made it the focus of much serious study. She made a living by collecting local fossils and selling them to interested visitors as well as scientists. There is some dispute as to the site of her home and her fossil shop. Many significant specimens found by her are in the major British palaeontological museum collections. She was involved in the first identifiable find of an icthyosaurus in 1811 and later of a plesiosaurus. Mary died in 1847, aged forty-eight, and is buried in St Michael's churchyard. Her grave stands to the north side of the church, which also contains a window dedicated to her.

Examples of local fossils can be seen in the Philpot Museum★. The museum was named after three other local fossilists, the **Philpot** sisters, **Mary**, **Margaret** and **Elizabeth**. They were contemporaries of Mary Anning, from a more genteel family, but they were happy to collaborate with her. From 1805 their home was at the top of Silver Street, then number 1, and now the Anchor Hotel. The hotel was also the setting for some illustrations by **Beatrix Potter**, the author of the popular children's books, who much later was once a guest in the house.

The local geology also shaped the lives of two other remarkable women. **Mrs Eleanor Coade**, and her daughter, **Eleanor Coade**, lived here, while Mr Coade operated a business, which his wife took over on his death in 1770. They had by this time moved to London, having acquired a business in Lambeth making what became known as Coade Stone. They had developed a formula for reconstituted stone. Eleanor the younger kept a house in Lyme. It stands on the hill, at the corner of Cobb Street and Pound Street. It is now called Belmont and its façade is decorated with ornaments in Coade Stone, showing that she too valued her own products.

Other visitors to the town included the author of *Our Village: Sketches of Rural Life, Character and Scenery* [1832], **Mary Russell Mitford**, whose stay in Broad Street is marked by a sign on the premises now Boots the Chemist's shop.

LYMPNE, Kent [see Map 1, F5]   **Margaret Damer Dawson**, the social reformer and women's police pioneer, died here in 1920 and was buried in the town.

LYNDHURST, Hampshire [see Map 1, G3]   In the south side of the graveyard of the church of St Michael and All Angels, lie the ashes of **Alice Liddell**, the Alice of Lewis Carroll's *Alice in Wonderland* [1865]. She died in 1934, and the plain inscription on the grave remembers her as Mrs Reginald Hargreaves.

LYTH HILL, Shropshire [see Map 1, E3] **Mary Webb**, the Shropshire regional novelist, lived at Spring Cottage for ten years from 1917. *The House in Dormer Forest* [1920] and *Precious Bane* [1924] were written in these last years of her life. Towards the end she spent as much time as possible here, to escape London and a failing marriage. Her heart was always in her native county.

M M

MALVERN, Hereford and Worcestershire [see Map 1, F3]   The Swedish singer, **Jenny Lind**, retired here to live at Wynd's Point, a large and now secluded Victorian house on the hillside near Little Malvern Priory. She had an international career, earning the affectionate nickname 'the Swedish Nightingale' when she settled in London on her marriage in 1852. She died in 1887 and was buried in the town cemetery in Great Malvern. Her plain gravestone, of granite from her native Sweden, lies to the right of the chapel.

MANCHESTER, Greater Manchester [see Map 1, E3]   This northern industrial city has been the home, workplace and campaign ground of many notable women. One of its earlier daughters was **Mother Ann Lee**, later leader of the religious group called the Shakers, Believers in Christ's Second Appearing. She was born into a blacksmith's family in 1736 in Todd Street, near the Victoria Railway Station, but much of the street has been demolished. She herself married a blacksmith, Abraham Standerin, but their four children all died in infancy. Already a Shaker, this convinced her of the evils of sex, which she then denied herself. A vision led her to cross the Atlantic with some devoted followers in 1774. There she was hailed in Shaker communities as the second coming of Christ, perhaps not so strange for the illiterate daughter of a blacksmith.

Mrs Gaskell made her home at 14 Dover Street [now gone] when she first moved here as a newly-wed in 1832. She was to spend forty years here, moving in 1842 to 121 Upper Rumford Street [also gone] and finally settling at 84 Plymouth Grove [now the University's Overseas Student Centre, with a plaque recording it as her former residence]. Her husband was the minister of the Unitarian Chapel in Cross Street. She involved herself in her husband's parish work and became familiar with the situation of working people and the poor. She set her first novel *Mary Barton: a Tale of Manchester Life* [1848] in the city factories. Its publication was greeted with uproar by the mill-owners who were portrayed in a very poor light. Her later works *Ruth* [1853], which shocked some of its readers by its sympathetic treatment of an abandoned unmarried mother, and *North and South* [1855] also drew on her insights into less privileged lives. In her best known work *Cranford* [1853], the city is referred to as Dumble. Her books made her a literary figure, and she received many visitors into her home at Plymouth Grove, including **Charlotte Brontë**, whom she came to know well and whose biography she wrote, **Jane Carlyle**, and the American author of the anti-slavery work *Uncle Tom's Cabin* [1852], **Harriet Beecher Stowe**.

Geraldine Jewsbury, **Frances Hodgson Burnett** and **Angela Brazil** are other writers with local associations. Geraldine Jewsbury kept house for her father and brothers in the city while writing her novels, including *Zöe* [1845], *The Half Sisters* [1848] and *Marion Withers* [1851]. She lived at 2 Birchfield Place, Higher Ardwick. She first met Jane Carlyle in 1841, and a close friendship developed between them and some of their correspondence survives. She left Manchester in 1853 to be near Jane in London. Frances Hodgson Burnett was born in 1849 at 141 York Street [the original house has been demolished but it stood in what is now Cheetham Hill Road]. A plaque on 361 Cheetham Hill Road indicates the house to which her family moved in 1852, its address then being 9 St Luke's Terrace. Her father died the next year, and financial circumstances forced them to find cheaper accommodaton. They finally emigrated to Tennessee in 1864, where she remained until 1880. She returned to Britain already acknowledged as a novelist, but made her name from her two children's works *Little Lord Fauntleroy* [1886] and *The Secret Garden* [1911]. Angela Brazil's writing success came from popular schoolgirl adventure fiction. Her own schooldays were spent at Manchester Preparatory High and Ellerslie Schools, both of which were sources for characters and action in her books.

Manchester's place in the fight for women's votes should be better known. A meeting held at the Free Trade Hall, Peter Street, in 1868 by the Manchester Women's Suffrage Society was a landmark; the cause of women's voting rights was the pressing item on the agenda, from then on many women and men devoted their time and energy to secure these rights. The forthcoming Women's History Resource Centre in the former Pankhurst family home at 62 Nelson Street and its neighbouring building, will pay full tribute to this struggle. **Emmeline Pankhurst** and her husband Dr Richard Pankhurst met in 1878, and Mrs Pankhurst immediately took up his political interests, beginning with the proposed Married Women's Property Act. While bringing up her children in London, where they moved to further the doctor's parliamentary ambitions, she continued her involvement in politics, alive to every issue of the day. She and her daughters returned to Manchester in 1898, when she was widowed; 62 Nelson Street became their home. Her three daughters **Christabel**, **Sylvia** and **Adela**, all made this their home base from then, until their involvement in the suffrage campaigns took them to London and elsewhere. In order to support her family, Emmeline took a job as registrar of births, deaths and marriages for the Rusholme district. She continued her work for the poor of Manchester, and became the first woman appointed to the Board of Guardians, the body which managed the workhouses for the destitute. She was herself a native northerner, having been born in the area in 1858. The Pankhurst home is undergoing comprehensive restoration, funded by women's organisations and various supporting bodies.

Christabel was the most academic of the three daughters. After attending Manchester High School for Girls on the corner of Oxford Road and Dover Street with her sisters, she entered Victoria University [now the University of Manchester] to study law. In 1906 she gained the top first class degree in her year, but was not permitted to practise at the bar on account of her sex. She also helped her mother at work, as Deputy Registrar. She and her mother founded the Women's Social and Political Union at 62 Nelson Street in 1903, after despairing of the established parties ever taking seriously the matter of votes for women. In 1907 she left for the capital where she was able to use her skills in organising the WSPU's Votes for Women campaign more effectively. However, this was not before she and her friend **Annie Kenney** had hit the headlines by being arrested outside the Free Trade Hall, Peter Street, in 1905. They had been heckling at a Liberal Party election meeting, and the penalty was a spell inside Strangeways Prison, Sherbourne Street. This was the first time that women had been apprehended for such political activity, and it began a trend which many women followed gladly for the Cause, even to the detriment of their health. In reports of their arrest the term suffragette was used for the first time. Following their example, **Emily Wilding Davison** also experienced prison life in Strangeways, in her extreme devotion to the Cause.

Sylvia was the second daughter, and her talents lay in the arts. She attended the Manchester College of Art, achieving many distinctions, including opportunities to study abroad. As with her sisters, she became committed to and involved in the women's movement at an early stage. She used her art for the cause, designing banners, posters and other campaign material. She, too, went to London, initially to further her art studies, and she went to prison there several times. She organised support for the Cause in London and contributed both articles and illustrations for several suffrage publications. Her own history *The Suffragette Movement – an Intimate Account of Persons and Ideals* [1931] remains a key source for understanding the campaign. She continued to fight for freedom and peace throughout her life. Her last cause was independence for Abyssinia, now Ethiopia, and she died there in 1960.

Adela, the youngest, was also involved in the fight for votes, both here and in London, but most of her active life was spent abroad. She chose a different route in the struggle for women's enfranchisement and went to live in Australia. There she was active in the peace movement, socialism and social work. She died in 1961 aged seventy-six.

Annie Kenney was from a very different background from the Pankhursts, whom she first met in 1905 when she joined the WSPU. She had started to work in the textile mills at the age of ten, going full-time three years later. She became active in the trade union movement, and studied several subjects through a correspondence course at the trade union college at Oxford. She became totally committed to the WSPU, also moving south to further the cause. Their achievements enabled **Mrs Emmeline Pethick-Lawrence** to stand as Labour Parliamentary candidate for Rusholme in 1918, the first occasion on which women could legally do so. Unfortunately, she did not win the seat.

Esther Roper was an early woman student of the city's Victoria University, graduating from Owen's College in 1891. She soon became secretary of the North of England Society for Women's Suffrage, a post she held until 1905. In 1896 she met **Eva Gore-Booth**, an Irish-born aristocrat who wrote poetry. They took an immediate liking to one another, having many interests in common. Eva moved north to share a house with Esther in 1897. Eva, never strong in health, felt that she must give her time and energy to the Cause, while she still had both. As it turned out, she had thirty years left for this work, and with Esther as her friend and partner she channelled her efforts to good effect unswervingly in pursuit of peace, equal rights and the abolition of capital punishment. They concentrated on the experience of working-class women. Eva died in 1926 and Esther twelve years later.

There were many others who worked locally for the Cause, notably **Lydia Becker**, who was born in Cooper Street in 1827. She was a founder-member, in 1867, of the Manchester National Society for Women's Suffrage, the earliest such organisation in Great Britain. She was instrumental in gaining women the right to sit on school boards in 1870. A persuasive orator, she addressed an audience in the city's Free Trade Hall on 14 April 1868, making the first public speech by a woman on the subject of votes for women. She edited the *Women's Suffrage Journal* from the inaugural issue in 1870 until her death in 1890. **Helena Swanwick** moved to Manchester on her marriage in 1888. She reported on all local women's issues as a journalist but later in life became more closely associated with pacificism. From 1909 she edited the *Common Cause*, the weekly paper of the National Union of Women's Suffrage Societies. **Margaret Llewelyn Davies** was general secretary of the Women's Co-operative Guild from its foundation in 1883 until 1915. Since its inception, women have always been active in the Co-operative Movement. The headquarters, a vast building of imposing decorated redbrick, stands proudly in Corporation Street.

The generation which first made strides in parliamentary politics produced **Ellen Wilkinson**. 'Red Ellen', as she was called later, was born in Manchester in 1891; she obtained a scholarship in 1910 to read history at the university here, graduating in 1913. Her early involvement in the Labour and Co-operative movements here was useful training for the time when she became the first woman to enter parliament for the Labour Party. Another pioneer who was not afraid to confront public disapproval was **Marie Stopes**, the campaigner for birth control. Her academic career as a palaeontologist led her to take a teaching post at the University of Manchester, where she was to be the first woman lecturer. Her own unsatisfactory first marriage led her to open as a subject for debate the topics of contraception and sex. **Alison Uttley**, known for her children's writing and as creator of Little Grey Rabbit, began her career as a science teacher after graduating from Manchester University in 1903. The artist **Helen**

22   Albion House, West Street in Marlow, Buckinghamshire, where Mary Shelley prepared *Frankenstein* for publication

Bradley painted in the Wilmslow area, greatly influenced by local artist L. S. Lowry.

In the arts, **Sarah Siddons**, the actress, spent a season performing here in 1776-7; **Dame Sybil Thorndike** began her acting career in repertory in the city. More recently the singer **Isobel Baillie**, who died in 1983, grew up here and ended her music career teaching at the College of Music where she had received her own voice training. The city has a lively arts life today.

The Pankhurst Appeal Committee has published a guided walk entitled *Women in Manchester: a Walk through the Past*, which follows the activities and achievements in the city of women individually and collectively. The Appeal Committee is raising funds to open the Pankhursts' home as a resource, research and exhibition centre for women's history and heritage.

MARKET BOSWORTH, Leicestershire [see Map 1, E3]   Market Bosworth Hall, now the Bosworth Park Infirmary, was the marital home of **Lady Florence Dixie**. She had married Sir Beaumont Dixie in 1875, but this did not confine her in any way. She was frequently abroad, pursuing her career as a journalist. She went on to become the first female war correspondent, covering the Boer War fought in South Africa in 1880-1.

MARLOW, Buckinghamshire [see Map 3, B1]   In 1817 **Mary Shelley** came to Marlow with the poet Percy Bysshe Shelley from Switzerland. She had gone abroad with him, when he left his wife. After his wife's death, they married and moved into Albion House, a gothic cottage in West Street beside the Grammar School playing fields, now divided into four dwellings. There is a tablet high on the building which records that Byron had a meeting here with Shelley: it makes no mention of the fact that Mary Shelley prepared her story, *Frankenstein, or the Modern Prometheus* [1818], for publication at Albion House. It proved to be an enduring classic, of which over thirty film versions have been made.

MAUTBY, Norfolk [see Map 1, E5] **Margaret Paston**, whose given name, Mautby, suggests that she was born in this community, belonged to an important local family. Her date of birth may be *c.* 1423. Her advantageous marriage in 1440 took her to Caistor and Paston and when her husband died in 1466 she returned here a rich widow. She was buried in the south aisle of the church, but the site can no longer be found. She penned many of *The Paston Letters*, written in the late fifteenth century and are now a unique record of the management of estates and property in medieval Norfolk.

MEASHAM, Leicestershire [see Map 1, E3] **Geraldine Jewsbury** was born here in 1812; her father had a business here, before he took the family to Manchester. She later became a significant woman of letters, writing six novels and numerous articles.

MELBOURNE, Derbyshire [see Map 1, E3] **Lady Caroline Lamb**'s uneasy marriage to William Lamb, later Lord Melbourne, the nineteenth-century Prime Minister, connected her with Melbourne Hall★, his family home. The glorious gardens, which were laid out by Le Notre, designer of the gardens at Versailles, seem to have provided little consolation for the sixteen-year-old bride. It is not known how much time she spent here, but a portrait and some needlework testify to her association.

MELTON MOWBRAY, Leicestershire [see Map 1, E4] This is another town in which **Anne of Cleves** acquired property from Henry VIII on their divorce in 1540. The building is now The Anne of Cleves restaurant in Burton Street, adjacent to the lovely parish church, but the signboard shows Henry VIII and not her. A daughter of the Melton area, who was taken abroad shortly after she was born in 1902, was **Beryl Markham**, the daring aviator who made the first solo flight across the Atlantic, from east to west, in 1936. She was a professional pilot and became Kenya's premier racehorse trainer, having her first success at the age of eighteen. Most of her life was spent in East Africa, and she gave a stirring account of her extraordinary life in her book *West with the Night* [1942]. She died in August 1986, sadly just weeks before the jubilee of her transatlantic flight.

MERE, Wiltshire [see Map 1, F3] **Lisbeth Eisner**, German socialist poet, spent her last years in this charming village. She died in 1949, away from the European political scene in which her husband had also been active.

MERTON   See **LONDON BOROUGH OF MERTON**.

MEY, Highland [see Map 2, A3]   The Castle of Mey, formerly called Barrogil, was saved from demolition in 1952 by **Queen Elizabeth, the Queen Mother**. She chose this fortress, which in the sixteenth century had been the seat of the Earls of Caithness, as her summer residence. It is perched on the cliff-tops, overlooking the Pentland Firth.

MICKLEHAM, Surrey [see Map 3, C2]   In 1793 **Madame de Stael**, together with other compatriots, was obliged to leave France. They had openly opposed Napoleon's regime. A group of them rented Juniper Hall, now a Field Studies Centre. The novelist and diarist **Fanny Burney** became acquainted with the exiles in 1792, while visiting friends in the neighbour-hood. One of the exiles was General d'Arblay, whom she married here the following year in the parish church. Their financial problems were solved to a certain extent by the success of Fanny's third novel *Camilla, or a Picture of Youth* [1796], which enabled them to buy a cottage at Great Bookham. The political situation allowed them to make their home in France in 1802.

Another writer of popular fiction to live here was **Marie Corelli**, born in 1855. Her home was Fern Dell, but this was before she had made her name as the author of romantic novels. At this stage she was still called Mary Mackay. She was thirty when she gave up all ideas of a career in music and began to write. It was in Mickleham that George Meredith wrote his best known work, *Diana of the Crossways* [1885], based on the life of **Caroline Norton**. The Honorable Caroline Norton, herself a writer, had a very unhappy life. When her marriage failed, she lost custody of her three children. Her relationship with Lord Melbourne was misinterpreted, and this was the problematic subject of Meredith's book. Meredith had made his home in the village from 1867. Through his position as a publisher's reader he supported several writers in their efforts to get published.

MIDDLE CLAYDON, Buckinghamshire [see Map 1, F4]   **Florence Nightingale** was a regular visitor to Claydon✻[NT], the country home of her married sister Parthenope Verney. There is a room dedicated to Florence's life and nursing achievements, showing many of her belongings and several decorations and awards presented to her.

MIDDLESBROUGH, Cleveland [see Map 2, D4]   The town can claim the Labour Party's first woman Member of Parliament. **Ellen Wilkinson**, named by the press 'Red Ellen', represented this constituency from 1924 until 1931. She later returned to Parliament as MP for Jarrow. Her entry to politics was through student societies and trade unionism. She joined the Independent Labour Party in 1913 and also the National Union of Women's Suffrage Societies, as she was concerned that working-class women should also strive for, and benefit from, the vote.

MILFORD HAVEN, Dyfed [see Map 1, F2]   The port, and associated community, was the result of investment and encouragement from Sir

23 Maxwelton House, Moniaive, Dumfries and Galloway, the birthplace of
Annie Laurie

William Hamilton, who founded it in 1793. His second wife, **Emma
Hamilton**, accompanied him during his stays here at Castle Hall, and
sometimes Lord Nelson joined them. All three are commemorated in the
town.

MILTON KEYNES, Buckinghamshire [see Map 1, F4] The Open
University, the so-called second chance university which has given many
women access to degree level education through broadcast and correspondence teaching, was established here in 1969. One of those who gave the
new institution much needed encouragement in its early years was **Jennie
Lee**, Labour Minister for Education. The University library is named after
her.

MIRFIELD, West Yorkshire [see Map 1, E3] The **Brontë** sisters all spent
some time at Miss Wooler's school at Roehead, near Mirfield. **Charlotte
Brontë**, as the eldest surviving sister, was the first to be sent in 1831.
During her year here she became close to her two dearest friends, Ellen
Nussey and Mary Taylor, whose families inspired some of her writing. In
her capacity as a teacher she returned in 1835, staying two years, during
which **Emily**, briefly, and **Anne** attended as non-fee-paying pupils.
However, Charlotte did not enjoy teaching, and was pleased to leave after

this comparatively short time. Anne later took a position as a governess in a private home [no longer standing] in Mirfield.

MONIAIVE, Dumfries and Galloway [see Map 2, C2] In 1682 **Annie Laurie**, the heroine of the Scottish ballad of that name, was born at Maxwelton House★, to the south of Moniaive. The song describes her romantic involvement with William Douglas, but she became the wife of Alexander Ferguson, a match which had her parents' approval. A portrait of her in Maxwelton House shows her to be a handsome woman; a small boudoir has been furnished to suggest her life here. As the opening lines of the song run, 'Maxwelton Braes are bonny, they're a' clad ower wi' dew.' The lines were set to music in 1835. This is a very attractive part of Scotland. Annie stayed in the area, her married home being Craigendarroch, further north up the valley. The coats of arms and initials of Annie Laurie and her husband are built into the walls and coupled with the date of their marriage, 1729. She died in 1764 and is buried in the ruined church in Kirklands graveyard which is situated between her two homes. She is also honoured in the United States of America. There is a chapel built in her memory in Los Angeles.

MONKSTADT, Isle of Skye, Highland [see Map 1, B1] **Flora MacDonald** grew up in the once substantial but now ruined Monkstadt House. These isolated crumbling walls create the right evocative atmosphere in which to contemplate the end of the Stuart claims to the Scottish throne.

MONMOUTH, Gwent [see Map 1, F3] **Emma Hamilton**'s colourful life brought her notoriety, fame, love and sadness. Posterity has claimed her through her association with Admiral Lord Nelson, the British naval hero. Monmouth Museum★ exhibits material relating to them both in the Nelson Collection.

MONTROSE, Tayside [see Map 2, B3] This Angus town may seem an unlikely place for the dancer **Lola Montez** to spend her school days. Her lifetime of travel started early, as her father was an officer in the British Army. Her education continued in Paris, which is more as one might expect. Her real name was Maria Dolores Eliza Rosanna Gilbert, and she was born in Ireland. She came to Scotland in 1826 after her mother's second marriage, to a Scot.

MORPETH, Northumberland [see Map 2, C3] The gravestone of **Emily Wilding Davison** in the churchyard here carries the moving and determined inscription 'Deeds, not Words'. Emily was buried here in 1913 after giving her life in the fight for votes at the race course at Epsom. Her funeral in London was huge, and several suffragettes including Emmeline Pankhurst were arrested at it under the 'Cat and Mouse Act'. Her sacrifice was not in vain, although all adult women did not get the vote until universal suffrage was granted in 1928. Emily's mother had run a sweet

24   The grave of Emily Wilding Davison at Morpeth, Northumberland

shop in the nearby village of Long Horseley, having herself made considerable sacrifices to give Emily a good education.

MUCH WENLOCK, Shropshire [see Map 1, E3]   The writer who drew heavily on the imagery and atmosphere of the countryside in this part of the county, **Mary Webb**, spent her formative years at the Grange. This rambling country house was the family home from 1882 until 1896. Mary was already writing poems during her childhood here, but she was in her thirties when her first novels were published

MYLOR, Cornwall [see Map 1, G2]   In 1916 **Katherine Mansfield**, the New Zealand writer, moved to this tiny fishing village with John Middleton Murry. It should have been of benefit to her health – she suffered from tuberculosis which eventually killed her – but she was unable to settle into the way of life here, and was always travelling up to London and Garsington. Eventually she moved back to the capital where she married Murry in 1918.

N N

NEAR SAWREY, Cumbria [see Map 1, D3]   In 1905 **Beatrix Potter** bought Hill Top*[NT], the small seventeenth-century farmhouse where many of her later children's books were written and illustrated. She had fallen in love with the area on a visit to the village with her parents in 1896. She paid for publication of *The Tale of Peter Rabbit* [1900] and its successor *The Tailor of Gloucester* [1902] before a professional publishing company became involved and brought her the degree of financial independence through which she was able to buy Hill Top. It is quite charming, and some of the furniture and fittings can be recognised from her picture books. She bought the neighbouring working farm a few years later, becoming herself a serious and highly-respected sheep farmer. In the meantime she had married and abandoned her writing. She eventually owned 4,000 acres which she left to the National Trust, together with Hill Top.

NELSON, Lancashire [see Map 1, D3]   **Selina Cooper**, a northern working-class suffragist whose involvement in the Labour Movement and women's rights has recently been rediscovered, took her first steps into a life of political action here. The town earned itself the nickname 'Red Nelson'. She concentrated on ways of improving the lot of local people, serving as member of the Poor Law Board of Guardians, as president of the Women's Co-operative Guild and as a magistrate. She died in 1946 aged eighty-two. Her papers, only recently collected, can be consulted in the Lancashire Records Office in Lancaster. Jill Liddington's biography of her, *The Life and Times of a Respectable Rebel* [1984], is an inspiring chronicle of a courageous, capable and committed woman.

NEW ABBEY, Dumfries and Galloway [see Map 2, D3]   The new abbey which gives this community its name is Sweetheart Abbey★, a substantial ruin in warm red sandstone. The abbey was built in the thirteenth century by the wealthy noblewoman **Dervorguilla**, Lady of Galloway, as a Cistercian house. Dervorguilla was the benefactor of Balliol College, Oxford, several other religious houses and the people of Dumfries. She had been inseparable from her husband in life, and when he died she had his heart embalmed and always kept it with her in a fine casket, until her own death in 1289. This was the 'sweet heart' after which the abbey is named. Dervorguilla and the heart were buried in front of the high altar of the Abbey Church, and the spot is marked. An earlier tombstone has been restored under cover in the south transept. She was known for her wisdom and generosity throughout Scotland.

25   27 Broad Street, New Alresford, Hampshire, the birthplace of Mary
Russell Mitford

NEW ALRESFORD, Hampshire [see Map 1, F4]   A plaque on 27 Broad
Street commemorates the birthplace of **Mary Russell Mitford** in 1787.
This was the family home until she was ten, when she had the remarkable
luck of winning £20,000 in a lottery. Unfortunately, the prize, an enormous
amount in 1797, went to her father's head. He moved the family to Reading
and the family adopted an extravagant new lifestyle. In the end it was only
through her success as a writer that they were able to maintain even a
modest household.

NEWCASTLE UPON TYNE, Tyne and Wear [see Map 2, D3]   The
fortunes of this north-eastern port were built upon the coal industry, which
had received royal support in the fourteenth century from **Philippa of
Hainault**, Edward III's queen. She had backed coal-mining on her own
estates in the north-east coalfields. **Mary Astell**, an early feminist born
1666, is thought to have been a native of Newcastle. Her life as a writer was
based in London. She deserves to be better known, on account of her
publication of *A Serious Proposal to the Ladies by a Lover of her Sex* [1694]. In
this she proposed the establishment of a college or residential academy
where women could pursue studies and enjoy the intellectual stimulus
which she herself had found in books and discussion. Although it attracted
some financial support, it was considered a threat to the Anglican Church,

and never materialised. Nearby, East Denton Hall was the home in the 1750s of **Lady Mary Wortley Montagu**, another enterprising feminist, whose unconventional life is recorded in her letters and her publications, though many were published anonymously or posthumously, for example her *Turkish Letters* [1763]. Here her guests included Johnson, Garrick and Reynolds; other friends included Pope and Gay, and, indeed, Mary Astell.

In Newcastle itself, **Mary Beilby**, a member of a family of glass enamellers, produced some beautiful works of art. She was born here in 1749, and, working in partnership with her brother William, they produced marvellous decorated drinking glasses and decanters. They both moved to Fife in 1778, but examples of their work can be seen in the Laing Art Gallery★. Journalism was the field in which **Nancy Spain** made her name; she too was a native of Newcastle, born in 1917. She took the opportunities offered by the new twentieth-century medium, television, and became one of Britain's first television personalities in the 1950s and 1960s, having earlier become well known through radio broadcasts. In addition to her freelance writing she started *She*, a new type of women's magazine, together with her lover, Joan Werner Laurie, and published several detective novels, such as *The Cat Strikes*. She and Joan Werner Laurie were killed in a tragic air crash, *en route* to the race course at Aintree in 1964. She began her career as a sports journalist, and sadly ended it while going to cover one of the British sporting calendar's biggest events, the Grand National.

NEWLYN, Cornwall [see Map 1, G2] When this small Cornish town again attracted artists before the First World War, **Laura Knight** came here in 1910, using the Trewarveneth Studio. Another attracted to the community here was **Dod Shaw**, who lived with her painter husband Ernest Proctor in Harbour View Terrace, a short row of granite homes at the top of a steep hill beside the Methodist Church. There is a very effective small art gallery, Newlyn Art Gallery★, which usually has some of their works on show in their high quality exhibitions.

NEWMARKET, Suffolk [see Map 1, E4] The Anglo-Saxon saint **Etheldreda** is said to have been born at Exning, a neighbouring village, in *c*. 630. This country market town has been famous as a centre of horse-racing since Charles II began to follow the sport here. Where he went, his mistress, **Nell Gwyn**, can always be counted on to have accompanied him, however much they tried to be discreet. The house in which she stayed in Palace Street is said to have been linked by an underground passage to the inn in which he lodged. It is the only house to have survived a fire which devastated the town in 1683. Horse-racing was a solely male preserve, and its dubious reputation led many churchmen with a taste for the sport to adopt a *nom de course* in order to participate fully and with impunity. **Lillie Langtry**, the Jersey-born actress and socialite, employed the same tactics and was the first woman to have a racing stable. This was at Etheldreda House, which she managed under the name Mr Jersey.

NEWTON TONEY, Wiltshire [see Map 1, F3]   The travel writer of the late seventeenth and early eighteenth century, **Celia Fiennes**, was probably born at the manor house in this village in 1662. Little is known of her life apart from what she recorded in her accounts of her travelling between *c.* 1682 and *c.* 1712. These records were not published in full until 1947, and they are a valuable source for economic and landscape history. Certainly, until her mother's death in 1691, the Manor was the home of her family which had supported the Roundheads in the Civil War. There is no trace remaining of the Manor, but most of her early journeys began and ended here. After the death in 1691 of her mother, who had accompanied her on her first travels, London tended to be her starting point. She was inevitably a Nonconformist and a Whig supporter. It might therefore seem surprising to find her memorial on the north wall in the Anglican flint church, St Andrews, recording her burial here, as she had wished, after her death in Hackney in 1741. As other members of her family are also remembered on the stone tablet, their position as leading local family would inevitably tie them closely with the church.

NEWTOWN, Powys [see Map 1, E3]   At Gregynog Hall, the sisters **Gwendoline** and **Margaret Davies** settled in 1920. They had inherited a fortune made from the Welsh coalfields. Collectors of nineteenth-century French paintings and patrons of contemporary artists, they were among the first British collectors to appreciate the work of the French Impressionists. From 1923 until 1940 they ran a private press which produced forty-two fine print books, all beautifully bound. Many musical events were staged here. However, they did not confine their spending to cultural and academic fields. Both women were also active in social philanthropy. Gwen died in 1951, and Daisy [as Margaret was known] in 1963. They left their home and its contents to the University of Wales. It is now a music and conference centre.

NORTH BERWICK, Lothian [see Map 2, C3]   At the end of the sixteenth century two women who were lay-healers were among those tried here as witches at a famous trial in which the King himself had felt threatened. **Geillis Duncan** was the servant of a town official, and she died in *c.* 1590, after naming **Agnes Sampson**, another lay-healer, as a witch and implicating her in a plot against James VI and I. She eventually confessed to performing various rites, and was executed with several others in 1592. Accusations of witchcraft were often levelled against women quite unjustly when a scapegoat was required in times of economic and other crises. It did enormous damage to the value placed on the healing, and other skills, of women, many of which went underground and are now sadly lost to us.

Off the coast can be seen the distinctive volcanic outcrop, the Bass Rock. The island is now a bird sanctuary, but in the past served as impregnable fortress on several occasions, including providing refuge for covenanters. Many women covenanters played leading roles and suffered imprisonment and execution for their beliefs in the reign of James VII and II.

NORTH STOKE, Oxfordshire [see Map 1, F4] **Dame Clara Butt**, the opera singer, died in this South Oxfordshire village in 1936. Her long career as a concert performer brought pleasure to many, and hers is still considered one of the greatest voices of all time. She and her husband lived from 1929 at Brook Lodge, north of the village opposite Mill House, moving to Prospect House, also in the street, where they spent their retirement. She was buried in the churchyard, west of the church. The church lighting was installed in her memory, and a plaque inside the building recording this bears the words 'Thou art to them a very lovely song.'

NORTHAMPTON, Northamptonshire [see Map 1, F4] One of the surviving Eleanor Crosses stands on the side of the Old London road, on the south of the town. It was extensively restored in 1984, and a booklet describing it fully was published by Northampton Borough Council to coincide with the preservation project: *Restoration of the Eleanor Cross* by W. J. Nicolson. It was in the adjacent Delapre Abbey★, now the County Records Office, that **Eleanor of Castile**'s embalmed body was placed overnight on its journey to Westminster Abbey in 1290. The abbey was a nunnery in the medieval period, and became a private house in the seventeenth century.

Two seventeenth-century daughters of the town made names for themselves, one on each side of the Atlantic, but a major fire in the town in 1673 wiped out traces of older properties and their associations. **Anne Bradstreet** was born into a local family in *c.* 1612. Her father Thomas Dudley was well placed as steward to the Earl of Lincoln, and she received a good education. The opportunity to establish a new lifestyle based on Puritan principles free from the harassment which many Dissenters endured in Britain at this time, must have been a powerful incentive. Anne had married a Nonconformist Simon Bradstreet in 1628, and together they sailed for Massachusetts two years later, where Anne wrote 'I found a new world and new manners, at which my heart rose.' She became the first English-speaking poet in America to have her writings published. Her brother-in-law had her poetry published in Britain as *The Tenth Muse Lately Sprung up in America* [1650] without her knowledge. The work was well received, and her reputation continued after her death in Andover, Massachusetts, in *c.* 1672. The other was **Anne Bracegirdle**, whose career was on the stage. She was born here in *c.* 1663 but acting in the Restoration plays took her all over the country in various acting companies.

More recently, **Margaret Bondfield** sat as a Labour Member of Parliament for Northampton from 1923 until the next year, eventually becoming the first woman to serve as a Cabinet Minister.

NORTHCHURCH, Hertfordshire [see Map 3, A2] The novelist **Maria Edgeworth** lived here as a girl during her holidays from the boarding school for young ladies in Derby, 1776-81. The former family home is now called Edgeworth House, and it stands on the main road. She began to write seriously after her family settled in Ireland in their traditional territory, Edgeworthstown.

NORTHIAM, Sussex [see Map 1, F4]   This East Sussex town became the home of the regional novelist **Sheila Kaye-Smith** in 1929. She and her husband converted their house, Little Doucegrove, from an oasthouse into a home and refuge. Converted to the Roman Catholic faith, they temporarily used a small room as an oratory. When this room was deemed hazardous, Sheila Kaye-Smith had a small church built in the grounds. It was dedicated to St Thérèse of Lisieux in 1935. The author died after a fall on the stairs from her study in 1956. She was buried in the small graveyard adjacent to her church. The countryside she loved provides the setting for all her novels, *Joanna Godden* [1921] being one of the better known that is still in print. She also wrote a guide to the area, *Weald of Kent and Sussex*.

NORTON CONYERS, North Yorkshire [see Map 1, D3]   The Jacobean house, Norton Conyers★, belongs to the same family as when **Charlotte Brontë** visited in 1839. It is a probable model for her Thornfield Hall, where much of the action in *Jane Eyre* [1847] takes place.

NORWICH, Norfolk [see Map 1, E5]   The county town of Norfolk rejoices in being a cathedral city and having a good crop of medieval churches within its walls. Many of these were built with the money earned by the woollen industry which had been given encouragement in the fourteenth century by **Philippa of Hainault**. She fostered trading links with her native Flanders by settling Flemish weavers here. **Juliana of Norwich**, also known as **Mother Julian of Norwich**, the author of *XVI Revelations of Divine Love* [1373], is known to have lived as an anchoress in a simple stone cell beside the church off King Street which is now dedicated to her. The appropriately plain Church of St Julian includes a small chapel celebrating her life. Her book is thought to be the first written in English by a woman. May 8 is marked in the Roman Catholic calendar as her festival day. Very little is known about this religious mystic who lived *c.* 1343–1413, but she received many visitors who drew inspiration from her example. These included **Margery Kempe**, who saw Mother Julian before starting out on her travels to the Holy Land. In the second half of the fifteenth century **Margaret Paston**, one of the authors of *The Paston Letters*, spent time in the city. Her husband had several properties here, including the Music House, on the opposite side of King Street and now an adult education centre, and Crown Court, off the much photographed Elms Hill which has retained its late medieval character. The Paston correspondence gives many insights into the life and business interests of a prosperous household at this time.

The cathedral naturally was the centre of much activity throughout its long history, and was also the focus of much genteel social life. In the 1880s, the naturalist **Margaret Fountaine** spent a great deal of time and emotion sketching in the cathedral precincts, in the hope of attracting the attentions of a rakish chorister who later cruelly misused her. Coming herself from a clerical family, her later escapades would have shocked many in her social circles. Her near contemporary, the campaigning reformer and pacifist, **Mary Sheepshanks**, reacted against the all-pervading influence of the cathedral, where her father was Bishop of Norwich. She was fortunate in that she had received a good education in Liverpool; she became an early woman student at Cambridge University, and thereafter rarely returned to her family.

Edith Cavell was also the daughter of a clergyman; she is commemorated both inside the cathedral, on a pillar, and outside where her remains were buried under a cross by the south-east transept wall after the First World War. In 1907 she returned to Brussels, where she had earlier taught as a governess, to set up a pioneering nursing school. She remained in Belgium when the First World War broke out, and treated all patients regardless of their nationality. She enabled many soldiers to escape the German army, and for her courageous resistance was ultimately executed in 1915.

There was also a strong Nonconformist community in Norwich. Gurney's Court, a courtyard house set back on Magdalen Street, has a plaque recording that two significant women were born there: **Elizabeth Fry** [née Gurney] in 1780 and **Harriet Martineau** in 1802. Elizabeth's was a leading Quaker family, and she grew up at Earlham Hall, now part of the University of East Anglia, set in a public park to the south of the city. She is best known for her prison reform work. Harriet belonged to a prosperous Unitarian family of Huguenot origins, and the Octagon Chapel on Colegate played an influential part in her early religious and intellectual life. Although afflicted by deafness, Harriet was well able to support herself by writing when her family's financial situation deteriorated, later being highly respected as a progressive journalist. She was particularly proud of her novel *Deerbrook* [1839], but her series of articles *Illustrations of Political Economy* [1832-4] made a greater impact. It demonstrated that women had a firm grasp of topics which had previously been regarded as the intellectual preserve of men. **Mary** and **Anna Sewell**, both Quakers, lived a simple life at 125 Spixworth Road when Old Catton was a separate village to the north of the city centre, from 1867. This was to be their home from *c.* 1860. Anna kept bees here, but increasing ill health confined her indoors, where she wrote *Black Beauty* [1877] before predeceasing her mother in 1878. Mary died here in 1884, herself having published much literature for children. *Black Beauty* exposed the cruelty inflicted on many horses in the Victorian era, and the moving story firmly established itself as a classic work for children.

Elizabeth Fry's family attracted the writer **Amelia Opie** to the Quaker way of life in 1825. She had met John Opie the portrait painter in 1797, marrying him the same year. They moved to London, where he found many sitters, but she returned when widowed to look after her elderly father. She was active in workhouse visiting and campaigning against slavery. She made her home on the corner of Castle Meadow and Opie Street. Her best known works are *Father and Daughter* [1801] and *Adeline Mowbray* [1804]; she also wrote much poetry. **Daisy Ashford** was another local writer. She wrote her precocious and perceptive gem *The Young Visitors* [1919] when she was nine, but it was not published until she was forty-eight. She died at Hellesdon, to the north-west of the city, in 1972.

Norwich is known in art history for the Norwich School of painters, though these were predominantly men. There were local women artists, notably **Phyllis Jessup** who married her fellow artist Sir William Beechey in 1793 and **Ann Charlotte Bartholomew**, who was a successful flower and miniature painter, after an early career as playwright and poet. The works of both are represented in the Castle Museum★, where also on display are some of the international butterfly collections bequeathed to the city museum by **Margaret Fountaine** when she died in the West Indies in 1940. She had made the request that one box should not be opened until 1978, one hundred years following the first entry in her diaries. In 1978, these diaries, which were found inside, were read for the first time. She gave an enthusiastic account of her collecting expeditions as well as recounting aspects of her romantic life which she knew would have scandalised her family, had they learned the full details. She comes across as a very appealing woman.

In a city in which so many strong women lived, it is most encouraging to find that the museums in the city are serious in their attitudes to the history of ordinary women's lives. They have produced a guide to the Bridewell Museum★ and Strangers Hall★, both of which display social history collections. The guide was also designed as part of an Open University course in women's studies and is testament to the way everyday objects can tell us much about the past lives of women whose history is not found in written sources. This booklet is *Women's Work and Leisure: a Guide to the Strangers Hall and Bridewell Museums*, G. Durbin and M. Day, The Open University, Milton Keynes, 1983.

NOTTINGHAM, Nottinghamshire [see Map 1, E4]   The heroic tales of Robin Hood, and his adversary the Sheriff of Nottingham, inevitably remind visitors of the band of outlaws who supported Richard the Lionheart in the unpopular reign of King John. **Maid Marion**, portrayed as the English noblewoman whom Robin married, is also remembered, and features in the display at the Gatehouse to the Castle Museum★. However, despite the status of folk heroine ascribed to her by local legend, she is most likely a figure absorbed into English folklore from the French tales. A new centre is being planned which will explain current theories. The castle, which is much altered, was the residence during the English Civil War of **Lucy Hutchinson**. Her husband was the Parliamentarian Governor responsible for the local garrison force, and her surviving accounts are an important source, not only for Nottingham's seventeenth-century history but also for insights into the guiding philosophy of the Puritans. Her writings were a personal memoir of her husband who died in 1664, never intended for publication, unlike her theological treatises and her translations of Latin poetry.

The museum also has paintings by **Laura Knight** who grew up in Nottingham in Noel Street, overlooking Forest Park, site of the annual Goose Fair. Her first home here was number 9, called Ethel Villa and which carries a plaque noting it as her former home. Her family, the Johnsons, later moved to a redbrick semi-detached house, number 35, now part of the Forest Park Hotel. The final family home was a cottage nearby. In 1890, at thirteen, she became a very youthful student at the School of Art. For a while after this, she and her sister Nellie lived in a cave under the Castle. The castle rock is riddled with caves, many of which were inhabited. An idea of their circumstances can be gained by a visit to the Brewhouse Yard Musuem★, on Castle Boulevard, which includes displays in some of the caves. Laura left the city on her marriage to Harold Knight in 1903.

NUNEATON, Warwickshire [see Map 1, E3]   This is the area associated with **George Eliot** born Mary Anne Evans. She was born in 1819 at Arbury Farm [now named South Farm] on the Arbury estate, where her father was the estate manager. Arbury Hall★ is a country house in the gothic style, and it was the Cheverel Hall in her first work of fiction *Scenes from Clerical Life* [1858]. It had been a refuge at the end of the sixteenth century for **Mary Fitton**, the supposed 'Dark Lady' of Shakespeare's *Sonnets*. She came from the Court to her sister's home here for some privacy when she was unmarried and pregnant, a situation which received little sympathy in Court circles.

The Evans family moved into a nearby farm, Griff House, a few months after the writer's birth. When she was not away at boarding school, this was her home until 1840. The farmhouse stands on Griff Lane on the old Bedworth road to the south of Nuneaton, on a roundabout. It has been greatly extended and is now a steak house. There is a commemorative plaque above the door of the old part. She received a full education, starting at a small Dame's School [no longer standing] just across the road from the farmhouse. At five she was sent to her first boarding school in the neighbouring village of Attleborough. From 1828 she boarded at Miss Wallington's school in Nuneaton. She moved to Coventry with her father in 1841. She had been baptised in the Church on Avenue Road in Chilvers Coton, now part of Nuneaton, and was a regular attender all the time that she lived at Griff House. There are several sites in the area associated with her novels.

The town of Nuneaton is now very proud of George Eliot, and a whole gallery in the Nuneaton Museum and Gallery★ in Rivesley Park is devoted to her life and associated material. A useful booklet *George Eliot Country* by Dorothy Dods [4th edition 1980] is published by the Borough Council and is a guide to many places which she knew and which she later used in her novels. The George Eliot Fellowship is raising money for a statue to be commissioned as a memorial.

O o

OATLANDS, Surrey [see Map 3, B2]   **Catherine Howard**, ill-fated fifth wife to Henry VIII, married the king in Oatlands in 1540. Despite the experiences of her four predecessors, she was not sufficiently wary of the political intrigues of the court, and paid for the consequences with her life barely eighteen months later. Within a year of her royal marriage, her name was being blackened in the king's hearing. Whether there was any truth in the accusations of promiscuity now levelled at her, it is impossible to say. In any case she appears to have been yet another pawn in the succession game, and, for her supposed indiscretions, she was executed in 1542.

OLD DAILLY, Strathclyde [see Map 2, C2]   In 1868-9 the poet **Christina Rossetti** stayed at Penkill Castle★, as the guest of the artist **Alice Boyd**. The fifteenth-century castle which is two miles north-east of Girvan was a source for her poetic inventiveness, and for the artistic endeavours of her brother and their friends in the Pre-Raphaelite brethren.

OLD KINNEFF, Grampian [see Map 2, B3]   In the church at Old Kinneff the Honours of Scotland, the crown, sceptre and sword, were hidden under the floorboards from 1652 until 1660, the restoration of the Stuarts, after being rescued by **Christian Fletcher**, the minister's wife, from the besieged castle at Dunnottar. There is a splendid monument to her husband, James Grainger, on the west wall, but no mention in its Latin text of her courageous part.

ORKNEY ISLANDS [see Map 2, A3]   **Mary Brunton**, a novelist much admired by Jane Austen, was born on the island of Burray in 1778. This island is now linked to Orkney's mainland to the north by the Churchill Barriers. Her family was of some importance in the islands, a community in Shapinsay, bearing the family name, Balfour. They certainly held estates there, Sound and Cliffdale.

OTTERBOURNE, Hampshire [see Map 1, F4]   This is the village where the prolific novelist, **Charlotte Mary Yonge**, spent all her life. She was born in 1823 at Otterbourne House, on the main road. Its façade remains as it was in her day, but the building has been converted into five flats. By the time that her younger brother and his wife had a growing family, Charlotte and her widowed mother moved further up the hill to Elderfield. This large white house, now a market gardening business, across the main road from St Matthew's Church, was to be her home until the end of her life. The church was very important to her, and much of the income from her more than 150 books was spent on it. She paid for the building of the lychgate. The incumbent was John Keble, who greatly influenced her life. She found strength in the Oxford movement's return to High Anglican services, and this comes through in her books. The most famous of her novels is *The Heir of Redclyffe* [1853], but few are read today. When she died in 1901 she was buried in the graveyard, near the south porch in front of Keble's memorial.

OXFORD, Oxfordshire [see Map 1, F4] Before there was a university here, Oxford was a significant market town. The success of **Matilda**, daughter of Henry I, in her campaign to secure the English throne against Stephen of Blois, began to run out in 1142. Her fight in pursuit of the Crown which her father had indicated should be hers began in earnest in 1139. In 1142 she was besieged at Oxford castle, of which little remains beyond the grassy mound in New Road. She managed to escape one winter night, fleeing across the frozen fields to Wallingford. She decided to give up the struggle and retire to France, where her husband held the Duchy of Normandy. She agreed to renounce her claims to the throne in favour of her son Henry II; she lived to see him succeed Stephen in 1154.

The first college, founded in 1249, was University College. Others soon followed, the second being Balliol College in 1263. Its founder was John de Balliol, who had married one of the richest women in Scotland, **Dervorguilla**. When she was widowed in 1269 she continued to support the college securing it a reliable income by buying estates for it, and laying down a code of conduct for the scholars. Another benefactor in the early days of the university was **Lady Margaret Beaufort**. She endowed a professorship in divinity both here and at Cambridge and herself gave lectures and wrote books in this subject. She further supported the academic world by helping William Caxton, the inventor of the printing press. Her contribution was recognised in the naming of one of the first women's colleges here, Lady Margaret Hall. Queen's College is named after **Philippa of Hainault**; it was founded in her honour in 1341 by her chaplain Roger Eglefield. **Elizabeth I** founded Jesus College, particularly for the academic education of Welsh students.

26   Charlotte Yonge's grave in St Matthew's Churchyard, Otterbourne, Hampshire

Women were first admitted to Oxford University examinations in 1870, later than at Cambridge. However, Oxford accepted women as full members of the University in 1920, nearly thirty years before its Cambridge rival. Ultimately there were five women's colleges, though in the 1970s the trend for mixed colleges was prevalent. An Association for the Education of Women was set up in Oxford in 1878 and it was directly responsible for the first women's colleges. Together with Lady Margaret Hall, Somerville College was also founded in 1879. It was named after **Mary Somerville**, the Scottish astronomer, geographer and mathematician who, when she died in 1872, left money specifically for the purpose of making available to able women the educational opportunities that she had been denied. It began as Somerville Hall, attaining full college status after ten years. The college has been associated with many women who made their mark in several fields. The first college secretary was **Mrs Humphrey Ward**. In 1856, her family had returned to England from Tasmania, her place of birth, and by 1865 had made their home in Oxford. After her marriage in 1872 she lived at 5 [now 17] Bradmore Road, off the Banbury Road. Although she worked all her life to improve the lot of women, she felt unable to support the struggle for women's votes, leading the Anti-Suffrage League which she founded in 1890. Her members felt that since the 1884 Reform Bill made the vote available more widely to men, women's interests would be better represented.

Several Somerville women produced fine literary works. The period 1910-15 nurtured some writers, whose works have not dated. **Vera Brittain**'s *Testament* trilogy included a biography of her friend and Somerville contemporary, **Winifred Holtby**: *Testament of Friendship* [1940]. Winifred herself became a journalist, which enabled her to pursue her interest in politics, and she herself was author of several fine novels set in her native north Yorkshire. Other fellow students included **Rose Macaulay**, whose better known works are *Tale Told by an Idiot* [1923] and *They Were Defeated* [1932]; **Margaret Kennedy**, author of *The Constant Nymph* [1924]; and **Dorothy Sayers**. Dorothy was born in the city in 1893, her father being headmaster of the Cathedral School, but the family soon moved to the Cambridgeshire Fenlands. She went up to Somerville on a scholarship in 1912, and stayed on in Oxford in her first job as a publishers' reader with the company Blackwell's. Her novels often had Oxford settings, and she made her popular aristocratic detective, Lord Peter Wimsey, a Balliol man. Her own college was the model for Shrewsbury College in *Gaudy Night* [1935]. The Dorothy L. Sayers Historical and Literary Society has published a walking tour of her Oxford. A research fellow at Somerville whose subject area was medieval Latin was **Helen Waddell**, who produced some sensitive translations of medieval works and herself wrote a period novel *Peter Abelard* [1933].

In the sciences, **Dorothy Crowfoot Hodgkin**'s research in chemistry gained her many scientific honours including Fellowship of the Royal Society [1947] and a Nobel Prize [1964]. **Barbara Ward**'s achievements were in economics, but she showed a special concern for Third World and environmental problems. More recently **Margaret Thatcher**, a Somerville graduate in chemistry, has taken a leading role in political life. Her recent opposite number in India, **Indira Gandhi**, also spent her student days at this college. Other early students include **Lady Ottoline Morrell**, **Eleanor Rathbone** and **Lady Rhondda**.

St Hilda's College was named after the seventh-century northern saint, **Hilda of Whitby**, who set up her religious house to be a centre of scholarship. Originally established in 1893 as St Hilda's Hall, an extension to St Hilda's College for Women Teachers which the pioneer of women's education **Dorothy Beale** had set up in Cheltenham, it became a college of the University in 1901. St Anne's has Somerville philosophy graduate **Iris Murdoch** as a fellow, teaching her subject. Outside the academic world she is better known for her novels, *A Severed Head* [1961] and the prize-winning *The Sea, the Sea* [1978]. **Ivy Williams** was a local girl, so when she began her law studies in 1896 she joined the Society of Oxford Home Students, forerunner of St Anne's College. In 1922 she earned the distinction of being the first woman called to the English Bar, but she chose not to practise as a barrister. Rather she shared her knowledge of law with Oxford students, as a member of the University's academic staff. St Anne's became an official college in 1952.

Eleanor Jourdain, herself one of the first women to study at Oxford University, became vice-principal of St Hugh's College, and lived with **Annie Moberley**, the first principal, at 4 Norham Road, in north Oxford. They were extremely close and in 1901 they shared a psychic experience at the Petit Trianon at the Palais de Versailles in Paris. They both independently sensed that they had been in the company of characters from the French Revolution. They later published an account as *The Adventure* [1911]. St Hugh's was founded in 1886 as St Hugh's Hall. **Dame Kathleen Kenyon**, the distinguished archaeologist, was a more recent principal. Lady Margaret Hall, founded in 1879, includes among its outstanding graduates the arabist, linguist and traveller **Gertrude Bell**, whose top honours in history were the first awarded to a woman. **Emily Wilding Davison**, the dedicated suffragette, also studied at Oxford.

The university dominated the city's life until recently, but there have been women not connected with the university who spent time here. The seven-year-old **Jane Austen** attended Mrs Crawley's school here with her sister Cassandra for some unhappy months in 1783. It was not a success, and they fared better at their next school in Reading. Another writer who lived in Oxford was the author of *Belinda* [1883], **Rhoda Broughton**, who moved to the city with her sister. From 1894 their home was 51 Holywell Street; on her sister's death in 1900, she lived in Riverview, a cousin's house in Headington. By the time she died there in 1920, her works were no longer considered so sensational. **Elizabeth Bowen**, a writer often associated with Ireland, lived in Old Headington, now a southern suburb of Oxford, from 1923, writing many short stories and her first novels here, such as *The Hotel* [1927] and *The House in Paris* [1935]. As daughter of the Dean of Christ Church, **Alice Liddell**, spent much of her childhood with academics. The mathematics tutor, Charles Dodgson, grew very close to her family, and, as Lewis Carroll, wrote *Alice in Wonderland* [1865] and *Alice Through the Looking Glass* [1872] for her. A small shop in St Aldates, opposite Christ Church, still calls itself Alice's Sweetshop after her. **Gertrude Tuckwell** the trade unionist was a daughter of Oxford, born in the city in 1861. Throughout her ninety years she worked unstintingly for the support of working women.

  Josephine Butler spent the first five years of her marriage in 1852 in Oxford. As her husband was a don, she saw much of the academic world but it did not blind her to the sorry circumstances of many of the local people. Rather, she espoused the cause of young women prostitutes and in Oxford began her campaign to change attitudes and the treatment of prostitutes for which she is now remembered.

P p

PADIHAM, Lancashire [see Map 1, D3]   **Charlotte Brontë** was a visitor to Gawthorpe Hall☆[NT] in the 1850s when the fine early seventeenth-century manor house was being altered by the fashionable architect, Charles Barry. Her hosts were Sir James and Lady Kay-Shuttleworth, whose family had occupied the Hall since *c*. 1330. Standing on the east of Padiham, itself not far from Burnley, then a centre for cotton-weaving, the Hall houses the **Rachel Kay-Shuttleworth** collection of embroidery and lace. Rachel Kay-Shuttleworth was the last of her family to live in the Hall. Born there in 1886, she devoted her life to the practice, teaching and appreciation of the art and craft of needlework. She built up a large and important collection for teaching from, and together with her library, it is constantly consulted by students and researchers. She arranged for the house and her collection to be left to the National Trust, which has ensured that her wish to make both available to the widest public is carried out.

PAINSWICK, Gloucestershire [see Map 1, F3]   The artist, **Margaret Gere**, moved here with her brother and fellow-artist Charles Gere, who had also been her teacher in Birmingham. After a stay in Italy she became particularly interested in tempera painting and specialised in painting flowers and figures.

PALGRAVE, Suffolk [see Map 1, E5]   The Blue Stocking and writer, **Anna Laetitia Barbauld**, came here in 1774 with her husband, of French Huguenot descent, to run a Nonconformist boarding school in the village. The building no longer stands. While here she wrote many of her works for children, having decided that the school texts then available were inadequate. In 1786 they went abroad before settling in London.

PASTON, Norfolk [see Map 1, E5]   The husband of **Margaret Paston** belonged to the major landowning family from here. After her marriage to John Paston in 1448, she became responsible for this estate on the north-east coast of Norfolk. She managed this property, and other estates in Norfolk, for her husband when his business took him to the capital for long spells. Their lively correspondence survives as *The Paston Letters*, and is a fascinating document of life in an unsettled period in English history, the Wars of the Roses in the fifteenth century. Their hall here is long gone but the barn in which their crops, a major asset, would have been stored, stands built in flint beside the church.

PEEBLES, Borders [see Map 2, C3]   Near the bridge on the High Street stands Bank House, home of **Anna Buchan**. As **O. Douglas** she wrote several works of fiction, some set in the Peebles area. She chose to use a *nom de plume*, to avoid comparison with her much published brother John. She set her novel, *Priorsford* [1932], in the town.

PEMBROKE, Dyfed [see Map 1, F2]   Pembroke Castle is still an impressive fortress. During the insecurity of the Wars of the Roses, **Margaret Beaufort**, widowed for the second time, spent almost fifteen years in the protection of her second husband's family. Her son Henry Tudor was born in the tower beside the gatehouse in 1457. She had always inclined toward a religious life, and her place at the centre of dynastic struggles was not her choice. However, when her son gained the English throne in 1485, the ensuing peace afforded her the opportunity to found religious and academic institutions and follow her own studious pursuits.

PENDINE, Dyfed [see Map 1, F2]   **Amy Johnson**, or Johnnie as she became known, took off on her flight across the Atlantic from east to west from Pendine Sands in 1933. The flight was not smooth but she and her husband, Jim Mollison, landed safely in North America. This was the first flight from mainland Britain in this direction. Although better known for her solo flight to Australia, Amy's flying career was very diverse, and included delivering military aircraft from factory to airstrip during the Second World War.

PENN, Buckinghamshire [see Map 3, A1]   The novelist, **Elizabeth von Arnim**, who published her works as 'by Elizabeth', is buried here, although she died in America. Hers was a very international life: born in Australia in 1866 [a cousin of Katherine Mansfield], she was educated in England. On her marriage to a Pomeranian count, she went to live on his estates in Europe, which she wrote about in *Elizabeth and Her German Garden* [1898]. Her other novels include *Pastor's Wife* [1912] and *Vera* [1921]. Towards the end of her life she lived in the United States, where she died in 1941. Her gravestone in Penn is incribed 'Parva sed apta', an epitaph which she wrote for herself. It translates as 'Small but effective'. She had adapted this as her own motto; she was very petite.

The graveyard of Holy Trinity Church is in two parts. In the main churchyard, in the south side, a flat gravestone commemorates two devoted and capable women. **Flora Murray**, who died in 1923, commanded the Military Hospital in London where her friend and colleague **Louisa Garrett Anderson**, a qualified surgeon, also worked. Louisa had followed her mother, Elizabeth Garrett Anderson, into medicine as a career and during the First World War was Chief Surgeon of the Women's Hospital Corps. She died in 1943. The grave, dedicated 'to the Dear Love of Comrades', also carries the wonderful inscription: 'We have been gloriously happy.'

The second part of the graveyard is in the former vicarage vineyard.

Here, by the central cross, **Alison Uttley** lies buried; the words on her simple tombstone aptly describe her as 'a Spinner of Tales'. She died in nearby High Wycombe in 1976, having come to live in the area in 1934. Although she is best known for her children's books and as creator of the character *Little Grey Rabbit*, her literary output was mainly adult works on rural subjects. *Country World* [1984] is a recently published selection of her autobiographical writings.

PENRITH, Cumbria [see Map 2, D3] The teenaged **Dorothy Words-worth** came to know her brother again when she came to live with their grandparents here for a year in 1778. She had spent the previous decade being brought up by other relations in Halifax apart from him. They were determined to maintain close ties after this, and ultimately spent almost their entire adult lives together. Their grandparents ran a drapery shop in the market place, but it has since been replaced. In the 1840s **Frances Trollope**'s financial situation was sufficiently settled, thanks to the unexpected success of her writing career, for her to have a house built in Penrith. However, she continued to spend much of her later life in Italy, and she died in Florence in 1863.

PENRYN, Cornwall [see Map 1, G2] **Mrs Delaney**, the inveterate eighteenth-century letter writer, spent her unhappy but thankfully short first marriage in the grey granite Roscrow Castle above the town. From her description it was oppressive, gloomy and in a poor state of repair when she arrived in 1718 as a young bride. It is long since demolished. However, the wild coast and countryside were sources of consolation, and her acquaintance with seashells, begun during her six years here, was to absorb her energies later in the then popular artform of decorative shellwork.

PENSHURST PLACE, Kent [see Map 3, C4] This marvellous fourteenth-century house, with its later additions in keeping with its earliest design, must have been a delightful place in which to spend one's childhood. **Mary Sidney** grew up here with her poet brother Philip Sidney, whose works she later edited and prepared for publication. Together they translated psalms. She left Penshurst Place★ and its enchanting gardens in 1575 to join the household of Elizabeth I at Hampton Court. She later became Countess of Pembroke through her marriage to Henry Herbert, Earl of Pembroke.

PENZANCE, Cornwall [see Map 1, G2] **Mrs Thrale**, now the widowed **Mrs Piozzi**, came to Cornwall as an octogenarian, with the specific aim of spending a cheap winter in healthy surroundings away from the expensive temptations of Bath, which she missed. It proved to be her last winter, but she had managed to save enough to return to the more 'civilised' social environment of Bristol in the early months of 1821.

PERLETHORPE, Nottinghamshire [see Map 1, E4] It is thought that **Lady Mary Wortley Montagu**, daringly unconventional daughter of the Earl of Kingston, was born here in 1689, though she was baptised Mary

Pierrepont in London. She certainly spent much of her childhood on the family estate. Her marriage to a diplomat took her to Turkey where her observations of the Turkish practice of vaccination led her to introduce it into Britain in 1718. In later life, after she had left her husband, she was an avid correspondent, keeping in touch with events in Britain. She also wrote poetry, including much satirical verse.

PERTH, Perthshire [see Map 2, C3] **Catriona Glover**, the fourteenth-century heroine, was immortalised as Catharine Glover in Walter Scott's work *The Fair Maid of Perth* [1828]. Her former home, in Curfew Row, was rebuilt in 1893 but maintains much of its period character in its present use as a crafts shop. **Effie Gray**, the Pre-Raphaelite muse, was born in 1828 and brought up at Bowerswell, now an elderly persons' home, to the north of the Tay, overlooking the Kinnoul river. Her father had a local law practice. She came to know John Ruskin, whose family used to spend their holidays in Perthshire. She married him in 1848, but, although she was an inspiration to him, it was not a happy union and was never consummated. She had also modelled for Ruskin's friend, the artist John Millais, and all three had spent a holiday together in 1853 during which Effie became close to Millais. In 1855 she married him and came back to live at Annat's Lodge, near Bowerswell, also maintaining a home in London. This was an idyllic marriage and she brought up eight children in great contentment. She died in 1897 and was buried in the old graveyard at Kinnoul on the banks of the River Tay.

PETERBOROUGH, Cambridgeshire [see Map 1, E4] The city is dominated by the Romanesque cathedral, in which **Catherine of Aragon** lies buried. She died nearby in 1536, having lived a wretched life after Henry VIII had divorced her. Her once distinguished tomb, appropriate to her queenly status with its effigy, was damaged in the Civil War. Another Queen, **Mary Queen of Scots**, who had been executed at Fotheringhay in 1587, was also given a decent burial here, with reluctant approval of the sovereign, this time Elizabeth I. After Mary's son, James VI and I, succeeded to the English throne in addition to his mother's Scottish realm, he had her body brought to London, where ironically her tomb stands in the same chapel as that of her rival Elizabeth I.

In the eighteenth century the first Canadian novelist, **Frances Brooke**, is thought to have spent part of her youth in Peterborough, but the precise circumstances are not known. She was born in 1724, and the claims on her as Canada's first novelist derive from the period she spent in Quebec where her husband was stationed during military service. Her *The History of Emily Montagu* [1766] was written there and introduced British readers to the Canadian scenery and climate. It was very well received in Britain.

PETERSFIELD, Hampshire [see Map 1, F4] The complicated associations in the life of **Emma Hamilton** begin with her marriage at the age of fifteen to Sir Harry Featherstonehaugh in 1770. He brought her to his family seat, Uppark☆[NT], which is five miles from the town. He soon tired of her and by 1781 she was living in London with a lover.

In 1849 Alice Sophia Cunningham was born in Petersfield where her father was the local Anglican minister. Her contribution to the lives of women was as a founder-member and first secretary of the Women's Co-operative Guild. By then, 1883, she had married and she is better known today as **Mrs Acland**. Her father moved to a rectory in Oxfordshire, where she met and married the Oxford don Henry Acland.

An educational experiment, unconventional in its day, took place at the Beacon Hill School which **Dora Russell**, and her husband Bertrand Russell, started in 1927. The idea behind this progressive school was that it should have a home-like, family environment in which children would all feel comfortable and want to learn. Dora was a firm believer in children's rights and later was a founder-member of the National Council for Civil Liberties. Dora ran Beacon Hill on her own from 1935 until the outbreak of war. The War Office requisitioned the premises in 1943, and Dora herself worked in London for the Ministry of Information.

PETERSHAM   See **LONDON BOROUGH OF RICHMOND**.

PLYMOUTH, Devon [see Map 1, G2]   This port has long and honourable associations with naval and military installations. **James Miranda Barry**, who, by disguising herself as a man, was able to train as a doctor in Edinburgh, joined the army medical service and in 1813 took up her first appointment as an army surgeon in Plymouth. Most of her career was spent abroad; she held senior posts in the West Indies and Canada. Her sex was not discovered until her death. **Mary Read** was equally unorthodox, but on the wrong side of the law. Thought to have been born in the Plymouth area *c*. 1690, this woman used her male disguise to serve in the navy and in the army. She eventually joined up with pirates *en route* for the West Indies, finding that one of their number was an Irishwoman, Anne Bonny, whose career had also thrived in male dress. They then reputedly stuck together through adventures in the Caribbean, before being taken prisoner and tried for piracy. They were both able to escape hanging by pleading pregnancy, but Mary died in prison *c*. 1721. How much of their story was embellished by ambitious journalists is not known. What is certain is that Mary was tough, adaptable and determined to look after herself.

The first woman to take up a seat in the British Parliament represented the constituency of Plymouth. **Nancy Astor** had accompanied her husband here from 1909 during the period when he was the local Member of Parliament. Their home in the constituency was on the Hoe, to the south of the town, at 3 Elliot Terrace. When her husband succeeded to his father's peerage, he was no longer eligible to sit in the House of Commons, so Nancy Astor stood as a candidate in the 1919 elections and won the seat. She held the seat until 1945, serving as Mayor of Plymouth during the war years. The city later honoured her with the Freedom of the City.

27   Marie Stopes' cottages which now house the Portland Bill Museum, Portland Bill, Dorset

POLPERRO, Cornwall [see Map 1, G2]   **Angela Brazil**, the prolific writer of schoolgirl adventure stories, bought a cottage in Polperro after the First World War. She loved the Cornish coast, of which she had a splendid view from The Haven. When she died in 1947, she left The Warren, a mile of coastal clifftop, to the National Trust, for the enjoyment of all.

POLSTEAD, Suffolk [see Map 1, F4]   **Maria Martin**'s cottage is pointed out to visitors as a reminder of the infamous murder case of the last century. As victim in an unpleasant case, Maria's story became widely known, and the case was eagerly followed in 1827. Her murderer William Corder was caught and hanged. The crime later became the subject of a melodrama, *The Red Barn Murder*, still popular with amateur dramatic societies. It shows the way women were abused in the rough justice of the last century. Maria's cottage survives but her gravestone was chipped beyond recognition years ago by morbid souvenir hunters. The red barn has long since been taken down.

POLWARTH, Borders [see Map 2, C3]   The church in the grounds of Marchmont House was the daily destination of the youthful **Lady Grizel Baillie** in 1684. Apparently very devout, the Scottish heroine was in fact bringing food to her father who was hiding in a vault to avoid his pursuers. Escaping detection for several weeks, Grizel Baillie was eventually able to arrange the escape to exile in Holland of her whole family, no mean achievement in the uncertain times at the end of the Stuart monarchy. Although her early courage has earned her the status of a folk heroine, in adult life, her ballads gained an equally wide reputation.

PORTHCURNO, Cornwall [see Map 1, G2]   **Dora Russell** spent the last years of her very active life at Carnvoel in Porthcurno. Right up until her death in 1986 Dora was involved in such causes as disarmament, women's rights and world peace. Her rural retreat did not cut her off from key issues of the day. Rather, she continued to accept speaking engagements and apply her great intellect and reasoning to the furtherance of her lifelong convictions. When she died her ashes were scattered here as she requested.

PORTLAND BILL, Dorset [see Map 1, G3]   This promontory on the south coast held great charm for **Marie Stopes**. Her retreat, The Old Lighthouse, Easton, would be a welcome place of quiet reflection away from the controversy surrounding her work for the availability of birth control. Having spent her academic life studying palaeontology, the fossil-rich coastline would also have held much interest for her. In 1929 she donated to the local community the two cottages which comprise the Portland Museum★. When she died in 1958 her ashes were scattered off the head of Portland Bill, as she requested.

PORTREE, Isle of Skye, Highland [see Map 2, B2]   **Flora MacDonald** said her final farewell to Prince Charles Edward Stuart at McNab's Inn, now the Royal Hotel, in Portree in 1746, having saved his life after Culloden. Her heroism and patriotism saved the Young Pretender, but later cost her a spell in the Tower of London as a prisoner.

PORTSMOUTH, Hampshire [see Map 1, G4]   The sailors' friend, **Agnes Weston**, founded her second home for seamen here in 1881. She was inspired by her religious beliefs to pursue a mission for sailors far from home.

PRESTON, Lancashire [see Map 1, D3]   Preston can claim three very different but equally distinguished daughters. **Anne Baynard**'s short but scholarly life began with her birth in Preston in 1672. She received a good classical education from her father and gained a considerable reputation as a woman of learning. She appears to have been attracted to mysticism, and died in London aged twenty-five, after meditating in a graveyard for two years.

The story of the early life of the singer **Kathleen Ferrier** is often told. She was born in Lancashire in 1912, taking her first job at fourteen as a telephonist. Although she had always played the piano, it was only when she was twenty-five that she began to use her voice professionally as a singer. She trained seriously from 1943, bringing pleasure to many as one of the best-loved singers of her day. Her family moved to London with her where her career developed quickly. However, it was cruelly cut short in 1953 by cancer.

Angela Brazil was the longest-living of these three Preston natives. She was born at 1 Westcliff Terrace in 1868, and reached her eightieth year. Her career as a writer of the schoolgirl fiction genre was very successful, and her later years were mostly spent in Coventry.

PWLLHELI, Gwynedd [see Map 1, E2]   **Hester Thrale** was born at Bodvel Hall in 1741 as Hester Salusbury. She grew up with an enduring love of Wales to which she returned often, especially after her second marriage. In 1763 her parents had obliged her to marry her first husband, a prosperous London brewer. Mr Thrale did not make her happy but he encouraged her social life which numbered in its circle Dr Samuel Johnson – she was the only woman for whom he had any intellectual regard.

Q Q

QUIDHAMPTON, Wiltshire [see Map 1, F3]   The writer **Edith Olivier** lived for many years at Daye House. The surrounding countryside was an inspiration for many of her works, such as *Moonrakings* [1930], a collection of Wiltshire stories. Daye House was the former dairy of the Wilton Park estate and Edith, her sister Mildred, and their friends converted it into a delightful home. Although she had enjoyed living at Teffont Magna, Edith was keen to return to the area where she had grown up. Her autobiographical work *Without Knowing Mr. Walkley* [1939] describes her literary friendships, her enjoyment of the art of conversation and her gentle rural lifestyle at Daye House.

R R

RAVENSCRAIG, Fife [see Map 2, C3]   The fifteenth-century Ravenscraig Castle★, to the north of Kirkcaldy, was built by **Mary of Gueldres**. In her short life she established herself as a competent partner for her husband, James II, King of Scotland, eventually holding the throne from 1460 for her son who was still a minor when James II died. The castle was full of romance for the writer **Anna Buchan**. At the end of the nineteenth century she grew up nearby in Pathhead, on a literary diet which included Sir Walter Scott's evocative poem about Rosabelle St Clair whose home was the castle.

READING, Berkshire [see Map 1, F4]   The Abbey School, in the Gatehouse of the former Benedictine Abbey, was run as a boarding school for young ladies by a Mrs Latournelle. Her former pupils included four future novelists. **Jane Austen** and her sister Cassandra became pupils there in 1784. The atmosphere was very relaxed, but it was not academically taxing, and after a year, the Austen parents decided to keep their daughters at home. **Mary Martha Sherwood** was a contemporary at the school with Jane. Later pupils included **Letitia Landon** and **Mary Russell Mitford**, whose family had moved to Reading on the strength of her winning a lottery. The Mitfords had bought the large redbrick house at 39 London Road, now a dental surgery, in 1797, and moved on to grander premises outside the town *c.* 1805. However, they were obliged to leave there in straitened circumstances in 1820. Mary continued to be very familiar with the town, which became the *Belford Regis* [1835] of her writings.

RENISHAW, Derbyshire [see Map 1, E3]   Renishaw Hall was the main family home of the prolific and innovative poet **Edith Sitwell**. Hers was both an eccentric and a wealthy upbringing. Born at the family's summer home in Scarborough in 1887, her first collection of poems, *The Mother and Other Poems*, was published in 1915. She is probably best known for *Façade* [1923], a novel piece set to music by William Walton, and the works she wrote in the Second World War: *Street Songs* [1942], *Green Song* [1944] and *The Shadow of Cain* [1947]. After the First World War a garden scheme for Renishaw Hall was designed by **Gertrude Jekyll** but Edith's father had his own ideas on planting, so little, if anything, remains of Gertrude's efforts.

RICHMOND, Surrey   See **LONDON BOROUGH OF RICHMOND**.

RICKMANSWORTH, Hertfordshire [see Map 3, A2]   Moor Park, now a

28   39 London Road, Reading, Berkshire, the home of Mary Russell Mitford

golf club to the south of the town, has very romantic associations.
Dorothy Osborne was able to hold clandestine meetings here with her
fiancé William Temple, while visiting her relations. Throughout their long
engagement her parents disapproved of the match. For six years they kept
up a correspondence which survives. These well-written letters are an
important source for the social history of their day. In 1654 they finally
married, and their honeymoon was spent here. When they settled in
Farnham they named their home after Moor Park.

ROBERTSBRIDGE, Sussex [see Map 1, F4]   The active feminist **Barbara
Bodichon** bought herself a house here called Scalands, which was to be a
retreat for herself and her friends. Her enlightened father had enabled all his
children to be financially independent from their twenty-first birthday, and
Barbara spent much of her time in London running a school and
campaigning for better opportunities for women. Buying a country home
was an unusual step for a single woman. She lived simply here, and
encouraged her friends and fellow-activists to renew their energies in the
calm of the lovely Sussex countryside. Among her guests was her friend
Gertrude Jekyll, whose earliest garden designs were for Scalands in 1880.
Other friends who enjoyed Scalands included **Bessie Rayner Parkes**,
whom she had known since childhood. Together they ran the *English*

Woman's Journal from 1858, and campaigned for the Married Women's Property Act and better education for women. As Barbara Leigh-Smith she married Dr Eugene Bodichon on the understanding that she would spend half the year in Britain involved in the pursuit of her various causes and would join him in Algeria for the rest of the time. The arrangement seems to have worked well. British women have benefited in so many ways from the total dedication of Barbara Bodichon, who died here in 1891.

ROBIN HOOD'S BAY, North Yorkshire [see Map 1, D4] The artist **Ethel Walker** owned a cottage Whitegates and the adjacent studio at the end of Tommy Baxter Street. She used to love coming from her London base to paint in this seaside village.

ROCHDALE, Lancashire [see Map 1, E3] Rochdale's famous daughter was the entertainer **Gracie Fields**. She was born here in 1898, and her career, which started when she was twelve, took her far from home. However, the people of Rochdale felt a strong affection for her and she is still warmly remembered in the town, though sadly her husband's nationality obliged her to settle abroad during the Second World War. Her last years were spent on the Italian island of Capri, where her villa is now a tourist landmark. She is commemorated locally by the naming of Rochdale's theatre after her.

ROCHESTER, Kent [see Map 3, B4]   **Dame Sybil Thorndike**, the great English actress, was brought up in Rochester, where her father was made a canon of the cathedral. She originally trained for a career in music but was soon 'treading the boards' as a rising star of the stage, touring in Britain and America. Her Saint Joan in the title role of Shaw's play was a *tour de force*. Shaw had created the play especially for her in 1924, and it remains a stirring and testing part for modern actresses. Rochester recognised Dame Sybil's contribution to British theatre and honoured her with the Freedom of the City.

RODMELL, Sussex [see Map 1, F4]   **Virginia Woolf** and her husband Leonard bought Monk's House☆[NT] in 1919. It is a traditional rural house, which the Woolfs altered and decorated with the help of Virginia's artist sister **Vanessa Bell** and Duncan Grant. The Woolfs never used the entrance facing the street as a front door, they and their guests always entered from the lovely garden. Their visitors included, in addition to Vanessa, **Vita Sackville-West** and **Ethel Smyth**. Monk's House was a weekend retreat for many of the Bloomsbury Group; part of its initial attraction was the enforced simple lifestyle without running water, electricity, gas, telephone, bathroom or inside loo. Over the years the Woolfs added a few modern conveniences, as the success of various books allowed: *Mrs Dalloway* [1925], for example, paid for the bathroom. Inside, furniture, pictures, books, and the decorative scheme all retain the atmosphere which appealed to the Woolfs. Virginia's bedroom is almost stark in its simplicity. Added on in 1929, it has to be reached by going out of the main building. It opens on to the garden, which both Virginia and Leonard enjoyed.

Virginia Woolf's mental state frequently gave her family and friends grave cause for concern. Hers was an intense and difficult creativity which sometimes plummeted in deep despair and depression. In such a state she set out, after leaving notes for Leonard and her sister, and headed for the river. Putting stones in her pockets she drowned herself. The pressure of wartime combined with her own tendency towards depression took its toll in 1941. Leonard lived on at Rodmell until his death in 1969. His ashes were scattered under the elm tree beyond the dew pond, where earlier Virginia's had been scattered. A bronze bust of Virginia by Stephen Tomlin stands on a low wall; it adds to the atmosphere a dignity and sense of place which is both affecting and confirming.

ROLVEDEN, Kent [see Map 1, F4]   **Frances Hodgson Burnett**, author of the now classic children's books *Little Lord Fauntleroy* [1886] and *The Secret Garden* [1911], lived here from 1898 until 1907 on her return from America. After two years at Great Maytham Hall, on the outskirts of the village, she divorced her husband, but her next marriage also proved unhappy. She devoted much of her efforts to a campaign, ultimately successful, for copyright legislation to protect authors' rights. She spent the last years of her life in America, where her books had also sold well. She died there in 1924, but is commemorated in the church in Rolveden.

Great Maytham Hall, which was her country home, was transformed after her tenancy to its present design by Sir Edwin Lutyens in 1909. **Gertrude Jekyll**'s career as a garden designer perfectly complemented Lutyens' work, and Great Maytham Hall is possibly a grand example of their joint creativity, the much-revered 'partnership'. The earlier walled garden may have been the inspiration for Frances Hodgson Burnett's popular *Secret Garden* but the recently restored terraced gardens cannot be attributed with certainty to Gertrude Jekyll's plantings. The Hall is now divided into very pleasant flats.

ROTHERFIELD, Sussex [see Map 1, F4]   **Sophia Jex-Blake**, whose family came originally from Sussex, chose to be buried here. She died in 1912 after a long fight to open the medical profession to women, eventually herself training women as doctors in Edinburgh and London. In 1869 she began to study medicine at the University of Edinburgh but the men students prevented her and four other women from completing their studies. Despite this she established her own practice in Edinburgh and even started her own Medical School for Women. Later she opened a special hospital for female patients with female doctors.

ROTHIEMURCHUS, Grampian [see Map 2, B2]   This relatively isolated highland community in Speyside offers some surprises for those in search of women's history. The Doune, the home of the Grants of Rothiemurchus, local landowners, is currently being restored to its former glory. It is a large stone house, with a huge Georgian wing overpowering the earlier tall and narrow tower house. From 1803 until 1827 it was the home of **Elizabeth Grant** whose wryly well-observed account of life in the beginning of the last century, *Memoirs of a Highland Lady* [published posthumously in 1898], still holds the reader with its light touch and wit. It was a childhood home of her niece the suffragist **Lady Jane Strachey**, herself both mother and mother-in-law to later suffragettes, Philippa Strachey and Ray Strachey. Lady Strachey edited her aunt's writings and arranged for their publication.

ROXBURGH, Borders [see Map 2, C3] **Mary of Gueldres** completed the work of her husband King James II of Scotland by the successful outcome in the siege of Roxburgh in 1460. James died suddenly whilst besieging the town at a crucial stage in his defence of the Scottish border country against the English. Mary's son was a mere nine years old when the king died, so Queen Mary took over, ending hostilities and proving an able diplomat and astute stateswoman until her own death three years later.

RUDSTON, Humberside [see Map 1, D4] Rudston House, a solid Victorian House in Long Street, was the birthplace and childhood home of **Winifred Holtby**. She combined her interests in politics and writing by becoming a journalist after graduating from Oxford. Her mother had been involved in local politics, becoming the first woman county councillor in Yorkshire, and Winifred Holtby's best known novel, *South Riding* [1936], is a sympathetic portrayal of the conflicts encountered by a woman attracted to politics which differ from her husband's. It is set in this area. Winifred Holtby died tragically young in 1935, and was buried in the west of All Saints churchyard beside the graves of the MacDonalds of the Isles. Her grave monument is an open book. There is also a memorial to her inside the church on the wall near the south porch and the font. The churchyard also contains the Rudston Monolith, an ancient feat of engineering which is well signposted.

RUGBY, Warwickshire [see Map 1, E3] The writer **Rose Macaulay** was born in the town in 1881, but much of her childhood was spent in Italy at a convent school, before she became a student in Oxford.

RUNCORN, Cheshire [see Map 1, E3] Runcorn has grown into a large community as a result of its designation as a development area. A landmark in its history was the establishment of a fort there by **Aethelflaed**, Lady of the Mercians, early in the tenth century when she secured for the Mercians territory which had been conquered by invading Danes. The fort would have commanded a view over the mouth of the River Mersey.

S s

ST ALBANS, Hertfordshire [see Map 3, A2] **Boudicca**, the Celtic leader who rebelled against the imposition of Roman rule which deprived her of her authority over her people, the Iceni, led them in an attack on the Roman colony of Verulamium. Excavations on the site of the Roman town have provided evidence of Boudicca's supporters burning Verulamium to the ground in AD 60. The Roman remains* can be visited. Her raid came at a time when the occupying army was overstretched in trying to subdue other parts of the island. Later settlement established the modern town of St Albans. In more stable times *The Boke of St.Albans* [1486] was printed here. It may well be the first book by a woman to appear in print, but there is still some doubt about its author's identity. The most popular candidate has been **Juliana Berners**, a noble woman born in *c.* 1368. She may have been Prioress at the Benedictine nunnery, to the south-east, on the site of which only a few later ruins remain. The book, subtitled *Julyan Barnes: Her gentleman's Academy of Hawking, Hunting, Fishing and Armouries*, shows her to be an expert in these areas. The name has been also used to support the case for male authorship.

The writings of **Anne Bacon** have been eclipsed by those of her son Sir Francis Bacon. She had, however, acquired a reputation as a scholar before her marriage in 1557, when she became mistress of Gorhambury, two miles to the west of St Albans. The ruins of her home survive in the grounds of Gorhambury House*, which is the home of her descendants. She translated key texts of her day from Latin into English, and influenced contemporary politics through her husband and her regular royal guest at Gorhambury, **Elizabeth I**. She died in 1610, but her grave in St Michael's Church in St Albans, unlike her son's, is unmarked.

Sarah Churchill, who later played a more direct role in the political life of her day, was born nearby at Sandridge in 1660. Thirteen years later the young Sarah Jennings began her preparation for court life as Maid of Honour to Mary of Modena, then Duchess of York. Moving easily in royal circles, she became the close friend and confidante of the future Queen Anne. This privileged relationship continued after her marriage to John Churchill in 1678, and Sarah Churchill used her influence to promote her husband's career. Her intimacy with the Queen did not survive beyond 1707, and Sarah, by now Duchess of Marlborough, felt more comfortable living abroad, returning only on the death of Queen Anne. Once Sarah Churchill had become a powerful wealthy woman she did not forget her place of origin and built the Marlborough Almshouses in Hatfield Road, St Albans, in 1736. This complex of brick dwellings, with two wings extending back, proudly boasts the fine coat of arms of its founder on the centre of the front façade; there was little modesty in Sarah Churchill, who lived on into her eighty-fourth year.

ST ANDREWS, Fife [see Map 2, C3] **Louisa Lumsden**, the most dynamic of the first five women students at Cambridge University, was invited to establish a school for girls in the town. She took up the challenge and founded St Leonard's School in 1877. Her fellow student from days at Hitchin, **Constance Maynard**, was an early member of the teaching staff. Louisa Lumsden's energy and encouragement of women to take charge of their own destiny led Constance to become first principal of Westfield College in London. Achievement in academic subjects was valued as highly as those in physical education and art and craft. The game of lacrosse was introduced in Britain as a women's sport after Louisa Lumsden had seen it played by native American Indians in North America. Ill health led her to resign in 1881, but by then she had had the satisfaction of sending her first pupil to Girton College, Cambridge. Women were admitted to the Scottish universities on equal terms with men from 1892, and Dame Louisa, as she became in 1925, maintained an active interest in the school and women's education throughout her life. With renewed vigour, she became founder-warden of University Hall, the women students' residence at the University of St Andrews, and was later honoured by the award of an honorary doctorate of law.

One early pupil at St Leonard's School, **Chrystal Macmillan**, went on to study science at Edinburgh University. She became active in the suffragette movement, pacifism and politics. In 1908 she had the distinction of being the first woman to address the House of Lords. She argued that women graduates, as well as male graduates, of Scottish Universities, should be able to vote for the anomalous Parliamentary seat representing these universities [it was abolished in 1948]. Although eloquent, on this occasion she was unable to persuade the Lords. Other former students played significant parts in the struggle for votes: **Mrs Chalmers–Watson**, an early medical graduate, and **Lady Rhondda** were instrumental in establishing *Time and Tide* as a key channel of communication for information and opinions on the changing status of women. From 1920 it was an important feminist weekly which affected and often led politics in new directions. The first woman to be a Deputy Speaker in the House of Commons, **Betty Harvie Anderson**, also spent her schooldays here.

Tradition has it that **Mary Queen of Scots** stayed briefly in a building which is now the school library. It has been preserved as Queen Mary's Bedroom★ with period furnishings. No specific date or reason for the visit is known, but St Andrews is likely to have featured regularly in the itineraries of the royal progresses through the realm.

ST ASAPH, Clwyd [see Map 1, E3] The popular Victorian writer **Felicia**

29   Talland House, Talland Road, St Ives, Cornwall, where Vanessa Bell and Virginia Woolf spent their summer holidays

Hemans came to the area as a child when her family moved to Wales from Liverpool. Her first home was Hen Wrych, Gwrych Castle, nearer the coast by Aberdale. The family certainly lived at Bronwylfa, now rebuilt. This house was to the north-east of the cathedral city on the hill. She came back there after her marriage. By 1825 the marriage had broken down, so, deserted by her husband, she left again for Liverpool. There is a bridge referred to locally as Mrs Hemans' bridge on the old Chester road where she used to compose her poetry. She wrote versions of romantic Welsh legends, introducing them to English readers, and also translated poetry from Portuguese and Spanish. She is commemorated in the cathedral on an inscribed stone in the south aisle and a window in the north wall of the chancel. Her works now reach a limited readership; many people will know the line, 'The boy stood on the burning deck', without perhaps realising that these are the opening words of Felicia Hemans' poem 'Casabianca', published in her collection *The Forest Sanctuary* [1829].

ST IVES, Cornwall [see Map 1, G2]   The childhood summers of sisters **Vanessa Bell** and **Virginia Woolf** were spent at Talland House, Talland Road. It stands high on the edge of the town, with a fine view across the bay to Godrevy lighthouse. Virginia probably had this view in mind when she wrote *To the Lighthouse* [1927]. Perhaps the best known former resident of St Ives is the sculptress **Barbara Hepworth**. She accompanied her children here as evacuees from London in 1939. Their first homes in Cardis Bay were Little Parc Owles, then in Dunluce House. After spells at Chy and Karis she bought the Trewyn Studio in the centre of the town in 1949, settling there permanently two years later. She also bought an old dance hall, which must have been ideal for working on large pieces. She died tragically in a studio fire in 1975. Since 1980 her studio on Barnoon Hill has been opened to the public as the Barbara Hepworth Museum★. The gallery area, the garden and her workshops all have her sculptures on show. It is a moving tribute to a gifted artist.

ST LEONARDS, Sussex [see Map 1, F4]   The author **Sheila Kaye-Smith** was born here in 1887 and spent most of her life in Sussex. Many of her fifty or more popular novels were set in the county. As a schoolgirl in the town she was drawn to Anglo-Catholicism through attending Christ Church. In 1924 she married its curate, and briefly moved to London. On her return to Sussex she made her home near Northiam.

 Mary Webb was another regional writer but her subject was Shropshire; she spent her last days in a nursing home in St Leonards, dying there in 1927. Since the age of twenty she had been bothered by ill health, which became aggravated in times of depression. She was buried in her beloved native county. These two writers had chosen a particular genre which later attracted the attention of Stella Gibbons. Her *Cold Comfort Farm*, also set in

30 Barbara Hepworth's studio in St Ives, Cornwall

Sussex, imitates and pokes gentle fun at the subject matter and style of both Sheila Kaye-Smith and Mary Webb.

SALISBURY, Wiltshire [see Map 1, F3]   The cathedral is the glory of Salisbury. The foundation stones were laid in 1220 and **Ela**, Countess of Salisbury in her own right, herself laid a stone. As a child she inherited her father's fortune, and was married at the age of ten to a well-connected nobleman, William Longespee. After she was widowed, six years later, she devoted herself to religious works. Inspired by visions, she established a monastery and a convent in Wiltshire, and became a nun. She lived to see the cathedral consecrated in 1258 and was herself later regarded as a saint.

Mary Sidney is buried in the Pembroke vault. She died in 1621, as her memorial on a pillar records. Typical of the period, it describes her by reference only to her relationship to men, as 'Sidney's sister, Pembroke's mother' but she was herself a significant woman. She came to live at Wilton, the large country house to the west of the cathedral city on her marriage to the Earl of Pembroke in 1577. She became the patron of several poets and the source of constant encouragement to one in particular, her brother Philip Sidney. She suggested the theme for his poem 'Arcadia', and contributed to its lines. She later edited it for publication after her brother's early death. She was well educated and accomplished, and she enjoyed the company of her brother's friends, including the poet Edmund Spenser whose character Urania is based on her.

A more recent literary figure to spend time in Salisbury was **Dorothy Sayers**. She attended the Godolphin School in the early years of the century, winning a scholarship from there to the University at Oxford in 1912. Another Salisbury resident has an important association with Oxford; **Annie Moberley** was the first principal of St Hugh's College. From 1866 she lived in the Bishop's Palace, ably assisting her father, the bishop, with the administration of the diocese. This proved invaluable experience after 1886 when she took up her appointment at Oxford.

SARK, Channel Islands [see Map 1, F1]   This tiny island was the domain of **Dame Sybil Hathaway**, Dame of Sark. She was a formidable but warm-hearted woman, whose hereditary home was La Seigneurie. She was the ideal figurehead for the local people during the German Occupation in the Second World War, fiercely determined to stay on the island, coping with an uneasy situation with dignity and earning the loyalty of the islanders and the respect of the occupying force. Her death in 1974 was much lamented.

SCARBOROUGH, North Yorkshire [see Map 1, D4]   **Charlotte Brontë** brought her sister **Anne** to this seaside resort in 1849, in the hope that the change of air would improve Anne's health. Anne was suffering from consumption, the same complaint which had killed their sister the previous year. The town had acquired its reputation as a health resort in the seventeenth century, but sadly Anne's health was beyond recovery. She died in May at a boarding house on the cliff, now built over by the Grand Hotel. A plaque outside the hotel, currently operating as a Butlins holiday complex, marks the site. She was only twenty-eight. She had suffered from tubercular problems all her life and is buried in the additional part of St Mary's Parish Churchyard, where her gravestone carries a carving of a draped urn, a typical symbol for a lost life in her time, and two books. These represent her two novels *Agnes Gray* [1847] and *The Tenant of Wildfell Hall* [1848]. The grave is well signposted and well tended. **Winifred Holtby**, a later writer of Yorkshire novels, attended Queen Margaret's School here before the First World War. She set some of her novels in the East Riding of Yorkshire. Like Anne Brontë, her own literary career was cut short by continued ill health. She died in 1935 at the age of thirty-seven.

   Edith Sitwell was born in 1887 at Wood End, her literary family's summer home in the Crescent. It is now Woodend Museum of Natural History★ and some items relating to the Sitwell family, including first editions, are on show in the library wing of the house. They were a much longer living and rather eccentric family. She and her two brothers all became writers, but she is best known for her innovative poetry, especially *Façade* [1923], which was accompanied by a musical score by William Walton. A collection of portraits of Edith Sitwell hang on the stairs and in the first floor gallery, and these show the striking ways in which she dressed and posed.

SCILLY ISLES, Cornwall [see Map 1, G1]   The novelist **George Eliot** spent the spring of 1857 on St Mary's Island. She wrote part of her first fictional work, *Scenes from Clerical Life* [1858], while staying with George Lewes at the post office. Another writer **Bryher**, who died in 1983, had taken her name from one of the other islands. Her family, the Ellermans, had a successful shipping company, and they rented a cottage on the island of Bryher which the author continued to visit regularly until her death. She spent much of her later life in Geneva, but between the wars lived in London with the American author Hilda Doolittle. Their lesbian relationship did not always run smoothly but it was a source of both strength and inspiration to each of them.

SCONE, Tayside [see Map 2, C3]   Scone was an important centre of government in medieval Scotland, although the present palace is a later building. **Annabella Drummond**, as Queen of Scotland, was more effective as a ruler than her husband Robert III and their sons, maintaining the realm intact, despite constant pressure from the English to the south. She died at Scone Abbey in 1401, but was buried in Dunfermline.

SEAHAM, County Durham [see Map 2, D3]   One of **Lady Byron**'s childhood homes was Seaham Hall [now a hospital]. Her family, the Milbankes, were local landowners. In 1815 her marriage to Lord Byron took place in the drawing-room of the Hall. The union was not a success. The couple parted after barely a year, and their daughter, **Ada Lovelace**, who was born just before this separation, never knowingly met her father.

SHEERING, Essex [see Map 1, F4]   **Elinor Glyn**, the romantic novelist with the flamboyant lifestyle, had a grand country home at Sheering Hall. Clearly she thrived in her glamorous social whirl, which included a period in Hollywood in the 1920s. When she died at nearly eighty years of age, she was buried in London.

SHEFFIELD, South Yorkshire [see Map 1, E3]   The city had already had a women's suffrage society for several years and hosted many suffragettes as speakers by the time **Adela Pankhurst** came as organising secretary of the Women's Social and Political Union's Sheffield branch in 1910. The branch headquarters was at 26-28 Chapel Walk, now Fenton's, a men's outfitters' shop. During the period in which she held this post she lived in Marlborough Road, in the Broomhill district. However, she had been active in Sheffield before this. In 1908 she led a crowd of suffragettes and unemployed people in an attempt to disrupt the Cutlers Feast, an annual dinner of the city's major employers and civic dignitaries. Adela's socialist views were not compatible with her mother's ideas, so in 1914 she went to live and work in Australia. She died there in 1961 after a long life dedicated to socialism and pacifism.

The history of the actions which Sheffield women have taken in order to further their rights and conditions are recorded in a booklet produced by the Sheffield Women's History Group in 1984: *Sheffield Women's History Walk: a guide to local women's history*. More of the places mentioned in this Gazetteer should produce booklets like this. The history is all there just waiting to be uncovered and made more widely known.

Amy Johnson, the pioneer aviator, may be the best known graduate of the University of Sheffield. She studied economics here from 1922. Her interest in flying did not come until she was living in London. Born in 1774, **Hannah Kilham** was a native of Sheffield whose pioneering took a very different form. Having shown early academic promise, she received no encouragement to pursue formal studies, but later in life, her commitment to Christianity brought her into contact with African peoples. She was among the first to make a serious study of West African languages. This was an integral part of her efforts to combat slavery. The outstanding result of her work as a missionary was her analysis of several languages, and her appreciation of the importance of their understanding for peaceable communications with peoples new to each other. She died at sea in 1832, during her third expedition to West Africa. Earlier, **Mary Queen of Scots** was a frequent but reluctant visitor to the area in the sixteenth century. During her seventeen years' imprisonment in England, the majority were passed in the custody of the Earl of Shrewsbury, whom she had to accompany when he made tours of inspection of his many business interests. She was confined locally on his estates of Sheffield Manor★ and Sheffield Castle for nearly fourteen years. Turret House, by Manor Lane, may also have been one of her places of confinement. Certainly the Earl's Sheffield properties were considered the most secure.

SHIFNAL, Shropshire [see Map 1, E3]   Weston Park★, the magnificent country house at Weston under Lizard, was built in 1671 by **Lady Wilbraham**. She was interested in Palladian architecture, and had her own ideas for adapting it to the English setting and building materials. Her margin notes in the 1663 edition of Palladio's *First Book of Architecture* testify to this. She was clearly instrumental in the design and building of the house, its stables and the contemporary rebuilding of the church. This capable woman died in 1705 and is buried in the church.

Hannah Cullick's origins were humble by comparison, but we know far more now about her life. She was born in Shifnal in 1833. Her scant formal education at the local charity school ended when she was eight years old. Her working life was spent in service, and it was as a household servant in London in 1854 that she met Arthur Munby, a poetry-writing lawyer. Theirs was an unusual relationship. She acted as his servant, not pubicly acknowledging that from 1873 she was his wife. Their situation at opposite ends of the social hierarchy would not have been understood in either her own or her husband's circle. As they were often apart, Munby encouraged Hannah to keep a diary, as he did. Both these works survive, although, at the request of both the authors, they were not made available until long after their deaths, for fear of scandalising their families. Hannah's writings were recently edited by Liz Stanley and published by Virago Press as *The Diaries of Hannah Cullick: Victorian Maidservant*, 1984. Photography was another of Munby's interests and many of his photographs of her survive, as well as those of other working women; these document many aspects of the lives of working women. From 1903 Hannah made her last home in a semi-detached cottage at Wyke Place, Shifnal. After her death there in 1909 she was buried in Shifnal Churchyard. The inscription on the kerbstones round her grave reads 'Hannah for 36 years wife and servant of Arthur Joseph Munby'.

SHREWSBURY, Shropshire [see Map 1, E3]   The family home of the regional novelist **Mary Webb** was Maesbrook, formerly the old village millhouse, in Meole Brace, to the south-west of Shrewsbury. She married Henry Webb in 1912 at the Meole Brace Church, where there is a commemorative plaque on the pew in which she worshipped from 1902 until 1912. She set many of her stories locally; Shrewsbury appears in them as Silverton. She followed her husband whose teaching jobs took him first to Somerset, but she was never happy away from her beloved Shropshire countryside and they returned as often and as soon as they could. Never very healthy, she died on the south coast in 1927 and was buried in Shrewsbury Cemetery. She had finally 'gone to earth' in the county she had made her own: *Gone to Earth* [1917] is the title of one of her better-known novels. Her work is regarded highly by the people of Shropshire and a Mary Webb trail has been published to guide her readers to places which featured in her life and her novels.

There are also local links with significant women before the Norman

31   Elizabeth Barrett Browning's house at 7–8 Fortfield Terrace, Sidmouth, Devon

Conquest. The relics of the Welsh saint **Winifride** were eventually brought here from Holywell where she died in *c.* 650. St Alkmund's Church, now substantially an eighteenth-century building, standing in Church Street, is thought to have been founded in *c.* 911 by **Aethelflaed**, the powerful Lady of the Mercians, who then ruled the Midlands.

SIDMOUTH, Devon [see Map 1, G3]   **Elizabeth Barrett Browning** came to live here in 1832 when her family had to leave Hope End. Their first home was in the terrace overlooking a bowling green with clear views out to sea. 7–8 Fortfield Terrace can be recognised immediately by the double-headed eagle in the pediment picked out in black. The house had briefly been occupied in 1831 by the Russian aristocrat Grand Duchess Helena, sister-in-law to the Tzar. It was a mark of the Duchess's popularity locally that the townspeople erected her crest, for her sole visit lasted barely three months. The following year the Barretts moved into a Regency house with large cedar trees in the gardens, on All Saints Road. At that time it was called Belmont, but is now the Cedar Shades Hotel. Elizabeth was afflicted with ill health and was often bedridden, but her health seemed to improve on the south coast. By 1835 the Barretts had moved to London, but Elizabeth's health inevitably suffered in the city.

SISSINGHURST, Kent [see Map 1, F4]   Sissinghurst Castle✲[NT] now has some of the loveliest gardens in England. **Vita Sackville-West** bought the castle in 1930 with her husband Harold Nicolson. Together they created the gardens among the remains of the Elizabethan house. They restored some of the castle buildings, making their home in the fifteenth-century South Cottage. Vita had her study in the Elizabethan tower, and among works written here were *The Dark Island* [1934], *Saint Joan of Arc* [1936], and *Pepita* [1937]. The room remains as it was when she used it as a retreat and source of inspiration. Visitors can glimpse inside the intimate atmosphere of book-lined walls, well-worn but much-loved simple furnishings, treasured objects from her travels abroad, well-thumbed cherished books, and mementos of family and friends, all testimony of a passionate life rich in experience, vision and feeling.

On the second floor of the tower the hand-printing press from her friend **Virginia Woolf**'s Hogarth Press is on view. Their close relationship inspired the literary output of both women. Vita dedicated her poem *Sissinghurst* [1931] to Virginia and it was published by the Hogarth Press.

The grounds are a joy to visit. They were organised into small beguiling enclosed areas specialising in different thematic plantings: the White Garden, the Rose Garden, the Nut Grove and the Cottage Garden are four examples. She encouraged plantings which concentrated on particular colours, such as the red and yellow garden by the South Cottage. Although the overall plan appears formal they have captured an atmosphere of intimacy. Vita did most of the plantings; the present display is the result of much experimentation. She was deeply involved with the gardens, while her husband took care of the restoration of the building. Their plans and documents relating to these projects are displayed in the Tower. Vita became gardening correspondent for the *Observer* newspaper, writing many articles on Sissinghurst and other gardens. Her own gardening diaries are being published. She died in 1962 in the sixteenth-century Priest's House, and is commemorated on an inscribed stone plaque on the tower.

SKIPTON, North Yorkshire [see Map 1, D3]   Skipton Castle★, standing beyond the gatehouse at the top of Skipton's High Street, cannot fail to impress. Stone letters silhouetted above the gateway spell out 'Desormais' [Henceforth] – the Clifford family motto. The fortifications include a deep moat and six immense and solid round towers. Inside, the heavily defended living quarters surround the cobbled courtyard. The castle, which withstood a three-year siege during the English Civil War, is in very good repair today, thanks in no small measure due to **Lady Anne Clifford**. Lady Anne was born in the castle in 1590 and as an adult fought through the courts to secure her father's estates as her birthright. Prevailing practice was that property passed to the male heir. As Lady Anne was the only surviving child, she did not relish the prospect of all the family possessions passing to a cousin. In order to finance her claims she made two judicious marriages to wealthy men, acquiring further titles as well. Ultimately she was successful, and she then concentrated her efforts of repairing and rebuilding her buildings, many of which had suffered during the English Civil War. Skipton Castle was just one of the northern properties which she restored and regularly visited, but she clearly had a special regard for it. Indeed she died while in residence in 1676.

She had a stone tablet inscribed in the entrance as follows: 'This Skipton Castle was repayered by The Lady Anne Clifford, Countess Dowager of Pembrookee, Dorsett, and Montgomerie, Baronesse Clifford, West Merland, and Vesie, Laddye of the Honour of Skipton in Craven, and High Sheriff Esse by inheritance of the Countie of Westmoreland, in the yeares 1657 and 1658, after this maine part of itt had layne ruinous ever since December 1648, and the Janvary followinge, when itt was thenn pulled downe and demolisht, almost to the foundacon, by the Command of the Parliament, then sitting at Westminster, because itt had bin a garrison in the then Civill Warres in England.' Clearly she had taken on a huge task and was proud of the finished product. Before she had tackled the castle she had restored the parish church, where her recent ancestors, including her father, had been buried. There are windowpanes bearing her initials AP – Anne, Countess of Pembroke – in the windows in the north wall.

A plaque on a building on the south side of the High Street records that in 1807 the actress **Harriot Mellon** played in the old Skipton Theatre which stood in the outbuildings of a former inn on the site. Later Skipton was the hometown in the mid-nineteenth century to the actress **Adelaide Neilson**, before her career blossomed in London.

SLEAFORD, Lincolnshire [see Map 1, E4]   **Frances Brooke** had already had several works published in England, notably *The History of Lady Julia Mandeville* [1763], before she accompanied her husband to Quebec. The first novel which she wrote there, *Emily Montagu* [1766], was the first novel to be written in Canada. On her return to Britain she wrote plays, some of which were performed. She spent some of her last years in Sleaford where she died in 1789 and was buried in the parish church. Her oval monument on the south wall of the chancel praises her thus: 'The union of superior literary talents with goodness of heart rendered her works serviceable to the cause of those virtues of which her life was a shining example.'

SLOUGH, Berkshire [see Map 3, B2]   **Caroline Herschel**, the astronomer, moved to Slough in 1786. She had left Bath with her brother William in 1782, on William's appointment as private astronomer to George III; it was more convenient to be near the royal residence at Windsor. They built their largest telescope, of forty feet, to the south of Slough at Datchet, and the king recognised Caroline Herschel's contribu-tion to her science by granting her an annual stipend of fifty pounds in 1787. She had her own telescopes which she used for her own observations. Their house on Windsor Road was named Observatory House, and the street to the north is now called Herschel Street. The house was demolished in the 1960s and has been built over with a modern office development. She continued to work

32   Ellen Terry's house at Small Hythe, Kent

with her brother, cataloguing and interpreting their findings, while keeping house for him until his marriage in 1788. She lived in Observatory Cottage, a building in the grounds of the House and later, among other places, in lodgings at Upton House, now 74 Upton Road. She never reconciled herself to William's marriage but remained closely involved with his family. Her discoveries included eight new comets, nebulae and other astronomical phenomena, and her published work received recognition from the Royal Astronomical Society which awarded her its Gold Medal in 1828 and later appointed her an honorary member. By then her brother had died and she had returned to her native Hanover. She remained there until her death in 1848. Her brother and nephew are both commemorated in the town, but Caroline's achievements have been shamefully neglected locally.

SMALL HYTHE, Kent [see Map 1, F4]   The actress **Ellen Terry** made her country home in the sixteenth-century timber-framed farmer's house which is now the Ellen Terry Memorial☆[NT]. Ellen Terry lived at Small Hythe Place, as it is known, from 1899 until 1928. She died in the bedroom which remains much as she had known it. Every room in the house is full of items associated with outstanding figures from stage history. Notably there are costumes worn by Ellen Terry in some of her major roles, but also photographs and prints and personal possessions of hers, earlier figures such as **Sarah Siddons**, her niece **Fanny Kemble** and **Adelaide Neilson**, other actresses and actors, and also of Henry Irving, the actor-manager whose career was closely tied to Ellen Terry's. The gardens and small orchard gave her much pleasure. The rose garden is maintained much as it was when Ellen lived there.

Her daughter, **Edith Craig**, herself active in the theatre as producer and designer, lived on here after Ellen Terry's death with two dear women friends: Christopher St John [her biographer] and Clare [Tony] Atwood, the artist. The trio organised the collection as a memorial to one of Britain's finest actresses, converting a barn there into a small theatre for annual commemorative performances. Ellen Terry had attended the nearby redbrick church, and her funeral was held in this airy, barn-like structure. She wanted no elaborate service or burial, though her remains are in London. Small Hythe Place with its small specialist library of theatre history and its many mementos is an appropriate tribute to a stage career spanning half a century.

SOUTH ACRE, Norfolk [see Map 1, E4] **Margaret Fountaine**, the naturalist whose later life was wild and dangerous by the standards of her times, was born in 1862 at the Rectory, which stands opposite the church which her father served. Her family lived here until the death of her father in 1877 obliged them to take up residence in Norwich. Her love of nature began in the surrounding countryside where she and her seven brothers and sisters enjoyed considerable freedom.

SOUTH SHIELDS, Tyne and Wear [see Map 2, D3] The actress, **Flora Robson**, was born in South Shields in 1902, into a family with maritime connections. Although the family finally settled in London when she was five, she always loved the sea, spending her last years in Brighton. When she died in 1984 her involvement with the theatre had lasted over sixty years.

SOUTH UIST, Western Isles [see Map 2, B1] The well-loved 'Highland Heroine', **Flora MacDonald**, was born on the island in 1722, but most of her childhood was spent on Skye. It was from the neighbouring island of Benbecula that she took Bonnie Prince Charlie to Skye in 1746 to escape from Scotland after his defeat. In the middle of the windswept ruins of her birthplace a cairn has been erected in her memory by Clan Donalk. It can be found to the north-east of Milton, on the west side of the A865 road.

SOUTHAMPTON, Hampshire [see Map 1, F4] Southampton has a long history as a key port of the south coast. **Anne Bradstreet**, who was to become the first English-speaking poet to have literary work written in North America published, put in here briefly in 1630 on her voyage with other early colonists to Massachusetts. **Jane Austen** and her family moved from Bath to Southampton, living at 2 Castle Square near the High Street from 1806 until 1809. Jane seems to have written little here. The Austens never really felt settled in Southampton and were much happier when they returned to the country, setting up home in Chawton.

Only twenty years later a pioneer of women's education and founder of Girton College, Cambridge, **Emily Davies**, was born in the town, also daughter of a cleric, but she soon moved to Gateshead.

SOUTHWOLD, Suffolk [see Map 1, E5] The historian **Agnes Strickland** retired to Reydon Hall, near the coastal town of Southwold, after a career as a writer which is best known for twelve volumes of *Lives of the Queens of England* [1840-8] and *Lives of the Queens of Scotland* [1850-9]. She died at the Hall in 1878, and is buried in the churchyard. Through her writings British history became more accessible to the general reader, and she may be regarded as pioneering research into women's history.

STAITHES, North Yorkshire [see Map 2, D4] The artist **Laura Knight** first visited this coastal village in 1896, but did not come to live here until her marriage to her fellow artist Harold Knight in 1903. They made their home at Roxby, nearby, until 1910 when they were attracted to the artists' colony which was growing up in Cornwall.

STANFORD ON TEME, Hereford and Worcestershire [see Map 1, F3] The author of *The History of the Fairchild Family* [1818-47], **Mary Martha Sherwood**, was born in the Rectory, now the Old Rectory, on the hill west of the bridge in 1775. This was her home until 1801, but she was sent away to a boarding school in Reading where three other women writers also received their education. Her large output of works, mainly for younger readers, included *Susan Gray* [1802] and *Little Henry and his Bearer* [1815].

STAUNTON HAROLD, Leicestershire [see Map 1, E3] **Selina Hastings**, whose support of the early Methodists astonished her aristocratic peers but provided a secure foundation for this reforming church, was born in 1707 at Staunton Harold Hall. The daughter of an earl, she became Countess of Huntingdon through her marriage. Her aid to the Methodists is often referred to as 'the Countess of Huntingdon's Connection'.

STEVENTON, Hampshire [see Map 1, F4] It was in the rectory here that **Jane Austen** was born in 1775. Her father was rector of St Nicholas' Church, where the family worshipped. The rectory was demolished long ago but the site in the field on the opposite side of the road below the church is suggested by the pump, known locally as Jane's Pump. Her childhood here with her six sisters and brothers was a very happy one. Her literary output started as she was growing up. Three of her major novels were written here, under different titles, but published much later: *Sense and Sensibility* [1811], *Pride and Prejudice* [1813] and *Northanger Abbey* [1818]. She was often away from home visiting family and friends, but it was still a wrench to leave Steventon when her father retired in 1801. Her reaction, on being told of the proposed move, would not have been amiss from some of her characters – she fainted.

Several members of her family were buried at Steventon, and the church has been restored in her memory by appreciation societies in Canada and the USA. *The Austens of Steventon*, Keith Irons, produced by the Jane Austen Centenary Committee, Steventon, 1975, gives an account of the family's local connections.

STEYNING, Sussex [see Map 1, F4]   The Chantry House on the village green was for nearly forty years the home and studio of the artist **Gluck**, who died in 1978. There is a plaque on the wall of her red brick house but it fails to record her long residence, rather, it mentions the comparatively short stay of the Irish poet W. B. Yeats. Born Hannah Gluckstein in 1895 into a Jewish family, she took her name Gluck from the Yiddish word for joy. A lesbian artist, she spent time in Paris in the circle of Romaine Brooks and Natalie Barney, but was equally happy painting at Lamorna in Cornwall. In the nearby village of Ashurst the writer **Michael Fairless** is buried in the churchyard. Born Margaret Fairless Barber in 1869, she died in 1901 at the age of thirty-two. Her books include *The Roadmender* [1905] and *The Gathering of Brother Hilarius* [1901].

STOKE-ON-TRENT, Staffordshire [see Map 1, E3]   The modern city comprises six towns which expanded with the pottery industry. The novelist **Mrs Craik** is associated with two of them. She was born Diana Mulock in 1826 at Longfield Cottage, Hartshill, north of Stoke town centre. It has long been demolished but it was her home from her birth until her family moved to Newcastle under Lyme when she was five years old. Her father became the minister of a local Nonconformist church, and settled the family initially in Lower Street, now a main thoroughfare, and then at 2 Mount Pleasant. She attended Bampton House Academy, soon becoming proficient enough in Latin to teach at her mother's school. The Mulocks left for the capital in 1846. Her most famous novel is *John Halifax, Gentleman* [1856], but she also wrote poetry and children's stories. A later writer, **Vera Brittain**, was born in Newcastle under Lyme in 1893.

The fortunes of the potteries fluctuated, and many women were dependent on them for their living. **Sylvia Pankhurst** painted a series of works depicting women employed in them, many doing very skilful and intricate work. She had studied art in London and used her talents for the cause of women's votes. She designed banners, badges and publications for the Women's Social and Political Union, and also a WSPU tea-service made in Stoke-on-Trent. In the twentieth century **Charlotte Rhead**, **Clarice Cliff** and **Susie Cooper** were very influential designers who created styles which supported many factories in the area. They came from very different backgrounds but shared a love of their material and confidence in their sense of design. Examples of their work can be seen in the City Museum and Art Gallery★ in Bethesda Street, Hanley.

Trentham Park and Gardens★, to the south of Newcastle, are all that remain of the imposing country seat of the wealthy Dukes of Sutherland. **Millicent Duchess of Sutherland** tried to redress the exploitation which had made her husband's family so rich. She encouraged and supported welfare and educational work, earning herself the local nickname Meddlesome Millie. However, her efforts were both productive and appreciated.

STRATFORD-UPON-AVON, Warwickshire [see Map 1, F3]   This is William Shakespeare territory, but literary women also lived here.

33   Marie Corelli's grave in
Stratford-upon-Avon, Warwickshire

However, possibly the best known cottage in England is **Anne Hathaway**'s Cottage★, at Shottery. Anne was the wife of the Bard, and no doubt a major influence in his life. The garden at the cottage was designed by **Ellen Willmott**, in 1920. The town was by then already well established as a place of pilgrimage for Shakespeare lovers. Two other historic buildings with Shakespeare connections are Mary Arden's House★, which includes an agricultural history museum, at Wilmcote, and Susannah Hall's home, Hall's Croft★. **Mary Arden** was Shakespeare's mother and **Susannah Hall** was his daughter. These properties are all well signposted.

To return to the women writers, firstly **Mrs Gaskell**, then called Elizabeth Stevenson, attended Avonbank School from 1825 for two years. This institution for young ladies, run by four sisters, the Misses Byerleys, would have been eminently suitable for the daughter of a widower, and she received a surprisingly good education here. **Jessie Boucherett**, an original member of the Langham Place Group of feminists, was a pupil in the 1830s. The building was demolished in 1866 but the terrace can be seen in the public gardens on the riverbank, now known as the Shakespeare Company Gardens.

Marie Corelli, a rather flamboyant figure whose style could be described as that of the sensational popular novelist, moved here in 1901 with her friend Bertha Vyver. Her early successes include *A Romance of Two Worlds* [1886], *Barabbas* [1893] and *The Sorrows of Satan* [1895]. She did write a few more bestsellers while living here at Mason's Croft in Church Street. The building now houses the University of Birmingham's Institute of Shakespeare Studies, a fact which might have pleased Marie Corelli more if her own works received equally serious study. The people of Stratford did not take this colourful character to their hearts. When she was not riding in the town in a scaled-down vehicle drawn by Shetland ponies, she was being transported on the River Avon in a gondola which had been brought over for her from Venice. She was not one to go quietly. When she died in 1924, she was buried near the western entrance to the town cemetery on Evesham Road; no plain modest marker for her grave but a splendidly triumphant angel pointing upwards to heaven.

There have also been many fine female Shakespearian actresses, and several are introduced in the Royal Shakespeare Gallery at the rear of the Royal Shakespeare Theatre. Among its collections are portraits in oil and stone of such significant portrayers of Shakespeare's women as **Sarah Siddons**, **Helen Faucit** and **Ellen Terry**, whose death mask is shown together with a cast of her hands. The display is both traditional and theatrical and covers very recent productions and living actresses through costumes, programmes, photographs and other memorabilia. The present theatre was built in 1932 to the designs of architect **Elisabeth Whitworth Scott**, who won the architectural competition.

SWALLOWFIELD, Berkshire [see Map 3, B1]   The last four years of **Mary Russell Mitford**'s life were spent in the two-storey, three bay redbrick house, now called Queen Anne's Mead at the far end of the village. She died in 1855, and is buried in All Saints' churchyard. A large stone cross was erected over her grave on the north edge of the graveyard by public subscription. Her writings had finally allowed her to pay off the debts which she had inherited from her father. She had some success with poetry, plays and a novel, but her most popular work has remained *Our Village* [1832].

SWANSEA, West Glamorgan [see Map 1, F2]   The Welsh are a nation of singers and the people of Wales adopted **Adelina Patti** as their own when the Italian singer retired to Craig-y-Nos, an eclectic nineteenth-century castle in the Vale of Swansea. The Patti Pavilion in Victoria Park is the Winter Gardens building from Craig-y-Nos which was re-erected here as a memorial to her. She died in 1919.

SWARDESTON, Norfolk [see Map 1, E5]   This country village to the south-west of Norwich was the birthplace in 1865 of **Edith Cavell**. Her upbringing in a Christian household greatly influenced her later work as a nurse. Her selfless dedication to care for the wounded of all nationalities, ignoring the divisive pressures of wartime, led to her courageous activities in Belgium in the First World War. She continued to nurse British wounded and helped them to escape from enemy territory. For this she faced the firing squad in 1915. Her moving words, 'Patriotism is not enough', are still quoted today. Her body was brought back to Britain and is buried in Norwich.

SWINBROOK, Oxfordshire [see Map 1, F3] A family of remarkable women, the six **Mitford** sisters, were brought up at Swinbrook, country home of their father, Baron Redesdale. He saw no need to educate girls, but despite lacking formal teaching they all went on to lead extraordinarily varied lives. **Nancy**, the eldest, a successful novelist, lies buried in the churchyard with her sister **Unity**, who is best known for her friendship with Adolf Hitler. Nancy died in 1973, having written several novels, among them *The Pursuit of Love* [1945] and *Love in a Cold Climate* [1949]. She spent much of her later years in France, and wrote biographies of important figures in French history such as *Madame de Pompadour* [1954] and *The Sun King, Louis XIV at Versailles* [1966]. Unity died in 1948. The other sisters are **Diana**, who was linked with the Fascist movement through her late husband Oswald Mosley; **Deborah**, who as Duchess of Devonshire has written about her home, Chatsworth, and her husband's family history; **Pamela** and **Jessica**, whose left-wing views led her to live abroad, latterly in the USA where she continues to write incisively and perceptively on contemporary subjects as a journalist and author.

SYDMONTON, Hampshire [see Map 1, F4] The poet **Anne Finch** is thought to have been born Anne Kingsmill at Sydmonton in 1661. Her works, especially *The Spleen* [1709], were admired by Pope whose name for her in his own poetry was Ardelia. She became Countess of Winchilsea after she married in 1684.

SYDENHAM See **LONDON BOROUGH OF LEWISHAM**.

T T

TAVISTOCK, Devon [see Map 1, G2]   **Mary Ellen Smith**, born in this country town in 1862, emigrated with her husband to Canada in 1891. When she was widowed in 1917 she took over her husband's constituency. Her political career prospered and she became, albeit briefly, the first woman in the British Empire, as it then was, to attain a cabinet position, serving as Minister without Portfolio in 1921-2 for British Columbia. Tavistock has yet to acknowledge this daughter's achievements.

TEFFONT MAGNA, Wiltshire [see Map 1, F3]   Fitz House, a warm stone farmhouse in beautiful gardens★ [gardens only], was rented by the writer **Edith Olivier**. She had long admired it and her dreams were fulfilled when she was able to live there for some years in the 1920s. She was the author of such novels as *The Love-child* [1927] and *Mary Magdalen* [1934], and prose works based on local lore and scenery such as her *Moonrakings* [1930].

TENBY, Dyfed [see Map 1, F2]   When **Gwen John**, the painter, was eight years old, in 1884, her family moved here permanently from Haverfordwest. The family home was Victoria House, 32 Victoria Street. Some of her early works were sketches of children at play on the sea shore. She left home in 1895 to study art in London, afterwards spending most of her life in France.

TEWKESBURY, Gloucestershire [see Map 1, F3]   **Mrs Craik**'s best known novel, *John Halifax, Gentleman* [1856], was set partly in the town and the surrounding countryside. An enduring tale of rags to respectability, its enormous popularity was a sure sign that Mrs Craik was in tune with the Victorian values then prevailing. The Bell Hotel, a fourteenth-century building at 52 Church Street, was the model for one in the book, the success of which put Tewkesbury on the map. A marble memorial to her in the abbey commemorates her contribution to the town. The vista of the abbey from the main street was opened up in 1940 when structures which previously obstructed the view were demolished. **Victoria Woodhull** died at her home nearby at Bredon's Norton and to commemorate her deep affection for this part of England, her daughter arranged for the abbey to be more visible in this way.

THEYDON BOIS, Essex [see Map 3, A4]   The formidable teacher and administrator **Frances Buss** founded North London Collegiate School for Girls in 1850, and was its headmistress for the next forty years. She believed

179

passionately in a full and academically rewarding education for girls, taught by professional women teachers. All her life, she determinedly pursued her aim of widening educational opportunities. She is forever linked with Dorothea Beale, founder of Cheltenham Ladies' College, as pioneers in this field. As the oft-repeated ditty suggests, they were totally dedicated to their chosen cause:

> 'Miss Buss and Miss Beale,
> Cupid's darts do not feel.
> They are not like us,
> Miss Beale and Miss Buss.'

They were single-minded in all their activities. Miss Buss introduced outdoor sports for her pupils at a field in nearby Epping. This was an area which she knew well, and when her energetic life ended in 1894, she was buried in St Mary's churchyard, up Piercing Hill. Her low pink granite gravestone lies to the south of the church, by the spire.

THORNTON, West Yorkshire [see Map 1, D3]   The three literary sisters **Charlotte**, **Emily** and **Anne Brontë** were born here in, respectively, 1816, 1818 and 1820. Their father was the curate of the Bell chapel from 1816 until the family moved to Haworth after Emily's birth. A plaque on 74 High Street marks their home, and a road, Brontë Place, is named after them.

THREE MILE CROSS, Berkshire [see Map 3, B1]   This small community was the inspiration for **Mary Russell Mitford**'s book *Our Village: Sketches of Rural Life, Character, and Scenery* [1832]. The family was reduced to very modest circumstances as a result of her father's mismanagement of her lottery win. From 1820 until 1851 she lived in a cottage, now in poor repair, on the main road, next to the Swan Hotel. The building is partly a Gospel Hall and partly The Mitford, changed much from the time when it was a popular tourist attraction. Mary Mitford also wrote other works – plays, poetry, short stories – here, as she was obliged to keep both her parents, as well as supporting herself. The 'rural sketches' first appeared as articles in various periodicals, such as the *Lady's Magazine*, in 1824. She later wrote plays and poetry, but the popularity of *Our Village* outlasted those other successes.

TICKERAGE, Surrey [see Map 1, C2]   The film actress, **Vivien Leigh**, latterly lived near Guildford at Tickerage Mill. Her biggest screen role was undoubtedly that of Scarlett O'Hara in *Gone with the Wind* [1939], for which she earned an Oscar. Her own life was not easy. Her last years, after her divorce from fellow actor Laurence Olivier in 1960, were increasingly dogged by depression. When she died at home here in 1967, her ashes were scattered on the millpond.

TIDMARSH, Berkshire [see Map 1, F4]   The painter and comparatively quiet member of the Bloomsbury Group, **Dora Carrington**, moved to

Old Mill House on the Tilehurst road in 1917, and set up home here with Lytton Strachey. The household in this large, brick building, partly painted white, was an unusual one. As she became more involved with Strachey, she painted less, which is our loss today, for she was immensely talented. Clearly Carrington, as she preferred to be known, was devoted to Strachey but in 1921 she married Ralph Partridge, who also joined the household at Tidmarsh Mill. Three years later they all moved to Ham in Wiltshire.

TILBURY, Essex [see Map 3, B4]   In 1588, when England was at war with Spain, **Elizabeth I** inspected her forces at Tilbury, which has always been of great strategic importance in defending London from enemy approach by river; the present Tilbury Fort★, an impressive fortification which can be visited, dates from the late seventeenth century. During Elizabeth's reign her support for the navy had established England as a premier naval power which in 1588 was to be tested by the Spanish Armada. It was here, during the War against Philip of Spain, that Elizabeth delivered her famous and rousing speech: 'My loving people. . . I am come amongst you, as you see . . . being resolved, in the midst and heat of battle, to live or die amongst you all; to lay down for my God, and for my kingdom, and for my people, my honour and my blood, even in the dust. I know I have the body and the frame of a weak and feeble woman but I have the heart and stomach of a king, and of a king of England too, and think foul scorn that Parma or Spain should dare to invade the borders of my realm.'

TOBERMORY, Isle of Mull, Strathclyde [see Map 2, B2]   The main town on the Isle of Mull became a retreat for **Isabella Bird** where she could be herself with her sister away from the limiting social life which she encountered in Edinburgh. In Edinburgh she was laid low with health problems but these barely affected her on her adventurous journeys, which were initially undertaken to improve her health. She embarked on her travels unchaperoned and described them with disarming frankness in her letters, which were later published. The titles of her published accounts show just how far she managed to go: *An Englishwoman in America* [1856], *Six Months in the Sandwich Islands* [1875], *A Lady's Life in the Rocky Mountains* [1879], *Unbeaten Tracks in Japan* [1880], *The Golden Cheronese and the Way Thither* [1883], *Journeys in Persia and Kurdistan* [1891], *Korea and her Neighbours* [1893] and *The Yaangtze Valley and Beyond* [1899].

   Her sister, Henrietta, to whom she was devoted and who was the recipient of her travel correspondence, spent the summers on Mull in a modest cottage. Isabella shared her love of the islanders and helped her welfare work on the island. When she died in Edinburgh in 1904, aged seventy-three, Isabella was buried in the Kirkyard here beside her sister.

TONG, Shropshire [see Map 1, E3]   It is certain that **Venetia Stanley** was born in the charming and historic village of Tong and that she died there in 1633. Tong Castle was her birthplace, childhood home and the scene of her early death at the age of thirty-three. She was a strikingly good-looking woman who attracted many suitors and the tributes of artists and poets. In 1625 she married the obsessional Sir Kenelm Digby. He was the author of *Choice Receipts in Physick and Chirurgery and of Cookery* [1669] and it is said that he insisted on feeding his wife dishes which he had specially prepared to ensure that her health and beauty was maintained. It is not recorded whether one of his plans went awry and that he inadvertently caused his wife's demise or whether the strains of having four children took their toll. She was buried in London, but her life is recorded on the Stanley family monuments in Tong Church.

Tong has also been suggested as one of the possible birthplaces in 1689 of the traveller and writer **Lady Mary Wortley Montagu**, although her baptism in London that year is undisputed. Her family, the Pierreponts, had estates here. In 1756 **Mrs Fitzherbert** was born at Tong Castle, during a visit there by her parents. Her given name was Maria Anne Smythe, and on her first marriage in 1771 she became Maria Weld. Thomas Fitzherbert, whom she married secondly, died in 1781 leaving her the name by which she is best known. She was then admired, loved and then neglected by the Prince Regent, the future George IV, who had in fact married her secretly. However, because she was a devout Roman Catholic and the rites of her Church had been followed at the ceremony, the wedding was not recognised by the monarchy; indeed the Prince denied it and in 1795 he married Caroline of Brunswick, who was considered a more suitable bride for an heir to the throne.

TORQUAY, Devon [see Map 1, G3]   This seaside resort attracted the Barratt family as being beneficial to the health of their eldest daughter **Elizabeth Barratt Browning**. She had already had three years of sea air at Sidmouth, but the following three years of London smog sent her to Torquay in 1838. She stayed at 1 Beacon Terrace, now the Regina Hotel, but then called Bath House. Sited on the corner of the old port, commanding good views, she made good progress, publishing several writings, such as *The Seraphim and Other Poems* [1838], until tragedy struck. Her brother, to whom she had been very close, was drowned in a yachting accident in 1840, and she was so affected by his death that she was unable to move to London until the next year. **Angela Burdett-Coutts**, the philanthropist, also came to Torquay for her health. She preferred to spend time by the sea rather than in damp and polluted London, and she regularly rented Meadwood House, 1 Hesketh Crescent, from 1857, until she took Ehrenberg Hall from 1861 until 1877. She supported many local ventures and causes, including the schools, the museum and the churches.

A more recent and extremely successful writer was born in the town fifty years later, in 1891. This was the writer of popular detective stories, **Agatha Christie**. She was taught at home, Ashfield, on Barton Road, on the hill looking down on the port, until she went to Paris for voice training in 1906. After living in Egypt, the outbreak of the First World War found her back in Torquay as a VAD, where she met and married her first husband, Archibald Christie. In 1971 another writer, **Stevie Smith**, died ten miles away at Buckfastleigh. Her cremation took place in Torquay. She had always liked seaside towns, though Brighton was probably her favourite.

TREFECCA, Powys [see Map 1, F3]   **Selina Hastings**, Countess of Huntingdon, having already given material support to many Methodist chapels and preachers, funded and opened in 1786 a training centre for Methodist ministers at Trefecca House, her ultimate aim being the reform of the Church of England through the ideas of George Whitefield. Methodists were not eligible to study at the two established universities, Oxford and Cambridge, as they would not subscribe to the Church of England, then a requirement for all students and staff. By 1792 new premises were found in Hertfordshire. College Farm, Trefecca, is the site of the first college.

TREMEIRCHION, Clwyd [see Map 1, E3]   **Hester Thrale Piozzi** had a home at Brynbella on the River Clwyd with her second husband, the Italian musician Gabriel Piozzi. She had known and loved this area as a child and had Brynbella built in 1790. This period in her life, which brought her more joy than her first marriage, ended when Gabriel Piozzi died here in 1809. She then retired to Bath but she is commemorated in the church here by a plaque in the north chancel.

TREVONE, Cornwall [see Map 1, G2]   This tiny community on the north Cornish coast was where **Dorothy Richardson** and her artist husband Alan Odle spent their winters from 1916 until 1938. Their financial circumstances as writer and artist were precarious, and they were obliged to rent out their London base while they stayed more cheaply in Cornwall. During most of this time Dorothy Richardson was writing her twelve-volume *Pilgrimage*, which draws on her own experience using a style now termed stream of consciousness. *Pointed Roofs*, the first volume, was published in 1915; the last, *March Moonlight* [1967], was not published until after her death.

TRULL, Somerset [see Map 1, F3]   **Juliana Horatia Ewing**, the writer of children's books popular beyond the Victorian period, was always plagued by ill health, and on her death aged only forty-four, she was buried in the churchyard of this village on the southern edge of Taunton. Her grave lies in the shade of a large tree north-west of the church. She created many enduring and very human characters. The junior version of the Girl Guides are named Brownies after her creations in *The Brownies and Other Tales* [1870], although originally the Baden-Powells called their young guides Rosebuds.

TUNBRIDGE WELLS, Kent [see Map 1, C4]   **Celia Fiennes** visited several spa-towns during her 'Great Journeys' in the late seventeenth and early eighteenth century, and was adequately qualified to judge them. Not all met her high standards, but Tunbridge Wells pleased her. The water was beneficial: 'The waters I have dranke many years with great advantage'; and the accommodation and amenities were acceptable: 'They have made the wells very comodious by the many good buildings all about it.' Many entertainments were provided, making it popular during the social seasons.

Tunbridge has more recently attracted those who seek a slower pace of life at the end of their days; some however gained a new lease of life. The philanthropist and pioneer of workhouse reform, **Louisa Twining**, moved here in 1893, after active campaigning throughout the country for social reform of the Poor Law, better conditions in workhouses and the representation of women on the Boards of Guardians. This proved to be no retirement for she was herself elected to the Board of Guardians for Tunbridge Wells, serving till 1896. She continued to write in pursuit of social reforms and to win power for women in local government. She died in 1912. The formidable doctor, **Sophia Jex-Blake**, who died the same year, had also retired here. She left all her property to **Octavia Hill**, to whom she had been very close, for Octavia to use in her various philanthropic enterprises: housing schemes in London and the National Trust.

Tunbridge Wells also drew political figures. After an equally active life, this time in Parliamentary politics, **Margaret Bondfield**, who was the first woman to hold ministerial office and later the first woman Privy Councillor, also spent some of her retirement here. She lived at a house in Southborough called Cultivers. **Sarah Grand**, known widely as 'Madame', lived here from 1898. She had already published several novels, of which *The Beth Book* [1897] is probably the best known today. She first joined the Women Writers' Suffrage League and later became president of the local branch of the National Union of Women's Suffrage Societies. Her political career continued when she moved to Bath in 1920. She was appointed mayor after living there only three years. **Lady Ottoline Morrell**'s political influence was considered subversive, as her homes in London and Garsington attracted known pacifists in the First World War. Her health suffered and she underwent a novel treatment at a clinic in Tunbridge Wells; the unorthodox treatment failed and she died in 1938. She was buried at her family's church in Holbeck.

TYNEMOUTH, Tyne and Wear [see Map 2, D3]   **Harriet Martineau** came to live in Tynemouth for health reasons in 1839. She continued to write, however; in addition to various children's works and her journalism, she wrote her novel *Deerbrook* [1839]. By 1844, her health had sufficiently improved for her to return to the centre of national life in the south. She had remained in touch with events and opinion throughout from her northern sickbed, and had published *Life in the Sickroom* [1843].

U u

UFFINGTON, Lincolnshire [see Map 1, E4]   **Lady Charlotte Guest** was born at Uffington House, daughter of the Earl of Lindsey. Despite being born into a privileged family with its attendant opportunities, she retreated into books, acquiring fluency in many languages, to avoid clashes with her mother's second husband. Her own marriage to Josiah Guest in 1833 enabled her to escape into a happy and busy life in Wales, where her success at learning Welsh led her to make important translations into English of Welsh classical literature.

ULVERSTON, Cumbria [see Map 1, D3]   Swarthmoor Hall★, near Ulverston, was the home of **Margaret Fell**, on her first marriage. She opened it to all sincere religious people; one of these was George Fox, who in 1652 converted her to the Quaker way of life. Her involvement in the beliefs of the Society of Friends was increased when she was widowed in 1758. She supported the persecuted Quakers through the Civil War and the Restoration, herself incurring prison sentences for allowing meetings to take place in Swarthmoor Hall. She married George Fox in 1669, and continued to organise and publish on behalf of the Friends, until her death in 1702. She ensured that women could play a full part in the activities and worship of the Friends. Margaret Fell was buried in Sunbreck burial ground beside Birkrigg Common, two miles from the Hall.

V v

VENTNOR, Isle of Wight [see Map 1, G4]   **Eleanor Marx** paid several visits to her father Karl Marx here, during his stays at 1 St Boniface Gardens for the good of his ailing health between 1881 and 1883. Her commitments in London gave her little time but her father much appreciated her coming to see him. She became his political heiress on his death in 1883.

Ventnor became a popular destination for Victorians, especially those with health problems. The American novelist and playwright **Pearl Craigie** suffered from ill health and sought a more salubrious climate on the island, although she still spent time in London where she had a career as a journalist. She left her husband in 1890 and published her first novel, written here, the following year. This was *Some Emotions and a Moral* [1891], when she first used her pen-name John Oliver Hobbes. Most of her later works were written at Ventnor. Her first home, Springhill Castle, has been demolished although the grounds now form the public gardens on the west of the town. She moved to Craigie Lodge in 1900, but it only received this name after her death here in 1906.

W w

WAKEFIELD, West Yorkshire [see Map 1, E3] In 1903 **Barbara Hepworth** was born at 15 Duke of York Street. Her family then moved into Hawthorne Bank [now 4 Hawthorne Grove], in the Alverthorpe area of the town. She was educated at Wakefield Grammar School for Girls where her talent for art was encouraged, enabling her to win a scholarship in 1919 to study art in Leeds. Wakefield also claims as its daughter **Maid Marion**, the folk heroine who, according to legend, helped and married the outlaw Robin Hood, during the reigns of Richard I and John at the end of the twelfth century. However, it is thought more likely that the character of Marion entered English folk tradition from French sources.

WALLINGFORD, Berkshire [see Map 1, F4] All that remains of the Castle★ which once dominated the town is the mound on which the keep stood, and odd walls, all now part of a public park and garden. Climbing to the top of the mound gives an appreciation of the commanding site. During the dispute over the English throne on the death of Henry I, his daughter **Matilda** ultimately conceded the crown to her cousin Stephen of Blois. She had been taken prisoner at Oxford at the end of 1142, and managed to escape across the snow-covered fields to the comparative safety of Wallingford Castle. Having the opportunity to assess her chances realistically, she left for France, living out her days in Normandy. She had, however, not relinquished everything to Stephen: his reign was followed by that of her son Henry II.

    Agatha Christie made her home in a large mansion, Winterbrook House, by the river. It was to be her base for the last thirty years of her long and productive life. Much of her detective fiction was written here. She also wrote other novels, autobiography and plays. Among her enduring characters are Miss Marples and Hercule Poirot, both much admired fictional detectives. She is buried in the next village, Cholsey.

WALLINGTON, Northumberland [see Map 2, C3] **Pauline, Lady Trevelyan**, lived in Wallington Hall★[NT], a country mansion, with features dating from its initial building in 1688. Major alterations were made in the following century and she supervised and contributed to the nineteenth-century additions and decorative schemes. She was herself a patron of contemporary artists, and her circle of friends included Ruskin and William Bell-Scott, the latter of whom she commissioned to paint the mural in the central hall. It was on an epic scale, and the turbulent history of the region is graphically portrayed. The Roman Empire's conquest of the north of Britain was hampered by the fiercely independant tribes in the border country; Hadrian's Wall did not prove a lasting defence. Local people sat as models for the painting, and Lady Trevelyan is depicted as a Briton cowed by the might of Rome. She painted some of the exquisite flower designs on the pillars and pilasters. She is also represented in a marble relief on the wall in the hall. It records that it was she who had the open courtyard roofed and decorated in its present form. She was also interested in contemporary literature. Her regular literary guests included the poet **Christina Rossetti**.

WALLSEND, Tyne and Wear [see Map 2, D3] The town takes its name from the fact that it was at the end of the Roman fortification, Hadrian's Wall, on the banks of the Tyne. It is now part of the conurbation of Newcastle, built up on the former strength of the shipping industry. In 1926 **Margaret Bondfield** won the Parliamentary seat of Wallsend for the Labour Party and held it for five years. It was a testimony to her achievements in politics and trade unionism that she received the support and respect of an area where traditional male values held sway. While representing Wallsend, Margaret Bondfield became the first woman to hold Cabinet Office. Her experience in trade unionism was invaluable to her as Minister of Labour.

WALLYFORD, Lothian [see Map 2, C3] **Margaret Oliphant**, the Scottish novelist, was born in Wallyford in 1828. Her father's work as a customs officer meant that the family moved away but she returned on her marriage to her cousin in 1857. She had already published her first novel in 1849 and her writing, usually with a Scottish setting, was to be her main source of income after being widowed in 1859.

WALMER, Kent [see Map 1, F5] Walmer Castle★ was the official residence of the Lord Warden of the Cinque Ports, an office held by William Pitt. It was his niece, the traveller and Arabist. **Lady Hester Stanhope**, who laid out the gardens in *c.* 1805. She had acted as Pitt's hostess and confidante in his years in government. In 1810 she set out for the Middle East where she travelled extensively and gained the respect of the Arabs. She died in Lebanon in 1839.

WALSALL, West Midlands [see Map 1, E3] Walsall had its own nursing pioneer, **Sister Dora of Walsall**. Inspired by the work of Florence Nightingale, and her own strong Christian convictions, she had joined an Anglican order, the Christ Church Sisterhood. In 1865 she was sent to help in nursing at Walsall Cottage Hospital at 4 Bridge Street. Although Sister Dora's work was to be only a temporary expedient, she returned later in the year to devote the rest of her life to the people of Walsall. From small beginnings the hospital acquired a reputation for its care of the victims of the many industrial accidents which occurred with relentless regularity. She was a good organiser and a compassionate nurse, who has been recognised as Walsall's equivalent to Florence Nightingale; she improved standards of hygiene and patient care, coped with the casualties of large-scale industrial disasters and stemmed the spread of disease, at a time when hospitals were notorious for spreading rather than limiting infection. In addition to her energetic nursing, which included a long epidemic of smallpox, Sister Dora was also active in Christian Missionary work in the Black Country. She died of cancer in a cottage in Wednesbury Road in 1878. Her well-attended funeral was held in St Matthew's Church, where she was greatly mourned. Her final resting place in the Queen Street cemetery is marked by a simple gravestone which bears the inscription: 'In memory of Sister Dora who entered into rest on Christmas Eve 1878.' The town had taken Sister Dora to its heart, and there is a statue of her in the town centre, and also inside the main hospital which has recently been re-named the Sister Dora Hospital in her memory. She is also commemorated in the church's east window.

WALTHAM CROSS, Hertfordshire [see Map 3, A3]   The town's name is taken from the cross erected here by Edward I in memory of his wife **Eleanor of Castile**. She had died in Harby in 1290, and the king had stone crosses erected in every town where her body had rested on its passage to its final site in London, in accordance with her deathbed wish. The style of the Eleanor Crosses has been revived regularly in war memorials and other commemorative monuments since.

WARE, Hertfordshire [see Map 1, F4]   It was at Ware in July 1553 that the unfortunate **Lady Jane Grey** was proclaimed Queen of England. Aged sixteen, she was an unwilling claimant, a pawn in the political games of her ambitious father, the Duke of Suffolk, and his friends, who did not want the Roman Catholic Mary Tudor to succeed to the English throne. Known as the 'Nine Days Queen', Jane's reign was short-lived. Mary Tudor spared her in 1553 but following her father's involvement in the Wyatt rebellion, Lady Jane was executed in 1554.

WARRINGTON, Cheshire [see Map 1, E3]   **Anna Barbauld** was educated at Warrington Academy, her father John Aiken having moved here from Leicestershire. The building which first housed the academy from 1752 until 1762 stands as Bridge Foot House, now a newspaper office; it has been moved a few yards from its original site. It was here that she met her future husband, Rochemont Barbauld, and formed her own ideas about schooling. The Barbaulds were married in 1774 and later ran their own school in Suffolk. Mrs Barbauld is remembered in the naming of Barbauld Street. Her niece, and later her biographer, **Lucy Aiken**, was born here in 1781. Both of them were brought up as Nonconformists; this greatly influenced their lives. **Sarah Grand**, also a writer, spent some of her unhappy marriage in Warrington. Encouraged by the success of her first novel *Ideala* in 1888, she left her husband for London, where she was welcomed by those active in women's causes. Among her feminist novels *The Heavenly Twins* [1893] touched many raw nerves as it exposed aspects of married life, sexuality and moral hypocrisy. She has been credited with the concept of the New Woman, and was herself an example of this new phenomenon.

WASHINGTON, Tyne and Wear [see Map 2, D3] Many Americans are drawn to Washington Old Hall because of its associations with the founding President of the United States. The new hall, a Victorian redbrick building nearby, was the birthplace and childhood home of **Gertrude Bell**. This remarkable woman, born in 1868, had a gift for language and an urge to travel. Both were fulfilled during her life in the Middle East where she undertook archaeological excavations, adventurous journeys of discovery into the Arabian Desert and intelligence work for the British government in the First World War. Her own accounts of her travels, such as *The Desert and the Sown* [1907], combine fine description and informed observations. She is commemorated on a plaque inside Washington New Hall, now a management centre for the National Coal Board.

WEEDON LOIS, Northamptonshire [see Map 1, F4] When **Edith Sitwell** died in 1964, she was buried in the churchyard extension plot, across the road from the church here. The stark stone plinth incorporates hands in bronze by the sculptor Henry Moore. A considerable poet herself, she had fostered many poets of the next generation and encouraged them by her own explorations of new verse forms and use of language.

WELBECK, Nottinghamshire [see Map 1, E4] **Margaret Cavendish**, Duchess of Newcastle, and her step-daughter **Lady Jane Cheyne** lived through the troubled times of the English Civil War. Jane held Welbeck with her sister for the Royalists with a small force from 1643 but, although able to save her brothers, her father's Welbeck estates were confiscated. Such political upheaval did not provide conditions in which Margaret Cavendish's attempts to study science seriously could flourish. She spent most of the period in exile in Holland where she met her husband, and other intellectual exiles, who gave her some encouragement to pursue scientific enquiry. She tried in vain in 1651 to recover the Duke's family estates at Welbeck, but eventually was able to settle there on the Restoration of Charles II in 1660. All this time she wrote and published her scientific ideas, which received little attention from the establishment, and that little was dismissive of her efforts. She retaliated by accusing men of keeping knowledge, and access to it, from women, excluding them from universities. She was latterly regarded as an eccentric, but considering her complete lack of academic background, she was an original thinker who saw no reason why men should have the monopoly on good ideas.

WELWYN GARDEN CITY, Hertfordshire [see Map 1, F4] The architect **Elizabeth Whitworth Scott** did architectural work in the innovative Garden City development. Her contribution is among those recorded in the museum there.

WEST DEAN, Wiltshire [see Map 1, F3]   The unconventional life of **Lady Mary Wortley Montagu** began when she eloped from her parents' home in Acton, now in London, with Edward Wortley Montagu in 1712. They married in this village which was well known to her from spending much of her childhood at her grandparents' home here. That house is long gone but the gardens now form part of the public park.

WESTON-SUPER-MARE, Avon [see Map 1, F3]   **Amelia Blandford Edwards**, Egyptologist and writer, came to this seaside resort to recuperate from an accident but she died here in 1892. She is buried in Bristol. Once intrigued by Egypt, it took over her life. She wrote about her travels there, lectured widely to publicise and raise money for the Egyptian Exploration Society and its excavations. In her will she left funds to endow the first chair of Egyptology in Britain, at University College London. The sea air did not suit the Shropshire novelist **Mary Webb** either. On her marriage in 1912 she had to leave her native county to follow her husband's career as a teacher in the town. Their first home together was 6 Landemann Circus, but within two years they were back in Shropshire as Mary could not settle here.

WHITBY, N. Yorkshire [see Map 2, D5]   After successfully running a convent in Hartlepool for ten years, **Hilda** was sent by the leading theologians to take charge of a double house, of nuns and monks, in c. 657. The ruins★, which survive on the clifftop on the south side of the mouth of the River Esk, date from a second foundation built on the same site in the eleventh century. Hilda established her religious community as a centre for scholarship, and its fine reputation enabled her to host the Synod of Whitby there in 664. This was a key conference of Christian leaders, bringing together the Celtic and Roman traditions of Christianity and forging a common way forward acceptable to both. The community was destroyed by Scandinavian invaders in 867, but Hilda's name lives on, as St Hilda of Whitby. She had encouraged England's first poet, Caedmon, by taking him into the abbey and teaching him to write. Other protégés became bishops and saints. Hilda died in 680 after a long illness.

The town prospered as a port, particularly with the establishment of the whaling fleet by the nineteenth century. The way of life made a strong impression on **Mrs Gaskell** who stayed at 1 Abbey Terrace in 1859, and set her novel *Sylvia's Lovers* [1863] here. The five-storeyed corner house commands a splendid view across the river to the abbey ruins.

Storm Jameson was born in Whitby in 1891 into a sea-faring family. Her two-volume autobiographical work *Journey from the North* [1982] sheds light on local life. She died in Cambridge in 1986.

WIGTOWN, Dumfries and Galloway [see Map 2, D2]   There is a memorial in the churchyard of ruined St Madulis Church to **Margaret McLaughlan** and **Margaret Wilson**. These two women were martyrs to the cause of the Covenanters in Scotland. In 1685 they were tied to a stake in the estuary of the River Blagdon at lowtide, left to drown there when the tide came in. Many Scottish Covenanting women died for their beliefs throughout the country. This was one of the more horrific ends to which some of them came. The Martyrs' Monument on the hill overlooking the town honours the memory of all local Covenanters. The Covenanters held that the freedom to follow one's own religious faith unimpeded was a civil right. This was the body of the Scottish National Covenant of 1638 and the Solemn League and Covenant of 1643.

WILLINGHAM, Lincolnshire [see Map 1, E4] The feminist and writer **Jessie Boucherett** was born in the Manor in 1825. After her schooling in Stratford-upon-Avon she did charitable work in nearby Market Rasen. Later she was an active member of the Langham Place Group of feminists in London, editing and funding the *Englishwoman's Review*. Her last days were spent in North Willingham, where she died in 1905. She is buried here.

WILTON, Wiltshire [see Map 1, F3] The centre piece of Wilton is Wilton House★, home of the Earls of Pembroke. There had been a religious house at Wilton in the tenth century. It is thought that **St Edith**, born in 962, was brought up there. Certainly she became a nun here herself, and as the daughter of King Edgar, lived in circumstances which contrasted with the simple life adopted in most convents. Some of her personal wealth was used to build St Denys' Church, where she was buried in 984. Her life had been one of exemplary devoutness; she refrained from any involvement in the dynastic struggles which followed her father's death, despite pressure to take the throne herself. Only twenty-two when she died, she was revered as St Edith of Wilton, and her body is said to have been preserved from decay by divine intervention.

On her marriage to the second earl in 1577, **Mary Sidney** became Countess of Pembroke and took up residence in Wilton House. She was the patron of many young writers, and actively encouraged her brother, Sir Philip Sidney. Many literary works were dedicated to her in gratitude, notably her brother's *Arcadia*. She herself was well educated and after Philip's death in 1586 she edited his writings and published many translations of her own. After being widowed in 1601 she spent little time here. The house today is an important survival of the architecture of Inigo Jones, who received this major commission after the destruction by fire in 1647 of the earlier house, and so little remains of the building Mary Sidney knew.

The writer on country life, **Edith Olivier**, was daughter of the local rector. She spent most of her life in the immediate vicinity, becoming mayor of Wilton in 1939 until 1941.

WIMBLEDON See **LONDON BOROUGH OF MERTON**.

WINCHCOMBE, Gloucestershire [see Map 1, F3] **Catherine Parr**, sixth and last wife of Henry VIII, survived his death in 1547, and almost immediately married as her fourth husband Thomas Seymour. They had wished to marry before the king interfered. They moved to Sudeley

34   Jane Austen's last home at 8 College Street, Winchester, Hampshire

Castle★, the manor of the Seymour family, but their long-awaited happiness together was short-lived. Catherine died in childbirth in 1548. Catherine's royal marriage was not so fraught with uncertainties as her predecessors, and she succeeded in reuniting the king's family. She acted briefly as Regent, during Henry's absence abroad, but sought no personal power. Her tomb is in the church of St Mary on the east side of Sudeley Castle. Its present monument is a later reconstruction; a mere fragment remains of the original.

Although some of the early building, including the banqueting hall, is now ruined, there are several rooms open to the public. There are many items and pictures on display relating to several of the Tudor queens. **Lady Jane Grey**, whose own fated reign had been engineered by the ambitious Sir Thomas Seymour, had served Catherine Parr as a very young lady-in-waiting and led the mourners at her mistress's funeral.

WINCHESTER, Hampshire [see Map 1, F4]   Winchester cathedral contains the remains and memorials to three significant women of letters. **Mrs Elizabeth Montagu** had devoted herself to the literary life after losing her only child in 1744. She was a leader in the Blue Stocking Circle of eminent women of the eighteenth century. Her business acumen enabled her to have homes both in London and in the country, where she hosted intellectual gatherings of scholarly women. Cultured men were also invited and, going against the custom of the day, were excused from wearing formal black stockings; blue stockings were acceptable, thus these social gatherings earned the name Blue Stocking salons. Samuel Johnson referred to her as the Queen of the Blues. She died in her London home in 1800 but was buried in the north aisle of the cathedral. Her memorial is on the north wall.

Jane Austen, who lived most of her life in Hampshire, was also buried in the north aisle. Her unostentatious memorial was composed by her brothers, and makes no mention of her writings. Clearly the male members of her family could not reconcile themselves to her literary success, although mention is made on the inscribed slab of 'the extraordinary endowments of her mind'. As a plaque on the building at 8 College Street, behind the cathedral, records, she died in 1817, after two months of illness, tended by her devoted sister Cassandra. Despite the inevitable weakness caused by Addison's disease, which eventually killed her, Jane wrote letters and worked on a novel until the end. Her unfinished *Sanditon* gently mocks the medical profession and its unnecessarily dependent patients, based, no doubt, on her own observations during her last illness.

Josephine Butler accompanied her husband to Winchester in 1876 when he became Canon to the cathedral. She founded a home for prostitutes and women in need, as part of her campaigning against the indignities of the Contagious Diseases Acts of 1864, 1866 and 1869. The long fight, which caused her and her supporters to be mocked and insulted, harassed and harangued, saw the eventual repeal of the acts in 1886.

Annie Moberley, founder-principal of St Hugh's College, Oxford, was born in Winchester in 1846. Her father was headmaster of Winchester College, the second oldest established institution which dominates the life of the cathedral city. This was her home until her father was made Bishop of Salisbury in 1866.

WINDSOR, Berkshire [see Map 3, B1]   Windsor is dominated by the royal residence of Windsor Castle★, and it attracted many associated with court life, including **Mrs Delaney**. Towards the end of her life, Mrs Delaney, the letter writer and flower artist, had become a close friend of Queen Charlotte, and she eventually was granted a royal pension and a cottage in St Albans Street, Windsor, after 1768 – one of the 'many signal marks of grace and favour from their majesties' recorded on her memorial tablet in London. Her artwork, which latterly specialised in cut-paper flowers of great precision, was much admired by the Queen.

Caroline Herschel also became a royal pensioner. She had come to England from her native Hanover in Germany to act as housekeeper for her brother, William, in Bath. As her own hopes of a singing career receded, she became more involved with William's astronomical interests. In 1782 they moved from Bath to the Windsor area, which was more convenient after William Herschel's appointment as personal astronomer to George III. Caroline herself was awarded an annual stipend by the king for her services to sidereal astronomy. She and her brother recorded and identified over 2,500 stars and star systems new to science. Their home in Old Windsor, Gray Hall, no longer stands. Their main large telescope was erected at Datchet and they moved to Slough, to be nearer it, in 1786.

Mary Robinson was less fortunate in her association with royalty. She had attracted the attentions of the then Prince of Wales, later George IV, in her role as Perdita in *The Winter's Tale*. Her career as an actress ended when she became his mistress. Once he had tired of her, she earned a living by writing novels and poetry. Although the Prince had left his neglected mistress an annuity, she died in poverty in 1800, and was buried in the churchyard of Old Windsor.

The royal residence, Windsor Castle, overlooks the town, and several prominent royal women are connected with it and its precincts. St George's Chapel, which houses many tombs of royalty, contains the magnificent organ screen of Coade Stone, the material manufactured by the successful company of the two **Eleanor Coades**. **Jane Seymour**, the third and most cherished wife of Henry VIII, died shortly after the birth of her son in 1537. As a slab on the floor of the choir records, she is buried with the King in a vault below the Garter Chapel. Certainly the most spectacular monument is the tomb of **Princess Charlotte** in the Chiswick Chantry at the west end of

35   Queen Victoria's mausoleum at Windsor, Berkshire

the north aisle. The popular princess, heiress to the throne as daughter of George IV, had been married in 1816 to Prince Leopold of Saxe-Coburg. She died the following year in childbirth, and the marble monument shows her spirit leaving her death-bed with that of her baby, meeting the angels. Its extravagant design fully expresses the overwhelming grief of a nation. She was much loved, and greatly mourned by the British people, who longed for a steady, sober and peaceable sovereign and had looked forward to her reign expectantly but in vain.

Below the Castle are the gardens of Frogmore, another home of royalty. As a young princess, **Queen Victoria** would take breakfast here with her uncle in the little gothic summerhouse. She loved the house and its grounds, and had a mausoleum built here in the Italian style for the body of her beloved Albert. She laid the foundation stone in 1862. When she died in 1901, she was placed in the same tomb. The carved statues show them lying in state side by side under the mosaic dome. Some other members of the family are also buried here, but it is very much a Victorian memorial to the premier Victorians. It can only be visited on a handful of days in the year, but it is well worth waiting to see.

Constance Spry, whose skill in artistic flower arrangement gained the ultimate accolade of the commission to decorate Westminster Abbey for the coronation of Queen Elizabeth II, established both her home and her school at Winkfield Place, outside Windsor. Constance Spry excelled in both fine flower design and culinary skill, raising both to the status of art for the new generation.

WINSLADE, Devon [see Map 1, G3]   **Lady Mary Chudleigh**, writer and publisher of early feminist poems and letters, was born in Winslade in 1656 as Mary Lee. The village was her home until her unfortunate marriage in *c*. 1685. Her unhappiness as a wife caused her to reflect on the position of women, and her written ideas, published first in *The Ladies' Defence* [1701], have the depth of feeling drawn from personal experience.

WISBECH, Cambridgeshire [see Map 1, E4]   The river, now often silted up, was the life blood of this fenland town. The Nene is tidal at this point, and water transport made Wisbech into a prosperous inland port. At the time of **Octavia Hill**'s birth in 1838 at 7 South Brink, her father was a cornmerchant, but two years later his business failed. The house of her birth is marked with a plaque, and it stands, fittingly, across the river from the Peckover House, a historic property opened to the public by the National Trust, which she had helped to found.

WITHAM, Essex [see Map 1, F4]   From 1929 until her death in 1957 **Dorothy Sayers** lived at 24 Newland Street, formerly the headquarters of the Dorothy L. Sayers Historical and Literary Society. She also had a flat in London, but gave it up after the Second World War. In addition to writing detective fiction, she published plays and some translations, but she is best remembered for her character Lord Peter Wimsey.

WITHYHAM, Sussex [see Map 1, F4]   The chapel housing the remains of the Sackville family stands to the north of the chancel of St Michael and All Angels Church on the hill. One of the simpler memorials is the slate tablet inscribed 'In memory of V. Sackville-West, C.H., poet, whose ashes lie below this chapel. Only child of Lionel, Third Baron Sackville.' **Vita Sackville-West** had died at Sissinghurst in 1962. Although her writings included novels, gardening articles and other works, it was as a poet that she wished to be remembered and for which she was made a Companion of Honour.

WITLEY, Surrey [see Map 3, C1]   **Helen Allingham**, the painter of charming English cottages and their country gardens, found in this village and the surrounding hamlets the models and inspiration for her water-colours. From 1881 she lived at Sandhills, to the south, spending part of the year there and part in London. **George Eliot** also had a country home in this area, in Wormley. She had moved here with her companion George Lewes in the 1870s but he died soon afterwards.

WOKING, Surrey [see Map 3, C2]   **Eleanor Marx** was cremated at Woking crematorium after her suicide in Sydenham in 1898. She had never come to terms with her unsatisfactory relationship with Edward Aveling, with whom she had lived from 1884. Although her involvement in political life and social reform absorbed much of her time and energy, the importance to her of her selfish lover took a heavy toll. The energetic composer and suffragette **Dame Ethel Smyth** died at Coing in 1944. She is remembered for combining both her passions in the composition of 'The March of Women' which became the anthem of the suffragettes; it was a theme from her opera *The Boatswain's Mate* [1916]. Her other major compositions include *The Wreckers* [1906] and her *Symphony in D*. Her work for women did not stop when the vote was won. She persisted in her efforts to gain recognition and work for women professional musicians.

WOODSTOCK, Oxfordshire [see Map 1, F3]   Blenheim Palace★, still the residence of the Dukes of Marlborough, was granted to John Churchill, first Duke of Marlborough, by a grateful nation, after his successful military campaigns in the War of the Spanish Succession in Europe. His wife **Sarah Churchill** had greatly influenced his rise to power through her close friendship with Queen Anne. She also shaped Blenheim Palace, although Vanbrugh, the most admired architect of the day, received the commission. It was begun in 1704, but not finished until after the Duke's death, during which time Sarah had sacked Vanbrugh and completed the building herself. This was architecture on a grand scale, and cannot fail to impress. After Sarah's split with the Queen in 1707, she and her husband eventually went to live on the Continent, only returning to Blenheim on Anne's death in 1714. Widowed in 1722, she lived to be eighty-eight, but her last years were spent between her homes in London, St Albans and Windsor. Her remains are laid to rest in the vault of the chapel in Blenheim Palace, next to those of her husband, with an elaborate carved memorial.

Sarah's granddaughter, **Lady Diana Beauclerk**, born in 1734, was raised at the Palace. Surrounded by the splendid works of art here, she was inspired to be an artist herself. Her upbringing of wealth and privilege made this a practical proposition and she worked in several media, but her fellow artists, generally male, regarded her as an amateur.

A much later member of the Churchill family, **Jennie Churchill**, wife of Lord Randolph Churchill, inherited Sarah's position of influence in public life, continuing to be popular till her death. Born Jennie Jerome, daughter of a rich American, she brought an international flavour to the political salons which she hosted. Her elder son, Sir Winston Churchill, born at Blenheim in 1874, was later Prime Minister, and it is his association with the Palace which is most fully exploited for visitors. Widowed in 1895, her life took a new direction, as editor and publisher of a magazine. Although she was married twice more, she is buried in St Martin's Churchyard, in the nearby village of Bladon, with her first husband and her son Winston.

WOOLBEDING, Sussex [see Map 1, F4]   An early marriage to a feckless businessman would have meant starvation for her and her seven children, if **Charlotte Smith** had wasted her literary talents. Fortunately her first poems, *Elegiac Sonnets* [1784], were well received, and she persevered. However, it was inevitable that a man of her husband's disposition would try to take advantage of her income, so she decided to separate from him, renting Woolbeding House by the River Rother. She found that novels were more profitable than poetry, and she concentrated on these after their encouraging reception, particularly *Emmeline* [1788] and *The Manor House* [1793]. Having achieved a measure of independence, she lived in various parts of Surrey and Sussex continuing to write until her death in 1806.

WOOLER, Northumberland [see Map 2, C3]   **Josephine Butler** had been fighting all her days for improvements in women's lives. When she was no longer able to take an active role, she retired to Wooler in 1890 to be near her family. She continued to write but her subjects were now memoirs, her own, her family's, and those of the saint who was an inspiration to her, St Catherine of Siena. She died aged seventy-eight in 1906 in the small stone semi-detached house, now called Fallowfield, at 10 Queens Road. A plaque above the door announces that the local women's group had placed it there.

WORCESTER, Hereford and Worcestershire [see Map 1, F3]   **Hannah Snell** was an unconventional daughter of Worcester. She was born in 1723, her father working as a hosier in the city. She is thought to have grown up in Friar Street, opposite the Tudor House Museum. At seventeen she was orphaned and left to her own resources. She felt that there was no future for her in Worcester and so moved to Wapping. This was the first of several moves; her career in the army and navy took her even further afield, to war and a life of high adventure.

Worcester was also home for two women artists. **Mary Martha Sherwood** had spent eleven years in India before coming to live in Worcester in 1816. She already knew the area, having grown up in a nearby village. She had already published several works for children, mostly of a didactic and moralising nature. Her most famous book was almost a bible for Victorian children: *The History of the Fairchild Family* [1818-47], though largely unknown today. Her family, of five children from her marriage and three orphans from India, lived first in Lower Wick, on the west edge of the city; the house is long demolished, but the housing estate built in the former grounds bears the name Sherwood Lane. Latterly she lived in Britannia Square, a charming Regency development to the north of the city. She died in 1851, ending a prodigious literary output for younger readers.

Worcester's other novelist was **Mrs Henry Wood**. She was born Ellen Price in the city in 1814; her father worked in the glove trade, the main source of employment at the time. She was a semi-invalid, and was brought up by her grandmother at Danesbury House [now an antique shop], on the corner of City Walls Road. The house was rebuilt in 1889, but her stay is recorded on a plaque; it is no coincidence that her first novel was called *Danesbury House*, published in 1860. In 1836 she married and thereafter was rarely in Worcester. However, one of her better known works, *Mrs Halliburton's Troubles* [1862], is set among the glovers of Worcester, the Helstonleigh in the book. *East Lynne* [1861] brought her the most public notice and success. These two women writers are commemorated in the cathedral, together with the more recent local writer, Francis Brett Young, on a plaque in the north transept.

The city was also reputedly the birthplace of **Vesta Tilley**, the music-hall artist, in 1864, and another star of the stage, **Sarah Siddons**, is thought to have attended school here in the eighteenth century. Her only opportunities for formal schooling occurred when her acting family was engaged on a long run.

WORTH, Sussex [see Map 3, C3]   The Arabist, **Lady Anne Blunt**, was more often abroad on her Middle East travels than at Crabbett Park, her husband's home. They imported fine Arab horses and established the premier Arab stud at Crabbett. Her last years were spent in Egypt, where she died in 1917.

WRINGTON, Somerset [see Map 1, F3]   **Hannah More** spent twenty comparatively quiet years at Barley Wood, a large house in its own grounds up Long Lane on a hill overlooking the village. She left in 1832 after a dispute with her servants. However, she died the next year, and is buried in the parish churchyard. A signpost points to the large flat gravestone which also records the lives of her four sisters, who helped her in her education and religious work. There is a statue of her inside the porch of the church, showing the village's acknowledgment of her work and writings. She was one of the younger generation of Blue Stockings, making a living from her

36   Bust of Hannah More in the
Parish Church at Wrington, Somerset

pen, apparently with such success that her income from writing totalled a
remarkable £30,000.

WYE, Kent [see Map 1, F5]   The writer and adventurer **Aphra Behn** was
thought to have been baptised here in 1640, but there is now reason to
believe she was born in nearby Harbledown, and more likely baptised there.
At an early age she accompanied her parents to South America, where she
married a Dutch colonist in 1658. She was able to use her command of the
Dutch language when she returned to Europe as a widow. She acted as a spy
for Charles II in Holland, but was badly recompensed. She resorted to her
pen for her living, writing popular plays such as *The Rover* [1681] and *The
Lucky Chance* [1686], mocking the foibles and deceits of men, and also a
novel *Oronooko, or the History of the Royal Slave* [1688]. It is certain that
another woman who earned a living by her pen, the writer and historian
Catherine Macaulay, was born in Wye, in 1731. Her family lived at
Olantigh, Wye, and she received a good education at home. She began
work on her eight-volume history of England while still in her twenties.
She married in 1760, and the first volume of her history came out in 1763.
Her contemporary Mary Wollstonecraft appreciated Catherine Macaulay's
contribution to feminism, *Letters on Education* [1790], and was influenced by
it in writing her own *A Vindication of the Rights of Women* [1793].

Y Y

YORK, North Yorkshire [see Map 1, D4]   The first Christian Roman Empress is said to have been **Helena**. She was either wife or concubine, the records are not clear, of the Roman Emperor Constantius, and was known by the name Flavia Julia Helena. York was a key city in the Roman Province of Britannia, its Latin name being Eboracum. Constantius died at York in 306, being succeeded by her son Constantine the Great, who valued his mother's opinions. Together with her son she converted to Christianity in 312, and the new faith was adopted as the official religion of the Roman Empire. She was devout, setting off in 325 on a pilgrimage to the Holy Land. She was said to have found the true cross. She was later canonised. The Saxon scholar saint, **Hilda of Whitby**, is said to have been baptised in York in 627 on Easter Day. She also played a significant part in the history of Christianity in Britain. In 664 she hosted the Synod of Whitby, at which the decision was taken to adopt the Roman Catholic rather than the Celtic form of the religion in Britain, with far-reaching consequences for the cultural history of the British Isles.

As the second city in importance in the Anglican church, York has produced another saint, though it is the Roman Catholic Church which honoured her. In Elizabeth's reign, there was an anti-Catholic backlash after the reign of Mary Tudor, and **Margaret Clitheroe** had been brought up as a Catholic by her parents; it soon became difficult to practise openly as a Catholic. She had married a butcher in 1571, and came to live in the Shambles. Three years later she became fully active as a Catholic, and her home was used as a secret place for worship, and hiding place for vestments and religious objects. She served prison sentences for not attending the Anglican churches, but ultimately the hidden door in her house was discovered by the authorities and she was sentenced to death. She refused to implicate her friends or follow the established church and was thus martyred on Ouse Bridge in 1586. Her house is now a shrine – its structure little changed. It is an affecting haven of quiet in a part of the city which is ever busy with shoppers and tourists. Margaret Clitheroe was canonised by the Roman Catholic Church in 1970.

York also produced one of the original Blue Stockings, **Mrs Montagu**. She was born Elizabeth Robinson in 1720 in the Treasurer's House✧[NT], behind the Minster. Her father had bought the house in 1721, selling off first one half in 1725 and then the second half in 1728. As a young girl she could only have been fascinated by the splendid clock which is still ticking

201

in the Great Hall. More recently, **Barbara Ward**, born in 1914, was brought up in the city. As an economist who cared passionately that the natural environment was a resource to be tended, shared and valued, she was honoured in 1976 with a life peerage. Thus having a voice in the House of Lords, she expounded her views and demonstrated her deep commitment to sensible and humane economics.

Z z

ZENNOR, Cornwall [see Map 1, G2]   **Barbara Bodichon** the pioneering feminist and one of the founders of Girton College in Cambridge had a country home here as well as her rural retreat at Robertsbridge in Sussex. This coastal community would be a refreshing contrast to London where she was a leading light of the Langham Place Circle from the 1860s.

LONDON

London

As England's capital city, London's cultural, economic and diplomatic importance has ensured that very many significant women were born here, lived, worked or ruled here, died, were buried or commemorated here. Often they were born into highly-placed families whose court or business interests demanded a London base. Others married into such circles, where, in turn, they were able to make their own mark. Yet others were obliged to come to the capital for their own ends – for schooling or study, for publishers or patrons, to take their campaigns to the heart of Government or to take up, at last, seats which they had earned in the Houses of Parliament. The Blue Plaques which the local authorities have erected on many buildings to mark places of birth, residence, death or other associations are a starting point for anyone interested in key figures from the past who spent time in the city. As yet, there are far fewer women than men identified, but several women have been thus commemorated. There are many more potential sites for such plaques, blue or purple or whatever colour, and what follows indicates some of the associations which could be pursued.

Inevitably much has been published on London's history and former inhabitants. There are a number of publications which deal with the place of women in London's past which will also be relevant to readers of this book:

Feminist History: a sponsored walk, Anna Davin, Rights of Women, London, 1980.
Feminist History Walk, Spare Rib Diary, London, 1983.
In our Grandmothers' Footsteps, Jennifer Clarke and Joanna Parkin, Virago, London, 1984.
London: a Feminist Local History and Holiday Guide, Susan Evasdaughter, Susan Evasdaughter, London, 1983.
The Pink Plaque to London, Michael Elliman and Frederick Roll, GMP Publishing, London, 1986.

The entries here are listed according to the boroughs, the administrative districts which make up the Greater London area. Distinct areas are broadly listed within their boroughs as appropriate, and cross references are made in the Biographical Index. Reference to the maps will clarify the sites. Map 3 on page xxviii shows the Greater London area and indicates the location of the London Boroughs. Map 4 on page xxx covers Central London, and indicates streets mentioned in the entry for the *City of Westminster* and also parts of the *City of London* and the Borough of *Camden*. Map 5 [page xxxii] indicates the area of the Royal Borough of *Kensington and Chelsea* and parts of the Borough of *Hammersmith and Fulham* by street.

The London Boroughs:

Barking
Barnet
Bexley
Brent
Bromley
Camden
City of London
Croydon
Ealing
Enfield
Greenwich
Hackney
Hammersmith and Fulham
Haringey
Harrow
Havering
Hillingdon

Hounslow
Islington
Kensington and Chelsea
Kingston upon Thames
Lambeth
Lewisham
Merton
Newham
Redbridge
Richmond
Southwark
Sutton
Tower Hamlets
Waltham Forest
Wandsworth
Westminster

As yet not every borough has a substantial entry, but it is expected that many more women will be traced in due course.

37 The Friends' Meeting House, Ilford Road, Barking, where Elizabeth Fry worshipped

BARKING, *London Borough of* [see Map 3, B4] This borough on the north side of the Thames in the east includes Dagenham and Barking.

Barking had as its original focus the Abbey built by *c.* 675 for **Ethelburga** by her brother who at the time was Bishop of London. She was Abbess and after her death and burial there three years later, she became the patron saint. Among later pilgrims and benefactors was **Matilda**, Scottish born wife of Henry I. The Abbey's religious life ended in 1539 with the Dissolution of the monasteries. Little now remains: only foundations and the fifteenth-century brick gatehouse. The former market town, seven miles from old London, has built up into a busy cosmopolitan suburb.

The Quaker reformer, **Elizabeth Fry**, spent some of her married life at Plashet [now in the London Borough of Newham], which her husband's family lost when their business fortunes waned. The house no longer stands, but the site of the burial ground in Barking, where she is buried, can be visited on Ilford Road. This small walled grassed area bears a plaque recording her burial but no actual grave is marked. The former Friends' Meeting House on the opposite side of the road is now Gurdwara Singh Saria Sikh Temple and is well signposted from the central shopping area of Barking. Elizabeth died in 1845, after devoting her adult life to the reform of prison conditions in Britain and beyond. Her advice was sought and followed in several European countries. She supported improvements in hospitals and asylums. She found the strength and energy for her commitment to this work in her deeply-held Quaker beliefs.

BARNET, *London Borough of* [see Map 3, A3]   Lying north of the River Thames beyond Hampstead Heath, the borough includes the districts known as Finchley, Golders Green, Mill Hill, Hendon, Hadley Green and Totteridge. The intrepid **Celia Fiennes** has left us her comments on Barnet, which she passed through in *c.* 1697: Barnet 'seemes to be a very sharpe aire, its a large place and the houses are made to entertain the Company that comes to drink the waters, which certainly if they be at paines to go once and see would have but little stomach to drink them.' In the course of her travels throughout the country she became a connoisseur of spas and watering places, and in her view Barnet did not merit much praise.

Finchley This is the parliamentary constituency of **Margaret Thatcher**, Britain's first female Prime Minister. She was first elected to the seat in 1959, and has held it ever since. She became leader of the Conservative Party in 1974, having previously held ministerial office as Secretary of State for Education.

Golders Green This area remained rural until development in the early years of the present century. A large plot was bought in 1902 as the site for a major crematorium and adjacent memorial gardens. Three women performers number among the many people who have since been cremated here: **Kathleen Ferrier**, the beautiful singer whose career was cut short by cancer in 1953; **Nellie Wallace**, the music-hall artiste, who died in 1948; and the Russian ballerina **Anna Pavlova**. Anna Pavolva settled in London in 1912 and her home, Ivy House, was the base for her international career. The house survives as one of the buildings of the Manor House Hospital on North End Road, overlooking Hampstead Heath. She was still dancing when she died in 1931 aged forty-nine.

Others cremated here include **Mrs Acland**, founder of the Women's Cooperative Guild, who died in 1935; **Margaret Bondfield**, Labour politician and first woman Cabinet Minister, in 1953; **Anna Freud**, the child psychologist whose ashes are in a casket near those of her father in the Ernest George Mausloleum; **Mary Macarthur**, the trade union activist who died at her home in Golders Green's Woodstock Road in 1921; **Margaret MacDonald**, unstinting worker for women's welfare, who died in 1911; **Marie Stopes**, the controversial promoter of birth control clinics and counselling, who died of cancer in 1958.

Mill Hill The great traveller of the late seventeenth century, **Celia Fiennes**, belonged to a well-connected Wiltshire family. Her accounts of her *Great Journeys* to many parts of England and Wales, some of which started in London, remain an important source for landscape history. She is known to have had a house in Mill Hill, but as yet it remains untraced. She is known to have owned Highwood Hill in 1730, when it was registered as a place for dissenters to worship. Celia was brought up as a Nonconformist and on her travels was interested to learn about the welfare of other Nonconformists.

BEXLEY, *London Borough of* [see Map 3, B4]   South of the river, this is the easternmost London borough. Within it are Erith, Bexleyheath and Bexley.

There will be many women of note from the past from the area covered by this borough and as their history is uncovered, it can add to our knowledge. Certainly there are creative women in this area now.

Bexleyheath The Red House in Red House Lane was designed for **Jane Morris**, newly married to William Morris in 1859. Jane, who had been a model for several of the Pre-Raphaelite painters, worked on the interior furnishings with William. She proved to be a gifted embroiderer and designer, talents which she later passed to her daughter **May Morris**. May was born in the Red House in 1862, but the Morris family moved to live in central London in 1865. The Morris household included among its guests in the early 1860s **Effie Gray**, who modelled for and married two artist members of the Pre-Raphaelite Brethren, and the poet **Christina Rossetti**.

BRENT, *London Borough of* [see Map 3, B2]   This borough north of the river includes Wembley and Willesden within its boundaries.

Willesden Where the borough borders on Hammersmith to the south, two large cemeteries on Harrow Road, together known as Kensal Green Cemetery, provide the final resting places for several women of importance. The larger cemetery, All Souls, was a commercial venture, started in 1832 to supply a desperate need in London for adequate burial space. Among those buried here were: **James Miranda Barry**, **Lady Byron**, **Anna Jameson**, **Fanny Kemble**, **Jane Loudon**, **Adelaide Procter**, **Louisa Twining** and **Lucia Vestris**. Madame Vestris, the opera singer, was among the earliest people to be buried there, in 1836. James Barry was able to pursue a successful medical career in military service by passing herself off throughout her life as a man. Her true gender was only discovered on her death in 1865, and her gravestone reveals nothing, naming her as 'Dr. James Barry, Inspector General of Hospitals'. She had held senior ranks in several colonies including South Africa, the West Indies and Canada. Lady Byron, the philanthropist and social reformer, was buried here five years earlier, in 1860, in the central circle. She too had had a scientific mind, but did not follow James Barry's route to study. Her interest in mathematics, which her daughter Ada shared, earned her the bemusement of her family and the nickname of 'Princess of the Parallelograms' and 'Mathematical Medea' from her husband, Lord Byron, the latter name after he had left her. She is named as Lady Noel Byron on the front of the Reformers' Monument. This is a dark granite pillar which stands next to Robert Owen's obelisk. **Frances Wright**, the Scottish-American utopianist who died in the United States in 1852, is also named on the front. Several other women's names were added in 1907: **Josephine Butler**, **Elizabeth Fry**, **Sarah Martin**, **Barbara Bodichon**, **Frances Power Cobbe**, **Lydia Becker**, **Margaret Llewelyn Davies** and **Beatrice Webb**.

The art critic Anna Jameson who died in the same year as Lady Byron, had been her close friend until an unexplained breach in 1853. Together they had led discussions on women's status, challenging the accepted ideas of the day, and starting the forerunner of consciousness-raising groups as we know them today. She set an example to the 'Ladies of Langham Place' and propounded the establishment of the *English Woman's Journal*. Among her works is *Characteristics of Women* [1832], also known as *Shakespeare's Heroines*, which she dedicated to her friend Fanny Kemble, member of the famous acting family. Fanny Kemble, the actress and abolitionist, was one of her discussants and admirers. Her grave, which is shared with her brother Charles Kemble, is a plain low horizontal slab beside the South Branch Avenue. She survived until 1893, her career spanning the Atlantic Ocean. Jane Loudon's contribution was in garden design, but she also wrote novels. In partnership with her husband, she designed the layout and plantings for many London squares. Adelaide Procter, who died of tuberculosis in 1864 aged only thirty-nine, was an original member of the Langham Place Circle, and her poetry featured in the *English Woman's Journal*, along with articles on feminism. Louisa Twining was another remarkable woman. A philanthropist and reformer, she worked to improve first the workhouses and then women's lives in general, recognising that women could contribute enormously by election to local authorities where they could speak out for themselves. She died in 1912, her grave marked with a prone white cross. This cemetery has some wonderful monuments and epitaphs. It is rewarding to explore unguided but maps are available. It covers a huge area but bicycles and slowly driven cars are welcomed.

To the west is St Mary's Roman Catholic Cemetery where **Mary Seacole** and **Alice Meynell** were buried. Mary Seacole was a remarkable woman, born in 1805 and brought up in Jamaica, in the West Indies. She practised the healing arts there, using traditional skills and achieving greater success than formally trained medical staff attached to the British Army. Her autobiography, first published in 1857, describes her life there and in Panama before she volunteered her services in the Crimean War. Her exhausting work in nursing and supplying the many basic needs of officers and men in the Crimea from 1854 to 1856 has been overshadowed by the contribution of Florence Nightingale. Yet the enterprise, energy and determination of this lone black woman deserves wider recognition. Her death in 1881 is recorded on her gravestone, decorated with the trees of her native island. Her grave, lying on the west side of the main north-south avenue near the chapel, is one of the best maintained in the cemetery. It was recently re-lettered by the Jamaican Nurses Association of Jamaica.

In complete contrast is the grave of Alice Meynell. Its simple headstone lies flat in the north-east section for plots 1700-2700 and is inscribed 'Alice Meynell, Died 1922'. Alice Meynell's conversion to the Roman Catholic faith in 1872 informed all her poetry and the writings. She and her husband contributed to the leading journals of their day, playing active roles in intellectual circles, but on a modest hard-earned income.

Paddington Cemetery is at the eastern border of the borough, off Willesden Lane. **Emma Paterson** the first woman delegate to the Trades Union Congress was buried here in 1886. Her neat flat gravestone can be located by the newly-planted weeping cedar tree beside it. In her forty-two years she had organised women workers in a wide variety of trades – upholstery, bookbinding, millinery, dress-making, printing – all were new to the idea of trade unions for women. Her abiding legacy is the TUC Women's Committee.

Kingsbury Before this area in the north of the borough became so built up, there was a small aerodrome in Stag Lane. It was here that **Amy Johnson**, the pioneering airpilot, learned to fly in 1928. Her enthusiasm for flying drove her to qualify as a ground engineer in addition to gaining her pilot's licence in 1929; both were invaluable in her new career as an aviator. Her long-distance flights, many of which broke records, made her a public figure, even making her the subject of a popular song 'Amy, Wonderful Amy'. Her expertise and experience were in great demand in the Second World War, long after her important flights from Croydon in 1930. Although women were not allowed to fly in combat, they provided vital service in delivering planes within Britain. It was on one of these flights that Amy Johnson lost her life in 1941 over the Thames estuary. Her body was never found.

BROMLEY, *London Borough of* [see Map 3, B3] This southern borough used to be part of Kent, which it now borders. It includes Beckenham and Sundridge.

Beckenham The first home of **Diana Mulock** following her marriage to a publisher in 1865 was Chilchester Lodge, in Wickham Road. She is now better known by her married name **Mrs Craik**. Five years later she moved nearer Bromley to the Corner House, Shortlands, where she lived till her death in 1887. She was a member of the congregation of St Mary's Church, Shortlands, and is commemorated inside as author of *John Halifax, Gentleman* [1856], which was written before she came to these parts. She is buried in Keston, beneath a Celtic cross in the churchyard. Her books were widely read on both sides of the Atlantic. **Enid Blyton**, who wrote for a younger readership, was educated locally, at St Christopher's School for Girls, which may have been a source for her schoolgirl stories. She trained and practised as a teacher herself, and drew heavily on that experience in her prolific writing for young readers. Well over four hundred books, many short stories, articles and poems, all for children, were published. These include adventures of the *Famous Five*, the *Secret Seven* and the *Noddy* books. Her works have appeared in one hundred and sixty languages. Although current educational theory finds much to criticise in her works, they remain a popular introduction to reading for many children.

Bromley Another children's writer who spent time in the area was **Richmal Crompton**. She taught classics at Bromley Girls' High School in the 1920s but retired through ill health. She had already had some success with her school stories, especially the *Just William* adventures, and she was able to build on this for her future living.

Chislehurst The French Empress, **Eugénie**, lived in exile at Camden Place, now a golf club, from 1870, when she and Napoleon III left Paris, until 1881. She had a chapel built at the church here for the bodies of her husband and son, but they were all eventually laid to rest in Farnborough.

Sundridge The sculptor **Anne Damer** was buried in the church here with, as she had requested, the ashes of her favourite dog, her studio apron, her mallets, chisels and other artist's tools. She had chosen a medium unusual for the few professional women artists at that time, but when she died in 1828, in her sixtieth year, her work in marble had achieved wide recognition and respect.

CAMDEN, *London Borough of* [see Map 3, B3] The district known as Camden town is at the heart of this borough north of Regent's Park. It includes Hampstead, Hampstead Heath, Bloomsbury and Camden Town.

Bloomsbury The area surrounding the University and the British Museum probably claims the sisters **Virginia Woolf** and **Vanessa Bell** as its best known former residents. In the early years of this century they were central figures of the Bloomsbury Group. The Stephen sisters, as they then were, set up home with their two brothers in various Bloomsbury townhouses after the death of their father in 1904. Vanessa, the elder sister, had already been studying art at the Royal Academy Schools. From 1905-7 they lived at 46 Gordon Square, to which Vanessa returned in 1911, by then married to Clive Bell. From 1907-11 the Stephens lived at 29 Fitzroy Square, marked by a blue plaque which names 'Virginia Stephen, novelist and critic', as its former resident. The next centre for the Bloomsbury Group was 38 Brunswick Square [no longer standing], but Virginia married Leonard Woolf in 1912 and by then the Group had begun to establish an alternative focus in the Sussex countryside. However, the London roots remained. After a period in Richmond Virginia Woolf and her husband ran their Hogarth Press at 52 Tavistock Square [now the site of the Tavistock Hotel] from 1924 until 1939. Their next premises, 32 Mecklenburg Square, were bombed in 1940 so they moved the Press to safety in Letchworth.

There were other writers living in the area. From 1896 until 1911, **Dorothy Richardson**, writer in the stream of consciousness style, had attic lodgings at 7 Endsleigh Street, just north of Tavistock Square. From here she worked as a journalist and freelance translator. She did not begin her mammoth work *Pilgrimage* [1915-67] until two years later. Her contemporary, the poet **Charlotte Mew**, was born at 10 Doughty Street in 1869. When she was nineteen, her family moved to the centre of Bloomsbury, to 9 Gordon Street, which was her home for the rest of her life. It was here that she committed suicide in 1928, grieving on the death of her sister. Women had always been important to her, and she had been extremely close to her sister. After a period of obscurity her poetry is now finding a new readership.

Earlier residents of Bedford Square include **Agnes Strickland**, whose literary output began with poetry but who was most successful as an historian of women; and **Lady Ottoline Morrell**, who hosted literary figures and pacifists at number 44, her London home, from 1908 and throughout the First World War. **Frances Trollope** was the author of novels and travel books, most notably *Domestic Manners of the Americans* [1832] which affronted the Americans, amused the British and started her on a hugely successful career as a writer. She spent her courtship and early married life in two houses in Keppel Street, until her husband's financial mismanagement necessitated a move to Harrow in 1818. **Mary Wollstone-craft**, the fiercely independent feminist writer, lived in Store Street in 1792, where she published *A Vindication of the Rights of Woman*, until she died in 1797. Store Street's tradition of feminist publishing continued when Pandora Press began there in 1982.

Emily Faithfull was not only a publisher but also a printer. In 1860 she set up the Victoria Press at 9 Great Coram Street. This was a brave venture, where she employed and trained women as printers. She was putting into action the aims of an organisation to which she belonged, the Society for Promoting the Employment of Women, and ignoring the hostility of male printers. Here she produced the *English Woman's Journal*, Britain's first feminist periodical, and later other tracts and journals concerned with women's issues. By June 1862 she was awarded the title Printer and Publisher in Ordinary to Her Majesty, by Royal Warrant.

Bloomsbury was also the site of many departments and colleges of London University. The novelist **Amelia Blandford Edwards** had been captivated by Egypt during a visit there in 1873. Thereafter she devoted her efforts to the study of Egyptian antiquities and founded the Egyptian Exploration Fund. She supported academic scholarship in this new field, and on her death in 1892 left her library and collection to University College, together with funds to establish a chair of Egyptology. In Gower Street, the Petrie Museum of Egyptian Archaeology★, named after her protégé who was first to hold the chair, shows the excavated results of her backing, now academically respectable. **Kathleen Lonsdale** studied physics as an undergraduate at Bedford College with such brilliant results that a research career was inevitable. Her studies in X-ray crystallography, mostly carried out at University College, earned her the respect of her fellow scientists and in 1945 she became the first woman to be awarded Fellowship of the Royal Society. Two other members of the University's teaching staff at the period when women were establishing themselves as serious academics were **Helen Waddell**, the medievalist, whose home was in Primrose Hill Road, north of Regent's Park, and **Marie Stopes**, a London graduate. Although better known for her campaign to make birth control advice freely available to women, Marie Stopes began her career as a lecturer in palaeontology. Marie Stopes House, at 108 Whitfield Street, now offers help and information in all matters concerning women's health, but in 1925 it was a very controversial birth control clinic. Marie Stopes had opened her first centre, the Mothers' Clinic for Birth Control, in 1920. She had recognised that the opportunity for women to control the number of their pregnancies would enable them to decide how best to use their energies and, if necessary, limit the size of their families. This was such a startling innovation that initially only married women were offered access to the information and counselling service.

The Slade School of Art, also part of University College London, was where several significant artists received their training. **Gwen John** spent four years here from 1895, before spending the rest of her life in France. **Dora Carrington** studied art at the Slade from 1910 until 1913. **Kate Greenaway**, **Ethel Walker**, **Paule Vézelay**, **Elsie Henderson** and **Margaret Gere** were other former students. **Eileen Gray**, the designer, who later specialised in lacquer work, had trained here in traditional media. Like Gwen John, most of her career was spent in France, where she branched out into furniture design, interior decoration and architecture. **Elisabeth Whitworth Scott** took her architectural training at the schools of the Architectural Association in the early 1920s.

Other graduates of the university include the novelist **Phyllis Bentley** and the suffragette martyr **Emily Wilding Davison**, who took a first class degree in mathematics. **Christina Rossetti**, the poet, was the daughter of a professor of Italian at the university. After ill health obliged him to retire, Christina and her mother tried to make an income by opening a school in Camden Town, but the venture failed. Towards the end of her life, she returned to Bloomsbury. Her last years, from 1876 until her death in 1894, were spent at 30 Torrington Square, as recorded on an elaborate bronze plaque on the building. *Goblin Market and Other Poems* [1862] and *The Prince's Progress and Other Poems* [1866] show her skill with words and verse forms, often aimed at younger readers.

Although she was a strong opponent of women's suffrage, **Mrs Humphrey Ward** worked hard to improve women's lives. In 1890 she established University Hall in Gordon Square as a meeting place for working women and men. It grew to include a play-centre and a school for invalid children. The enterprise developed into a settlement and was provided by the University with a splendid purpose-built art nouveau building in Tavistock Place. After her death in 1920 it was renamed the Mary Ward Centre. Although most often remembered as author of *Marcella* [1894] and *Helbeck of Bannisdale* [1898], Mrs Humphrey Ward was president of the Anti-Suffrage League from 1908, convinced that women's lives could be changed without the vote. She felt that women could make the greatest impact in their own homes, setting examples to the next generations, and that the exposure to public life which would come with enfranchisement would only dilute their influence, with adverse consequences. Her London home from 1881 until 1891 was at 61 Russell Square, since superseded by the Imperial Hotel.

The Pankhurst family home, further round the Square, has met a similar fate. The Votes for Women movement made its presence forcefully felt in the capital, where many of its key figures had homes. **Mrs Emmeline Pankhurst** rented a large house, 8 Russell Square [now part of the Russell Hotel], on the corner of Bernard Street, from 1888. According to **Sylvia Pankhurst**: 'The house was soon to be a centre for many gatherings, of Socialists, Fabians, Anarchists, Suffragists, Free Thinkers, Radicals and Humanitarians of all schools.' In her history of the struggle for women's enfranchisement, *The Suffrage Movement* [1931], she describes growing up there with her sisters **Christabel Pankhurst** and **Adela Pankhurst**. From earliest childhood, all three were involved in their parents' political campaigns, but they enjoyed the same illicit fun and games as other children, playing in the gardens in the centre of the Square to let off steam. Their parents' friends and guests included **Harriet Stanton Blatch**, **Annie Besant** and the exiled French communard **Louise Michel**, who in 1866 had been a founder of France's first feminist organisation, the 'Société Pour la Revendication des Droits de la Femme'. By 1893 the combined effects of Mrs Pankhurst's ailing business venture, Emerson and Company, an interior decorating shop, and the high cost of living in London obliged the Pankhursts to return to the north.

Millicent Garrett Fawcett was another leader of the campaign for women's votes who lived in this part of London. Her home was at 2 Gower Street. Here she died in 1929 after more than sixty years working for improvements in women's situation. Indeed she claimed to have been a woman suffragist from her cradle. An original member of the London Society for Women's Suffrage of 1867, she worked also hard for the Married Women's Property Act of 1882. It was her belief that 'men cannot be truly free so long as women are held in political subjection'. She did not agree with the militant tactics of the Pankhursts' Women's Social and Political Union. Nonetheless she was wholly committed to the issue of suffrage for women, holding the presidency of the National Union of Women's Suffrage Societies from 1897-1918, and living to see extension of the franchise to all women over twenty-one in 1928. Her achievements are commemorated in the Fawcett Library, the most significant resource for the study of women's history in Britain. In addition to its large book and journal holdings, it has an important archival collection of printed ephemera and other material relating to the women's movement since 1572, all of which can be consulted in the City of London Polytechnic, Old Castle Street, in the City of London. The London Society for Women's Suffrage still campaigns for women's rights under the name of the Fawcett Society, which it adopted in 1953.

From 1909 there was another nest of suffrage workers nearby at 51 Gordon Square, which a blue plaque identifies as the home of Lytton Strachey. However, his mother **Lady Jane Strachey**, his sister **Philippa Strachey** and his American sister-in-law **Ray Strachey** were all active campaigners for the Cause. Ray Strachey worked very closely with Millicent Garrett Fawcett, later writing her biography, *Millicent Garrett Fawcett* [1931] and a history of the modern women's movement *The Cause* [1928].

Over the centuries Gower Street has been the home of many women active in various other fields. **Sarah Siddons** resided here for five years from 1784, by now an established actress with a devoted London following. **Margaret Bondfield** and **Mary Macarthur** shared a flat here from 1903. Margaret Bondfield had already begun her full-time commitment to trade unionism by the time Mary Macarthur joined her from Scotland to become secretary of the Women's Trades Union Congress League and founder of the National Federation of Women Workers. In Congress House, Great Russell Street, **Emma Paterson**, first female delegate to the Trades Union Congress in 1875, is commemorated by a wooden tablet; the sycamore wood came from the tree in Dorset under which the Tolpuddle Martyrs first proposed organising a union of workers. **Gertrude Tuckwell** is also remembered here. She was secretary of the Women's TUC League from 1893 until 1903 and active for over thirty years in union work. The Gertrude Tuckwell collection of papers and pamphlets can be consulted here by appointment.

The educational pioneer **Frances Buss** opened a school with her mother in Kentish Town in 1845. She moved this to Camden Town in 1850. It was to become the North London Collegiate School, still one of London's most respected schools for all aspects of girls' education. She devoted her life to the school, which has since moved further north in London, and the cause of women's education. She was a contemporary of **Dorothea Beale** with whom she studied at Queen's College in Westminster. Their names are always linked as the leaders of the movement for an academic training for girls.

Hampstead Now a much sought after place for London homes, it was once a country village by the famous heath. **Katherine Mansfield** lived at 17 East Heath Road, looking out across the Heath. Sadly the problems caused to her health by tuberculosis meant that she had to spend much of her time abroad, during which she made plans for this home. However, her death in France in 1923, at the age of thirty-four, ended her short but very influential literary life. **Flora Mayor**, who published her novels as F. M. Mayor, lived longer but, until recently, her literary reputation has been, undeservedly, eclipsed. Her family home was in Kingston upon Thames but she and her much-loved twin sister lived from 1927 at 7 East Heath Road. Flora died there in 1932, and her sister invited Flora's friend from student days, the pacifist **Mary Sheepshanks**, to move into Flora's rooms, but the arrangement soon ended, by mutual agreement.

They were by no means the only women writers to live in Hampstead. **Joanna Baillie** had moved to London from Scotland in 1784. She had

38   Bolton House, Windmill Hill, Hampstead: the home of Joanna Baillie

started to write seriously after her father's death in 1778. She brought her mother and sister to be near her brother, but the income from her own writing was their main support. Her poetry and plays, including the group published as *Plays on the Passions* [1798], proved very popular. She settled in Hampstead in 1802 and in 1806 established her base at Bolton House, a fine brick bulding up Windmill Hill on a little green, which became a meeting place for many key figures: **Maria Edgeworth**, **Mary Somerville**, William Wordsworth and Sir Walter Scott. The village 'feel' is still strong here and Joanna Baillie would easily recognise it today. She died there in 1851 and is buried in the graveyard of St John's, the parish church. Her tabletop grave is surrounded by railings, standing at the south-east of the church. A later writer was also buried in the parish churchyard: **May Sinclair**, who died in 1946 after a prolific career which produced poetry and prose, fiction and works of criticism. *The Three Sisters* [1914], *The Tree of Heaven* [1917], *Mary Olivier: a Life* [1919] and *The Life and Death of Harriett Frean* [1922] are among her better-known novels.

The street leading from Hampstead High Street to the church is Church Row. When **Anna Barbauld**, who was later to join Joanna Baillie's circle, returned from an extended stay on the Continent, she made her home at number 8. Here she wrote pamphlets, literary criticism and educational works, moving to Stoke Newington in 1802. A few doors along, at 18, lived her niece and biographer, **Lucy Aikin**, another author who concentrated on works of history. In addition to her *Memoirs of Mrs Barbauld* [1825], she wrote *Epistles on Women* [1810]. She was very close to Joanna Baillie and was buried next to her in the parish churchyard. She died in 1864, in her eighty-fourth year. **Mary Webb**, the Shropshire novelist and poet, was never happy during her stay in London; she lived from 1921 at 12 Hampstead Grove. She returned to her home county whenever she could. She did manage to do some writing at Grove Cottages, and her best known work, *Precious Bane* [1924], was largely written here in 1923.

Down the hill from the church on the west runs the road called Frognal. The very popular singer **Kathleen Ferrier** lived at number 97, for the last ten years of her life. She died of cancer in 1953 after a singing career which had started late but won many affectionate admirers. From 1885 another much loved character, **Kate Greenaway**, whose enchanting illustrations continue to feature in children's books, lived in the house designed for her by the architect Norman Shaw. With its tall chimneys, hanging tiles and leaded lights, it has recently been refurbished, and can be distinguished by a blue plaque. She died here, at 39 Frognal, in 1901 and is buried in Hampstead Cemetery. Hampstead Cemetery in Fortune Green Road is also the last resting place of **Gladys Cooper**, who died in 1971. Her career as an actress lasted sixty-six years on stage and later in films. She also managed the Playhouse Theatre. Her long career was crowned by her creation as a Dame of the British Empire in 1967.

East of the centre of Hampstead village Downshire Hill runs down from East Heath Road. **Hilda Carline** was born into an artistic household, living at 47 Downshire Hill. Her two sisters, Anne and Nancy, were also artists, as was their father George Carline. Hilda's unorthodox marriage to her fellow-artist Stanley Spencer – she lived with him at Cookham – brought her little lasting happiness. The sculptor **Barbara Hepworth** practised her art at 7 Mall Studios in 1928. Hampstead had already attracted several artists as residents. Barbara Hepworth lived here with her first husband John Skeaping, and after 1931 with her second Ben Nicolson. In 1939 she evacuated with her children to Cornwall and that county became her home until her death in 1975. The South African feminist writer, **Olive Schreiner**, lived briefly at 8 Downshire Hill, another neat early nineteenth-century building. Parliament Hill, the southern part of the public area of Hampstead Heath, stands nearby, overlooking London. It was saved as an open space in 1899 by the fund-raising efforts of **Octavia Hill**, as one of her schemes to make the country air more readily available to poor inner city dwellers. It is one of several spots traditionally said to be the burial place of the Celtic leader **Boudicca**. Although she inflicted defeats on the Roman defenders of Colchester, St Albans and London in AD 60 and 61, the superior might of the Roman army overcame her forces in 62, some-where north of London. She committed suicide, preferring death to slavery.

Still nearer to the city centre stands **Anna Freud**'s home, at 20 Maresfield Gardens. The plaque on the building records that her father Sigmund Freud spent his last year here, but it was her home from their arrival in England from Austria in 1938 until her death in 1982. From her twenties she had been her father's indispensable partner; in her own right she was a first-class psychoanalyst, specialising in children's behaviour. As Jews, they soon realised the danger of continuing their work in Vienna, and their move to England was a necessary wrench. From *c*. 1939 she worked at and eventually ran the Hampstead Child Therapy clinic. She kept much of her home as it was when her adored father died. It is now open to visitors as the Freud Museum★, charting her considerable contribution to her field as well as her father's contribution to his. A wall of impressive framed certificates awarded by learned bodies is testimony that her own very significant contributions received due recognition from her academic and professional colleagues. The memorabilia also show her home life and interests, including her loom. In parallel Netherhall Gardens another lifelong partnership began. This was where **Beatrice Webb**, Fabian and chronicler of social conditions, started her married life with fellow worker Sidney Webb in 1892. They went on to found the London School of Economics and the influential journal, the *New Statesman*.

Swiss Cottage Nearer central London than Hampstead, at 7 Harley Road, the contralto **Clara Butt** lived from 1901, having married the baritone Kenneth Rumford the previous year. This was their home until 1929. Clara Butt had made her debut in London when she was sixteen and stayed on for further study at the Royal College of Music. Her powerful voice was legendary, and she gave recitals throughout Britain. She retired to the country at Wallingford for her last years.

CITY OF LONDON [see Map 3, B3]   The square mile of central London which is called the City is now the centre of the banking and investment world. It includes the earliest areas of settlement in London's history, and despite the dominance of multi-storey office developments, many historic churches and buildings survive today, some having already withstood the devastation of the Great Fire of 1666. The history of London is well explained in the Museum of London★ in London Wall, and it is worth noting that the museum houses the Suffragette Fellowship Collection which can be consulted by appointment. Some material from this collection is on permanent display – badges, sashes, campaigning literature and photographs. The Fawcett Library is also in the City, maintained in the City of London Polytechnic, Old Castle Street. Its subject matter is the women's movement from the sixteenth century to the present.

Temple Bar is the western boundary of the City. Two impressive columns divide the Strand, in Westminster, from Fleet Street in the City. This main route linking the commercial and government centres of the capital narrows to become Fleet Street, long associated with journalism and the press. *Time and Tide* was one of the most interesting publishing ventures established in Fleet Street. It was founded at 88 Fleet Street in 1920 by a group of seven women. These were three former schoolfriends, **Mrs Chalmers-Watson**, **Lady Rhondda** and **Helen Archdale**, together with **Helen Gwynne-Vaughan**, Mrs H. B. Irving, Christine Maguire and **Elizabeth Robins**, author of the play *Votes for Women* [1907]. They were concerned that women should not become complacent because the post-war government had granted voting rights to women of thirty years and over. The work of the suffrage movement was incomplete, and feminist issues must still be aired and striven for. The new voters were to have an independent weekly which would inform them of concerns central to women's lives, expressing the opinions of differing political lines. Contributors to this influential feminist journal included **Rebecca West**, **Vera Brittain** and **Winifred Holtby**, all women prepared to speak out and defend their feminist views. The story of the journal and its contributors is told with extracts in *Time and Tide Wait for No Man* [Dale Spender, Pandora Press, London, 1984].

In the City's early history, one woman defended herself and her people in blood. Severe damage was inflicted on the embryonic Roman settlement, Londinium, in AD 61 by the determined Celtic queen **Boudicca**. She led her warriors from their traditional tribal territory in East Anglia to pursue the colonising Romans. The invaders did not respect the rights of her daughters to inherit their dead father's realm, and in fact the Romans treated her, her family and her people, the Iceni, appallingly. Her revenge was fierce, and after Colchester and St Albans, London was her next target. Archaeological excavations in the City have uncovered evidence of burning which may well be her legacy.

Equally independent in spirit and deeds was **Mary Frith**, better known today as **Moll Cutpurse**. She became something of a folk heroine in her own lifetime after her exploits as thief and highwaywoman were immortalised in *The Roaring Girl*, a comedy written in 1611 by Thomas Middleton, still revived from time to time. She is said to have been born in the Barbican, Aldgate, one of the fortified gateways to the medieval city, into a shoemaker's family, but she found the attractions of crime irresistible. After a spell in Newgate Prison, now the site of the Central Criminal Court on the corner of Newgate Street and Old Bailey, she latterly ran a pawn shop in Fleet Street. Here she made a comfortable income, dying in 1659 aged *c*. 75. She is supposedly buried in St Bride's at the east end of Fleet Street. The church was remodelled by Sir Christopher Wren in the 1670s, and damaged by bombs in the Second World War. St Bride's is the church of the printing, publishing and newspaper industries and several of the seats have dedications to women, including **Octavia Hill**, the social reformer, and the Society of Women Writers and Journalists, which was founded in 1894. There is also a terracotta head of a young girl. This represents Virginia Dare, who was the first English child to be born in North America. Her parents had been parishioners of St Brides before leaving for the new colonies. Their daughter was born in Virginia in 1587.

Moll Frith's near-contemporary, **Mary Sidney**, later Countess of Pembroke, was born into quite different circumstances. Her marriage to Henry Herbert, Earl of Pembroke, in 1577 brought her further advantages than those she already had from her own privileged upbringing. One of her properties was Crosby Place, where she was living in 1609. As a wealthy widow by 1590 she was in a position to sponsor writers and involve herself in her own literary projects. She died here of smallpox in 1621. Most of Crosby Place has been demolished, but architectural features have been incorporated in the premises of the British Federation of University Women, a fitting tribute to a very learned woman. Another literary contemporary, **Katherine Philips**, lived in Fleet Street, where she died of smallpox in 1664. She spent half her life in London and half in Wales. It was in Wales that she wrote poetry with her circle of women friends. Their name for her was 'Matchless Orinda'. Her collected poems were published in 1667, although some had appeared in print in her lifetime.

In the medieval and early modern period the Guildhall★ was the centre of civic government for the City. Trade and other practices were regulated from here as was the controlling of gold and silversmithing. **Anne Taunqueray**, a silversmith of Huguenot stock, was active in the City in the 1720s and 1730s. **Hester Bateman**, another fine craftswoman in silver, registered her own hallmark in 1774. Their work still attracts interest. The

Guildhall was also the setting for major trials. The Protestant martyr **Anne Askew** was tried here in 1546. **Lady Jane Grey** was sentenced at the Guildhall in 1553 for threatening the stability of the kingdom. The sentence was carried out the next year.

Two centuries later in 1813, Newgate Prison, where conditions were always dire, was visited by **Elizabeth Fry**. Despite bringing up a large family of her own, she had the energy to play a leading role in the Quaker community. Coming from a prominent Norfolk family, she had married a Quaker merchant in 1800 and for several years lived with him in Mildred's Court, Poultry – the continuation east of Cheapside. A plaque marks the site of the premises, which also housed the Fry family's tea, coffee and spice warehouse. Her strong reaction to the miserable unhygienic conditions inside Newgate Prison, long since demolished but remembered in Newgate Street, spurred her to begin her life's work in prison reform. She organised education for children in prison, paid work for women prisoners and religious discussions and readings. Her commitment to prison reform and other humanitarian causes took her to all parts of Britain, and to continental Europe, where in Germany she became involved in nursing training. Newgate had been the public hanging place from 1783. A victim of its predecessor, **Elizabeth Barton**, was buried in 1534 in Christ Church Greyfriars, the Newgate Street church which was razed to the ground in the Great Fire of 1666.

Like the Fry family, many Nonconformists living in the City were involved in business enterprises. A burial ground for these Dissenters was created in Bunhill Fields, now between Bunhill Row and City Road. **Eleanor Coade**, who died in 1796, and her daughter and partner in their successful reconstituted stone concern, also **Eleanor Coade**, who died twenty-five years later, were both buried there. Many public buildings in London have decorative features in Coadestone. **Susanna Wesley**, who towards the end of her life lived with her son John, is one of the few to whom a monument remains. She died in 1742, justly called the 'Mother of Methodism'. She had brought up twenty children, including the key figures in the Methodist movement. Her memorial stands under the trees, off City Road, in the company of male religious and literary figures. At 47 City Road, now called Wesley's House★, a collection of Wesleyana pays tribute to the early Methodists.

The City also includes two central institutions of the English legal world. The two Inns of Court standing within the square mile are the Inner Temple and the Middle Temple. The male control of the training and practice of law ensured the exclusion of women until relatively recently. Women were admitted in 1919; the first woman to be called to the Bar was **Ivy Williams**, in 1922. However, she preferred to extend women's opportunities by teaching law at Oxford University, so Helena Normanton became the first woman to practise as a barrister, being called later the same year. This does not mean that there were no women in this part of the City. **Mary Lamb** was baptised in the Temple Church, to the south of Fleet Street, in 1764.

She spent her early childhood nearby at 2 Crown Office Row. The plaque which marks the building names her brother with whom she later collaborated on their best-loved work *Tales from Shakespeare* [1807]. They were obliged to move to Holborn in 1795.

Doughty Street is in the north-west corner of the City, just off Gray's Inn Road. Its most famous resident was Charles Dickens, whose home at number 48 for just two and a half years has been lovingly preserved. On the other hand **Charlotte Mew**'s much longer association with number 10 has been completely ignored. This New Georgian poet was born here in 1869 and did not leave until 1888, when her family moved to Gordon Street. Her poetry is now receiving renewed attention; it is only right that her former home should receive some recognition.

Most of the wharves have gone from the City's Thames waterfront, but their names remain in street names and in one church. St Benet's Paul Wharf, in Upper Thames Street, provided the last resting place for **Delarivier Manley**. She led an unconventional life for a woman of her times, pursuing a successful career in journalism, editing *The Examiner* after Swift in 1711. It was then a Tory paper. Her well-observed and socially critical novels, such as *The New Atalantis* [1709], and plays were uncomfortably thinly disguised in their commentary on current politics and personalities, but she managed to avoid libel suits. In her own life she openly lived with her lovers, having learned early that marriage did not always provide the security claimed for it. She died in 1724, in her early fifties, while living with her last lover, her publisher, at his house on Lambeth Hill.

She certainly would have been in sympathy with the struggle for women's suffrage of two centuries later. One of its most poignant and emotional gatherings was the funeral in 1913 of **Emily Wilding Davison**. Always in the forefront of any dangerous action, this suffragette martyr died as a result of throwing herself under the King's horse at the Derby, a horseracing highlight of the social calendar. Thousands of women, dressed in black or purple or white, bearing purple irises, blood-red peonie roses and laurel wreaths, accompanied the coffin to St George's Church, Hart Street, near Fenchurch Street Station, and then to King's Cross Station. All the suffrage societies were represented, many trade union organisations, colleges, and people from all walks of life. Her grave in the parish churchyard in Morpeth, Northumberland, bears the inscription 'Deeds, not words', the only possible epitaph for this woman whose sacrifice still moves even the uncommitted. One of the more active Victorian feminists, **Emily Faithfull**, started her own printing and publishing venture, the Victoria Press, in 1860. By 1862 it expanded and she moved it to 83 Farringdon Street, using a steam printing press. She employed, trained and cared for her women employees, and considered that printing and bookbinding were fine trades for women. She published a variety of periodicals: *Victoria Magazine*, *West London Express*, *Work and Women* as well as printing the *English Woman's Journal* for the Langham Place Group. She also wrote herself. In 1874 she founded the Women's Printing Society with the trade unionist **Emma Paterson** who learned printing here.

The early importance of the City is manifest in William the Conqueror's fortification, the Tower of London★. Guarding the south-east corner of the walled town, it commands views of the river traffic and crossings as well as the surrounding area, now densely built up. The complex increased in size and defensive strength in the succeeding reigns, and it has been the scene of many key incidents in British history. Not a few have involved women.

The Tower of London has served most notoriously as a prison for individuals who were deemed to threaten the safety of the Realm. Women prisoners included royalty, and the best known perhaps are two who incurred the displeasure of Henry VIII, himself frustrated by his lack of a male heir. Having cut off his people from the Roman Catholic Church in order to divorce his first wife, Henry then imprisoned his second wife, **Anne Boleyn**, in the Tower having charged her with various, probably invented, infidelities. She was condemned to die along with members of her family and supposed lovers. Before her execution Henry had their marriage dissolved. Generally, convicted prisoners were executed beyond the walls on Tower Hill as a public example, but special dispensation permitted certain aristocrats to die in the Tower. The small green marks the place where Anne Boleyn was executed in 1536, and where six years later **Catherine Howard** met the same fate. She was Henry's fifth wife, and, like her predecessor and cousin Anne Boleyn, she too failed to produce a male heir. Similar charges of infidelity were brought against her and after less than two years of marriage she was also executed. Their remains are buried in the church beside the green, St Peter ad Vincula, but there are conflicting rumours about Anne's heart, said to be buried both at East Horndon in Essex and near Thetford in Norfolk.

One of Henry's opponents, originally a valued advisor and friend, was Thomas More. His conscience would not allow him to support Henry's first divorce action, and in 1535 he paid the price of the king's displeasure with his head. His daughter, **Margaret Roper**, defied the king by having her father's head taken down from where it had been publicly exhibited in order to arrange a fitting burial. She was imprisoned in the Tower when Henry found out, but she was released and lived out her days in peace.

Henry had also felt threatened by a challenge to his legal authority in the matter of ending his first marriage from an unexpected source. The **Holy Maid of Kent**, as **Elizabeth Barton** became known, did not have the education or social privileges which were taken for granted in most of Henry's supporters and critics. She was from a very humble background in Kent but religious ardour, speaking prophecies while in trances and supposed healing powers brought her to the attention of powerful figures who encouraged her to speak out against the king's attempts to dissolve his first marriage. She became a political pawn, but on the losing side. In 1534 she was executed outside the Tower at the Tyburn, with those who had tried to use her for their own ends.

Henry VIII's Tudor successors also used the Tower for containing women considered as threats to the Crown. **Mary I** had **Lady Jane Grey**, the tragic 'Nine Days Queen', imprisoned after Lady Jane's ambitious relatives had put her forward as a claimant to the English throne in 1553. Although Mary released her, she was soon back inside as a prisoner, and this time beheaded in 1554 with the men who had expected to gain by her accession. Lady Jane is buried in St Peter ad Vincula. Mary also briefly had her sister **Elizabeth** interned here, viewing her and her adherence to their father's protestant church, as potentially unsettling. Once on the throne herself, Elizabeth saw rivals to her own power. **Elizabeth Talbot**, also known as **Bess of Hardwick**, spent part of 1547-8 inside the Tower, having incurred the Queen's displeasure by arranging a tactical marriage for one of her daughters. In 1610, the child of that union, **Arabella Stuart**, whose parentage endowed her with claims, seemingly plausible, to both the Scottish and English thrones, paid the price of entering into a marriage guaranteed to anger the sovereign, now James VI of Scotland and I of England. An abortive attempt to escape abroad landed her in the Tower, where after four years of imprisonment, she died in 1615.

Dynastic threats from the Stuarts continued into the middle of the eighteenth century. The part played by the Scottish heroine **Flora MacDonald** in enabling Charles Edward Stuart to escape capture in 1746 was discovered, and at the age of twenty-five Flora MacDonald found her first experience of England an unpleasant one. She was imprisoned in the Tower, but soon released in 1747 when the Hanoverian monarchy declared a general amnesty for all Stuart sympathisers.

Some women started, rather than ended their lives in the Tower of London. The garrison and officials often had wives and families living with them within the walls. **Lucy Hutchinson** was born within the Tower in 1620 when her father, Sir Allen Apsley, was its lieutenant. It was the sort of building complex she was to know intimately in adult life when she was married to the Governor of Nottingham Castle.

There have, of course, been many other women of importance associated with the City. The publications of **Isabella Beeton** have, both directly and indirectly, touched the lives of several generations of Britons, through the many editions of *Mrs Beeton's Book of Household Management* [1861]. Isabella Beeton was born in Milk Street above her father's linen store in 1836, but she grew up in Epsom. The actress **Mary Betterton**, who guided the career of **Anne Oldfield**, married her fellow-actor Thomas Betterton from Cripplegate in 1662. In the same area, the cabinet-maker **Anne Hepplewhite** ran the business of designing and making fine furniture which remains associated not with her but her husband.

Holborn To the north-west of Temple Bar lies the road called Holborn, which gives its name to this district. **Ann Radcliffe**, author of gothic novels popular in Jane Austen's day, was born in 1764 at 19 Holborn. This was her home until her parents moved to Bath in 1771. **Dorothy Osborne**, whose letters describe a devoted courtship in the troubled times of the English Civil War, finally married William Temple in 1654 at the church of St Giles-in-the-Field, in St Giles High Street. The marriage was a long and happy one, clearly worth the six years of waiting. **Margaret MacDonald**'s marriage to the future Labour Prime Minister, Ramsay MacDonald, was equally successful but cut short by her early death in 1911. While living at 3 Lincoln's Inn Fields she brought up six children of her own, actively supported her husband's political work, founded the Women's Labour League and was fully involved in local women's welfare work. A bronze statue depicting her surrounded by small children stands in the public gardens and incorporates a bench: 'The seat is placed here in memory of Margaret MacDonald who spent her life in helping others.'

Mary Lamb and her family first came into the Holborn area in 1795. It was still convenient for the Inns of Court, where her brother Charles and their father were employed. They had lodgings at 7 Little Queen Street, now built over by Holy Trinity Church, Kingsway. Their stay here was short-lived as Mary's ensuing history of recurring bouts of insanity started when, in an unstable state, she killed her mother. From then on she spent periods in asylums, but she was fortunate in her brother, whose care enabled her to pass as little time as possible in institutions and encouraged her in her writing.

CROYDON, London Borough of [see Map 3, B3] Formerly part of Surrey, Croydon was the biggest town in the county. It had its own civil airport, one of the first in Britain, and the buildings still stand on the east side of the Brighton Road. It was from here on 5 May 1930 that pioneer aviator, **Amy Johnson**, took off for her record-setting flight to Australia. She became the first woman to fly the route solo, landing in Darwin on 24 May. She had undertaken this marathon less than a year after her first solo flight. Her plane was a gipsy moth which she had named *Jason*, and it survives in the aviation collection of the Science Museum in South Kensington. In the 1930s aviators were pioneering new routes and trying to better flight times. Amy later flew to Capetown and back twice, breaking records both with both flights, in 1932 and 1936 respectively.

More recently, in 1985 and 1986, **Wendy Savage** has been the focus of a campaign to improve maternity care, especially in relation to the mother's involvement in choosing the method of delivery. Despite attempts by male colleagues to discredit the woman-centred practices of this gynaecologist and obstetrician, Wendy Savage has been cleared of charges of mishandling births in her efforts to help women with minimal interference with instruments, drugs and new technology. Her supporters were from all over

Britain, not just in the immediate area served by the London Hospital, and demonstrated to the male-dominated profession that women need to have their own voices heard when decisions about delivery methods are made. Wendy Savage received her school education at Croydon High School before going to the University of Cambridge to study medicine.

EALING, *London Borough of* [see Map 3, B2]   This suburban district lies in West London, north of the river. The contemporaries **Anna Jameson**, the writer and art critic, and **Lady Byron**, the philanthropist, participated in an early consciousness-raising group which met in Ealing in the 1850s. Members included **Emily Faithfull** and **Barbara Bodichon**. Foremost in their discussions was the economic and social independence which could be achieved by women when employment and educational opportunities were open to them. The friendship between Anna Jameson and Lady Byron also ended abruptly at this time, but the reasons for this are not known. They both died in 1860. Lady Byron had sponsored Ealing Grove, a school of industry and agriculture for fourteen years from 1834.

Mrs Fitzherbert, later the morganatic wife of the Prince Regent who became George IV, was an early occupant of Castle Hill Lodge, near what is now West Ealing. Her marriage to the Prince, held in secret in 1785, was never officially acknowledged, but she always regarded it as a legal union. She did not, however, embarrass the Prince in any public way; rather she turned increasingly for consolation to her Roman Catholic faith.

ENFIELD, *London Borough of* [see Map 3, A3]   This administrative district lies to the north of the capital, the former country town of Enfield being its present centre. It includes Edmonton and Palmer's Green within its compass.

Edmonton, a parish within the borough but to the south of Enfield itself, was where **Mary Lamb** moved in 1833 after six years in Enfield village. Not far from Lower Edmonton station, Lamb's Cottage stands near the corner of Church Street and Lion Road. This was to be her last home with her brother Charles, who died the following year. She survived him by thirteen years, and is buried with him in All Saints' churchyard. Their gravestone remains in its original position to the south-west of the church in an area now paved. They had collaborated in the writing of *Tales from Shakespeare* [1807], which remains popular with younger readers as an introduction to the plays of William Shakespeare. They also wrote *Mrs Leicester's School* [1809], to which Mary was the major contributor.

Enfield In Enfield Town the sense of the past is preserved in Gentlemen's Row, a group of charming cottages near the church in the old village, where **Mary Lamb**, with her brother Charles, came to live in 1827. Their first home was the building, marked with a plaque, now called Clarendon Cottage; however, Mary's continuing ill health prevented her from coping with the management of their household, so after two years they moved nearby to Westwood Cottage, the weatherboarded house at 85 Chase Side, where they were catered for by their landlady and landlord until 1833.

Palmer's Green The poet **Stevie Smith** spent most of her life in this twentieth-century residential suburb in what she described as a 'house of female habitation'. This was 1 Avondale Road, a redbrick Victorian end-of-terrace house. She moved here from Kingston upon Hull in 1906 at the age of five to live with her mother, her sister and her aunt. It was this aunt who featured so often in her writings, such as *Novel on Yellow Paper* [1936]. *Not Waving But Drowning* [1957] is her best known collection of poetry. Towards the end of her life she enjoyed giving readings of her verse in her own quirky style. As a girl she attended Palmer's Green High School, where the actress **Flora Robson** was a fellow-pupil.

GREENWICH, *London Borough of* [see Map 3, B3] This Thames-side borough on the south bank is probably known best for the imposing archictecture of the Royal Naval College and the National Maritime Museum, if not for the zero meridian of longitude and Greenwich Mean Time. Its importance as a naval centre has overshadowed other aspects of the history of Greenwich, and the other districts in the borough such as Eltham and Blackheath.

Blackheath This developed into a middle-class Victorian suburb, with its share of schools for young ladies. It was one of these that **Elizabeth Garrett Anderson** atended as a girl in the 1840s. She soon became aware that the education which she received there was inadequate preparation for the medical training which she eventually succeeded in following. Later her younger sister **Millicent Garrett Fawcett** also became a pupil. She married soon after her formal education ended, and at the age of twenty joined the women's suffrage committee; this was the start of sixty years of dedicated service in the cause of votes for women.

Greenwich A Tudor palace was sited here and Henry VIII, whose reign was to lay the foundations for the British navy, often held court here. His two daughters, during whose reigns the navy was to develop further, were born at Greenwich Palace. **Mary I**, known also as Mary Tudor, was born to Henry's first wife **Catherine of Aragon** in 1516. Her sister, **Elizabeth I**, was born to his second wife, **Anne Boleyn**, in 1533 and it was she who, as queen, oversaw the transformation of the Royal Navy into an effective marine force which routed the Spanish Armada and secured England's position as the premier sea power for years to come. The palace was demolished in 1662, though some vaults remain, incorporated into the part of the Royal Naval College called Queen Anne's Block.

On the slope behind the college, and now forming part of the National Maritime Museum, stands the Queen's House★, itself a landmark in architectural history. Begun in 1616, it was built for Anne of Denmark, wife of James I and VI, and completed for Henrietta Maria, wife of their heir Charles I. It was designed by Inigo Jones who thus introduced the Palladian style into Britain.

Eltham Also another palace popular with the Tudors stands within today's Borough of Greenwich. It was then in the Kent countryside with many attractions for the sovereigns. **Margaret Roper**, the intellectual daughter of Henry VIII's friend and advisor Thomas More, who fell from favour by sticking to the laws of the Church of Rome and opposing Henry's divorce, had settled into Well Hall, at Eltham, after her marriage. She herself had risked the king's wrath by taking the head of her executed father to be buried decently. According to one tradition, she buried him here. Well Hall Pleasaunce, now a small public park by Eltham Well Hall station, was part of her garden. Its successor building, also now largely demolished, was the home of the popular children's writer, **Edith Nesbit**, from 1899 until her family had grown up in 1922. One of the original members of the Fabian Society she hosted literary and political gatherings here as well as writing works such as *The Wouldbegoods* [1901], *The Five Children and It* [1902] and *The Railway Children* [1906]. She published them as E. Nesbit.

Woolwich **Lilian Barker**, the twentieth-century prison reformer who established a professional service for the care of women offenders, first demonstrated her great capacity for organisation and management in the First World War. She was ultimately responsible for the vast female work force which was employed at Woolwich Arsenal on munitions and other work in the war years. She introduced basic welfare measures and general improvements in the working conditions. During this period she lived in Shooters Hill Road.

HACKNEY, *London Borough of* [see Map 3, B3]   The borough of Hackney lies to the north-east of the City of London, and includes Stoke Newington and Shoreditch and the East End within its boundaries.

Hackney Hackney's social status has changed over the centuries. In the seventeenth century the poet **Katherine Philips** was sent to be educated in Hackney. It is likely that **Celia Fiennes**, the traveller, had a home in Hackney, but its site is not known. What is certain is that she died in Hackney in 1741, in her seventy-ninth year. At her request she was buried at her Wiltshire home in Newton Toney.

In the nineteenth century Hackney's population increased as a variety of new industries offered employment. Towards the end of the century, social conditions were deteriorating and concerned individuals tried to stop this decline. In 1884 Toynbee Hall was opened at 28 Commercial Street. This was the first of the so-called settlements which attracted students and others who wished to share the advantages they had gained by birth and education. They lived in the poorer districts, taking a great interest in the welfare of their neighbours and offering a variety of social services and informal educational courses for all-comers. Many early women graduates took this route to a career in social work. The American pioneering social reformer and pacifist **Jane Addams** was profoundly influenced by her visit to Toynbee Hall in 1887. It inspired her to set up her own settlement at Hull House in Chicago, setting an example to America by her especial concern for the welfare of immigrants.

Sylvia Pankhurst worked for the Women's Social and Political Union here, founding the East London branch in 1912. By 1914 she became disaffected as she felt that working-class women did not have an adequate voice in the organisation. She then set up a separate East London Federation of Suffragettes and supported it wholeheartedly throughout the remainder of the campaign for votes. The wealthy philanthropist **Angela Burdett-Coutts** was also concerned about the effects of poverty in this crowded part of the city and she supported new housing schemes, evening classes and social clubs. One landmark which bears testimony of her activities is the drinking fountain in Hackney's Victoria Park. It was erected in 1867 at her expense, at a cost of £7,000.

Hoxton Hoxton's two famous daughters made their names in quite different fields. The extrovert **Marie Lloyd** was born at 55 Graham Road in 1870. She had already made her mark as a singer by the time she was twenty. For many people Old Time Music Halls and Marie Lloyd are inseparable. She lived her life to the full, combining a successful career as a performer with a lively personal life. **Kate Greenaway**, born in 1846 in Cavendish Square, had equal success in her chosen career as an illustrator. Her attractive drawings which continue to be popular are viewed now in a nostalgic reverence for the past which renders them timeless.

At the beginning of the twentieth century **Edith Cavell** was employed as a nurse at St Leonard's Hospital in Nuttal Street. It was then still a workhouse, an institution for the destitute. She left in 1907 to take up an invitation to establish a training centre for nurses in Belgium

Stoke Newington This part of London was formerly a village with a strong tradition of Nonconformism. This is probably why **Mary Wollstonecraft** was attracted to establish a school here, where she was also born, thinking it might fare better than in Islington where earlier, in 1783, she had begun such a venture with her sister. The site of the school is known only to have been Newington Green. It did not last long and Mary was obliged to find other employment, this time as a governess. She was, however, to use the experience in some of her later writings, such as *Thoughts on the Education of Daughters* [1787].

Another woman who spent time running a school also ended up in Stoke Newington. This was **Anna Laetitia Barbauld**, who settled at 113 Stoke Newington Church Street in 1802. Her husband's mental illness made him increasingly difficult to live with so she undoubtedly moved here to be near her brother, who lived across the street, and his daughter, **Lucy Aikin**, to whom she was very close. Mrs Barbauld died here in 1825 and is buried in Abney Park Cemetery, just to the north of her home. She had written *Evenings at Home* [1792-6] with her brother John Aikin; it was a collection of writings and entertainments for children. **Catherine Booth**, the founder of the Salvation Army, was also buried there. She had shared her husband's Christian missionary work, preaching with him throughout Britain. When they decided to settle, it was in London's East End that they felt most needed.

HAMMERSMITH AND FULHAM, *London Borough of* [see Map 3, B3] Lying on the north bank of the Thames, the Borough of Hammersmith and Fulham is becoming more fashionable and includes Fulham.

Fulham The position of Fulham between Westminster and the outlying royal palaces of Hampton Court and Kew made it a convenient address for those involved in court life. King's Road has developed as a major thoroughfare through Fulham from being Charles II's private route. His well-liked mistress, the actress **Nell Gwyn**, is said to have set up home in Sanford Manor House, but she is also associated with other London properties. **Mrs Fitzherbert**, whom many regarded as a royal mistress, had a house, long demolished, on Parson's Green, on the north side of new King's Road. She, however, always claimed to be the legal wife of the Prince Regent, recognised by her church, if not by Parliament. For dynastic reasons, the Prince married **Caroline of Brunswick**. The union was not a success, punctuated as it was by rows and crises. By the time her husband held the throne as George IV, she found herself in an unenviable position. She had separated from the king, and was tried for adultery, the pivotal event in the 'Queen Caroline Affair', which split the country down political lines. The king's morals were hardly above reproach: his many liaisons were well known. Caroline deserves some sympathy as the victim of the double standards which prevailed at that time. She died at Brandenburg House in 1821, days after being excluded from the king's coronation. Not surprisingly, she chose to be buried in her native Brunswick. The site of the house on Crisp Road has been built over but she is commemorated in nearby Queen Caroline Road.

Hammersmith The prolific romantic novelist, **Marie Louisa de la Ramée**, lived with her mother and grandmother by Ravenscourt Park at Bessborough House, 11 Ravenscourt Square, now marked with a plaque. It was her home from *c*. 1857-66, but, having a French father she was often abroad. She wrote *Held in Bondage* [1863], *Under Two Flags* [1867], *Two Little Wooden Shoes* [1874] and over forty other novels under the pen name **Ouida**, and later the success of her works was regarded with jealousy by her rival Marie Corelli. However, when Ouida settled permanently in Italy, she continued to publish in Britain, eventually nearly fifty novels. A sudden drop in popularity and her own careless extravagance led to her death in poverty at Lucca in 1908.

Eight Hammersmith Terrace, an eighteenth-century house on the bank of the Thames, was **May Morris**'s London home from 1890. While living here she was active in the early socialist movement as well as teaching embroidery at the Central School of Arts and Crafts and carrying out commissions, designing and producing work for William Morris and Co. She administered the embroidery side of the firm's work. She also did silversmithing and organised a number of Arts and Crafts exhibitions. In 1907 she was elected first secretary of the Women's Guild of Artists. She spent the summers at Kelmscott Manor and in the 1920s gave up the lease in Hammersmith to take up permanent residence in the country.

HARINGEY, *London Borough of* [see Map 3, A3] This borough, due north of Islington and Hackney, is bounded on the east by the River Lea. It includes Highgate, Wood Green and Tottenham.

Highgate The explorer, anthropologist and travel writer, **Mary Kingsley**, grew up at 22 Southwood Lane, where her family moved shortly after her birth in 1862. She was able to make up for the absence of a formal education by having the freedom of her father's library, and their cottage's long garden. When she was twenty, her family moved to Cambridge to enable her brother, not her, to pursue studies at the university.

Probably the best known site for notable figures in this area is the wonderful Highgate Cemetery, which is in two parts, on either side of Swaine Lane. Below St Michael's Church, buried in the West or 'Old' section, which can only be visited on special days, is a crop of writers amid the ivy, brambles and high grasses. **Mrs Henry Wood** lies beneath a splendid marble tomb, in the Roman style high on the Lebanon circle of catacombs, named after the large cedar tree growing there. She had died in 1887, when the Victorians were still drawing on many architectural styles from the past for funerary masonry. **Christina Rossetti**, best known for her poetry, was buried with her family; her grave is harder to track down, but a short track has been beaten to it off the path round the oval plot. The neglected-looking Rossetti memorial is surmounted by a quatrefoil with a monogram of interlaced initials, surrounded by headstones which lean at despairing angles. Christina's name can be read near ground level. **Ann Charlotte Bartholomew**, who, in addition to her literary career, was an accomplished miniature painter, was also buried in the west section of the cemetery, as was **Radclyffe Hall**. Radclyffe Hall's life was dominated by two strong lesbian relationships, the experience of which dominated her life and particularly, the writing of *The Well of Loneliness* [1928]. She was buried in the catacomb circle in the tomb of her first lover, Mabel Veronica Batten, and her epitaph was written by the second, Una, Lady Trowbridge. A trust has recently been set up to restore the memorial tomb. Both graves are hard to locate but well worth spending time to seek out in this wonderful and intriguing cemetery.

The East or 'New' section of Highgate cemetery can be visited anytime during daylight hours. It has long been a focus for pilgrimages to the grave of Karl Marx. It is in this same grave that the ashes of his daughter, **Eleanor Marx**, 1855-98, were buried after her suicide. She was as active in politics as her father, and in her own right was a leading exponent of socialism. Her talents extended to literary translations and organisational skills, and a fine committee member. Nearby stands the polished granite obelisk which marks the last resting place of **George Eliot**, commemorated in both her pen-name and her married name, Mary Ann Cross. She had married John Cross in 1880, but died shortly afterwards. Those with more time to spend will find *Highgate Cemetery: Victorian Valhalla* by F. Berker [1984, London, John Murray] a helpful guide. A group of sterling volunteers, the Friends of Highgate Cemetery, has taken on the marathon task of recording and restoring, as far as is practical, the cemetery buildings, monuments and grounds, and it welcomes new members.

Holly Lodge Gardens, off Highgate West Hill, is a reminder of the site's previous building, Holly Lodge. In 1809 it was bought for **Harriot Mellon**, the actress who in 1822 became the richest woman in Britain on the death of her first husband, the banker Thomas Coutts. The children of his first wife never accepted that their father's fortune had been left solely to Harriot. She was not greedy, and used her money generously but wisely. On her own death in 1837, she had named the 23-year-old **Angela Burdett-Coutts** as her heiress. Miss Coutts determined to use her fortune for the direct benefit of the underprivileged, and embarked on carefully thought-out, well-managed works of philanthropy. She often lived at

Holly Lodge, a building near Holly Village. This small, beautifully landscaped development of small gothic style houses was designed as a model village and included a model farm. The gatehouse in to Holly Village has two statues over it, and bears a bold inscription recording Angela Burdett-Coutts' foundation. She herself is represented by the statue on the right, that on the left is of Mrs Brown, whose friendship with the founder began when she became Miss Coutts' governess. There are several memorials to Miss Coutts in London, such as the drinking fountains which she paid for. She was also extremely interested in the welfare of the peoples of Britain's colonies and supported welfare work and industries overseas.

Tottenham Haringey can also claim another well-travelled daughter. **Kate Marsden** was born in Tottenham in 1859. Sterling Way is built over Silver Street where she grew up. She trained as a nurse in the local hospital and served in Russia in 1877, caring for the wounded of the Russo-Balkan Wars. She did not settle on her return to England, and after an unsatisfactory period in New Zealand she returned to Russia. In 1891 she set out to establish a leper hospital in Siberia, and succeeded at the cost of her own health. She returned to Britain in 1897 an invalid. However, she published an account of her harrowing travels, *On Sledge and Horseback to Outcast Siberian Lepers* [1893]. She died in 1931.

Eleanor Jourdain, an early woman student at the University of Oxford, began her own distinguished career in education at Tottenham High School. She later became Vice-Principal of St Hugh's College, one of the women's colleges at Oxford.

HARROW, *London Borough of* [see Map 3, A2]   This borough in the north-west centres on the old village of Harrow on the Hill but also includes Pinner and Stanmore.

At the heart of *Harrow* village is Harrow School, an old established school for boys, which provides an education for an elite. Education at Harrow School has been seen as a stepping stone to a secure and powerful future. So much so that those who could not afford to have their sons attend as boarding pupils would move to the neighbourhood so that they could afford the day-pupil fees. This is how **Fanny Trollope** came to live here. Her husband's career seemed to lurch from one crisis to another, forcing him to move from central London. In 1817 he rented Julians, a house with a farm, in Harrow on the south side of the hill. The house, now considerably altered, was big and was to be Fanny's home till the next financial crisis obliged them to move into a smaller farmhouse, Julians Hill, now demolished. In 1827 they had to move again, this time to Harrow Weald. By this time, her third son Anthony, later known as a writer, was attending

Harrow School as a day boy. Fanny had earlier met and taken a great liking to the Scottish social reformer **Frances Wright**, who now appeared as a welcome but unexpected guest. Her description of the Utopian colony for ex-slaves which she had set up in Tennessee inspired Fanny to visit the New World. Thinking she could rescue the family fortunes she set off in 1827 with three of her children to accompany Frances to the United States. Her business ventures there were not a success and after various hardships, she returned to the little house in Harrow Weald, said to have stood on the corner of Weald Lane and the High Street. Here her efforts to support the family financially were rewarded. She published an account of her impressions of the United States in 1832. *Domestic Manners of the Americans* was an immediate sellout: her fifty-second year proved to be the start of a literary career which produced many popular works, mostly novels and travel writing. She moved to Italy permanently in 1844 dying there aged eighty-three, as well known then as her now more famous son.

About ten years later, the young **Annie Besant** came with her widowed mother and her brother to live near Harrow School. Her father had died in 1852, when she was five, and her mother decided she would take in as boarders pupils from the school. The house, a former vicarage situated between the church and the school, no longer stands, but it was large enough to take several boys and a schoolmaster as well as the Besants. Annie's education benefited from the presence of a tutor, but she later became a boarder herself at Charmouth in Dorset, coming home only for the holidays.

Pinner **Isabella Beeton** lived in Victorian Pinner after her marriage to the publisher Samuel Beeton. Her *Mrs Beeton's Book of Household Management*, first edition 1861, was to become a bible preaching pragmatic domestic order. Editions continue to be issued, which, though the content may have been revised beyond recognition, remain standard works in their field. The extent of her achievement is the greater, considering that she was under thirty years old when she died.

Ivy Compton-Burnett was born in Pinner in 1884, but her large family soon settled permanently in Hove. Her novels often have domestic settings, sometimes stifling but always acutely observed. They include *Brothers and Sisters* [1929] and *Manservant and Maidservant* [1947].

HAVERING, *London Borough of* [see Map 3, A4] This easternmost borough on the North bank of the Thames includes villages which used to be in the county of Essex: Havering-atte-Bower, Romford and Upminster, all by now well built up. There must be many women of interest who have spent significant parts of their lives here, and we hope to learn about them from readers.

HILLINGDON, *London Borough of* [see Map 3, B2]   This is one of the larger boroughs, lying on the west of Greater London. Within its area are Harefield, Uxbridge, Northwood, Ruislip, Harmondsworth and Heathrow Airport. This is an area which must have provided homes to many fascinating women, and it is hoped that readers will be able to identify them for a revised edition of this Gazetteer.

HOUNSLOW, *London Borough of* [see Map 3, B2]   Hounslow is a borough in West London on the north bank of the Thames looking across the river to Kew Gardens. It encompasses Brentford, Chiswick and Isleworth as well as Hounslow itself.

Chiswick This charming Thames-side village was a popular place to live in the seventeenth and eighteenth centuries. Among its fashionable residents was **Barbara Villiers**. She was a noted beauty who was well established at the court of Charles II as the king's mistress. As such, she had great influence over the king, which, in turn, made her unpopular with the politicians. Her last years were not very secure. She spent them at Walpole House on Chiswick Mall, on the river bank. She had acquired the titles Countess of Castlemaine and Duchess of Cleveland, leaving several children to inherit them. She thus merited a splendid funeral on her death in 1709. She was buried in St Nicholas Church, Chiswick.

Chiswick Mall's popularity has continued into the twentieth century. Two writers who have lived here are **Nancy Mitford**, who lived for some time in Rose Cottage, and **Margaret Kennedy**, author of *The Constant Nymph* [1924], occupied number one. Nancy Mitford spent her later years in France, where her knowledge of French history led her to write biographies of *Madame de Pompadour* [1954] and *The Sun King, Louis XIV at Versailles* [1966]. Her best known novels are *The Pursuit of Love* [1945] and *Love in a Cold Climate* [1949].

Isleworth Beautiful Syon House★ stands in fine landscaped gardens bordering the Thames, but it has been much altered by later architects of high repute, since it was the prison of **Catherine Howard**, fifth wife of Henry VIII, before her execution in 1542. The same fate awaited **Lady Jane Grey** in 1554. Her troubles started at Syon House when she was offered the English throne in 1552. Pressure was put on her by her ambitious family to accept, and shortly afterwards her reign of nine days began.

ISLINGTON, *London Borough of* [see Map 3, B3]   Due north of the City, Islington grew from a village, with Islington Green and the High Street as its centre, into a residential area in the eighteenth and early nineteenth century, a development of mainly terraced town houses. Such a house is 64 Duncan Terrace, home from 1823 of **Mary Lamb** and her brother. The house, in their time called Colebrook Cottage, bears a plaque on which only Charles' residence is recorded. They moved further north to Enfield after four years. She had written her best known book *Tales from Shakespeare* [1807] with her brother before her mental illness recurred more persistently.

Sadler's Wells Theatre was re-established by the theatre manager **Lilian Baylis** in 1931, after she had set the Old Vic firmly on its feet. She lived to see it accepted as one of London's major stages for opera and ballet, which she aimed to make as accessible as the great dramas for which the Old Vic has earned its reputation. The original Sadler's Wells was a spring which became an early popular spa, fortunate in its proximity to London. The letter writer **Lady Mary Wortley Montagu**, who pioneered vaccination and other health practices, is said to have given Sadler's Wells the publicity in the 1730s which attracted royalty to it. Among the entertainments provided was a music theatre of fluctuating fortunes. This was the forerunner of Lilian Baylis' enterprise, which still has a spring rising below it.

Islington has recently gained a reputation for progressive educational innovation. However, there were earlier educational experiments. **Mary Wollstonecraft** tried to set up a school here with her sister in 1783. It was not a success, but they were not deterred. Instead they opened another school in Stoke Newington. Mary later wrote up her feminist theories as *Thoughts on the Education of Daughters* [1787].

Holloway Holloway Prison, a redbrick gothic edifice in the north of the borough in Parkhurst Road, admitted its first suffragettes in 1906. Originally built in 1852 for both female and male offenders, by 1902 its inmates were exclusively women. Suffragette occupants include **Mrs Emmeline Pankhurst**, her three daughters **Christable**, **Sylvia** and **Adela**, **Mrs Pethick-Lawrence**, **Emily Wilding Davison**, the Cause's first martyr, and **Annie Kenney**. There were suffragettes incarcerated here almost continually from 1911 until the outbreak of war in 1914. In the end over one thousand women received prison sentences, several were repeatedly imprisoned, especially after the so-called 'Cat and Mouse Act' of 1913. By this Prisoners' Temporary Discharge for Ill-health Act, women could be released if their health declined as a result of hunger-striking or similar, to be re-arrested as soon as they were seen to be active again. It was an invidious situation which only ended with the outbreak of the Great War in 1914.

They never succeeded in persuading the government that they were political prisoners. Many of the militant suffragettes were convicted of the so-called 'Outrages', which included setting fire to pillar-boxes, breaking windows, slashing works of art in galleries. When they went on hunger strike, prison staff were instructed to force-feed the prisoners, a most unpleasant experience, which had lasting ill-effects on the health of many. **Lady Constance Lytton** was first imprisoned in 1909. During a subsequent spell in gaol she was released because of her heart condition. To prove that this was in fact on account of her position in society as a well-connected aristocrat, she later had herself arrested in Liverpool under a different name, to the severe detriment of her health. She published a report of her contrasting experiences as *Prisons and Prisoners, Some Personal Experiences by Constance Lytton and Jane Warton* [1914], thus exposing the double standards of the authorities. **Ethel Smyth**, the composer, was also imprisoned as a suffragette. She had written the suffrage anthem 'The March of Women', and she conducted rousing choruses of this sung by her fellow-prisoners with her toothbrush through the window of her cell.

At the end of the First World War **Constance Markievicz**, the first woman to be elected to a seat in the British Parliament, was a prisoner in Holloway Prison. An Irish nationalist and leader of Sinn Fein, she was arrested when the struggle for Irish independence was at its height. In the 1918 election she was elected to represent the St Patrick's Division of Dublin, but she refused to take up her seat, having no allegiance to the British Crown. She had founded the Irish Women's Franchise League in 1908.

Marie Stopes was not arrested for opening her first controversial birth control clinic in North Holloway in 1921. Although it caused great argument and offended the churches it was not an illegal enterprise. It soon supplied the demand for birth control advice and information which Marie Stopes knew existed from personal experience. Her determination to spread her message has changed the lives of future generations of women who are now able to plan their families.

St Pancras **Lilian Barker**, whose life's work was to improve the conditions and organisation of women's prisons and girls' reformatories, was born west of Holloway in Kentish Town Road in 1874, but her career was not established early enough to help the suffragettes.

Polygon Road is built on the site of the Polygon, a fifteen-sided housing development where **Mary Wollstonecraft** lived and died in 1797. She had recently married William Godwin, but died shortly after the birth of their daughter **Mary Godwin Shelley**. Mary Wollstonecraft, whose unconventional life provided a model for Amelia Opie's novel *Adeline Mowbray* [1804], was buried in St Pancras' Churchyard. The square block of her monument, over which Mary Shelley and Percy Bysshe Shelley first admitted their mutual love, remains. Although she did not know her mother, Mary Shelley felt very close to her, and in 1851 had her parents' remains removed to Bournemouth where she herself is buried with them.

KENSINGTON AND CHELSEA, *Royal Borough of* [see Map 3, B3]
Within the Royal Borough, which housed royalty in its two palaces, there
are, in addition to the former villages of Kensington and Chelsea, other
well-known districts such as Earl's Court and Knightsbridge.

Chelsea, which in parts still has a village feel to it, was the site of the Royal
Palace of Chelsea, reached easily by boat or royal barge. Henry VIII often
took his court to Chelsea Palace [now gone], and Sir Thomas More built his
home nearby. His daughter **Margaret Roper** received her broad education
while living with her father 1524-34. Their manor house no longer survives
and Cheyne Walk and the surrounding streets are probably built on their
estate. The premises of the British Federation of University Women in
Danvers Street are built near the site, and incorporate part of **Mary
Sidney**'s City home, Crosby Place, as the dining hall. Chelsea Manor
House, also long since demolished, was a wedding gift from Henry VIII to
his sixth and last wife, **Catherine Parr**. She brought the young
Elizabeth I here, and the studious **Lady Jane Grey** joined her household.
Catherine later died in the manor house in 1548. Henry's fourth wife, **Anne
of Cleves** also died here eight years later. In many ways she was the most
fortunate of his wives. After their brief marriage and relatively amicable
divorce in 1540, she lived on good terms with the king, having been granted
the title 'the King's Sister'. She had a fair divorce settlement, and survived
him by nine years. The site of the Manor House is covered by Chelsea
Manor Street and Flood Street, where **Dame Sybil Thorndike**, the fine
actress, had her London flat in Swan Court. She died there in 1976.

Chelsea Old Church, dedicated to All Saints, stood at the heart of village
life. Early worshippers who lived in the parish included **Margaret Roper**,
Lady Jane Cheyne, **Mary Astell**, feminist pamphleteer, **Anne
Chamberlayne** and **Elizabeth Blackwell**, botanical illustrator. Most are
commemorated within the church. Anne Chamberlayne was a woman
soldier active in the 1690s. Lady Jane Cheyne, who herself saw action in the
Civil War when she defended her family's Welbeck estates, was a generous
parishioner. She paid for the church to be re-roofed. A sculpture dedicated
to her can be seen inside. The church stands where Old Church Street joins
Chelsea Embankment. **Octavia Hill**, the energetic social reformer and
philanthropist, managed Hertford buildings in Old Church Street as a
community of flats for elderly women. It was one of several properties in
different parts of London for which she took responsibility.

Chelsea's history includes various periods as a fashionable place to live. In
the nineteenth century it attracted writers. Cheyne Walk, built over the
Chelsea Manor estate and named after Lady Jane Cheyne, housed several.
Mrs Gaskell was born at number 93 in 1810, as a plaque records. Her
mother died within a short time and Elizabeth Stevenson, as she then was,
was sent immediately to be brought up by relatives in Knutsford.
Number 91 was the home of **Margaret Fairless Barber**, whose essays and
short stories were published under the pen-name **Michael Fairless**. Her

health was poor and she moved to Steyning in the hope that sea air would bring improvement. The detective fiction writer **Agatha Christie**, originally from Torquay, made her London home in Chelsea. It is now called Christie Cottage. **George Eliot** having finally conformed and married in 1880, died at number 4, a few weeks later. **Alison Uttley** taught science in Chelsea in the Edwardian period. From 1908 until her marriage three years later she had lodgings in Cheyne Walk. The success of her *Little Grey Rabbit* books [first published in 1929] enabled her to abandon her teaching career.

Just off Cheyne Walk, at 24 Cheyne Row, **Jane Welsh Carlyle** settled with her husband in 1834. The house☆[NT], a national monument since 1895, bears a grand plaque in memory of him but Jane had most definitely made her mark inside on him and their circle of literary and political friends. Hers was not an easy life; Thomas Carlyle being an awkward and demanding character. He was very dependent on her and her death in 1866 affected him deeply. She had died in her carriage in Hyde Park after a dog she was exercising had been struck by another vehicle. There are many portraits of her in the house, as well as her furniture, belongings and copies of her letters. She was a constant letter writer and kept up correspondence with numerous friends and relations. She inspired great affection, and **Geraldine Jewsbury**, a frequent guest, moved from Manchester to be near her. The house also contains some water-colours and sketches of the rooms by **Helen Allingham**. Number 10 Cheyne Row, marked with a plaque, was the home of **Margaret Damer Dawson**. Although trained as a musician she was active in animal welfare work in the first decade of this century. However, her lasting achievement was to found the Women Police Volunteers, in 1914, forerunners of today's British policewomen.

Chelsea has also acquired a reputation as an artists' colony. **Dame Ethel Walker** had her home and studio at 127 Cheyne Walk [no longer standing] from 1910 until her death in 1951. Her younger contemporary **Ethel Sands** worked at 15 The Vale, on the north side of King's Road from 1920 until she died in 1962. By this time she had renounced her American citizenship for British. James McNeill Whistler belonged to an earlier generation of Chelsea artists. His mother, **Anna McNeill Whistler**, crossed the Atlantic in 1863 to live with him at 7 Lindsey Row. She was the model for his painting 'Arrangement in Black and Grey' [1872], now in the Musée du Louvre in Paris. It has long been familiarly known as 'Whistler's Mother'; thus she became immortalised, although she undoubtedly also had a powerful influence over the artist and his circle.

To the north-east of Cheyne Walk, behind high walls, is the Chelsea Physick Garden★, only recently opened to the public on a regular basis. It is entered from Swan Walk, and still belongs to the old trade guild, the Society of Apothecaries. It is an oasis of tranquillity and to enjoy its shade and colour is to forget the bustle of city life all around. **Elizabeth Blackwell** lived in Swan Walk, a street of fine eighteenth-century houses which belie her circumstances. Her husband was imprisoned for debt and she was eventually able to secure his release after publishing in 1739 *A Curious Herbal*, a collection of five hundred of her illustrations of plants from the Physick Garden. She was fortunate in finding as a sponsor Sir Hans Sloane, whose name is given to several fashionable streets in the area. **Mrs Delaney**, the chronicler of eighteenth-century society, also used the plant life of the Physick Garden as models. Her chosen medium was cunningly cut and coloured paper which she used to create extremely accurate flower collages, what she termed 'paper mosaicks'. She did not take up this artform until 1772 and practised it skilfully for a decade; as she was as old as the century, this was testament to her continuing artistic inventiveness. She certainly seems to have invented this medium. The British Museum has a collection of these works. In the present century the poet **Dame Edith Sitwell** lived in Swan Walk, overlooking the garden. She made her home here from 1917 until 1919. During this period her experimental work *Façade* [1923] was first performed.

Royal Hospital Road passes on its south side the Chelsea Royal Hospital. It was built in 1682 by Christopher Wren. It is said that **Nell Gwyn**, Charles II's most popular mistress, had suggested the idea to the king. However that may be, she is known to have been a benefactor of it. She was familiar with almshouses in her native Hereford. As an institution for invalided and pensioned soldiers, it comes as a surprise to learn that **Christian Davis** was an inmate there before she died in 1739. She had disguised herself in order to enlist as a soldier. She wanted to follow her husband who had been more or less abducted away from their native Ireland into the British army. She eventually found him, after seeing active service herself abroad and being wounded more than once. **Hannah Snell** led an equally adventurous soldiering life in disguise. Her formal military career ended in 1750 but she received a King's Pension in recognition of her service in India. She was an outpatient here, but ended her days in a mental institution. Both these female soldiers are buried in the hospital grounds here, but their graves are unmarked.

Parallel to Royal Hospital Road, and north of it, runs King's Road, Charles II's route to London, though probably better known this century for its trendsetting shops in the 'Swinging Sixties'. One of its earlier inhabitants led an unconventional private life which would have raised few eyebrows in the 1960s. The actress **Ellen Terry** had a London home at number 215 from 1904 until 1920. Her long, much admired acting career was more satisfying than her personal life, and she latterly spent a great deal of time at her country home at Smallhythe in Kent. The Princess **Seraphine Astafieva**, another star of the stage, this time of the ballet stage, lived and taught at 152 King's Road. A Russian aristocrat, she had trained with the Imperial Ballet in St Petersburg, but after a successful career, she chose to establish herself in London in 1914 and devote herself to teaching. The premier ballerinas Dame Alicia Markova and Dame Margot Fontaine both benefited from her teaching as did **Marié Rambert**, the Polish-born founder of the Ballet Rambert. The impressive entrance way sits uneasily

on what is now a restaurant complex called the Pheasantry; her association
with Diaghilev's Company is acknowledged in the naming of the lively
Diaghilev Café. Pheasants had been kept in the gardens of the original
building, hence its present name.

Other performers also lived in Chelsea. **Jenny Lind**, 'the Swedish
Nightingale', lived at 189 Old Brompton Road, to the north. Her large
house, on the corner of the Boltons, stands next to the telephone exchange.
It is now a housing aid centre. She had married her accompanist Otto
Goldschmidt in 1852. Together they founded the London Bach Choir. Her
career as leading soprano culminated in her appointment in 1883 as
Professor of Singing at the Royal College of Music. She retired to Malvern.
At different times, two actresses resided at 15 Tedworth Square: first **Lillie
Langtry** and later **Mrs Patrick Campbell**, both of whom moved with
ease in very elevated social circles. **Fanny Kemble**'s closing years were
spent at 26 Hertford Square. Part of the great acting family which included
her famous aunt Sarah Siddons, Fanny belonged to an earlier generation of
actresses. From her acting debut in 1829 at the age of twenty, she kept in the
public eye. Her talents were wider than the stage. She was a prolific poet
and writer, and after a difficult marriage in America, she eloquently
denounced slavery. She lived in Hertford Square for six years from 1884.

Brompton cemetery on the south side of Old Brompton Road is one of
London's large Victorian cemeteries. Some important women lie buried
here, most notably, perhaps, **Emmeline Pankhurst**. Her grave, generally
with fresh flowers on it, is a tall Celtic cross, on the east side of the central
avenue. She died in London in 1928 just after the passing of the second
Representation of the People Act. It gave women and men of twenty-one
years and over the full and equal voting rights for which she and her
daughters had campaigned so vigorously and with total commitment.
Further south on the central avenue near the domed chapel is the grave
monument, surmounted by a statue of a draped female, commemorating
the American romantic novelist **Blanche Macchetta**, who died in 1898.
Among other women interred here are **Lady Sydney Morgan** and
Geraldine Jewsbury. Lady Morgan [born Sydney Ownson] was an Irish
novelist, her best known work being *The Wild Irish Girl* [1806, reprinted by
Pandora Press in 1986]. She died in 1859. Geraldine Jewsbury had come to
London to be near her friend Jane Carlyle. On Jane's death in 1866 she
assisted Thomas Carlyle to prepare his biography of his wife. She had
earlier helped Lady Morgan write her memoirs, and on her own death in
1880 she chose to be buried in the same grave here. The actress **Helen
Faucit** died in her Welsh home in 1898 but she is also buried in this
cemetery.

Kensington Formerly a village in Middlesex conveniently close to London,
Kensington has been developed from the beginning of the nineteenth
century. To the north of Old Brompton Road, the district is known as
South Kensington, famous for its museums. **Beatrix Potter**, who spent a

rather sad and isolated childhood at 2 Bolton Gardens, was educated privately at home, but was allowed to spend time in the British Museum [Natural History]★ nearby. There she studied and drew with great accuracy animal and plant specimens, skills which she later used very effectively when illustrating her much loved books for children, known collectively as *The Tales of Beatrix Potter*. The popular characters Mrs Tiggywinkle, Jemima Puddleduck, Jeremy Fisher, Peter Rabbit and Pigling Bland are her creations. This house was her home from her birth there in 1866 until she married in 1913. Many of her original illustrations are in the collections of the Victoria and Albert Museum★, which also houses the English ceramics bequeathed by **Lady Charlotte Guest**. As Lady Charlotte Schreiber after her second marriage, she started to collect English porcelain and pottery, one of the first collectors in this field. Although it is a very mixed collection, it contains some fine pieces.

North again from Bolton Gardens is Barkeston Gardens, where the actress **Ellen Terry** had another London home at number 22. It leads to Courtfield Gardens. Novelist **Antonia White**, who died in 1980, lived at 42 towards the end of her life. Her best known work *Frost in May* [1933] has deservedly been re-published. Running parallel to Cromwell Road is Longridge Street where **Marie Corelli** lived when she began her career as a sensational romantic novelist under that name. She was born Mary Mackay, and had moved to 47 Longridge Street after her father's illness. They resided here from 1883, and all her successful works, such as *A Romance of Two Worlds* [1886] and *Barabbas* [1893], were written here. She moved to Stratford upon Avon in 1900. A successful author of a different and more serious type of novel, **Ivy Compton-Burnett**, shared a London flat at 5 Braemar Mansions, in Cornwall Gardens on the other side of Cromwell Road, with her cherished companion Margaret Jourdain from 1934. Margaret died in 1951, but Ivy stayed on until her own death in 1969.

Kensington High Street runs from east to west, still a main shopping street. On its north side is Campden Hill. The novelist and feminist **Violet Hunt** welcomed into her home as a lodger fellow-author Ford Madox Ford from 1912. The plaque on South Lodge, which is on the corner of Tor Gardens and Campden Hill Road, makes no mention of his literary landlady, whose novels include *The Maiden's Progress* [1894] and *White Rose of Weary Leaf* [1908]. The plaque on 50 Campden Hill Square, however, gives due acknowledgment of its significant female resident, **Evelyn Underhill**. Living here from her marriage in 1907 until 1939, she wrote poetry and religious works, notably *Mysticism* [1911].

Radclyffe Hall, writer of poetry and novels, was brought up by her grandmother in Addison Road, which links Kensington High Street with Holland Park Avenue. When she came of age in 1901 she became financially independent, having received a generous inheritance. She then bought and moved into a house in Campden Hill Terrace, just off Kensington Church Street to the east, and studied at King's College. The sensitive account of lesbian love and pain in *The Well of Loneliness* [1928] involved her in a courtcase. The book was judged obscene and for many years it was unobtainable. The scandal created has overshadowed her many other works in verse and prose, such as *The Unlit Lamp* [1924] and *The Sixth Beatitude* [1936].

The building which first made the Kensington area a respectable place to live was Kensington Palace★. It initially became a royal residence in 1689. It was built for **Mary II** and her husband William III. **Queen Anne**, Mary's sister and, unexpectedly, heir to the throne in 1782, lived here while sovereign. Her close friend **Sarah Churchill**, who had been a Lady of the Bedchamber, became, on Anne's succession in 1702, Mistress of the Robes, Groom of the Stole and, more importantly, Keeper of the Privy Purse. Their intimate relationship is characterised by their choice of names for each other: Anne was 'Mrs Morley' and Sarah was 'Mrs Freeman' in their letters, allowing them equal status. This closeness did not last, as the ambitious Whig-sympathiser Sarah Churchill, who had become Duchess of Marlborough in 1702, fell from favour, much to the delight of the Tories. The argument which finally ended Sarah's influence took place in the Queen's Closet in the State Apartments★. The palace remained one of Queen Anne's preferred residences and she died there in 1714.

Victoria was the next queen to rule Britain in her own right. She was born in 1819 in what is now called the north drawing-room. She was brought up in the palace, and various rooms where the young princess lived, played and slept can be visited, and some of her possessions seen. She inherited the throne in 1837 through her father, who was brother of William IV.

Among those who set up home in this area was **Elizabeth Inchbald**, whose last years were spent at Kensington House. She led a very independent life, supporting herself by acting and writing. Once she had established herself as a novelist and playwright she was able to give up her stage career. Her first successful novel was *A Simple Story* [1791] and has recently been republished by Pandora Press. She died in 1821 after barely two years of retirement at Kensington House. **Marguerite Gardiner**, Countess of Blessington, also had a residence in Kensington. Her career as a society hostess began in earnest when Lord Blessington, whose mistress she had been for some years, was able on his wife's death in 1818 to become her third husband. Together they travelled on the continent in some style, meeting up with famous figures of the day. These included Count d'Orsay, with whom she became involved. In 1829 her husband's death left her well provided for but in order to continue entertaining in her extravagant style she wrote novels which brought her a good income. Her salons at Gore House, Kensington Gore, which she hosted from 1836 until her bankruptcy obliged her to flee the country, were legendary. She and Count d'Orsay escaped to France in 1849 where she died soon after. The Royal Albert Hall is built on the site, looking over Kensington Gardens and Hyde Park.

Kensington Square, with its late seventeenth-century townhouses, stands just south of the east end of Kensington High Street. More recent residents include the notable actress, **Mrs Patrick Campbell**, whose home for seventeen years was at number 33. A native of Kensington, she took up acting professionally when her husband was unable to find work. Having made her name on the London stage in the title role of *The Second Mrs Tanqueray* [1893], her career was sufficiently established for her to move into Kensington Square in 1898. From here she conducted her famous correspondence with her friend and admirer George Bernard Shaw. It was for her that he wrote the memorable role of Eliza Doolittle in his play *Pygmalion* [1914]. Later, the remarkable family of the novelist **Nancy Mitford** had a London home in the Square, although the Mitfords' country home at Swinford is the better known.

To the north, Palace Gate leads off Kensington Gardens. A blue plaque indicates number 2 as the home of Sir John Everett Millais, one of the artists at the centre of the Pre-Raphaelite circle. **Effie Millais**, his wife, had modelled for and inspired several of its members. After a short-lived and unhappy marriage to John Ruskin, she became the wife of Millais. Living mostly here but partly in her native Perthshire, she brought up eight children and led a contented and gentle life.

The remarkable American, **Victoria Woodhull**, moved into 17 Hyde Park Gate in 1882. Her controversial life in the United States had driven her to seek a new home in Britain. Most of the uproar was caused by her outspoken support for free love. It earned her the title 'Mrs Satan'. She was always in the public eye, having been a travelling clairvoyant and the publisher, with her sister, of a journal *Woodhull and Claflin's Weekly*. She and her sister, Tennessee Claflin, were the first women to practise as stockbrokers in the United States. An ardent, if extreme, suffrage campaigner, Victoria was the first woman to stand as a candidate for the Presidency of the United States. Although she had had a curious experience of marriage in America, she accepted the proposal of a quiet and respectable Englishman, John Biddulph Martin, and settled in Kensington and Bredon's Norton for over forty years. Sir Leslie Stephen was living at 22 Hyde Park Gate in 1882 when his daughter, **Virginia Woolf**, was born there. No mention is made on the plaque of her birth or the childhood residence there of her older sister **Vanessa Bell**; both of them were to be leading figures in literary and artistic circles. **Enid Bagnold** is another writer whose association with this street remains unmarked; she spent her married life at number 29. Probably best known as the author of *National Velvet* [1935] and the play *The Chalk Garden* [1955], she was a versatile and prolific writer.

Knightsbridge Hans Place held great charms for **Jane Austen** who spent some months in 1814 and 1815 at her brother's home at number 23. As a girl she had attended a school for young ladies in Reading which gave a rudimentary education to other future novelists. There was a similar institution at 22 Hans Place and some of its pupils also made contributions to English literature: **Mary Russell Mitford**, author of *Our Village* [1819];

Lady Caroline Lamb, better known as the distracted lover of Lord Byron, but herself a competent novelist and author of *Glenarvon* [1816]; **Letitia Langdon**, the poet who was born in Hans Place in 1802, and **Fanny Kemble**. Fanny Kemble was a member of the famous acting family which included her aunt Sarah Siddons, but she was also a published author, strongly critical of American slavery, which she had seen during her marriage to a plantation owner in the 1830s and 1840s. Her *Journal of a Residence in a Georgian Plantation* [1863] describes the horrors of slave life which she witnessed when accompanying her American businessman husband on a visit to his estates. This led to fundamental disagreements which in turn ended the marriage. Fanny lived to be eighty-four and published various autobiographical writings towards the end of her life. She died in 1893.

There were also twentieth-century women writers living in Knightsbridge. Forty-nine Lowndes Square was home to **Hilda Doolittle** and **Bryher**. Hilda Doolittle was an American-born poet who had first come to Britain in 1911 and joined the literary circle of Ezra Pound. She gained a reputation for her imagist poetry, written in the name **H.D.**, and it is as H.D. that she is best known today. She moved into Lowndes Square in 1934, having ended her marriage and having already become close to Bryher. Their lesbian relationship lasted over forty years but they did not always live together. Bryher moved in in 1940 and they experienced the blitz together in London. It is described in Bryher's *The Days of Mars: A Memoir 1940-46* [1972]. Residing here was particularly productive for H.D. She wrote *The Gift* and her *Trilogy* [1944–6], a work as powerful as T. S. Eliot's *The Four Quartets*. In 1933, at Bryher's instigation, H.D. underwent psychoanalysis with Sigmund Freud, of which her *Tribute to Freud* [1965] is a remarkable account.

Pimlico The district called Pimlico borders on the City of Westminster and is currently enjoying a vogue as a desirable residential area, convenient for central London. **Vita Sackville-West** and her husband Harold Nicolson had their first London home together at 182 Ebury Street. Vita Sackville-West's gardening articles in the *Observer* newspaper attracted a devoted regular readership but she preferred to be thought of as a poet and novelist.

KINGSTON UPON THAMES, *Royal Borough of* [see Map 3, B2] The Royal Borough of Kingston, on the south-west edge of the metropolitan area, was an important market town in the county of Surrey. **Charlotte Despard**, the suffragette and campaigner for social reform, was elected as a Poor Law Guardian for Kingston upon Thames in 1890. Such offices were among the first open to women and experience of this type of public work proved invaluable to many women involved in the suffrage and other political struggles. Charlotte Despard was more actively involved with the poor in Wandsworth, where she also championed the cause of the Irish and votes for women. Although **Flora Mayor** was aware of the plight of the poor of Kingston in her role as daughter of a local cleric, it did not play a large part in her life. Born in 1872, she grew up in a genteel and relatively prosperous family, living most of her life at Queensgate House, on Kingston Hill, overlooking Richmond Park. Following schooling at Surbiton High School, she studied at Cambridge University. After a brief and undistinguished acting career, she published as F. M. Mayor some well-observed fiction, notably *The Third Miss Symons* [1913] and *The Rector's Daughter* [1924]. Her accounts of the devalued existence of unmarried women were keenly accurate and drew attention to the indignities and suffering of capable but frustrated and oppressed women whose potential was generally completely dismissed.

LAMBETH, *London Borough of* [see Map 3, B3]   Lambeth, on the south bank of the Thames, now includes the districts of Brixton, Kennington, Clapham and Streatham.

Lambeth Lambeth Palace, the London home of the Archbishop of Canterbury, senior cleric of the Church of England, is at the heart of Lambeth. Traditionally churches were places which offered sanctuary where secular authorities could not interfere. During the 'Cat and Mouse Act', in force in 1913, suffragette **Annie Kenney** sought sanctuary unsuccessfully at the Palace, interviewing the Archbishop. Her aim had been to enlist the Church's support for women's enfranchisement. He called in the police and she was again arrested. Six days later she returned; finding the gates barred to her she lay down on the ground. Having been released after hungerstriking, she had medical help with her, but she was still taken away to the local hospital. This was one of several incidents designed to embarrass the establishment, and the Women's Social and Political Union derived further publicity for the Cause.

In the fifteenth century, **Margery Kempe**, a Norfolk woman whose religious visions inspired her to undertake a journey to the Holy Land, sought the blessing here of the then Archbishop of Canterbury. The Church had little esteem for this ill-educated woman. Nonetheless she successfully reached the Holy Land and on her return described her travels in *The Boke of Margery Kempe*, a remarkable account, which, since she was illiterate, she dictated in *c.* 1420. In nearby St Mary-at-Lambeth Church, now housing the Museum of Garden History★, **Gertrude Jekyll** is credited in the displays as a leading influence in modern garden design and planting.

The South Bank has become a Mecca for the arts now, and its artistic foundations may rightly be said to have been laid by **Emma Cons** and her niece **Lilian Baylis**. Emma had become active in the reformed housing projects of her old schoolfriend Octavia Hill, and had succeeded in raising enough money to buy property in Lambeth. She managed the property, Surrey Lodge, herself, concerning herself with the welfare of the tenants. She did not drink alcohol herself, and took action to discourage her tenants, by acquiring in 1880 a redundant music-hall, which was to become known as the Old Vic, on the corner of Waterloo Road and Webber Street. She called it the Royal Victoria Coffee Music Hall and here she organised lectures and concerts, with coffee the only refreshment on offer. The lecture programme developed into a separate institution, Morley College, by Westminster Bridge Road. **Mary Sheepshanks**, the energetic pacifist, was its first vice-principal and effective lynchpin; the college continues to offer a wide programme of educational activities for working adults.

The theatrical side blossomed from 1898 when Lilian Baylis took over responsibility for its management for her aunt. Emma's energies were needed elsewhere and by then she was one of the first women representatives on London County Council. Lilian Baylis was a member of a musical family which moved from London to South Africa eight years earlier and she responded to her aunt's request for assistance. When she was in sole charge on Emma's death in 1912, she further expanded the scope of the Old Vic to include ballet and opera as well as plays and music programmes. **Sybil Thorndike** played Shakespearean roles there throughout the First World War. The high standard of drama created demand for a permanent company at the Old Vic, so by 1931 it was time to look elsewhere for housing ballet and opera. **Lilian Baylis** established Sadler's Wells in Islington. From her return to London she made her home at 27 Stockwell Park Road, among the audience she aimed to serve. When she died there in 1937, her ashes were scattered, as she requested, in East London Cemetery. The Old Vic later became the National Theatre in recognition of its standing in British theatre and is now housed in riverside premises. It is a fine memorial to the achievements of these two women.

Another lasting memorial to a woman's determination to succeed is at St Thomas's Hospital. It was here on the Albert Embankment that **Florence Nightingale** set up the Nightingale School of Nursing, taking in its first students in 1860. Using guidelines based on her own nursing experience in the Crimean War, she established a training programme that remains the basis of modern professional nursing around the world. Soon hospitals, nursing homes and workhouse infirmaries throughout the country had trained nursing staff, as similar training was provided at other centres. The trainees are still called Nightingale Nurses, and a Florence Nightingale Museum Trust has been established to set up a museum of nursing history which will be worth visiting. Earlier **James Miranda Barry** had determined to become a doctor, but she had to resort to a lifetime's disguise as a man in order to follow her chosen profession. In 1812 she trained as a surgeon at Old St Thomas's Hospital, which stood on the north bank of the Thames, before joining the army medical service.

The Royal Festival Hall now covers the site on Pedlar's Acre where the two **Eleanor Coade**s ran their very successful factory. Coade Stone was a reconstituted stone, made to a special formula. It could be cast to produce architectural ornaments which still decorate houses, churches, tombs and schools throughout Britain. The venture was a joint venture of mother and daughter, after the death in 1770 of Mr Coade. There was still a factory on the site in the 1940s.

Brixton The Second World War heroine **Violette Szabo** grew up in Brixton, although she was born in France in 1921. Her Anglo-French parents had ensured that she continued to speak French, and her wartime marriage to a French soldier served to maintain her fluency. After being widowed in 1941, she volunteered for special missions in enemy territory. Knowing the risks, she was taken prisoner on her second undercover trip to France, enduring torture and intense interrogation before being executed in Germany in 1945. A plaque on her childhood home, 18 Burnley Road, commemorates her bravery and patriotism: 'She gave her life for the French Resistance.'

Kennington **Edith Nesbit**, the author of much loved books for children, was born at 38 Lower Kennington Lane in 1858. Hers was a very happy childhood, and her works recall this and the lives of her own children. *The Five Children and It* [1902], *Phoenix and the Carpet* [1904] and *The Railway Children* [1906] are among her books still read today.

Streatham **Hester Thrale**'s parents arranged for her to marry Henry Thrale, MP for Streatham, in 1763 when she was twenty-two. It may have been an advantageous match from her parents' point of view but she was never very close to her husband. However, she was a dutiful wife, living at Streatham Place, their country home. Here their regular guests included **Fanny Burney** and Samuel Johnson. Hester became the leading literary hostess of her day. Nothing now remains of Streatham Place which was dismantled in 1863, though the summerhouse was removed and eventually re-erected on Hampstead Heath. She was encouraged to write by Samuel Johnson, whom she met in 1764. They became close friends and her learning and intellect earned his respect, a considerable achievement as he had little time for women. The relationship ended after her second, far happier marriage to an Italian singer in 1784. She gave up Streatham Place in 1795 when she and Mr Piozzi settled in her native Wales.

Dorothy Richardson, also an addicted writer, in the stream of consciousness style, died in 1957, completing twelve volumes of her *Pilgrimage* [1915-67]. This was a series of semi-autobiographical novels in which much of the narrative appears as the unspoken thoughts and feelings of Miriam Henderson, the central character, in an unstructured but telling way. This device has since been used by other twentieth-century novelists such as Virginia Woolf, Marcel Proust and James Joyce. Dorothy Richardson was buried in Streatham Park Cemetery. Her grave marker names her as Dorothy Miriam Odle, and justly describes her as 'a pioneer among novelists'. She published her work as D. M. Richardson, usually taken to be derived from her maiden name Dorothy Miller Richardson; here she appears to have identified so closely with her fictional heroine that she has been given the middle name of Miriam. In 1917 she had married an artist Alan Odle.

West Norwood Cemetery, in Norwood High Street, is now Lambeth's Borough Cemetery. It provides the last resting place of **Isabella Beeton** and **Eleanor Rathbone**. Mrs Beeton died aged only twenty-eight in 1865, leaving as a continuing legacy her mammoth work on domestic matters, *Mrs Beeton's Book of Household Management* [1861]. She first published it in instalments in a magazine produced by her husband Sam. She had no formal domestic science training, but she had gained much useful experience from running her own small household. Her book, though frequently revised, remains in print. Eleanor Rathbone worked more publicly for the improvement of family life. As the Independent Member of Parliament representing the Combined Universities, a seat which was discontinued after the Second World War, from 1929, she fought for the introduction of the Family Allowance Act of 1945 to give women with dependent children some financial security of their own. Her book *The Disinherited Family* [1924] was extremely influential and focused on the importance of child-rearing to the nation's future and women's key role. She died in 1946 after a lifetime supporting improvements for women, and was buried here.

LEWISHAM, *London Borough of* [see Map 3, B3]   This south London borough stretches from Deptford on the Thames to Catford and Sydenham in the south.

Deptford Two Scots sisters, **Margaret** and **Rachel McMillan**, had already been concerned about the government's neglect of the issue of child health, in both Bradford and Scotland. In 1902 Margaret opened her first clinic in Bow and, encouraged by the response and with the help of Rachel, she opened a health centre for children which combined a large safe outdoor play area and well-appointed washing facilities. It was known as the Rachel McMillan Open Air Nursery School. Both sisters were convinced of the contribution of hygiene to health and pioneered many precepts of pre-school education. After Rachel's death in 1917 Margaret worked towards proper training for nursery education and succeeded in 1930 in establishing the Rachel McMillan Training College.

Lewisham During their work in the Borough, the McMillan sisters lived from 1910 until 1913 at 127 George Lane, just off Lewisham High Street. Lewisham's best loved daughter was **Gladys Cooper**, the actress. She was born in Lewisham in 1888. In addition to a long and admired stage career, she successfully managed London's Playhouse Theatre for sixteen years. **Marie Lloyd**, the comedienne, also lived locally. Despite her public face of cheerfulness, her first marriage in 1887 was unhappy and unsettling. Her home was then on the corner of Lewisham High Road and Wickham Road, in Brockley.

Sydenham **Eleanor Marx** was able to buy a house here, The Den in Jews Walk, in 1895, having received an inheritance on the death of Friedrich Engels, the friend and collaborator of her father Karl. She was a dedicated socialist in her own right, and a tireless worker for the deprived. Unhappiness in her relationship with Edward Aveling led her to commit suicide in 1898.

MERTON, *London Borough of* [see Map 3, B3]   The south London Borough of Merton includes Mitcham, Morden and Wimbledon. It was formerly in Surrey.

Merton **Emma Hamilton**, whose relationship with Admiral Lord Nelson was considered scandalous at the time, appeared to have caused little pain to her husband Sir William Hamilton. She had a daughter in 1801, named Horatia Nelson Thompson, who was officially described as the Hamiltons' adopted daughter, in deference to prevailing moral codes. Indeed the four of them seem to have established a contented household in Merton. Their home, Merton Place, where in 1803 Sir William died, no longer stands. The River Wandle ran through part of the estate, and Emma had it diverted and nicknamed it the Nile, to commemorate her lover's famous victory in Egypt in 1798. Emma's happiness came to an end on Nelson's heroic death at the Battle of Trafalgar in 1805 and her life was lived out in sorrow. She died in France in 1815 and is buried at Calais.

Wimbledon Best known as the venue for the annual All England Lawn Tennis Championships which began in 1877, Wimbledon records the achievements of women tennis players in the Lawn Tennis Museum★. Women have had their own competitions here from 1884. It is one of the few sporting competitions in which women have participated actively since almost its inception. Their successes are chronicled in *Ladies of the Court: a Century of Women at Wimbledon*, Virginia Wade, Atheneum, London, 1984. **Dorothea Douglass** was an early winner with an outstanding record: she was the Women's Singles Champion in 1903, 1904, 1906, 1910, 1911, 1913 and 1914. Although the game has changed since then women continue to provide spectators with first-rate entertainment, displaying impressive skill and power.

Margaret Rutherford, the fine character actress, was a pupil in the 1900s at Wimbledon High School. Originally trained for a music career, she persevered in her determination to act, ultimately attaining national and international recognition. The historical novelist **Georgette Heyer** was a native of Wimbledon. Her works were extremely well researched, and she became an authority on her favourite period, the Regency era. An earlier writer **George Eliot** spent part of 1859 and 1860 living at 31 Wimbledon Park Road. At that time the house was known as Holly Lodge. It was here that she wrote *The Mill on the Floss* [1860]. She openly shared her life with George Lewes, a married man, which was then regarded as scandalous. They had made the decision to live together in 1854 and, realising the far-reaching implications of their new partnership in the Victorian moral climate, they initially lived abroad. On their return they were predictably shunned by society. However, their mutual love and support sustained them and close friends still valued their friendship. Among these supporters was the ardent feminist Barbara Bodichon, later the inspiration for George Eliot's *Romola* [1863], set in medieval Italy. They were always both welcomed by the intellectual community but only towards the end of their lives were they accepted in other social circles.

NEWHAM, *London Borough of* [see Map 3, B3]   The borough, which is in the east on the north bank of the Thames, includes Canning Town, East and West Ham, Stratford and some of the former docklands.

West Ham   The area has a long tradition of Nonconformist worship. **Elizabeth Fry**'s marriage brought her into a wealthy merchant family, also Quakers. Her family already had interests in East Ham, so the district was not new to her. She lived in the Fry country home, Plashet, from 1809 until the family fortunes suffered in 1829. The house was demolished in 1883, but is recalled in the naming of a residential area beside East Ham's High Street. Elizabeth Fry would not recognise the village today, now built up as a busy London suburb.

Stratford   The village of Stratford was transformed into a significant settlement on a major road to the capital when **Queen Matilda** had the Bow Bridge built over the River Lea *c.* 1110. It linked the east side of the river with Bow, in what is now the Borough of Tower Hamlets.

REDBRIDGE, *London Borough of* [see Map 3, A3]   Redbridge is a north-east London borough, lying on the southern edge of Epping Forest. Within its administrative district lie Woodford and Ilford.

Ilford **Dame Kathleen Lonsdale** showed her academic ability early. In 1914 she was awarded a scholarship at the local girls' school, London County High School. From there she embarked on an outstanding career as a scientist specialising in crystallography. Her list of scientific publications is impressive and her achievements were marked by her election to Fellowship of the Royal Society in 1945. Many other academic honours followed.

Woodford Green **Sylvia Pankhurst** moved to Woodford Green in 1924, by which time she was a full-time writer. Her home from 1930 until 1956 when she left for Ethiopia was West Dene, 3 Charteris Road, but the house no longer stands. Although she is generally associated with the struggle for the enfranchisement of women, which she documents in *The Suffragette Movement* [1931], she supported other causes: internationalism, maternity provision, freedom of speech, the welfare of the peoples of India and Ethiopia. In 1935, with others, she had 'the bomb monument' erected in Woodford High Road, opposite the Horse and Well public house, as a protest against air warfare. She died in Addis Ababa in Ethiopia in 1960.

RICHMOND, *London Borough of* [see Map 3, B2]   Richmond, which used to be in the county of Surrey, straddles both sides of the Thames in London's south-west. It comprises several royal parks and palaces and former villages, most of which still give the impression of compact communities. These include Kew, Twickenham, Ham, Petersham and Richmond itself. When travel by water was often the quickest and safest means of transport, it made sense to have palaces with access to the Thames.

Barnes In the seventeenth century, Barnes was a comparatively isolated community. It attracted the northern intellectual **Anne Baynard**. She was a well-educated woman and early feminist. Deeply-involved in philosophical thinking, she passed the last two years of her life in meditation in the graveyard of St Mary's Church. She was buried at the east end of the churchyard in 1697. The exact site has not been traced, although the inscription from her lost monument has been recorded:

> 'Here lies that happy maiden who often said
> That no man is happy until he is dead,
> That the business of life is but playing the fool,
> Which hath no relation to saving the soul;
> For all the transaction that's under the sun

Is doing of nothing – if that be not done.
All wisdom and knowledge does lie in this one.'

East Sheen George Eliot, whose relationship with George Lewes was never socially acceptable in Victorian eyes, lived in East Sheen for four years and her first published works of fiction were written here: *Scenes of Clerical Life* [1857], and *Adam Bede* [1859]. Initially, in 1855, they stayed at 7 Clarence Row, thought to be the site of the Bull Inn. They then moved into 8 Park Shot, near the Old Deer Park. The photographer **Julia Margaret Cameron** lived in East Sheen when she first settled in England in 1848. She had been born and raised in Ceylon [now Sri Lanka], but brought her own children up in Britain. It was one of her daughters who gave her a camera in 1864, when she was forty-eight years old. Her understanding of the camera's possibilities enabled her to produce the artistic portraits for which she is recognised today. Her models included her own household and friends such as the poet Alfred, Lord Tennyson. Much of her photography was taken on the Isle of Wight in her summer home there.

Ham The most important building in this pretty village is Ham House★, an architectural gem from the seventeenth century. It was built in 1610, but the present house is mainly the work of **Elizabeth Murray**, Countess of Dysart and Duchess of Lauderdale. Her father had acquired it in 1637, and she inherited it on his death in 1650. At this time she was married to Sir Lionel Tollemache, living mainly at his Suffolk home, Helmingham Hall. However, she was a well-educated and determined woman, and pursued her own interests. These included her father's title which she eventually won the right to hold herself and pass on to her heirs. She was always close to the political affairs of the day, surviving the uncertainty of the Commonwealth, the Restoration and the Glorious Revolution by shrewd alliances. Her second marriage in 1671 was to John Maitland, Duke of Lauderdale, and it was during this marriage that she created the house which can be visited today. Women contributed to architecture at this time more as commis-sioners of buildings rather than as architects or designers themselves. Indeed architecture was only just emerging as a profession separate from building, and it was to be another three centuries before women became actively involved. The redbrick house is laid out on an H-shaped plan with Elizabeth's work a filling in of the south side to double the size of the building. The interior has splendid decorative schemes, which, together with the furnishing, give a full impression of Elizabeth's taste and lifestyle. The gardens are preserved in period style with appropriate plantings and are charming.

A particularly attractive smaller building, Ormley Lodge, was made available to **Mrs Fitzherbert** for her third honeymoon. In 1785 she consented to marry the Prince of Wales, later George IV. The wedding was a closely guarded secret, and was never officially recognised by the Prince nor sanctioned by the government. She always considered herself as his legal wife and remained true to that, despite the Prince's other relationships and his royal wife. In the next century the lodge was the home of the teenaged **Catherine Sinclair**, Victorian children's writer and benefactor of many good causes. Her best known book *Holiday House* [1839] broke new ground in that its story was written for the wholehearted enjoyment of younger readers rather than the didactic preaching which was the general aim of other children's fiction. Her adult writings included essays, novels, and descriptive travel books.

Hampton Court The magnificent redbrick Hampton Court Palace★ began as a private home built on the north bank of the river for Cardinal Wolsey in 1515, until he felt obliged to present it to his sovereign Henry VIII in 1529. Then its association with some significant women began, naturally with some of Henry's wives. By then Henry had already met his second wife **Anne Boleyn**, who is remembered in the fine brick gateway named after her and in her initials which feature in much of the structure of the Great Hall. His anxieties about the lack of an heir developed into 'the King's Great Matter' which ultimtely led to the separation of England from the Church of Rome, the establishment of the Church of England, with the sovereign at its head, and his divorce from **Catherine of Aragon** and his marriage to Anne Boleyn in 1533. This marriage failed to provide a male heir which he so desired, and so was followed by a third, to **Jane Seymour** in 1536. Jane was Henry's favourite wife, and sadly she died here giving birth to Edward VI the next year. **Anne of Cleves**' marriage in 1540 lasted barely six months to be followed immediately by the king's fifth marriage, to **Catherine Howard**, a lady-in-waiting to her predecessor. Her reign was another short one, falling from favour late in 1541 and losing her head in 1542. She and Jane Seymour are said to haunt the Palace as ghosts. Henry's sixth wife, **Catherine Parr**, married him in 1543 and succeeded in making the royal household a happier place. She was more mature, having already been widowed twice, and brought together Henry's three children and Anne of Cleves in remarkable harmony.

Henry appointed the Flemish artist **Lavinia Teerlinc** as court painter in 1545. Her work was then regarded more highly than that of Hans Holbein, whom she followed into this position. She continued to serve the next three sovereigns. Her speciality was portrait miniatures, several of which have survived.

Henry had greatly enlarged the Palace, and his successors enjoyed it in this style, including **Mary I** and **Elizabeth**. **Mary Fitton** and **Mary Sidney** would have attended to Elizabeth here as her ladies-in-waiting. Further architectural changes were made by Christopher Wren for **Mary II** and her husband William III. Mary died here of smallpox in 1694, five years after coming to the throne. She had the famous maze planted and her sister **Queen Anne** had the lower orangery built. There was little court use of the Palace thereafter, and it was **Queen Victoria** who in 1839 arranged for the state apartments to be open to the public, as they still are. The complex is huge and there remain some private dwellings within it. One of these was a 'grace and favour' apartment made available to **Olave Baden-Powell** towards the end of her life. She used it from 1942 until 1973.

In the previous century the young **Caroline Norton** was raised by her widowed mother in another such apartment, the only truly happy period in a tortured life. Her later suffering resulted in the struggle for the recognition · of the rights of married women. The young Caroline Sheridan became the wife of George Norton in 1827. When it was clear that the marriage was failing she tried in vain to keep her three sons with her, but the law decreed otherwise. Her activities to right this injustice included her publication *The Natural Claim of a Mother to the Custody of her Children* [1836]. It eventually led to the passing of the Infant Custody Act of 1839. Yet the battle was not over for her. She was already a published author of poetry, plays and novels, but, as a married woman, she was not entitled to keep the income they earned; instead it went to her husband who made her no allowance. She then published *English Laws for Women in the Nineteenth Century* [1854], highlighting the invidious position of married women in relation to property and the iniquitous situation of divorced women. Ultimately her voice influenced the 1857 Divorce Act and the Married Women's Property Act of 1870.

Kew The world famous Royal Botanical Gardens★ at Kew were founded in 1759 by Princess Augusta, although the research activity which is now so important did not begin until 1841. The gardens are the park of Kew Palace★, also known as the Dutch House. Inside are many items dating from its occupation by George III. **Mrs Delaney**, who was very close to Queen Charlotte, enjoyed the flowers at Kew. It was through her that **Fanny Burney** was appointed as Assistant Dresser to the Queen in 1786. Fanny never felt at ease in such intimate royal society and resigned as soon as she decently could.

The plants are not the only treasures at Kew Gardens. Among the covered displays is the **Marianne North** Gallery★. Marianne North had studied plants for drawings in the glasshouses at Kew. On becoming independent in 1869, when her father died, she decided that she would like to paint these exotic species in their natural environment. Her botanical travels took her to distant corners of the world: Japan, Sarawak, North and South America, South Africa, Australia and India. She painted wherever she went and was the first person to describe some new species, some of which were given her name. The authorities at Kew were so impressed with her work that they willingly accepted the gift of her paintings and the gallery, which she paid for herself.

Edith Holden's talents as a nature artist have only been recognised posthumously. Sadly in 1920 she drowned in the Thames near Kew probably while collecting material to paint. Her charming illustrated diaries were published as *The Country Diary of an Edwardian Lady* in 1977 and doubtless she would have been surprised at the commercial success of not only the Diary but also the many domestic products decorated with her sketches which established a popular furnishing style based on a nostalgia for country life. Her last years, after her marriage, were spent in London and it may be that she never really adjusted to life in the capital.

Mortlake On the south side of the Thames, to the north of East Sheen, Mortlake has the Roman Catholic Cemetery on North Worple Way, attached to St Mary Magdalen. Its most impressive memorial is the Arabian tent made in concrete, standing lifesized. It was put up in 1890 by **Isabel Burton** as the grave monument to her husband whom she had accompanied on diplomatic missions to Brazil, Syria and Trieste and other travels in the Middle East and India. Sir Richard is better known for his published works, especially his translations of the *Arabian Nights*. Isabel, however, had quite a few adventures herself and also wrote, notably her husband's biography after his death. She had lived in North Worple Way to supervise the construction of the grave marker. She died in 1896 and was buried here with her husband.

Petersham **Elizabeth Murphy**, ambitious owner of Ham House, was buried in St Peter's Church in Church Lane in 1698. Inside, the box pews have been retained. The precocious writer **Daisy Ashford** was born in the village in 1881. Her best known book, *The Young Visiters*, still regarded as a classic, was written when she was only nine years old, but not published until 1919. It is still in print.

Richmond Richmond stands by Richmond Hill, overlooking the Royal Park of Richmond. All that remains of Richmond Palace, where **Elizabeth I** died in 1603, is a brick gateway. Maids of Honour Row, on Richmond Green, was built in 1724 to house the maids of honour of the then Princess of Wales, Caroline of Ansbach, George II's consort.

Some notable literary women lived in the town, none of whom could be described as bowing to convention. **George Eliot**, regarded by many contemporaries as a social outcast for openly living with a married, though separated, man, George Lewes, stayed where Richmond borders on East Sheen. **Mary Braddon**, the writer of sensational novels, had also outraged the social mores by living with her publisher, John Maxwell. However, she was able to marry him after his wife's death in 1874 and was at home in Lichfield House [where Lichfield Court now stands], Sheen Road, when she died in 1915. By then she had written more than seventy novels, some of which are said to have been set in Richmond. Her most famous work was *Lady Audley's Secret* [1862] which caused a sensation on publication and was a financial success. She was buried in the Parish Church of Saint Mary's, where she is commemorated by a tablet on the wall. **Virginia Woolf** moved to Richmond from Bloomsbury in 1914. At first she and her husband stayed at 17 The Green, before settling the following year in Hogarth House in Paradise Road. They took its name for their Hogarth Press which produced in 1918 as its first imprint **Katherine Mansfield**'s *Prelude*. They returned to Bloomsbury in 1924.

Twickenham West of Richmond, across the Thames, Twickenham still boasts some attractive historic buildings. **Lady Mary Wortley Montagu** was an early literary resident. She stayed briefly in Heath Road at Savile House [no longer standing] but she was always restless. Much of her adult life was spent abroad, especially after she left her husband in 1739. She was a prolific correspondent and many of her letters, which describe her life in France and Italy as well as her experiences as young wife to a diplomat at the Turkish court, were published in 1763, the year after her death. Marble Hill House★, a Palladian mansion built in 1728 for **Henrietta Howard**, mistress of George II, is another architectural gem. Henrietta was a contemporary of Lady Mary Wortley Montagu and was later created Countess of Suffolk. She was one of the more discreet of royal mistresses. A later resident was **Mrs Fitzherbert**, morganatic wife of George IV. A devout Roman Catholic, Maria Fitzherbert would not agree to being his mistress; after their quiet wedding in 1785 she always considered herself his legal wife and was much grieved by his later marriage to Caroline of Brunswick. Little Marble Hill was one of the homes of **Lady Diana Beauclerk**, the gifted amateur artist. She had decorated the interior herself. She sold it in 1780, and two years later it was destroyed.

Probably the most remarkable building in Twickenham is Strawberry Hill. Horace Walpole transformed a mere cottage into a gothic revival fantasy, which became a meeting place for literary personalities in the second half of the eighteenth century. Lady Diana Beauclerk provided some of the illustrations for his verse tragedy *The Mysterious Mother* [1768]. He valued his female friends highly and was most generous in his support of them. The actress **Kitty Clive**, who had specialised in comedy, was his neighbour. He gave her life-rent to Little Strawberry Hill [now gone], which was renamed Cliveden in her honour. She died there in 1785 and was buried in the church of St Mary the Virgin where she is commemorated in verse on a wall-mounted memorial stone. Considering the social status of many in the acting profession theirs was an uncommon friendship. He later sponsored two sisters, **Mary** and **Agnes Berry**, whom he had met in 1787. They both wrote but Mary is the better known because on Walpole's death in 1797 she edited his works. In 1791 he had established the sisters in Little Strawberry Hill, which they inherited on his death. They also were named as his literary executors. Walpole helped his cousin too, the sculptor **Anne Damer**, by making a small building in his garden available as a studio. She was left Strawberry Hill in Walpole's will, and was a neighbour and friend to the Berrys, until she moved away in 1811. Strawberry Hill★ is now a teacher training college and can be viewed by appointment. Anne Damer enjoyed living in Twickenham and her later house, bought in 1817, was the fine redbrick building called York House.

SOUTHWARK, *London Borough of* [see Map 3, B3]   Taking its name from the cathedral district, this borough on the south bank includes Bermondsey, Camberwell, Dulwich, Peckham and Rotherhithe.

Dulwich This quiet suburb once was home to some very radical women. **Louise Michel**, the French revolutionary socialist and communard, was obliged to flee France in 1890. She had already spent several years in a penal colony in the South Seas for her militancy during the civil unrest in Paris during 1870 and 1871. She had earned the nickname 'La Petroleuse' on account of her use of incendiary bombs. She found a refuge in East Dulwich after her involvement in French strikes. After maintaining political contacts in Britain, she was able to return to France, where she died in 1896. The trade unionist **Annie Besant**, who may have known Louise through their mutual friends, the Pankhursts, lived at 39 Colby Road. She first rented it in 1874. She had become a socialist and worked tirelessly to improve the situations of women and children in London and later in India. She wrote *An Autobiography* in 1893, but lived on until 1933. In *Why I Became a Theosophist* [1889] she expounded the thinking of the Theosophical Society, a secular movement influenced by Eastern Philosophies and led by Madame Helena Blavatsky.

Peckham **Maria Susan Rye**, an early social worker, undertook the care of neglected children by opening a home for waifs and strays in her native Peckham. Her activities broadened when she concluded that such children would have a better life in the New World. She therefore arranged emigration and placement in Canada of many children. At the time she was convinced of the benefits to the children, although this approach would be hard to defend today.

Southwark Originally a suburb of London, Southwark could be reached by old London Bridge, then the only one crossing the Thames. In addition to Southwark Cathedral, it was known for its prisons. **Charlotte Smith**'s husband was imprisoned as a debtor, and she was obliged to spend some months with him at the prison in Scovell Road [now gone] with their children in *c.* 1784. It was an experience which she never wished to repeat and after it she supported her family herself with her own writings. Her first success was *Elegiac Sonnets* [1784] and she branched out from poetry into novels which were also well received. Her contemporary **Hester Thrale** was more financially secure, thanks to her husband's brewery in Park Street. The present brewery is not the original. Nothing remains of Mr Thrale's premises, nor of their townhouse which stood in the same street. Their main home was Streatham Place in what is now the Borough of Lambeth. Samuel Johnson stayed with the Thrales when they were in residence in Southwark. He regarded Hester Thrale as the only intelligent woman of his acquaintance and valued her opinions highly. After his death she published anecdotes about his life, showing how intimately they had known one another. Their friendship did not survive her second, very

ated locally in the popular Anchor Pub on Bankside. As a very sociable woman, she might have appreciated this, though she would rarely have visited such places herself.

Southwark was also the homeground of Mary Wollstonecraft's friend, another feminist writer **Mary Hays**. She was born in 1760 and, like many radical thinkers, she was brought up in a Nonconformist household. She put forward her views of women's lot and proposals to change it, in print. She also published a six-volume work on women and their achievements in 1803, to prove that women in the past had contributed in many significant ways: *Female Biography, or Memoirs of Illustrious and Celebrated Women of All Ages and Countries, Alphabetically Arranged*. Other works include her feminist novel *Memoirs of Emma Courtney* [1796], reissued by Pandora Press in 1986.

SUTTON, *London Borough of* [see Map 3, B3]   Formerly part of the county of Surrey, Sutton includes Carshalton, Cheam and Beddington.

Sutton In 1900 **Dora Russell**'s family moved to Sutton. As Dora Black she attended Sutton High School, an intensely academic school for girls. The education which she received here enabled her in 1912 to win a scholarship to study at the University of Cambridge.

TOWER HAMLETS, *London Borough of* [see Map 3, B3]   This East End borough still has a high population density. It covers Clerkenwell, Whitechapel, Limehouse, Stepney, Poplar, Bow and Bethnal Green. The area attracted much philanthropy, in attempts to alleviate the often miserable conditions in which many East Enders lived. Housing projects, modelled on those of **Octavia Hill**, were organised, settlements, which gave well-educated women and men the experience which started them on a path towards social reform, were set up. The first of these settlements, Toynbee Hall in Commercial Street, was visited by the American social reformer and pacifist **Jane Addams** in 1888. It inspired her to start Hull House, a similar venture in Chicago in 1889. Some settlements were linked to women's university colleges, which sent a few graduates there and arranged fund-raising through former students working in other fields. For many it was the first step in a career in social work. It has to be said that patronising attitudes were in evidence, but a great deal of fine work was done, especially in drawing attention to the appalling housing and working conditions endured by so many. Jane Addams kept in touch with Europe and her reaction to the First World War led her to become the founder-president of the Women's International League for Peace and Freedom.

Sylvia Pankhurst was also active in the East End of London. In 1914, as a reaction against the middle-class bias of the Women's Social and Political Union, she started the East London Federation of Suffragettes, whose membership was mainly working class. She produced *Woman's Dreadnought* as the weekly voice of her new organisation.

Clerkenwell Exmouth Street, off Commercial Road, was the site of another London spa. In 1779 **Selina Hastings**, Countess of Huntingdon, opened her first chapel here, then called Spa Fields, and she lived in the house which she had built next door to it. The Countess of Huntingdon's Connection, as her patronage of early Methodism was referred to, ended on her death here in 1791, but the chapel and house survived until their demolition one hundred years after their completion.

The Elizabethan poet **Emilia Lanier** is thought to have died in Clerkenwell in 1645. A poet in her own right, she is also thought by some scholars to have been the inspiration for Shakespeare's sonnets addressed to his 'Dark Lady'. Her poetry, originally published as *Salve Deus Rex Judaeorum* [1611], has recently been reprinted as *Poems of Shakespeare's Dark Lady* [1978].

Poplar **Annie Besant** held her first elected office as a member of the School Board in Tower Hamlets in 1889. She was a leading light in the Matchgirls Strike in 1888 at the Bryant & May factory in Fairfield Road. The strike was one of the first succesful actions taken by women workers. They were employed in the factory on the banks of the River Lea, making matches, and exposed to the hazards of working with chemicals. Annie Besant's action with the matchgirls sought improved pay and working conditions and drew attention to the industrial disease 'phossy jaw', a form of cancer associated with phosphorus.

Mary Hughes was an example of the type of woman who devoted herself to those among whom she lived at 71 Vallance Road. As the plaque on her home records, 'Mary Hughes [1860-1941], friend of all in need, lived and worked here 1927-1941.' The London Hospital in the Mile End Road was the focus of a women's campaign for more understanding treatment in maternity care in 1984 and 1985. The consultant **Wendy Savage**, a respected medical researcher and academic, as well as a practising gynaecologist and obstetrician, was the focus of the campaign. Her practice of involving her patients in the decision-making in managing births, and using the latest high technology only in the event of potential danger to the health of the mother and child or at the request of the mother, received little sympathy from her male colleagues. She was suspended from her position at the hospital while an investigation into alleged professional negligence looked at her record. Throughout this period she received support from women from all over Britain who felt as strongly as she did that the women concerned should as far as possible have choice and control in the conduct of their labour. In 1986 Wendy Savage was cleared of all allegations of negligence. Her case had brought public attention to the insidious unnecessary use of new methods of delivery, introduced often for the convenience of doctors without reference to the wishes of the patients. The debate has aired many connected concerns and will have long-term benefits for woman-centred developments in childbirth. Although this was inevitably a stressful period for Dr Savage, this strong woman has raised many important issues and drawn together the vocal support of many women.

Spitalfields This area was famous in the seventeenth and eighteenth centuries for the silk weaving industry. Many Huguenot refugees were employed locally. **Susanna Wesley**, later known as 'the Mother of Methodism', was raised in this quarter, before her marriage to Samuel Wesley, an Anglican cleric. She brought up her own children, including the founders of the Methodist form of Christian belief and worship John and Charles Wesley, at Epworth in Lincolnshire. When this new sect gained adherents, many Huguenots were attracted by its doctrines and simplicity, not unlike the form of Protestantism that their families had followed in France before the Revocation of the Edict of Nantes in 1685 led them to seek safety in Britain.

Stepney The Flemish artist **Lavinia Teerlinc** served as court painter from the reign of Henry VIII until her death in Stepney in 1576. Her appointment had covered four reigns, which is testimony to the high opinion in which her works, mainly portrait miniatures, were held. In *c.* 1713 the woman soldier **Phoebe Hassall** was born in Stepney. As her gravestone in Brighton records, she saw active service abroad, a remarkable life for a woman at this period. She served with the Fifth Foot [Royal Northumberland Fusiliers] in Europe, claiming to have been wounded in Flanders.

Whitechapel In 1836 **Elizabeth Garrett Anderson** was born into a merchant family in this area. Her father's business prospered and when she was five years old the family moved to Aldeburgh in Suffolk. It was there that she grew up, along with her much younger sister **Millicent Garrett Fawcett**. Elizabeth became the first British woman to qualify and practise as a doctor in Britain, against considerable opposition from the male medical profession. She concentrated on women's health, and helped to open medical careers to women.

WALTHAM FOREST, *London Borough of* [see Map 3, A3] Waltham Forest is a northern borough which includes part of Epping Forest, one of the former Royal Forests. Former villages within its administrative territory include Walthamstow, Wanstead and Chingford.

Chingford To the north of this small town on the edge of the forest stands Queen Elizabeth's Hunting Lodge★, the Epping Forest Museum. The attractive timber-framed building was built for **Elizabeth I**, who enjoyed the sport of hunting. Epping Forest had been a royal deer forest long before Queen Elizabeth enjoyed the sport in the late sixteenth century. It is thought that the lodge was a building from which spectators could view the hunt in progress. The museum explains how the forests were managed to preserve the game for those privileged to hunt there.

Epping Forest may also claim the site of **Boudicca**'s last battle against the Romans in AD 62. There is a hillfort at Ambersbury Bank which may have been the scene of the clash between the highly professional Roman army and Boudicca's loyal Celtic supporters. After her defeat she took poison; the several reputed burial sites vary from under Paddington Station to Anglesey and Newmarket Gap.

Walthamstow The work of **Jane** and **May Morris** can be seen at the William Morris Gallery★, Water House, Lloyd Park on Forest Road. They both produced designs and embroideries of their own as well as working on commissions for William Morris and Co. May successfully managed the needlework side of her father's firm and made her own valuable contribution to the Arts and Crafts Movement. She also espoused socialism. The gallery includes photographs, artwork and other memorabilia of the Morris family.

WANDSWORTH, *London Borough of* [see Map 3, B3]   The borough of Wandsworth, south of the river, includes Battersea and Putney as well as Wandsworth.

Balham The well-loved character actress **Margaret Rutherford** was born at 15 Dorton Road, Balham in 1892. Her acting career started late but lasted well into her seventies when she played robust elderly women, notably Agatha Christie's detective Miss Marples. Many of her later parts have been immortalised in films like *Passport to Pimlico* [1949], *Miss Prism* [1958] and *The VIPs* [1963], as well as screen versions of Agatha Christie's fiction.

Battersea **Charlotte Despard** stood as a parliamentary candidate for the Battersea constituency in 1918, the year in which the right to vote was given to women of thirty years and over. She was not successful but she had been determined to stand, for the fight for women's votes needed to continue. Women still did not have equality of voting rights and there were no women in Parliament. It was not until 1928 that all women and men of twenty-one and over could vote.

Putney Westwards along the Thames, in suburban Putney, **Ivy Compton-Burnett** was laid to rest. On her death in 1969, her body was cremated here, where her ashes are now buried in Putney Vale Cemetery. Her literary output of twenty novels in forty years included *Pastors and Masters* [1925], *Men and Wives* [1931], *Parents and Children* [1941] and *Manservant and Maidservant* [1947]; each is finely crafted and well observed. They survive the test of time.

Putney Heath provided one of the English homes of the Victorian art photographer **Julia Margaret Cameron**. She spent her youth and last years in Ceylon [modern Sri Lanka], but brought up her own children in Britain. Her family also had a home on the Isle of Wight which is where she had her studio after discovering the delights and potential of photography in 1864. Her home in Carslake Road, just off the heath, no longer stands.

Ethel Smyth's talents lay in music. She was educated in Putney before she persuaded her family to allow her to study at the Leipzig Conservatoire, from 1877. She found that the music profession was a male domain, in which she nonetheless made her mark with several of her compositions. However her native country was slower to recognise her gifts than the continental counties. She devoted two years of her life to the British struggle for women's votes, providing the stirring anthem 'The March of the Women' for the cause. The theme formed the overture to her opera *The Boatswain's Mate* [1916].

Charlotte Despard was another early parliamentary candidate, for the Labour Party. She had joined the suffrage campaign comparatively late in life, in her sixties. Her membership of the Women's Social and Political Union was brief. She resigned in 1907, disapproving of Mrs Pankhurst's style of leadership, and she founded the Women's Freedom League that year. It produced its own paper *The Vote*, and she was the first president. She lived in Nine Elms, a district of extreme poverty and neglect and she started her own welfare scheme to help women and their children, with social clubs, discussion groups, health clinics, childcare and youth activities. There was a large Irish community and she became very sympathetic to their cause, supporting Irish independence. She moved to Ireland in 1921, having adopted the ideals of Sinn Fein. She died in Belfast in Northern Ireland in 1939 in her ninety-fifth year.

WESTMINSTER, *City of* [see Map 3, B3]   Westminster is the district in the heart of London where there must be more history per square foot than anywhere else in Britain. The area covered is less than four square miles.

Within its boundaries are fashionable, extravagant, notorious and historic quarters, crowned by the Palace of Westminster: Belgravia, Mayfair, Soho, St James's, the West End, Whitehall.

Adelphi The original terrace here was built by the eighteenth-century architect Robert Adam. **Angelica Kauffmann** was among those commissioned to decorate the interiors of these fine townhouses. One of its many notable residents was the artist **Lady Diana Beauclerk**. She was born into the aristocracy and had the time to practise her art, mainly in pastel and 'soot water'. Although she exhibited, many viewed her work as that of an amateur. Nearby is Buckingham Street where **Constance Markievicz** was born in 1868. Although she later became the first woman elected as a Member of the British Parliament, she did not take up her seat in protest against the Irish situation. She was an Irish patriot and Republican who endured imprisonment for her support of Irish independence. She was serving a prison sentence at the time of her election.

Bayswater This district to the north of Hyde Park seems to have attracted several literary women. **Ann Radcliffe**, writer of gothic novels, was buried in St George's Fields in 1823. The burial ground has been cleared to create a small playground behind Hyde Park Place, and her tombstone is one of those moved up against the wall. Her book *The Mysteries of Udolpho* [1794] started a vogue for novels with supernatural settings and gothic horrors. In 1849 **Harriet Martineau** was staying at 17 Westbourne Street when she met **Charlotte Brontë**, admirer of Harriet's novel *Deerbrook* [1839]. Charlotte was visiting London to see her publisher about *Shirley* which was just being published. Harriet was by now settled in Ambleside but continued to keep in touch with London life. When **Geraldine Jewsbury** moved to London in 1857 to be near her friend Jane Carlyle, she lived in this area.

At the turn of the century the poet and journalist **Alice Meynell** was a resident of Bayswater. During 1890-1905 she lived at 47 Palace Court. A blue plaque marks her home. During her residence here two anthologies of her verse were published – *Poems* [1893] and *Later Poems* [1902] – and also collections of her essays such as *The Rhythm of Life* [1893]. The novelist **Ivy Compton-Burnett** lived at 59 Leinster Square from 1912 until 1929. She had already published her first novel, *Dolores* [1911], but she wrote no more until *Pastors and Masters* [1925] and *Brothers and Sisters* [1929], both of which were written here. Her friend and companion Margaret Jourdain, a knowledgeable collector of English decorative arts, moved into number 59 with her in 1919 and they stayed together until Margaret's death in 1951, although they moved from here to Kensington in 1934.

In Porchester Terrace, the road to the west of Leinster Square, **Jane Loudon** made her home in the lovely brick house at number 3. Here she and her husband, John, worked together on various garden design and planting projects. Although the plaque on the wall names him more prominently, her own published works on gardening saved them from bankruptcy. She wrote for women about the pleasures and practicalities of gardening, having already written a successful novel before her marriage in 1830. When her husband died in 1843, she made a career of gardening journalism and was the first editor of the influential magazine *The Ladies' Companion: at home and abroad*. She had been granted a Civil List Pension of £100, but it was not enough to live on. As the plaque acknowledges, the Loudons' work in London gardens greatly enhanced them.

Jane Strachey, who sympathised with the women's suffrage movement, spent much of her married life at 69 Lancaster Gate. Her family included other active suffragists: **Philippa Strachey**, her daughter born in 1872, and **Ray Strachey**, her American daughter-in-law and the author of a history of the struggle for women's enfranchisement, *The Cause* [1928]. A colourful public figure of late Victorian and Edwardian Britain was **Jennie Churchill**, American wife of the politician Lord Randolph Churchill. Their London home from 1883-92 was 2 Connaught Place. Three years later she was widowed, but she continued in the London limelight. An energetic woman of great charm, she nursed in the Boer War, briefly ran her own magazine and married twice more. **Elinor Glyn**, the novelist and film-script writer, was equally flamboyant. She lived for three years from 1934 at 11 Connaught Place. She had first come to public notice with her bestselling novel *Three Weeks* [1907].

Charing Cross This area is named after the last cross put up by King Edward I to mark the overnight resting place of his dead wife's body on the route from Harby to Westminster Abbey. **Eleanor of Castile** died in 1290, and had been much loved by the king. Charing may be a corruption of *chère reine*, the French for 'dear queen'. The present monument, which has been moved more than once, is a Victorian reconstruction of Edward's original which was pulled down in 1647. *84 Charing Cross Road* is the title of the published letters of American bibliophile **Helene Hanff** to the proprietors of the bookshop at that site. In ordering books from there for the USA she began a long correspondence in 1945 which has achieved its own literary merit.

Under Hungerford Bridge there is an important resource for women. This is Hungerford House, known as A Woman's Place. It houses on the first floor the Feminist Library, which is building up a collection of books and printed matter on women's issues, history and literature. The ground floor provides meeting places for women's organisations and a variety of support networks.

The Church of St Martin-in-the-Fields is the eighteenth-century church in Trafalgar Square near the National Gallery. Before it was remodelled in 1722, **Nell Gwyn**, Charles II's popular actress–mistress, was buried in the old building, but the site of her tomb is no longer identifiable. She died in 1687, Charles having died two years before, supposedly with the immortal dying words 'Let not poor Nellie starve'. Having first encountered the theatre as an 'orange-girl', selling fruit to the audience at the age of thirteen, she had her own stage career before being taken into the patronage of the philandering king. Although he had other liaisons, Charles' affection for the good-hearted, down-to-earth Nell outlasted them all. Worshippers have included **Mary Tudor** in the sixteenth century and **Vera Brittain** in this century. The church was one of several attacked by militant suffragettes in 1914, and it suffered a direct hit by bombing in the Second World War. Although some churchmen were sympathetic to the women's cause, in general the Church of England was seen as a leading part of the male establishment which obstructed the women's demands for voting rights.

Covent Garden The former market area has long been at the heart of the capital's theatrical activity. The old church of St Paul's is known as 'the actors' church' and many key figures of the British stage are commemorated inside. Among the fine actresses remembered here are: **Edith Evans**, **Vivien Leigh**, **Flora Robson**, **Margaret Rutherford**, **Ellen Terry**, whose ashes have been placed in a caged casket in the south wall, and **Sybil Thorndike**. **Lilian Baylis**, whose success as manager of the Old Vic and Sadler's Wells Theatre, is also recorded here. **Marie Lloyd** 'from 1884 Queen of British Music Hall' and **Gracie Fields** represent music on stage and **Marie Rambert**, who came to Britain in 1915, is commemorated for her contribution to ballet in Britain. It is worth looking at all the memorials on the walls as other areas of stagecraft are also recognised here.

The theatres of Covent Garden featured at important points in the careers of these and earlier figures. The Royal Opera House staged **Sarah Siddons**' farewell performance in 1812 and her niece **Fanny Kemble**'s debut in *Romeo and Juliet* in 1829. **Helen Faucit** first appeared in London there in 1836, and shortly after this, in 1839, **Madame Lucia Vestris** took over the management of the Opera House with her partner for eight years. **Adelina Patti**, the Italian singer, made her London debut on this stage in 1861. She was an immediate success and continued to sing there until 1895.

The Theatre Royal, Drury Lane, is one of the older London theatres. It is actually sited off Drury Lane in Catherine Street. **Nell Gwyn**, actress and favourite of Charles II, is thought to have grown up in the Covent Garden area and certainly became 'streetwise' at an early age. She sold oranges at the Theatre Royal before making her debut on its stage at the age of fifteen in 1665. Once she was under the patronage of the King her lifestyle changed completely and she spent much of her adult life at court. As one of the royal mistresses, she maintained a high profile throughout his reign and was rewarded with titles for her children and a generous annual grant. The theatre was also the venue for **Sarah Siddons**' first London appearance in 1775 in Shakespeare's *The Merchant of Venice* where she played a memorable Portia. In 1905 it was the setting for **Ellen Terry**'s jubilee performance where her long stage career was honoured by many fellow professionals. **Vesta Tilley** was equally popular but her speciality was male impersonation. She sang in many music-hall productions but her successful career really started in pantomime at Drury Lane. The eighteenth-century comic actress **Kitty Clive** went onto the stage in 1728 as a raw seventeen year old, and the next year began a long acting association with David Garrick. In a career lasting over forty years she played all the major women's roles in comedy and was a first-rate entertainer.

Two eighteenth-century careers followed a remarkably similar path initially. Both **Elizabeth Inchbald** and **Mary Robinson** came from Suffolk, and had London stage careers before supporting themselves as novelists. Elizabeth had several London lodgings, one in nearby Russell Street. She earned a good living from her novels and plays. Her best known work is probably *A Simple Story* [1791]. Mary Robinson was not quite so fortunate. While acting in Shakespeare's *The Winter's Tale* at the Theatre Royal, Drury Lane in 1779, she caught the attention of the Prince of Wales. From then on he named her Perdita after her role in the play, and she became his mistress. However, she was soon discarded in favour of others, and she became very bitter about this treatment. Once her acting career was over she wrote novels but was never able to live in the style she would have liked, dying in poverty at the age of forty-two. She lodged in Great Queen Street in 1774.

The Freemasons' Hall in Great Queen Street is the successor building to the one in which a crucial meeting took place in 1840. The World Anti-Slavery Convention met here. This was a gathering of mainly British and American abolitionists who were working on both sides of the Atlantic to end the system of slavery. The first sessions almost broke up in disarray when British delegates were horrified to learn that the Americans proposed to grant full delegate status to women representatives. As women were among those most active in the cause of freedom for slaves in the United States, it seemed more than reasonable that American women should present their views. However, this was overruled, and the result was an historic meeting of two exasperated women **Elizabeth Cady Stanton** and **Lucretia Mott**. Both American, they did not previously know one another, but immediately found that they shared more than just a sense of outrage. They were both determined to embark upon a course which would lead to equal rights for women in all matters. From then on they pursued their aims, organising the first Women's Rights Convention at Seneca Falls, New York State, in 1848. The Freemasons' Hall should be marked as the birthplace of the present struggle for women's rights.

Marylebone Possibly one of the most famous London addresses associated with a woman is Wimpole Street. **Elizabeth Barrett Browning** and her family moved to 99 Gloucester Place [marked with a plaque] from Sidmouth in 1835. The Barretts moved three years later to 50 Wimpole Street. A very popular play *The Barretts of Wimpole Street* depicts Elizabeth's life here with her father, brothers and her much-loved dog Flush, who also has the title role in Virginia Woolf's work *Flush: A Biography* [1933]. Elizabeth's health problems caused her to be considered an invalid and her overpowering father restricted her freedom. She had turned to literature and poetry as a result, and much of her work was published. About this time she was again suffering from ill-health so she returned to Devon, this time to Torquay. When she returned in 1841, she led a secluded existence. In 1845 she met Robert Browning, a fellow poet who admired her work but of whose attentions her father disapproved. The romantic story of their elopement in 1846 is well known. They secretly married in Marylebone Parish Church, across Marylebone Road, and left immediately for Italy, taking Flush with them. Her father never forgave her, but her health improved dramatically. She continued to write, and she and Robert had a son born in 1849. She returned briefly to London, staying at 52 Welbeck Street, and again in 1855 at 13 Dorset Street, and she died in Florence in 1861.

Nearby, Wigmore Street provided the first married home of **Emma Hamilton** after her marriage in 1791 to Sir William Hamilton. They lived here only briefly before Sir William's ambassadorial duties took them again to Naples where she eventually met Horatio Nelson, her famous lover. Marylebone Church had served in 1798 as the scene for the wedding of the Norwich writer **Amelia Opie** to John Opie, a society artist. Another writer who lived near Elizabeth Barrett Browning's former haunts was **Rose Macaulay**. After 1926 she made her home in Dorset Street. *Tale Told by an Idiot* [1923] and *The Towers of Trebizond* [1956] are among her better known novels.

The actress **Marie Tempest** grew up in 9 Park Crescent, on the south side of Marylebone Road. She returned in adulthood to this splendid crescent of townhouses, designed by the architect Nash. From 1899 until 1902 she resided at 24 Park Crescent. This was during a turning point in her career; she decided to concentrate on comedy parts after a great success on the music stage. She had originally trained as a singer in the Royal College of Music. It proved to be a sensible decision, and she developed as a comedienne. The role of Judith Bliss in *Hay Fever* was written specially for her in 1925 by Noël Coward and the play is still frequently performed. The poet **Christina Rossetti** was born at 38 Charlotte Street, Marylebone, in 1830. The site has been built over, and 106-110 Hallam Street, between Portland Street and Portland Place, has a plaque on the front which marks it as the birthplace of her brother two years earlier, but no mention is made of her own life and achievements.

In Portland Place itself **Frances Hodgson Burnett**, whose best known works were written for children, especially *Little Lord Fauntleroy* [1886] and *The Secret Garden* [1911], lived at number 63, now indicated by a blue plaque. It was her London residence for five years from 1893. Her other works were adult fiction, but perhaps her most enduring achievement was to fight a lawsuit which ultimately ensured protection of copyright for future writers in all fields. Thanks to her efforts the British Copyright Act was passed in 1911. Her years in England came to an end in 1901 when she divorced her second husband and returned to the USA. Marriage was equally unsatisfactory for **Lady Byron**, an earlier resident of the same house. As Anne Isabella Milbanke she was pursued here by Lord Byron, the poet, prior to their marriage at her family's northern home in 1815. The union did not survive the birth of their mathematically-inclined daughter **Ada Lovelace**. At the south end the street leads into Langham Place.

The group of women known as the 'Ladies of Langham Place' had their base at number 19. Here **Barbara Bodichon**, **Bessie Rayner Parkes**, **Jessie Boucherett** and **Adelaide Anne Procter** and other like minded women met to work towards greater opportunities for women in all spheres. From the rooms that they rented here they published a feminist magazine, the *English Woman's Journal*, in 1858 which charted the progress of campaigns for women's rights to votes, education, jobs, legal status, and explored other women's issues. For this enterprise the Langham Place Group received valuable encouragement from **Anna Jameson**. In 1866 it became the *Englishwoman's Review*, edited by Jessie Boucherett. She was in a financial position to support the journal personally through difficulties; indeed she virtually subsidised its publication.

In 1859 the Society for the Promotion of Women's Employment was founded at Langham Place. It aimed to help women to get satisfying work by making them more employable. This often meant providing training or seeking out prospective employers. Many of those who benefited were single women from middle-class homes who may have had some education but their families had not expected them to work, as marriage and its attendant responsibilities usually kept them occupied. However, there were many women who remained single, sometimes from choice, but were keen to gain their own financial independence or contribute to the wider community in a job which was fulfilling and productive. The role of governess or lady's companion had became an accepted position for single women or widows, but this was rarely financially, emotionally or intellectually rewarding. One of the early beneficiaries of the Society was **Maria Susan Rye**, who by 1859 was organising a copying service for the legal profession. She went on to help other women emigrate to the colonies to take up jobs overseas. More about the members and activities of the Ladies of Langham Place can be found in *Barbara Leigh Smith Bodichon and the Langham Place Group*, edited by Candida A. Lacey, Routledge & Kegan Paul, London, 1987.

A short term resident of Langham Place was the novelist **Marie Louise de la Ramée [Ouida]**. For three years from 1867 she had rooms in the very grand Langham Hotel, now used as offices for the British Broadcasting Corporation. The income from her more successful works of light fiction, such as *Held in Bondage* [1863] and *Under Two Flags* [1867], enabled her to reside in warmer climates in Europe. She enjoyed living and entertaining extravagantly, and was unable to adjust her lifestyle to a dminishing income when her type of writing went out of fashion. She died in poverty in Italy in 1908.

Adelaide Anne Procter's home was very convenient for Langham

Place. She lived at 38 Harley Street with her father, who moved in literary circles. She herself had been writing poetry and prose from an early age and her contributions to the *English Woman's Journal* followed many to earlier periodicals, including Charles Dickens' weekly journal *Household Words*. One of her better known poems is 'A Lost Chord' [1858]. Adelaide Procter died of tuberculosis in 1864, shortly before her fortieth birthday. Her home has been built over and the site is part of a larger building, number 30.

Across the street at numbers 43 to 49, is Queen's College for Women, which had been founded in 1848 by the Governesses Benevolent Institution, and which provided education for women who wished to be more effective as governesses and therefore deserving of better pay. **Dorothea Beale** was one of the first to register as a student. She taught mathematics there, and by 1854 was the head of the college, resigning after two years, to continue her chosen career elsewhere. Her name is usually linked with that of **Frances Buss**, another pioneering educationalist. Frances Buss attended evening classes at the college, before setting up an academic girls' school in London herself. Among Queen's College's former pupils were: **Sophia Jex-Blake**, who was a pioneer of medical training for women; **Louisa Twining**, the philanthropist; **Margaret Llewelyn Davies**, early secretary of the Women's Co-operative Guild; **Gertrude Bell**, who later travelled and carried out archaeological excavations in the Middle East, and whose portrait bust stands in the entrance corridor; and writer of short stories **Katherine Mansfield**. Katherine had come over from her native New Zealand with two sisters in order to attend the school. They boarded next door at 41 for four years from 1903. **Florence Nightingale**'s first major nursing responsibility was for the Sanatorium for Sick Governesses, run by a committee of 'fine ladies' [her description], in 1853. It was sited at number 1 Harley Street.

There are some fine squares in the Marylebone area, one of the grandest being Portman Square. **Elizabeth Montagu**, the wealthy Blue Stocking, had a large mansion built for herself in 1782. Then called Montagu House, it was designd by the premier neo-classical architect of the day, 'Athenian Stuart', and took up the north-west corner of the square. Unfortunately it was knocked down in the Second World War, but number 22 marks its site. Here, she was at the centre of an intellectual circle of women, whose gatherings men were invited to attend. The men were able to come dressed informally in blue stockings, rather than the more formal attire which custom and fashion generally demanded. This dress requirement gave the name to the salons which Mrs Montagu hosted here and at her other properties. All the key thinkers and writers of the late eighteenth century met here from time to time, with women taking an equal, and generally leading, part in all the discussions. Mrs Montagu died here in 1800.

In the nineteenth century **Mary Seacole** was briefly resident at 26 Upper George Street, off Portman Square, in more modest surroundings. This woman has been sadly neglected by history, though her story is no less remarkable than that of Florence Nightingale; indeed her achievements were more so. As a black woman who was very much her own mistress, she always put the suffering of others before her own. In the West Indies and Central America she had cared for many Europeans as well as Indians and Africans, helping them to overcome the effects of climate and disease using traditional skills and commonsense. She had cured many British military personnel and knew that she had much to offer when the Crimean War began in 1854. She made her own way to Britain, and then on to the Crimea when the army refused to help her. Her entrepreneurial spirit enabled her to provide many necessities for the serving soldiers and officers. Her offers of assistance were rejected by Florence Nightingale; nonetheless she cared for many sick and wounded men, earning their gratitude and affection. When the war was over many influential people provided testimonials to her good work, and although she received some public acknowledgment, she was not granted the recognition that she deserved. She published her autobiography *The Wonderful Adventures of Mrs Seacole* in 1857.

Blandford Square has provided homes for two very independent-minded women. The writer **George Eliot** lived at number 16 from 1860 until 1865. During this period *Silas Marner* [1861] and *Romola* [1863] were published. Although *Romola* was set in fifteenth-century Italy, its heroine was modelled on the life of **Barbara Bodichon**, whom George Eliot much admired. Barbara Bodichon was born at 5 Blandford Square in 1827, which remained her London home for much of her life. Multi-talented and always active in the cause of women's opportunities, she was one of the leading 'Ladies of Langham Place', and a generous supporter of the early women's university colleges. She married Eugene Bodichon, making it a condition of their marriage that she should be able to spend half the year in Britain working for her causes. The other half of the year was spent in Algeria. Both these women would have enjoyed the company of an earlier feminist **Lady Mary Wortley Montagu**. Traveller, letter writer and free thinker, Lady Mary was equally unconventional in her lifestyle and her relationships with men. Her home was at 5 Cavendish Square from 1723 until 1738, when she too went abroad for some footloose years. She was one of the great letter writers of her century, and much of her correspondence was published in 1763, the year following her death.

Baker Street, now a major thoroughfare into London's West End, has earned some fame through association with the fictional detective Sherlock Holmes. However some equally dynamic real characters lived in the street. A plaque on 120 Baker Street notes it as the residence of William Pitt the Younger in 1803-4, when he was Prime Minister. His niece **Hester Stanhope** lived here with him as hostess, housekeeper and confidante. He valued her support and advice highly and had persuaded Parliament to give her a generous pension on his death in 1806. Today she does not get any recognition on the plaque, yet she later went on to become a renowned traveller in the Middle East. **Madame Tussaud**, the French woman whose fame as a modeller in wax was already known before she came to Britain in

1802, settled in Baker Street. She had been obliged to use her skills to make deathmasks of victims of the French Revolution, and she herself was put in prison. As soon as the situation allowed it, she and her eldest son took their Waxworks Exhibition on tour throughout Britain, eventually setting up a permanent display in Baker Street on the site now covered by the headquarters of Marks and Spencer. Some of her own work can still be seen in Madame Tussaud's Waxworks Exhibition★ in Euston Road. She made her home at 58 Baker Street from 1833 until her death in 1850. She had continued to make wax sculptures until handing the business over to her sons in 1842 when she was over eighty. The actress **Sarah Siddons**, who also had a long career, spent her last years at 27 Upper Baker Street, dying there in 1831. The development of the underground station necessitated the alteration of the site.

Nearer Marble Arch is Upper Berkeley Street where **Letitia Elizabeth Landon**, a writer of poetry and novels, including *Ethel Churchill* [1837], lived at number 28. She went to West Africa on her marriage in 1838, dying soon after her arrival – she may have committed suicide. The achievements of **Elizabeth Garrett Anderson** whose home was at number 20 are better remembered. She resided here from 1860 until 1874. Although many obstacles were put in her way, she succeeded in qualifying as a doctor, the first woman to do so in Britain, and she combined this with a full family life. She was not able to follow the more orthodox male route via university medical school; none were open to women. Instead she learned through nursing, private tuition and by taking the examinations of the Society of Apothecaries. In the end she obtained her MD qualification in Paris, but was registered with the British Medical Association in 1877. She specialised in the treatment of women and children, and a hospital which she had founded for their care now bears her name. The Elizabeth Garrett Anderson Hospital in Euston Road, where **Elsie Inglis** worked briefly, continues to provide medical care for women by women. Elizabeth knew that other women also wanted to be doctors and she worked to create opportunities for them, helping **Sophia Jex-Blake** to set up the London Medical School for Women where she taught and which she later administered as Dean. **Elizabeth Blackwell**, the first British woman to receive a medical degree, was offered the first chair of gynaecology at the London Medical School for Women. She had graduated in 1849 from Geneva College in New York State, in the USA, and had been obliged to practise medicine there as she was not then accepted by Britain's male medical establishment. However, she accepted the London chair in 1875 and continued her highly respected career in Britain.

Elizabeth Garrett Anderson did not confine herself to medical work. She was one of the first women, together with Emily Davies, to be elected to the London School Board in 1871. Her future husband was also a member. They went on to have three children, but she continued to work for women, supporting the Women's Suffrage movement with her sister Millicent Garrett Fawcett, and having as early as 1865 collected signatures supporting John Stuart Mill's bill to give women property owners the vote. She had her first small clinic in 1860 in Seymour Place. A contemporary of hers, who shared her concern for the welfare of the poor, **Emma Cons**, lived at 139. The blue plaque describes her as philanthropist and Founder of the Old Vic, but she also did valued social work in Southwark. She was a friend of the social reformer **Octavia Hill** who managed her first housing scheme in Nottingham Street's Paradise buildings. **Louisa Garrett Anderson** followed her mother into the medical profession. She and her friend, **Flora Murray**, both achieved responsible positions in the First World War – Louisa became Chief Surgeon of the Women's Hospital Corps and Flora was commander of the Military Hospital in London. Their mutual support enabled them to carry out their duties during the added pressure of wartime with skill, dedication and leadership that set an example to all their colleagues.

Mayfair Mayfair is the very select area between Oxford Street and Piccadilly. Several women of interest were married in the eighteenth-century church of St George's, Hanover Square, which actually stands in St George Street. **Emma Hamilton** became the second wife of Sir William in 1791, after which she was soon quite at home in the Court of Naples where he was ambassador. **Caroline Norton**'s disastrous marriage to George Norton started with the ceremony here in 1827. When the relationship deteriorated, she lost the care of her children and began her long and painful struggle to recover them. Ultimately she was responsible for some much needed divorce law reform and the Married Women's Property Act which gave married women the right to own and manage their own property. Prior to this, their belongings were regarded as owned by their husbands. Mary Anne Evans, by now a rich widow, became **Mrs Disraeli** here in 1839. Later, as wife of the Prime Minister she was known to all as Mrs Dizzy and exerted a beneficial influence on him. In 1880 another **Mary Anne Evans**, better known by her pen-name, **George Eliot**, married John Cross. The church was also the target in 1914 of one of the militant suffragettes's bombings: the Anglican Church was identified as a key institution of the establishment which condoned the oppression of women.

In Hanover Square itself **Mary Somerville**, the mathematician had a home from 1815 until 1840. The leading woman trade unionist **Emma Paterson** was born at 12 Hanover Square. Her father was the headmaster of St George's Parish School. **Harriet Martineau** pursued a successful career in journalism, little handicapped by her deafness and other health problems. She was a regular reviewer for *Monthly Repository* and a contributor to *Westminster Review, Household Words* and the *Edinburgh Review*. When in London she stayed in nearby Conduit Street.

There are a number of streets running north-south into Piccadilly. **Lola Montez**, the dancer who had so many interesting husbands and lovers, lived for part of 1849 in Half Moon Street. Clarges Street, to the east, was where the intellectual and translator **Elizabeth Carter** died in 1806. After being widowed in 1818, **Fanny Burney** came to live in the narrow-five-storeyed townhouse at 11 Bolton Street, the next road to the east. She had always been very sociable and she continued to be so but more gently. Her writing by this stage was mainly letters, diaries and a biography of her father. She moved from here in 1828. **Jane Marcet**, the Swiss-born writer who introduced the concepts of contemporary science to a wider readership in the early nineteenth century lived in Stratton Street towards the end of her life. She died there in 1858; her ninetieth year.

The large house, number 1 Stratton Street, became the home of the actress **Harriot Mellon** when she married the fabulously wealthy banker Thomas Coutts in 1815, much to the horror of his children by his first wife. Despite the family disapproval, she made her husband very happy. Needless to say there was further outrage when she exclusively inherited his fortune. She married, as her second husband, the Duke of St Albans, thus adding a title to her wealth. When she died in 1837 she left her entire estate to Thomas Coutts' granddaughter, **Angela Burdett-Coutts**, on condition that she took the name Coutts as an additional surname. The big house on the corner of Piccadilly had been the childhood home of Angela until her grandfather's second marriage; it was part of the inheritance which made her the richest woman in Britain. From the beginning she decided that the majority of her money would be spent for the good of others, and she was determined that this disbursement would be done wisely, more effectively than the generous attempts of her step-grandmother, and for those with the greatest need.

Further east on Piccadilly itself stands the Albany, a large complex of apartments whose recent former residents have included the historical novelist **Georgette Heyer** and the actress **Edith Evans**. The neighbouring building is the Royal Academy of Arts which was founded in 1768. **Angelica Kauffmann** was a founder member, involved in this fine arts body in its original premises in Pall Mall.

The health of **Florence Nightingale**, the pioneering nurse, had suffered in the course of her work caring for the wounded and the sick at Scutari during the Crimean War, but she did not let this prevent her from pursuing her plans to create a trained nursing profession. She became increasingly invalided but wrote reports, lobbied and set up nursing schools in Britain, Europe and the colonies. She died at her home at 10 South Street, off Park Lane in 1910 in her ninety-first year. The house has been demolished but a blue plaque indicates its successor. There is also a blue plaque on number 15 South Street, but it is unlikely that its former occupant **Catherine Walters** had much in common with her contemporary Florence Nightingale. Described as the last Victorian courtesan and nicknamed 'Skittles', she had a very different attitude to life. This was her home from 1872 until her death here in 1920. Upper Grosvenor Street remains as fashionable an address as it was when **Adeline Horsey de Horsey** was born at number 8 in 1824. Well connected by birth, she built on this advantage in her marriages and her flamboyant lifestyle, eventually becoming a countess twice over.

The Grosvenor Chapel in South Audley Street was built in 1730. It is the final resting place for that restless early feminist and letter writer, **Lady Mary Wortley Montagu**. She died in 1762, aged seventy-three. The exact site of her grave is not known. **Elizabeth Carter**, a later Blue Stocking who died in 1806 is also buried in the chapel. In 1820, **Caroline of Brunswick**, the figure at the heart of the 'Queen Caroline Affair', stayed in this street while a decision was made about her divorce from George IV. Caroline's status caused a political rift where the people and the Whigs supported her, but the Tories, then in power, were behind the King. The divorce came through, and so she was never crowned Queen. One South Audley Street was the London home of the Ellerman family. They also had a home on the island of Bryher, one of the Scilly Isles, and the novelist Winifred Ellerman took the name **Bryher** from there. She met her lesbian lover, **H.D.**, the poet in 1919. Their close relationship lasted until H.D.'s death in 1961, but for much of the time Bryher lived abroad. She died in 1983 aged eighty-nine. South Audley Street is also where the University Women's Club is sited. It is in a townhouse at 2 Audley Square and was founded in 1886 to serve women graduates in the same way as the established gentlemen's clubs served men: by providing dining facilities, accommodation, reading rooms, discussion rooms etc. **Emily Davies**, the campaigner for women's higher education, was a founder member. She died in adjacent Upper Brook Street in 1921 where the sculptor **Anne Damer** died in the same street one hundred years earlier, in 1828.

Ebury Street links Chelsea with Victoria Station, running right through Pimlico, and has been very fasionable in the twentieth century. **Vita Sackville-West** spent the early years of her married life with Harold Nicolson at 182 Ebury Street, but she escaped back to her beloved Kent countryside whenever she could. Nearby is Chester Square, where the author of the celebrated science fiction *Frankenstein* [1817], **Mary Shelley**, was living at number 24 when she died.

Paddington The Italian ballerina, **Marie Taglioni**, spent much of her professional life on tour throughout Europe. On retiring from the stage she taught in Paris. In 1875, already seventy, she opened a ballet school in London. It was then that she lived at 14 Connaught Square, near Marble Arch. **Elinor Glyn**, novelist and film-script writer, had a London home from 1934 until 1938 at 11 Connaught Place, by this time a very fashionable address. On the north side of Connaught Street is Portsea Place, where the South African feminist novelist **Olive Schreiner** stayed. Number 16 was her home during 1885-7. She had come to Britain to find a publisher for her writing. Using the pen-name **Ralph Iron**, *The Story of an African Farm* [1883] was an immediate success. The climate did not suit her however, and she spent the winters on the south coast.

Woodchester Square covers Westbourne Farm, former home of the actress **Sarah Siddons**. She lived here for twelve years from 1805, and retired from the stage during this period. When Sarah Siddons died in 1831 she was buried at St Mary on Paddington Green. A seated statue of her gazes out over the busy Westway, A40 [M] from the churchyard. In the 1840s the farm had another theatrical resident, **Madame Vestris**. Her forte was theatre management, although she had performed on stage in several types of entertainment. She managed the Olympic, Covent Garden and Lyceum Theatres with varying degrees of success.

In Maida Vale, to the north, two gifted writers and friends, **Winifred Holtby** and **Vera Brittain** shared a flat. The four years from 1923 until 1927 were hectic ones for both of them, busy as they were with careers in journalism and their own writing. Vera Brittain's biography of Winifred *Testament of Friendship* [1940] is a moving account of a remarkable, energetic and committed life.

Regent's Park George Eliot settled at The Priory, 21 North Bank, on the bank of the Grand Union Canal. The house, which was to be her last home with George Lewes, has been demolished, but the site lies off Lodge Road. By now their relationship caused less scandal, at least in the intellectual circles in which they moved, and they entertained here regularly. However, this all changed when Lewes died in 1878. She had done the writing for several of her later novels here, including *Middlemarch* [1872] and *Daniel Deronda* [1876]. Another writer who took a male pen-name, **Henry Handel Richardson**, also lived and wrote in this area. This Australian novelist made her home from 1910 until she was widowed in 1934 at 90 Regent's Park Road. Here she wrote *Australia Felix* [1917], *The Way Home* [1925] and *Ultima Thule* [1929], collectively known as *The Fortunes of Richard Mahoney*.

St James's St James's Palace lies in the centre of this district, situated between Piccadilly to the north, Green Park to the west and St James's Park to the south. The Palace was built by Henry VIII and the succeeding sovereigns regularly held court here, many modernising and extending the building, until Victoria preferred Buckingham Palace. **Mary I** died here in 1558. **Mary II** and **Anne** were often here. The presence of the palace attracted prominent members of the court to make their London home nearby. Marlborough House, built in 1710 by **Sarah Churchill**, when she became Duchess of Marlborough, and clearly needed to be near Queen Anne, stands back from Pall Mall and Marlborough Gate. Now an official government house used for Commonwealth meetings and considerably altered, Sarah had commissioned it from the best architect of her day, Christopher Wren, but she sacked him half-way through the project and completed it herself. In the nineteenth-century Lancaster House, then called Stafford House and also now used by the government, was considered by Queen Victoria to be grander than her own royal residence, as she told **Millicent Duchess of Sutherland**, whose home it was. The Dukes of Sutherland were immensely rich, having vast estates in Scotland. Millicent did her wifely duty by supporting her husband socially, in a very grand style here, but she tried to give back to the people of Sutherland, who had been exploited by her husband's forefathers, some benefit from that accumulation of wealth. She was a charming and resourceful woman whose position as an aristocrat's wife made her extremely influential and invitations to her London home were much sought after.

Pall Mall is the wide street on the north side of St James's Park. It was very convenient for royal mistresses. **Nell Gwyn** was set up in number 79, identified by a plaque, and it remained her property until her death in 1687. **Mrs Fitzherbert** who was a discreet, but not officially acknowledged wife of the Prince Regent, had number 105 as her main London residence from 1789 until 1796. **Princess Charlotte**, the popular heiress of George IV, was married at Carlton House [no longer standing] in 1816. The people held great hopes of a more conventional and moral monarchy with her as sovereign, but these were short-lived. She died in childbirth the following year. Aristocratic residents of the street included the beautiful **Jane Duchess of Gordon**, who stayed here from the 1780s until 1801, entertaining and influencing Tory politicians.

The nearness of George III's court to Pall Mall also had less orthodox appeal for **Patience Wright**. She called herself 'The greatest Yankee Patriot in London'. She opened her waxworks in Pall Mall in 1772, having come from the American colonies with her three children. She had strong opinions on everything, and she was not afraid to share them. Her waxworks became a social centre which George himself visited on several occasions. However once she had given him her views on the status of his American colonies it was clear that there would be no more royal visits. While she modelled her wax sculptures, she gleaned all sorts of information which she passed on to her American visitors. Her sitters included the historian **Catherine Macaulay**. Patience never succeeded in returning to the independent United States for which she had worked with such dedication, dying in London in 1786.

There were other artistic occupants of Pall Mall, including the portrait painter **Mary Beale**, who died here in 1699. **Maria Cosway**, an artist who worked in several media, lived in Schomberg House, of which a wing remains as number 90, after her marriage to Richard Cosway in 1781. She had arrived in England from Italy, and was encouraged to paint by Angelica Kauffmann. She specialised in miniature painting, becoming a more successful artist than her husband. She travelled on the Continent and became a close friend of Thomas Jefferson. In 1804 she left Britain for good, and eventually set up a school for young ladies in France. The art of **Sarah Mapp** was in setting human bones. Her skill, practised also in Epsom, gained her many influential clients. Nicknamed 'the Shape mistress', she took lodgings in Pall Mall before her death in Seven Dials in 1739.

The delightful **Mrs Delaney** lived in St James's Place from 1770 until her move to Windsor. When her adored second husband died in 1768, she returned from Ireland to London, living first in St James's Street, but soon settling round the corner for fifteen contented years. She had taken up the art of paper cutting to make flower collages of extraordinary botanical accuracy. Indeed she can be said to have invented this artform. Her work, which absorbed much of her energies, is in the collections of the British Museum. When she died in 1788 she was as old as the century. She was buried in St James's Church, Piccadilly, as noted on the north wall. In 1699 **Mary Beale**, a professional artist, was also buried here but there is no memorial to her.

The French Empress **Eugénie** suffered from the ill-considered political moves of her husband Napoleon III. 1848 was a year of unrest throughout Europe, and she and Napoleon escaped to Britain. They spent that year at 1c King Street. A century earlier, the writer **Charlotte Smith**, who also endured difficult times on account of her husband whom she eventually left, was born when her parents were living in King Street in 1749. King Street leads into St James's Square.

The impressive building at number 4 St James's Square was the London headquarters of **Nancy Astor**'s 'Cliveden Set'. Here she was at the centre of a political and social circle which was entertained in grand style from 1912 until 1942. Lady Astor, an American by birth, was the first woman to take a seat in the House of Commons, as Member of Parliament for Plymouth from 1919. Although she is closely associated with her country home, Cliveden, she served her constituents well, maintaining a home in Plymouth and keeping a high profile in local politics. **Marguerite Gardiner**, the recklessly extravagant Countess of Blessington, spent her early married life at number 11, now built over by Chandos House. Number 12 was from 1833 the home of **Ada Lovelace**, the mathematician daughter of Lady Byron.

St John's Wood This area lies to the north of Regent's Park. The religious leader, **Joanna Southcott**, was buried in the churchyard of St John's Wood Church, in the High Street. She had come to London from her native Devon in 1802, driven by various religious experiences, dreams and visions. She settled here in 1804, at the centre of a millenarian cult which attracted many followers. Although past child-bearing age, a phantom pregnancy was interpreted as the forthcoming birth of a new Messiah. She was later discredited but her following survived her death in 1814, and even exists today. **Emily Davies**, a leader of women in the secular world, moved to London in 1862, having already met the Ladies of Langham Place and Elizabeth Garrett Anderson, in whom she had found kindred spirits. Once in the capital she was able to pursue her twin projects: votes and higher education for women. As the plaque on her home, 17 Cunningham Place records, she went on to found Girton College, Cambridge, via her own small college in Hitchin. She lived in the area from 1862 until 1887. **Annie Besant**, who worked for the improvement of the quality of life for all, lived in Avenue Road. She had hit the headlines by leading the Matchgirls Strike at Bryant & May's East London factory in 1888 and initiating the first women's trade union, the Matchmakers' Union. She later joined the

Theosophical Society and spent her last years in India supporting women and seeking self-determination for the people of the subcontinent. From 1890, the property at 19 Avenue Road became the headquarters of the Theosophical Society. Its founder was a Russian, **Madame Helena Blavatsky**, and Annie became her disciple. The Irish poet W. B. Yeats met Madame Blavatsky, whom he described as 'a sort of female Dr Johnson'. She had travelled widely and the religious and philosophies of Asia made a great impact on her thinking. Both she and Annie Besant wrote prolifically about theosophy for a wider public.

Other local residents included three writers. **Mrs Henry Wood** had her London home in St John's Wood Park from 1867 until her death in 1887. **Dorothy Richardson** spent the summers from 1916-38 in the top rooms of 32 Queen's Terrace. In winter she and her artist husband would sub-let them, and move to Cornwall. Throughout this period she worked on her multi-volume autobiographical novel, *Pilgrimage* [1915-1967], in the style now known as stream of consciousness. **Katherine Mansfield**, author of short stories, spent the summer of 1915 at 5 Acacia Road, but it was a time of sadness for her. Her brother, to whom she was very close, died in the Great War, after spending his leaves here. She could not bear to stay on with so many memories.

From 1919 the artist **Laura Knight** settled in the capital taking a studio in St John's Wood. She and her husband, Harold, made 16 Langford Place their permanent home. Dame Laura died there in 1970. The sculptor **Clare Sheridan** also had a studio in this part of London. **Gluck**, the artist who chose a name to mask her gender so as not to compromise her standards, had studied art at St John's Wood School of Art. She was born into the Gluckstein family, and her professional name stems from her surname but it also means happiness or good fortune. She painted all her life, and bullied the manufacturers of artists' materials to improve the standards of paints and pigments.

Soho This area has long had a reputation for notoriety, but there was a time when it was considered a respectable place to own or rent accommodation. It lies between Regent Street and Charing Cross Road and is defined on the south-east by Leicester Square and on the north-east by Oxford Street.

Golden Square, laid out in 1681, is one of the earliest squares in Soho. **Lady Mary Wortley Montagu**, who had a home at 19, now an office, was one inhabitant who raised more eyebrows in her time than she would now. After eloping to marry Edward Wortley Montagu in 1712, much of her life was spent travelling on the Continent, having acquired a taste for adventure abroad during her husband's post as ambassador in Turkey, accounts of which survive in her correspondence. Before she finally left her husband, her essays and political writings kept her in the public sphere, and her views on the role of women were widely read, but did not get the attention they deserved. In 1739 she went abroad again, in an extended exile, returning only when her husband died in 1761. **Angelica Kauffmann**, the professional artist, lived at 16 Golden Square from 1767 until her marriage in 1781 took her to Italy.

To the north, **Madame de Stael** spent part of her exile from Napoleon's France at 30 Argyll Street in 1814, as a plaque records. She had been outspokenly critical of his regime and was banned from French soil in 1804. **Sarah Siddons**, the actress had accommodation in Great Marlborough Street from 1790 until 1804, by then established as a great lady of the theatre.

Soho Square is contemporary with Golden Square. **Mary Braddon**, author of such sensational novels as *Lady Audley's Secret* [1862] and *Aurora Floyd* [1863], was born at her parents' home in the square in 1837. **Eleanor Marx**, an active and ardent socialist in her own right, was born in 1855 at 28 Dean Street, known for its association with her famous father.

Other past residents of Soho include three contemporaries, all known for their writings. **Fanny Burney**, the only one whose residence is commemorated, lived with her father in St Martin's Street, off Leicester Square, from 1774 until 1789. A public library now stands on the site, and a plaque inside names it as her former home; here she wrote her best-selling first novel *Evelina* [1778]. Its success led her to publish her next work *Cecilia* [1782] in her own name. She also helped her father with his writings. It seems appropriate that the building is now a library, but it is a pity that it is only the other former resident, male, Sir Isaac Newton, who is honoured on the exterior of the building. In Leicester Square **Elizabeth Inchbald** had rooms at various times during her career as actress, playwright and novelist. Her first novel *A Simple Story* [1791] is said to have been written in Frith Street.

The skeleton of St Anne's Church, Wardour Street, is all that remains of the building in which **Hester Thrale** was first married in 1763. It was not a marriage of her choice, rather one that her parents considered to their advantage. Her husband was a prosperous brewer, and so Hester was assured a comfortable, if confining, future. Only the towers and three walls remain; it is strange to see a carpark where she must have walked reluctantly down the aisle. The ashes of a later writer of detective fiction **Dorothy Sayers** are housed in the room at the base of the tower. She had been involved with the work of the parish of Soho during her years in London. She died in 1957.

Leicester Square is now mostly associated with film premiers but live performances were also a feature of the area. The ballet dancer **Adeline Genée** had her London debut in 1897 at the former Empire Theatre. This proved to be the start of a ten-year residency as top artiste there. The theatre closed in 1927. **Mary Linwood**'s artistic talents took another form. In 1806, to national acclaim, this Leicestershire artist exhibited her woolwork 'Paintings' at Savile House, now the site of the Empire Cinema. The theatre manager **Madame Vestris** is thought to have been born in Soho in 1797, but the precise location is not known.

Strand The Strand is the wide street leading into Westminster from the east, serving as the major thoroughfare between the City of London and the City of Westminster and a convenient address for both. The actresses **Sarah Siddons** and **Elizabeth Inchbald** both lodged there. Sarah Siddons stayed at 149 in 1782, returning to the London stage, having firmly established her reputation in Bath and Bristol. She was an instant success and her career was now assured. Her contemporary, Elizabeth Inchbald, had other talents and by 1805, when she was in lodgings with a milliner at 63 The Strand, she was able to support herself more than adequately as a playwright and novelist. She remained here for four years. **George Eliot** was a later literary resident, living at 142 from 1851 until 1855. Her landlord was also her employer, the publisher John Chapman; she worked for him as an editor and contributor to *Westminster Review*. It was through Chapman that she met her lover and companion George Lewes.

The Church of St Clement Danes, which stands as an island in the middle of the Strand, gives its name to Clement's Inn, a narrow street to the north. The office at 6 Clement's Inn of Mr and **Mrs Pethick–Lawrence** served as headquarters of the suffragette movement. Emmeline Pethick-Lawrence was a very efficient treasurer of the Women's Social and Political Union, and both she and her husband edited *Votes for Women* which was published from here. Frederick Lawrence had early demonstrated his commitment to the equality of women and men by combining his wife's surname with his own on their marriage. **Christabel Pankhurst** regularly stayed with them when her heavy programme of lectures and rallies throughout Britain brought her to the English capital. A modern office block, Mobil Court, now stands on the site but a plaque on the side of the building records its links with the Suffragettes.

Louisa Twining, the philanthropist, grew up in the area of the Strand. Her family's tea company still trades at 216. She began her social work with the local poor, eventually instituting reforms in the workhouses, the last resort of the destitute. Her improvements made workhouses throughout the country more humane, and she involved more women in their management as Poor Law Guardians. **Gabriela de la Balmondière**, the poet and socialist, married Robert Cunninghame Graham at the Strand Registry Office in 1878. Her real name was Caroline Horsfall but she was always assumed to be French, a pretence which she kept up all her life and which her husband only revealed just before his death in 1936, thirty years after her death.

Westminster Old Westminster is the district immediately surrounding Westminster Abbey and the Houses of Parliament. Its long tradition as seat of power dates from the eleventh century. The street leading to it from the north is Whitehall, now dominated by government offices and today synonymous with government. One of these, Dover House, now the Scottish Office, was the home of **Lady Caroline Lamb**, a novelist in her own right, but better known as the distracted lover of Lord Byron.

Glenarvon [1816] is a dramatic, highly colourful version of their story. The impressive mansion was then called Melbourne House, her husband being Lord Melbourne. She died here in 1828, never having settled after her brief affair with Byron.

Ten Downing Street is the famous address which British Prime Ministers have had as their official residence since 1735. This modest townhouse, home since 1979 to Britain's first woman Prime Minister, **Margaret Thatcher**, is where the Cabinet, the group of key ministers of the government, meet and policy decisions are made. Other significant women, married to politicians, such as **Mary Disraeli**, have also lived here, influencing the course of politics through their illuminating comment and considered judgments. *Wives of Downing Street* by Kirsty McLeod [1976, London, Collins] describes some powerful former residents. The building has inevitably been the focus for many campaigns, notably in 1908 when members of the Women's Freedom League picketed the street and 1909 when suffragettes chained themselves to the railings outside number 10 to show how serious women were in their struggle for votes.

The Houses of Parliament, in the Palace of Westminster, were, of course, also the target of the campaigns for votes for women, beginning in earnest from the private member's bill put forward in 1866 in the House of Commons, the Lower House, by John Stuart Mill. The bill was supported by many articulate women, including the Ladies of Langham Place, who had helped by obtaining signatures for a petition. Had it been successful, it would have been considered by them only as a first step. It proposed that women who held property in their own right and paid taxes should qualify for the franchise in the same way as male property owners and tax-payers. This would have granted voting rights to a small minority of women, effectively excluding married women whose property, under prevailing English law, had become their husband's on their marriage. Although it failed, it roused more women to pursue this and other rights of women.

Women had tried to gain access to the debating chamber more directly in the past. On one occasion, in 1739, a group of formidable women were determined to hear the debates on the relationship between Britain and Spain, arising from trading in the Spanish colonies. **Lady Mary Wortley Montagu**, **Selina Hastings** and **Mrs Delaney** were among the party which, having been shut out of the gallery, interrupted proceedings by banging loudly and persistently on the doors. Then, after keeping quiet so that those inside thought that they had dispersed, they charged in as soon as the doors were opened. They commented on the debate noisily, frustrating the debate further. Lady Mary Wortley Montagu was able to leave the country later that year, feeling she had shown Parliament that women were prepared to make opportunities to confront politicians.

The greatest publicity for the Votes for Women campaign came through the actions of the militant suffragettes, led by **Emmeline Pankhurst**, her daughter **Christabel** and many others in their Women's Social and Political Union. Suffragettes regularly chained themselves to the railings surrounding the Houses of Parliament and were regularly arrested. Their activities intensified until the outbreak of the First World War in 1914, when they ceased, and women devoted their energies to the peace movement or to support the war effort. Others have told their story well, including **Sylvia Pankhurst** in *The Suffragette Movement* in 1931 and **Ray Strachey** in *The Cause* [1928]. There was more than one view on how to win the vote. The Women's Freedom League was a breakaway militant group founded by Charlotte Despard in 1907. Its members were committed to non-violent militancy and were great demonstrators. In 1908 they chained themselves to the grille in the Ladies Gallery in the House of Commons and interrupted the debates with their shouts of 'Votes for Women'. [The grille is now in the collections of the Museum of London.] In 1909 they picketed outside the building all summer long. The non-militant suffragists having their own organisations, combined under the National Union of Women's Suffrage Societies. Indeed, not all women were in favour of having voting rights, and there was an equally strong Anti-Suffrage League led by **Mrs Humphrey Ward**. It is an inspiring story, full of frustrations, disappointments, opposing views, leadership disputes, yet showing the strength of women acting together, disregarding class differences, making decisions, establishing enduring friendships, sometimes sacrificing their home lives and often their bodies, and ultimately achieving voting rights for women. The government passed the Representation of the People Act in 1918, giving women of thirty years and over the vote. This was extended in 1928 to all women of twenty-one and over, matching at last the voting rights of men. **Emmeline Pankhurst** had the satisfaction of knowing that this particular women's struggle had been won just before her death the same year.

The next step was for women to represent the people in Parliament. Women could stand for election from 1918, early candidates including the indefatigable **Christabel Pankhurst**, **Charlotte Despard** and **Emmeline Pethick-Lawrence**. The first to win a seat, despite a prison record, was **Constance Markievicz**, the Irish Nationalist whose introduction to politics had been through the commitment to the suffragette movement of her sister **Eva Gore-Booth**. She represented Dublin's St Patrick's constituency, Eire still being governed by Britain in 1918; however, both a prison sentence and her refusal to take the oath of allegiance prevented her from taking up her place in the House of Commons. Three years later, the independent Republic of Eire was established, rewarding her efforts and those of the other Irish patriots.

In 1919 **Nancy Astor** was the first woman to take up a seat. The constituency of Plymouth, Sutton, had been represented by her husband, but on his father's death he inherited his father's peerage, and was no longer eligible to sit in the Commons. She proved a tough, persistent and effective Member of Parliament, keeping her seat until she retired in 1945. She could hold her own in debate, championing many women's causes. In 1929 **Margaret Bondfield** became the first woman to obtain the status of

39 The Pankhurst Memorial, Victoria Tower Gardens, Westminster, City of Westminster

Cabinet Minister. She was Minister of Labour in the Labour government and then a Privy Councillor. **Eleanor Rathbone**, a Member of Parliament from 1926, took up the cause of women in the home, eventually seeing the Family Allowance Act passed in 1945, which gave home-based women some state-financed independence. **Jennie Lee** was a worthy successor and more recently has taken a seat in the House of Lords as Baroness Lee of Ashridge. **Betty Harvie Anderson**, whose parliamentary career spanned twenty years, became a Conservative Deputy Leader of the House, the first woman to hold this office. As yet no woman has been appointed Leader of the House.

Women were also long denied access to the House of Lords, the Upper House in the high Victorian Palace of Westminster. In 1908 the Scottish suffrage campaigner and advocate **Chrystal Macmillan** became the first woman to address the Lords. The graduates of the four older Scottish universities had the right to vote for their own member of parliament, but the new women graduates were excluded. She was unsuccessful in her attempt to persuade the Lords of the just claims of these female graduates to vote. Undeterred she worked all her life to improve the legal rights of women and children and to prevent war through her membership of the

Women's International League for Peace and Freedom. In 1923 **Lady Rhondda**, a viscountess in her own right through her father, tried without success to take her seat in the House of Lords. Peeresses have only had this right since 1958. Recent peeresses include **Barbara Ward**, Baroness Jackson of Lodsworth, and **Sue Ryder**, Baroness Ryder of Warsaw in Poland and Cavendish in the County of Suffolk.

In the park immediately to the west of Parliament's Victoria Tower, a bronze statue of **Emmeline Pankhurst** pays tribute to the many women who fought for the Cause. Bronze medallions on either side show respectively a portrait head of her daughter **Christabel Pankhurst** and the badge designed by **Sylvia Pankhurst** which was given to each of the thousand and more suffragettes who suffered imprisonment. These included the American campaigner **Alice Paul**, who in 1923 laid the foundations for the United States' Equal Rights Amendment. She participated fully in the activities of the militant suffragettes, enduring six prison sentences before returning to the United States in 1910. As president of the National Women's Party, she led the attempt to change the sacred wording of the Federal Constitution to include women. She did not live to see this passed although she died only in 1977. The Amendment has still not been accepted by the requisite number of states. The badge shows a broad arrow superimposed on the arms of Westminster, a portcullis gate. It is a moving work which continues to inspire.

Not far to the east, in Caxton Street, off Victoria Street, Caxton Hall still stands. It also has its place in the history of the Cause. Several 'Women's Parliaments', organised by the militant suffragettes, were held annually, both as a forum for debate and as a demonstration of solidarity and strength. The Suffragette Fellowship has erected a plaque of bronze 'to commemorate the courage and perseverance of those men and women who, in the long struggle for votes for women, selflessly braved derision, opposition and ostracism, many enduring physical violence and suffering.'

Victoria Street was also a residential road, and the botanical artist **Marianne North** had a studio and a flat there where she lived and painted when not travelling abroad on her expeditions. Birdcage Walk on the south of St James's Park may be considered the northern limit of today's Westminster. **Caroline Norton**, whose unhappy marriage deprived her for many years of her children's company, lived here at Storey House. Experiencing at first hand the injustices of matrimonial laws which gave husbands complete control over their wives, their wives' property and their children, Caroline Norton initiated changes which ultimately resulted in divorce law reforms, and the Married Women's Property Acts of 1870 and 1882.

Westminster Abbey is the magnificent centrepiece to the Westminster district. Dating from Edward the Confessor's eleventh-century foundation, it is an immense building in the gothic style, attracting huge numbers of visitors, mainly by its associations with royalty and royal occasions, such as coronations and weddings. Many male worthies are also buried here, such burials having long since been regarded as a sign of great achievement. Many significant women have also been honoured in this way, and it is with them that we are concerned here. It is worth noting that while some are actually interred here, others, commemorated here for their achievements, are buried elsewhere.

Starting with an early example **Matilda**, Henry I's Queen was buried in the abbey on her death in 1118. **Eleanor of Castile**, the adored and much lamented queen of Edward I, was buried here in 1290. Her body was brought from Harby, where she died, each overnight stop *en route* being marked by the erection of an elaborate stone monument, now called Eleanor Crosses. Her final resting place is below a bronze-gilt effigy of herself, dressed in robes, lying at shoulder height on a raised sarcophagus in the Chapel of St Edward the Confessor, **Philippa of Hainault**, Flemish wife of Edward III, had proved to be a good choice of consort. She was diplomatic, encouraged the country's economic activities and supported the king in military and peaceful encounters. On her death in 1369, she was buried in the blue marble tomb in this Chapel. Sadly, it has suffered from past vandalism.

In Henry VII's Chapel, at the far east end of the abbey, Henry's mother, **Margaret Beaufort**, was buried on her death in 1509. Her effigy in bronze in the south aisle portrays her as quietly capable. She had supported her son in the Wars of the Roses, which after the Battle of Bosworth in 1485 established the Tudor succession. She had turned to study and the support of the universities, devoting much of her own inherited wealth to both Oxford and Cambridge, to founding schools and charitable hospitals, and sponsoring William Caxton's far-reaching invention, the printing press. She is the first of many important royal women to be buried in the Chapel. On the north side **Mary I**, Mary Tudor, elder daughter of Henry VIII, is buried. She reigned five years 1553-8, an unsettling period when she tried to re-establish links with the Roman Catholic world, and ally with Spain. Her half-sister and heir, **Elizabeth I**, was, in contrast, a supremely successful and effective female sovereign. Her long reign, forty-five years, saw many changes, including, as is recorded on her monument, 'having restored religion to its original sincerity, established peace, restored money to its proper value'. She shares a tomb with Mary, a 'double-decker' four-poster construction.

In the south aisle of Henry VII's Chapel, **Mary Queen of Scots**, Mary Stuart, was buried by her son James VI of Scotland who inherited the English throne in 1603 from Elizabeth I. Mary had always presented a threat to Elizabeth and it was Elizabeth who had the Scots queen executed at Fotheringhay in 1587. On his accession as King James I of England, James had his mother's body removed from Peterborough, and re-interred here among her peers, under a heavily ornate four-poster canopy of stone. This is in complete contrast to the next queens to rule Britain in their own right: **Mary II** and **Anne**. Both are buried without memorial in front of the altar. **Elizabeth of Bohemia**, Mary Stuart's unhappy granddaughter, was also interred in Mary's tomb, as was the equally luckless **Arabella Stuart**.

In the south aisle of the presbytery lies the only one of Henry VIII's wives to be interred at Westminster, his fourth wife **Anne of Cleves**, whom he married in January 1540 and divorced six months later. It was a surprisingly amicable arrangement, and Anne outlived him by ten years, dying in 1557.

St Paul's Chapel contains a monument to the benefactor and founder of a Cambridge College, **Frances Sidney**, Countess of Sussex, who died in 1589. The north transept had the monuments to **Margaret Cavendish**, Duchess of Newcastle, scientist and writer, who died in 1673 and is shown holding a book, probably one of the many which she had written herself.

The south transept is known for its concentration of literary figures as Poets' Corner. The current tradition of honouring deceased poets here really began in the middle of the eighteenth century, but the first woman was not formally commemorated in the Abbey until **Jane Austen**'s memorial was erected. Her successor women novelists, the three **Brontë** sisters, **Charlotte**, **Anne** and **Emily**, share a tablet of remembrance, as in life they shared their writing.

In the cloister [which Helen Mott has called the women's enclosure!] two seventeenth-century women associated with the stage are buried. As early actresses were considered to be socially and morally suspect, it should come as no surprise that they were not granted burial within the abbey itself. **Aphra Behn**, whose adventurous life provided her with topics for her robust plays roundly criticising the treatment by men of women and often holding men up to ridicule, died in 1689. Her grave is marked on a paving slab on the floor by the door connecting the abbey church with the east walk of the cloister. Virginia Woolf has said that every woman writer should lay flowers on the grave of Aphra Behn. Some of her plays, including *The Rover* [1688] and *The Lucky Chance* [1686], have been revived recently and compare well with the male works of the same period. Further along the east walk, another slab marks the grave of **Anne Bracegirdle**, an actress who earned a fine reputation for Shakespearean roles, and for whom many of Congreve's female leads were written. She is thought to have died in 1748. She had been brought up by another actress who did merit burial in the abbey, **Mary Betterton**, whose remains were interred in 1712 beside those of her husband and fellow actor Thomas. Anne Bracegirdle survived her main rival, **Anne Oldfield**, now placed in the south aisle of the nave, having died in 1740. This Anne was not granted a marker on account of her unconventional marriage arrangements. By 1831 when **Sarah Siddons** died, acting was a respectable, and, indeed, in her case venerable, profession for a woman. A rather severe draped portrait bust of her was erected in the crowded east aisle of the north transept, in recognition of her great talent.

The aristocratic contemporaries of the seventeenth-century actresses, **Dorothy Osborne** and **Frances Stuart**, were also finally laid to rest here, their status guaranteeing them tombs and monuments within the abbey church itself. Dorothy Osborne died in 1695, having married her adored Sir William Temple and spent idyllic years as his wife, despite six long years of courtship strongly opposed by her parents. She is commemorated in the south aisle, and by her correspondence which was published in 1947. Frances Stuart, the beautiful Duchess of Richmond and Lennox, was buried in the vault beneath the south chapel leading off Henry VII's Chapel, having died in 1702. There is also a curious effigy of her in the abbey's museum.

Angela Burdett-Coutts, the wealthy philanthropist who did so much for London's poor, especially the children, was the last person actually to be buried within the abbey; for sometime before her death only cremated remains were accepted. The decision to forego the requirement for cremation then in force caused a few clerical feathers to be ruffled but it was a mark of the esteem in which she was held that her burial was permitted in 1906. The site is marked by a black marble stone in the floor. Her dedicated public generosity was rewarded in her own lifetime with two significant honours: in 1871 she was granted a peerage; in the following year she became the first woman to be given the Freedom of the City of London. Two other social reformers, **Beatrice Webb**, and her husband and fellow sociologist Sidney Webb, are commemorated in the floor of the west end of the north aisle. Beatrice died in 1943, a long-standing member of the Fabian Society. Her ashes and those of her husband were placed in the abbey in 1947. **Olave Baden-Powell**, founder of the Girl Guide movement, is remembered on the floor of the south aisle, with the words 'Give thanks'. When she died in 1977, she was laid to rest beside her husband in Kenya. **Millicent Garrett Fawcett**, 'who won citizenship for women', as it says on her monument, is commemorated with her husband in the Chapel of the Holy Cross.

BIOGRAPHICAL
INDEX

A A

ACKLAND, VALENTINE 1906–1960. Poet, essayist. Lived in Dorset, museum in **Dorchester**. *This Narrow Place*, Wendy Mulford, Pandora Press, London, 1988.

ACLAND, ALICE SOPHIA; née CUNNINGHAM 1849–1935. Founder of the Women's Co-operative Guild; born in **Petersfield**; grew up in Oxfordshire, founded Guild in **Hebden Bridge**, cremated in **London [Barnet]**, ashes laid near **Exeter**.

ADAMS, FANNY 1859–67. Child victim. Lived and died in **Alton**.

ADDAMS, JANE 1860–1935. American social reformer, pacifist. Lived mainly in Chicago but visited **London [Hackney** and **Tower Hamlets]**. *American Heroine, the Life and Legend of Jane Addams*, Allen F. Davis, Oxford University Press, Oxford, 1970; *Jane Addams of Hull House 1860–1935*, Margaret Tims, Allen & Unwin, London, 1961.

AETHELFLAED; ETHELFLEDA *c*. 870–918. Ruler of Mercia and military leader. Successful military activity in **Runcorn**, **Derby** and **Leicester**; religious benefactor to **Shrewsbury**; buried in **Gloucester**. 'Aethelflaed, Lady of the Mercians', F. T. Wainwright, in *Scandinavian England*, Odense University, Odense, 1975.

AIKIN, LUCY 1781–1864. Writer and biographer. Born in **Warrington**; lived in **London [Camden, Hackney]**; buried in **London [Camden]**, *A Memoir of Lucy Aikin*, anonymous, 1864.

ALDERSON, AMELIA. See OPIE, AMELIA.

ALLINGHAM, HELEN 1848–1926. Water-colour artist. Studied in **Birmingham**; sketches in **London [Kensington and Chelsea]**; lived from 1881 at **Witley**. *The Happy England of Helen Allingham*, Helen Allingham, Bracken Books, London, 1985.

ANDERSON, BETTY HARVIE. See HARVIE ANDERSON, BETTY.

ANDERSON, ELIZABETH GARRETT 1836–1917. Pioneering physician and, later, local government politician. Active life in **London [Westminster]** and **Aldeburgh**, where she was buried. *Elizabeth Garrett Anderson*, Jo G. Manton, Methuen, London, 1965; *Elizabeth Garrett Anderson, 1836–1917*, Louisa Garrett Anderson, Faber & Faber, London, 1939.

ANDERSON, LOUISA GARRETT 1873–1943. Surgeon. Active in **Guildford** and **London [Westminster]**; buried in **Penn**.

ANNE, QUEEN 1665–1714. Queen of Great Britain and Ireland in her own right 1702–1714. Most of her active life spent in **London [Kensington and Chelsea, Westminster]**; introduced horseracing to **Ascot**; commemorated in **Barnsley**. *Queen Anne*, Edward Gregg, Routledge & Kegan Paul, London, 1980; *Queen Anne*, David Green, Collins, London, 1970.

ANNE OF CLEVES 1515–57. Queen of England. Came to England in 1539; lived at **Edenbridge**; property in **Lewes** and **Melton Mowbray**; buried in **London [Westminster]**.

ANNING, MARY 1799–1847. Pioneer geologist. Lived, worked, died and buried in **Lyme Regis**. *Mary Anning*, Richard Curle, Dorset Natural History and Archaeological Society, Dorchster, n.d.

ARCHDALE, HELEN; née RUSSEL. Feminist publisher. Educated in **St Andrews**; published in **London [City]**.

ARDEN, MARY 1556–1608. Mother of William Shakespeare. Home near **Stratford-upon-Avon**.

ARNAUD, YVONNE 1892–1958. French actress, whose stage career was most successful in Britain. Theatre at **Guildford** named after her.

VON ARNIM, ELIZABETH; née MAY BEAUCHAMP 1866–1941. Australian novelist who lived in England and Pomerania, France and USA. Buried in **Penn**. *Elizabeth: the author of 'Elizabeth and her German garden'*, Karen Usborne, Bodley Head, London, 1986.

ASHFORD, DAISY, MRS MARGARET DEVLIN 1881–1972. Writer. Born in **London [Richmond]; lived in Norwich**. *Daisy Ashford: Her Life*, R. M. Malcolmson, Chatto & Windus, London, 1984.

ASKEW, ANNE 1521–46. Reformer and Protestant martyr. Born near **Grimsby**; spent time in **Lincoln**; martyred in **London [City]**.

ASTELL, MARY 1666–1731. Writer and campaigner for women's rights. Grew up in **Newcastle upon Tyne**; lived, wrote, died and buried in **London [Kensington and Chelsea]**. *The Celebrated Mary Astell*, Ruth Perry, University of Chicago, Chicago, 1986; *The First English Feminist: 'Reflections on Marriage' and Other Writings by Mary Astell*, Bridget Hill [ed.], Gower Publishing Co, Aldershot, 1986.

ASTOR, NANCY WITCHER, VISCOUNTESS ASTOR; née LANGHORNE 1879–1964. American whose marriage brought her British citizenship. Politician. Member of Parliament for **Plymouth**; centre of the influential 'Cliveden Set' in **London [Westminster]** and **Cliveden**; buried at **Cliveden**. *Nancy: The Life of Nancy Astor*, Christopher Sykes, Collins, London, 1972; *Nancy Astor: a Life*, Anthony Masters, Weidenfeld & Nicolson, London, 1981.

ATWELL, MABEL LUCIE 1879–1962. Writer and illustrator of children's books. From 1948 lived at **Fowey** where she died.

AUSTEN, JANE 1775–1817. Novelist. Born at **Steventon**; attended schools in **Oxford** and **Reading**; lived in **Bath, Southampton** and **Chawton**; visits to **London [Kensington and Chelsea]**; spent holidays in **Lyme Regis** and **Dorking**; last days and burial in **Winchester**. *A Portrait of Jane Austen*, David Cecil, Constable, London, 1978; *In the Steps of Jane Austen*, Anne-Marie Edwards, Arcady Books, Southampton, 1979, *The Life of Jane Austen*, John Halperin, Harvester Press, Brighton, 1984; *The Jane Austen Handbook*, J. David Grey [ed.], Athlone Press, London, 1986.

B B

BACON, ANNE; née COOKE 1528–1610. Translator of theological works. Brought up at Gidea Park; married life at **Gorhambury**; buried at **St Albans**. *The Grimstons of Gorhambury*, Norton King, Phillimore, Chichester, 1983.

BADEN-POWELL, OLAVE ST CLAIR 1889–1977. Founder of Girl Guides movement. Youth in Dorset; married life at **Bentley**; flat in **London [Richmond]**; commemorated in **London [Westminster]**; buried in Kenya. *Window on My Heart*, Olave Baden-Powell, Hodder & Stoughton, London, 1973.

BAGNOLD, ENID ELGERINE; LADY JONES 1889–1981. Novelist and playwright. Childhood in the West Indies; adult life in **London [Kensington and Chelsea]**.

BAILLIE; LADY GRIZEL; née HUME 1665–1746. Scottish heroine and songwriter. Heroism at **Edinburgh** and **Polwarth**; exile in Holland; married life and burial at **Gordon**.

BAILLIE, ISOBEL 1895–1983. Singer and teacher. Born in **Hawick**, trained and taught in **Manchester**.

BAILLIE, JOANNA 1762–1851. Writer. Born in **Bothwell**; educated in **Glasgow**; lived and buried in **London [Camden]**. *The Life and Work of Joanna Baillie*, M. S. Carhart, 1923.

BALMONDIERE, GABRIELA DE LA; GABRIELA CUNNINGHAME GRAHAM; née CAROLINE HORSFALL 1858–1906. Writer, traveller, socialist. Born in Yorkshire; early adulthood overseas; married in **London [Westminster]**; married life based at **Gartmore**; died in Spain; buried on **Inchmaholme**. *Robert and Gabriela Cunninghame Graham*, Alexander Maitland, Blackwood, Edinburgh, 1983.

BANKES, MARY, LADY; née HAWTRY d. 1661. Royalist heroine. Defender of **Corfe Castle**.

BARBAULD, ANNA LAETITIA; née AIKIN 1743–182. Writer and poet. Born in **Kibworth Harcourt**; educated in **Warrington**; taught in **Palgrave**; lived in **London [Camden and Hackney]** and is buried in **London [Hackney]**. *A Memoir of Mrs Anna Laetitia Barbauld with many of* *her Letters*, G. Ellis, 1874; *Georgian Chronicle: Mrs Barbauld and Her Family*, Betsy Rogers, Methuen, London, 1955.

BARKER, LILIAN CHARLOTTE 1874–1955. Prison reformer. Born in **London [Islington]**; lived and worked in **London [Greenwich]**.

BARRETT, ELIZABETH. See BROWNING, ELIZABETH BARRETT.

BARRY, JAMES MIRANDA 1799–1865. Doctor and military figure. Medical education in **Edinburgh**; surgery training in **London [Lambeth]**; military post in **Plymouth**; retired to and buried in **London [Brent]**. *The Perfect Gentleman: the Remarkable Life of Dr James Miranda Barry*, June Rose, Hutchinson, London, 1977.

BARTHOLOMEW, ANNE CHARLOTTE 1800–62. Writer and artist. Born in **Lodden**; paintings in **Norwich**; buried in **London [Haringey]**.

BARTON, ELIZABETH 'The Holy Maid of Kent'. *c*. 1506–34. Religious leader. Born in Kent; executed and buried in **London [City]**. *The Holy Maid of Kent*, Alan Neame, Hodder & Stoughton, London, 1971.

BATEMAN, HESTER; née NEEDAM *c*. 1709–93. Silversmith. Active in **London [City]**. *Hester Bateman*, D. S. Shure, 1959; 'Woman Silver-smiths, Hester Bateman' in *Collectors Guides*, E. J. G. Smith, 1969.

BAYLY, ADA ELLEN; 'EDNA LYALL' 1857–1903. Writer and novelist. Born in **Brighton**; lived and wrote in **Lincoln**; buried in **Bosbury**.

BAYLIS, LILIAN MARY 1874–1937. Theatre manager. Born in London; adolescence in South Africa. Returned to work in **London [Lambeth and Islington]**; lived in **London [Lambeth]** from 1898; died there; commemorated in **London [Westminster]**. Niece of EMMA CONS, who introduced her to theatre management. *Lilian Baylis: the Lady of the Old Vic*, Richard Findlater, Allen Lane, London, 1975.

BAYNARD, ANNE 1672–97. Scholar. Born in **Preston**; last years and burial in **London [Richmond]**.

BEALE, DOROTHEA 1831–1906. Educational reformer. Educated at schools in Paris and **London [Westminster]** where she also taught; other teaching posts in **Casterton** and **Cheltenham**; also active in **Oxford**. *How Different From Us: a Biography of Miss Buss and Miss Beale*, Josephine Kamm, Bodley Head, London, 1958.

BEALE, MARY; née CRADOCK 1633–99. Artist. Born and married in **Barrow**; lived and painted in **London [City and Westminster]** from *c*. 1655; buried in **London [Westminster]**. *The Excellent Mrs Mary Beale* [Exhibition catalogue], Elizabeth Walsh and Richard Jeffree, Inner London Education Authority, London, 1975.

BEAUCLERK, LADY DIANA; née SPENCER 1734–1808. Artist. Childhood at **Woodstock**; homes in **London [Westminster** and **Richmond]**;

visited **Bath** and **Brighton**. *Lady Diana Beauclerk: Her Life and Work*, B. Erskine, 1903.

BEAUFORT, MARGARET; COUNTESS OF RICHMOND AND DERBY *c.* 1443–1509. Scholar, writer and patron. Brought up in Dorset, lived in **Pembroke**; benefactor of **Holywell**, **Oxford** and **Cambridge**; visitor to **Buckden**; latterly lived in Surrey; buried in **London [Westminster]**.

BECKER, LYDIA ERNESTINE 1827–90. Suffragist. Born, lived, worked in **Manchester** and **Altham**; died and buried in Switzerland. *Lydia Becker*, M. Holmes, 1913.

BEETON, ISABELLA MARY; née MAYSON 1836–65. Writer on domestic matters; journalist. Born in **London [City]**; adolescence in **Epsom**; married life and journalist career in **London [Harrow]**; buried in **London [Lambeth]**. *Isabella and Sam: the Story of Mrs Beeton*, Sarah Freeman, Gollancz, London, 1977.

BEHN, APHRA; née JOHNSON 1640–89. Writer, playwright, spy. Born at **Harbledown**, Kent; baptised in **Wye**; buried in **London [Westminster]**. *Reconstructing Aphra: a Social Biography of Aphra Behn*, Angeline Goreau, The Dial Press, Oxford, 1980; *The Passionate Shepherdess: Aphra Behn 1640–89*, Maureen Duffy, Cape, London, 1977.

BEILBY, MARY b. 1749. Artist in glass and enamel. Lived and worked in **Newcastle**. *Those Ingenious Beilbys*, James Rush, Barrie & Jenkins, London, 1973.

'BELL, CURRER, ELLIS and ACTON'. See BRONTË, CHARLOTTE, EMILY and ANNE.

BELL, GERTRUDE MARGARET LOWTHIAN 1868–1926. Scholar, explorer, archaeologist, linguist. Born in **Washington**; educated in **London [Westminster]** and **Oxford**; rest of her life spent travelling in the Middle East. *Gertrude Bell*, Harry V. F. Winstone, Jonathan Cape, London, 1978.

BELL, VANESSA; née STEPHEN 1879–1961. Artist. Born and brought up in **London [Kensington and Chelsea]**, with her sister VIRGINIA WOOLF, with summers in **St Ives**; lived in **London [Camden]** with the Bloomsbury Group; country home at **Firle** from 1916; buried there; painted murals at **Berwick**. *Vanessa Bell*, Frances Spalding, Weidenfeld and Nicolson, London, 1983; *Bloomsbury Portraits: Vanessa Bell, Duncan Grant and their Circle*, Richard N. Shone, Phaidon, Oxford, 1976.

BENTLEY, PHYLLIS 1894–1977. Writer. Lived and wrote in **Halifax**; educated in **Cheltenham** and **London [Camden]**; supporter of **Haworth** Parsonage. *O Dreams, O Destinations*, Phyllis Bentley, 1962.

BERNERS, JULIANA; JULYAN BARNES. Writer. *C.* 1388–*c.* 1414. Lived and wrote in **St Albans**.

BERRY, MARY and AGNES 1763–1852 and 1764–1852. Writers and editors. Brought up in **Kirkbridge**; lived and buried in **London [Richmond]**.

BERTHA *fl.* 567–612. Religious pioneer and ruler. French princess whose marriage in 596 brought her to **Canterbury**; also buried there.

BESANT, ANNIE; née WOOD 1847–1933. Fabian socialist; sex reformer, Theosophist, Indian nationalist. Childhood in **London [Harrow]**; studied at **London [Camden]**; active in politics and Theosophy, lived in **London [Southwark]**; led striking Matchgirls **London [Tower Hamlets]**; died in India. *Eminent Victorian Women*, Elizabeth Longford, Weidenfeld and Nicolson, London, 1981; *The First Five Lives of Annie Besant* and *The Last Four Lives of Annie Besant*, Arthur H. Nethercote, Rupert Hart-Davies, London, 1961 and 1963; *Annie Besant: an Autobiography*, Annie Besant, T. Fisher Unwin, London, 1893.

BESS OF HARDWICK. See TALBOT, ELIZABETH.

BETTERTON, MARY; née SAUNDERSON *c.* 1637–1712. Actress. Lived in **London [City]**; buried in **London [Westminster]**.

BEVAN, BRIDGET. See VAUGHAN, BRIDGET.

BIRD, ISABELLA; MRS BISHOP 1831–1904. Traveller, explorer, writer. Born in **Boroughbridge**; lived in **Edinburgh**; buried in **Tobermory**. *A Curious Life for a Lady*, Patricia M. Barr, Penguin, London, 1985.

'BLACK AGNES'. See DUNBAR, AGNES.

BLACKWELL, ELIZABETH *fl.* 1737–47. Writer and illustrator of herbal plants. Born in Scotland, possibly **Aberdeen**; lived and illustrated plants in **London [Kensington and Chelsea]**.

BLACKWELL, ELIZABETH 1821–1910. Medical practitioner and doctor. Born in **Bristol**; brought up in Kentucky, qualified as the first woman doctor in Geneva, New York; set up medical treatment and training centres in New York for women; returned to set up own practice in **London [Westminster]** where she also taught gynaecology; moved to **Hastings**, where she died; buried in **Kilmun**. *Lone Woman: the Story of Elizabeth Blackwell, the First Woman Doctor*, Dorothy C. Wilson, Hodder and Stoughton, London, 1970; *Opening the Medical Profession to Women*, Elizabeth Blackwell [M. R. Walsh ed.], Schocken Books, New York, 1977.

BLATCH, HARRIET STANTON; née STANTON 1856–1940. American suffragist. Born in United States; married life in **Basingstoke**; active in **London [Camden]**; continued women's rights struggle in the United States, where she died.

BLAVATSKY, HELENA PETROVNA; MADAME BLAVATSKY; H.P.B. 1831–91. Russian-born Theosophist leader. Headquarters in **London [Westminster]**.

BLESSINGTON, COUNTESS OF; MARGUERITE GARDINER; née POWELL 1789–1849. Salon hostess; writer. Originally from Ireland, held salons and wrote novels in **London [Westminster** and **Kensington and Chelsea]**; died in France. *Lady Blessington in Naples*, Edith Clay [ed.], Hamish Hamilton, London, 1979.

BLUNT, LADY ANNE; née KING-NOEL 1837–1917. Traveller and writer. Lived in **Esher** and **Worth**; travelled abroad, died in Cairo, buried there. *A Pilgrimage of Passion: the Life of Wilfred Scawen Blunt*, Elizabeth Longford, Weidenfeld and Nicolson, London, 1979.

BLYTON, ENID MARY 1897–1968. Writer of children's books. Born and brought up in **London [Bromley]**. *Enid Blyton: a Biography*, Barbara Stoney, Hodder & Stoughton, London, 1974.

BOADICEA. See BOUDICCA.

BODICHON, BARBARA; née LEIGH SMITH 1827–91. Social and educational reformer, women's rights campaigner, artist. Born in **London [Westminster]**; lived, worked and campaigned in **London [Westminster]**; retreats in **Robertsbridge** and **Zennor**; spent time in Algeria; founded women's college in **Cambridge**. *Barbara Bodichon 1927–91*, Hester Burton, Murray, London, 1949; *Barbara Leigh Smith Bodichon and the Langham Place Group*, Candida Ann Lacey [ed.], Routledge & Kegan Paul, London, 1987.

BOLEYN, ANNE *c.* 1507–36. Ruler, and second wife of Henry VIII. Born in **Blickling**; grew up at **Edenbridge**; court life in **London [Richmond]**; died and buried in **London [City]**; heart buried in **East Horndon**. *Anne Boleyn*, M. L. Bruce, Collins, London, 1972; *Anne Boleyn*, Carolly Erickson, Macmillan, London, 1984.

BONDFIELD, MARGARET GRACE 1873–1953. Trade unionist, politician and cabinet minister. Born in **Chard**; worked in **Brighton** and **London [Westminster]**; Member of Parliament for **Northampton** and **Wallsend**; retired to **Tunbridge Wells**; cremated in **London [Barnet]**. *A Life's Work*, Margaret Bondfield, Hutchinson, London, 1949.

BOOTH, CATHERINE; née MUMFORD 1829–90. Founding leader of Salvation Army. Born in **Ashbourne**; early evangelism in **London [Hackney]**; first sermon in **Gateshead**; major missionary work in **London [Hackney]**; retired to Clacton; buried in **London [Hackney]**. *Catherine Booth: the Story of Her Loves*, Catherine Bramwell-Booth, Hodder & Stoughton, London, 1970.

BOUCHERETT, JESSIE EMILIA 1825–1905. Feminist activist, writer. Brought up in **Willingham**, educated at **Stratford-upon-Avon**. Worked for women's causes in **London [Westminster]**; last years and death in **Willingham**.

BOUDICCA; also known as BOADICEA d. *c.* 62. Celtic ruler and warrior.

Led Iceni tribe in attacks on **Colchester**, **St Albans** and **London [City]**. Several sites traditionally associated with her burial, including **London [Camden** and **Waltham Forest]**. *Boudicca*, Graham Webster, Batsford, London, 1978; *Rebellion Against Rome*, Plantagenet Somerset Fry, Terence Dalton, Lavenham, 1981.

BOWEN, ELIZABETH DOROTHEA COLE 1899–1973. Writer. Born and brought up in Ireland; educated in Kent; lived in **Oxford** and died in **Hythe**. *Elizabeth Bowen: Portrait of a Writer*, Victoria Glendinning, Weidenfeld & Nicolson, London, 1977; *Elizabeth Bowen*, Patricia Craig, Penguin, Harmondsworth, 1986.

BOWES-LYON, ELIZABETH. See ELIZABETH, QUEEN MOTHER.

BRACEGIRDLE, ANNE *c.* 1663–1748. Actress. Born in **Northampton**; travelled throughout acting career; died and buried in **London [Westminster]**.

BRADDOCK, BESSIE; née ELIZABETH MARGARET BAMBER 1899–1970. Labour politician. Active life in her native **Liverpool**.

BRADDON, MARY ELIZABETH; MRS MAXWELL 1837–1915. Novelist, poet, playwright. Born in **London [Westminster]**; lived at **Emery Wood** and also **London [Richmond]** where she died and was buried.

BRADLEY, HELEN 1900–79. Artist. Lived and worked in **Manchester**.

BRADSTREET, ANNE; née DUDLEY *c.* 1612–72. Poet. Born in **Northampton**; emigrated to New England from **Boston** and **Southampton**. First English-speaking woman to have poetry published from America. *Anne Bradstreet: 'the Tenth Muse'*, E. W. White, Oxford University Press, New York, 1971.

BRAZIL, ANGELA 1868–1947. Writer of books for girls. Born in **Preston**; educated in **Manchester**; last years and death in **Coventry**; country homes at **Llanbedr** and **Polperro**. *The Schoolgirl Ethic: the Work and Life of Angela Brazil*, Gillian Freeman, Allen Lane, London, 1976.

BRITTAIN, VERA MARY 1839–1970. Writer, pacifist, journalist. Born in **Stoke on Trent**; educated at **Oxford**; lived in **London [Westminster]**. *Testament of Youth* and *Testament of Experience*, Vera Brittain, Virago, London, 1977 and 1978 [reprints].

BRONTË, ANNE; 'ACTON BELL' 1820–49. Writer. Born at **Thornton**, lived mostly at **Haworth**; educated briefly at **Mirfield**; died and buried at **Scarborough**. *Anne Brontë*, Winifred Gerin, Nelson, London, 1959.

BRONTË, CHARLOTTE; 'CURRER BELL' 1816–55. Writer. Born at **Thornton**; childhood, youth and adult life mainly at **Haworth**; educated at **Cowan Bridge** and **Mirfield**, where she later taught; visitor to **Birstall**, **Gomersal**, **Manchester**, **Norton Conyers** and **Padiham**; died and buried at **Haworth**. *The Life of Charlotte Brontë*, Mrs Gaskell [1857], Penguin, London, 1975 [reprint]; *Charlotte Brontë: the Self Conceived*, Hélène Moglen, University of Wisconsin Press, Madison, 1984.

BRONTË, EMILY JANE; 'ELLIS BELL' 1818–48. Writer. Born at **Thornton**; **Haworth** was her home for the rest of her life; educated at **Cowan Bridge** and **Mirfield**; taught at **Halifax**; died and buried at **Haworth**. *Emily Brontë*, Winifred Gerin, 1978; *Emily Brontë: the Artist as a Free Woman*, Stevie Davies, Carcanet Press, London, 1985.

There is much published on the lives and works of the BRONTË SISTERS, individually and collectively. Some general works are *The Brontës and Their World*, Phyllis Bentley, Thames & Hudson, London, 1969; *The Brontës*, Tom Winifrith, Macmillan, London, 1977; *Everyman's Companion to the Brontës*, Barbara and Gareth Lloyd Evans, Dent, London, 1982. The Brontë Society's headquarters is the Brontë Parsonage, Haworth, Keighley, West Yorkshire, BD22 8DR.

BROOKE, FRANCES; née MOORE 1724–89. British-Canadian novelist. Born in Lincolnshire; youth in **Peterborough**; married life included 1763 travel to Quebec; last days and grave at **Sleaford**.

BROUGHTON, RHODA 1840–1920 Writer. Born near **Denbigh**; childhood home **Broughton**; then moved to North Wales and **Oxford**.

BROWNING, ELIZABETH BARRETT; née ELIZABETH BARRETT 1806–61. Poet and writer. Born in **Kelloe**; childhood at **Hope End**; convalesced at **Sidmouth** and **Torquay**; lived in **London [Westminster]**; died and buried in Florence, Italy. *Elizabeth Barrett Browning*, Alethea Hayter, Longmans, Harlow, 1965; *Elizabeth Barrett Browning: a Portrait*, Isabel C. Clarke, Darby Books, 1985 [original publication 1929].

BRUNTON, MARY; née BALFOUR 1778–1818. Novelist. Born in **Orkney**; married life in **Haddington** area and **Edinburgh**, where she is buried.

BRYHER; ANNIE WINIFRED ELLERMAN 1894–1983. Writer. Took her name from one of the **Scilly Isles**, where she had a summer home; family home in **London [Westminster]**; often lived abroad, but spent the Second World War in **London [Kensington and Chelsea]**. *The Days of Mars: A Memoir 1940–46*, Bryher, 1972.

BUCHAN, ANNA; 'O. DOUGLAS' d. 1938. Novelist. Youth near **Ravenscraig**, later years at **Peebles**. *Unforgettable, Unforgotten*, Anna Buchan, Hodder & Stoughton, London, n.d.

BUCHAN, ELSPETH; née SIMPSON 1738–91. Religious leader. Born and raised in north-east Scotland; religious involvement in **Irvine**; died in **Auchengibbert**.

BURDETT-COUTTS; ANGELA GEORGINA, BARONESS 1814–1906. Philanthropist. Born and spent much of her life in **London [Westminster** and **Camden]**; charitable work in **London [Hackney]**; wintered in **Torquay** and **Brighton**; died and buried in **London [Westminster]**. *Lady Unknown: the Life of Angela Burdett-Coutts*, Edna Healey, Sidgwick & Jackson, London, 1978; *Made of Gold: a Biography of Angela Burdett-Coutts*, Diana Orton, Hamish Hamilton, London, 1980.

DE BURGH, ELIZABETH; ELIZABETH DE CLARE *c.* 1291–1360. Benefactress. Founder of colleges in **Cambridge**.

BURNETT, FRANCES ELIZA HODGSON 1849–1924. Writer for children and adults; born in **Manchester**; emigrated to USA in 1864; returned to live in **London [Westminster]** and **Rolvedem**; last years and death in USA. *Waiting for the Party: the Life of Frances Hodgson Burnett*, A. Thwaite, Secker & Warburg, London, 1974.

BURNEY, FANNY [FRANCES]; MADAME D'ARBLEY 1752–1840. Novelist and diarist. Born and early years in **King's Lynn**, lived in **London [Richmond]** and **Windsor**; married life first in **Great Bookham**; moved to France; came back to Britain living in **Bath** and **London [Westminster]**; buried in **Bath**. *Fanny Burney*, Sarah Kilpatrick, David & Charles, Newton Abbot, 1980; *The History of Fanny Burney*, Joyce Henlow, Oxford University Press, Oxford, 1958.

BURTON, ISABEL, LADY 1831–96. Traveller and writer. Born, lived and wrote in **London [Richmond]**, but travelled extensively in four continents; died and buried in **London [Richmond]**. *The Wilder Shores of Love*, Lesley Blanch, John Murray, London, 1954.

DE BUSH, PAULISE. Dress historian and collector. Home and costume collection near **Exeter**.

BUSS, FRANCES MARY 1827–94. Educational pioneer. Born, educated, taught in **London [Camden** and **Westminster]**; buried in **Theydon Bois**. *How Different From Us: a Biography of Miss Buss and Miss Beale*, Josephine Kamm, Bodley Head, London, 1958.

BUTLER, ELEANOR, LADY 1745–1829. Irish writer and recluse. Born in Ireland; educated in France; eloped to **Denbigh**; settled in **Llangollen**. *The Ladies of Llangollen*, Elizabeth Mavor, Penguin, Harmondsworth, 1973; *A Year with the Ladies of Llangollen*, Elizabeth Mavor [ed.], Viking, London, 1984.

BUTLER, JOSEPHINE ELIZABETH 1828–1906. Activist in women's issues, campaigner against slavery and for education. Born in Northumberland; lived and campaigned in **Oxford**, **Cheltenham**, **Liverpool**, **Leeds** and **Winchester**; last years in **Wooler**; buried in **Kirknewton**. *Significant Sisters*, Margaret Forster, Secker & Warburg, London, 1984; *Josephine Butler: Flame of Fire*, E. Moberley-Bell, Constable, London, 1962; *A Singular Iniquity: the Campaigns of Josephine Butler*, Glen Petrie, Macmillan,

London, 1971; *Josephine Butler: the Forgotten Saint*, Joseph Williamson, Faith Press, Leighton Buzzard, 1977.

BUTT, CLARA, DAME 1873–1936. Singer. Brought up and trained in **Bristol** and **London [Camden]**; retirement and burial in **North Stoke**. *Clara Butt: Her Life-Story*, Winifred Ponder, Da Capo Press, New York, 1978.

BYRON, LADY ANNE ISABELLA NOEL; BARONESS WENTWORTH; née MILBANKE 1792–1860. Philanthropist and social reformer. Born in **Durham**; married at **Seaham**, one of her childhood homes; lived at **Kirkby Mallory**, another home in **Esher**, visited **Exmouth** and **Brighton**; supported work in **Bristol**; buried in **London [Brent]**. *Lady Byron Vindicated: a History of the Byron Controversy*, Harriet Beecher Stowe, London, 1870 [reprinted Haskell, 1970].

C c

CAMERON, JEAN *fl.* 1745. Scottish heroine. Lived in **East Kilbride**.

CAMERON, JULIA MARGARET; née PATTLE 1815–79. Photographer. Born in Calcutta; educated in England and France; lived and married in India; returned to Britain in 1848; had homes in **London [Richmond, Wandsworth]** and **Freshwater**; spent her closing years in Ceylon, where she is buried. *Julia Margaret Cameron*, Amanda Hopkins, Virago, London, 1986.

CAMPBELL, MRS PATRICK; 'MRS PAT'; née BEATRICE STELLA TANNER 1864–1940. Actress. Native of **London [Kensington and Chelsea]**, where she later had homes; educated in French and English schools; professional stage debut in **Liverpool**; theatrical career mainly in London; died in obscurity in France. *Mrs Pat*, Margot Peters, Bodley Head, London, 1984.

CARLINE, HILDA; LADY SPENCER 1889–1950. Artist. **London [Camden]** childhood shared with her sisters; married Stanley Spencer with whom she lived and was buried in **Cookham**.

CARLYLE, JANE WELSH; née WELSH 1801–66. Writer. Born and grew up in **Haddington**; first home after marriage in **Edinburgh**, then **Craigenputtoch**; moved to **London [Kensington and Chelsea]** in 1834, where she died; visitor to **Manchester**; buried in **Haddington**. *From Threshold to Rooftree: the Haddington Home of Jane Welsh Carlyle*, Pentland Press, Haddington, 1984; *I Too Am Here: Selections from the Letters of Jane Welsh Carlyle*, Alan and Mary Simpson [eds], Cambridge University Press, Cambridge, 1977; *Jane Welsh Carlyle: Letters to Her Family 1839–1963*, Leonard Huxley [ed.], John Murray, London, 1924.

CAROLINE, QUEEN 1768–1821. Consort and political problem. Born in Brunswick; married her cousin, Prince of Wales, in 1795; left England in 1814; returned on becoming Queen in 1820 to **London [Westminster]**, but died shortly afterwards in **London [Hammersmith]**; buried in Brunswick. *Caroline: a Biography of Caroline of Brunswick*, Thea Holme, Hamish Hamilton, London, 1979.

CARPENTER, MARY 1807–77. Educational reformer. Born in **Exeter**, but her family moved to **Bristol** in 1817; here she lived, worked, died and is buried. *Mary Carpenter and the Children of the Streets*, Jo Manton, Heinemann Educational, London, 1976.

CARRINGTON, DORA 1893–1932. Artist. Trained and painted in **London [Camden]**, frequent guest of LADY OTTOLINE MORRELL's at **Garsington**; moves to **Tidmarsh** and later **Ham** where she died and was buried. *Carrington: Paintings, Drawings and Decorations*, Noel Carrington, Thames & Hudson, London, 1983.

CARTER, MRS ELIZABETH 1717–1806. Scholar, translator, writer. Born and mostly lived in **Deal**; visitor to **Bath**; spent many winters of her later life in **London [Westminster]**, where she died and is buried. *Sisters of the Quill*, Alice A. Hufstader, Dodd Mead, New York, 1978.

CARTIMANDUA *fl.* 1st century AD. Celtic ruler. Leader of the Brigantes, headquarters at **Aldborough**.

CATCHPOLE, MARGARET 1762–1819. Australian pioneer. Born in Suffolk; early life in service; gaoled in **Ipswich**. *Margaret Catchpole*, N. Donkin, *Australians in History* series, 1974.

CATHERINE OF ARAGON *c.* 1485–1536. Queen of England, first of Henry VIII's six wives. Birth and childhood in Spain; married life firstly in **Ludlow** and secondly in **London [Greenwich]**; awaited divorce at **Ampthill Park**; after divorce imprisoned at **Buckden**, and **Kimbolton**, where she died; buried in **Peterborough**. *Catherine of Aragon*, G. Mattingly, 1944.

CAVELL, EDITH LOUISA 1856–1915. Nurse; humanist. Born in **Swardeston**; governess in Belgium, before nursing in **London [Hackney]**; returned to nurse in Belgium where she died heroically; buried and commemorated in **Norwich**. *Edith Cavell*, Rowland Ryder, Hamish Hamilton, London, 1975.

CAVENDISH, GEORGIANA; DUCHESS OF DEVONSHIRE; née SPENCER 1757–1806. Influential political hostess. Born at **Althorp**; married life at **Chatsworth** and in **London [Westminster]**, where she died; buried in **Derby**. *Georgiana, Duchess of Devonshire*, Brian Masters, Hamish Hamilton, London, 1981.

CAVENDISH, LUCY; née LADY LUCY LYTTLETON 1841–1926. Educational and social reformer. Born at **Hagley**; honoured by **Leeds** university; commemorated by **Cambridge** university. *The Diary of Lady Lucy Cavendish*, J. Bailey [ed.], 1927.

CAVENDISH, MARGARET, DUCHESS OF NEWCASTLE; née LUCAS 1623–73. Scientist; writer. Born in Essex; much of her married life spent in exile in France and Holland; on return to England, settled at **Welbeck**, where she died; buried in **London [Westminster]**. *Margaret the First: a Biography of Margaret Cavendish, Duchess of Newcastle*, Douglas Grant, University of Toronto Press, Toronto, 1957; 'The Duchess of Newcastle' in *The Common Reader*, Virginia Woolf, Hogarth Press, London, 1925.

CHALMERS-WATSON, MRS; née ALEXANDRA MARY GEDDES Doctor, administrator and feminist publisher. Educated in **St Andrews**; graduated in **Edinburgh**; war service at **Guildford**; published in **London [City]**.

CHAMBERLAIN, BRENDA 1912–71. Artist and writer. Lived on **Bardsey Island**.

CHAMBERLAYNE, ANNE *fl.* 1690. Soldier. Commemorated in **London [Kensington and Chelsea]**.

CHARLOTTE, PRINCESS, PRINCESS OF WALES 1796–1817. Beloved heiress of George III. Born in **London [Westminster]**; married life at **Esher**; buried in **Windsor**. *Prinny's Daughter: a Life of Princess Charlotte of Wales*, Thea Holme, Hamish Hamilton, London, 1976.

CHEYNE, LADY JANE; née CAVENDISH 1621–69. Royalist activist. Family home, which she defended, at **Welbeck**; married life in **London [Kensington and Chelsea]**, where she is buried.

CHICHESTER, ROSALIE CAROLINE 1865–1949. Collector. Whole life spent at **Barnstaple**.

CHRISTIE, AGATHA MARY CLARISSA; née MILLER 1891–1976. Crime writer. Early life in **Torquay**; 'disappearance' to **Harrogate**; lived and wrote in **London [Kensington and Chelsea]**; home in **Wallingford**; buried at **Cholsey**. *An Autobiography*, Agatha Christie, Collins, London, 1977; *Agatha Christie: a Biography*, Janet Morgan, Collins, London, 1984.

CHUDLEIGH, LADY MARY; née LEE 1656–1710. Feminist writer. Probably born at **Winslade**; married life at **Higher Ashton**, where she died and was buried.

CHURCHILL, JENNIE; née JEROME 1854–1924. Married life and burial at **Woodstock**.

CHURCHILL, SARAH, DUCHESS OF MARLBOROUGH; née JENNINGS 1660–1744. Social and political leader, businesswoman. Birth and childhood in **St Albans**; married life in **London [Westminster]** and **Woodstock**, where she is buried. *Sarah, Duchess of Marlborough*, David Green, Collins, London, 1967.

CLIFF, CLARICE 1899–1972. Artist and designer in ceramic. Active life in **Stoke on Trent**. *Clarice Cliff*, Peter Wentworth-Shields and Kay Johnson, L'Odeon, London, 1976.

CLIFFORD, LADY ANNE, COUNTESS OF DORSET; COUNTESS OF PEMBROKE and MONTGOMERY 1590–1676. Builder, landowner. Built and fortified castles in **Appleby**, **Brougham**, **Brough**, **Barden Tower** and **Skipton**, living at each in turn; born at **Skipton**; died at **Brougham** and buried in **Appleby**. *Proud Northern Lady*, Martin Holmes, Philimore Press, London, 1975; 'Lady Anne Clifford. . . A Re-appraisal', R. T.

Spence, in *Northern History*, University of Leeds, 1979.

CLIFFORD, ROSAMUND DE; 'FAIR ROSAMUND' d. *c.* 1176. Reputedly born at **Clifford**; buried at **Godstowe**.

CLITHEROE, SAINT MARGARET; née MIDDLETON 1556–86. Roman Catholic martyr. Born, lived and martyred in **York**.

CLIVE, CATHERINE [KITTY]; née RAFTOR 1711–85. Actress. Career in **London [Westminster]**; retired and died in **London [Richmond]**.

CLOUGH, ANNE JEMIMA 1820–92. Social and educational reformer. Born in **Liverpool**; childhood in USA; campaigned in **Leeds**; taught in **Liverpool** and **Ambleside**; administered college in **Cambridge**.

COADE, MRS ELEANOR d. 1796. Businesswoman and manufacturer of Coade Stone. In business with her husband in **Lyme Regis**, and later with her daughter ELEANOR COADE in **London [Lambeth]**; buried in **London [Camden]**. Fine example of her product at **Windsor**.

COADE, ELEANOR d. 1821. Businesswoman. Grew up in **Lyme Regis**, maintained a home there after going into business in **London [Lambeth]** with her mother, beside whom she was buried in **London [Camden]**.

COBBE, FRANCES POWER 1822–1904. Journalist, writer, campaigner for women's issues, especially against wife abuse, anti-vivisectionist. Born and brought up in Ireland, brief formal education in **Brighton**; worked in **Bristol** with MARY CARPENTER; campaigned in **London**; retired to **Dolgellau**. *The Life of Frances Power Cobbe*, Richard Bentley, London, 1894.

COMPTON-BURNETT, IVY 1884–1969. Writer. Born in **London [Harrow]**; lived with her family in **Hove**; took a degree in **London [Kensington and Chelsea]**, later living there with Margaret Jourdain. *Ivy When Young: the Early Life of Ivy Compton-Burnett*, 1974, and *Secrets of a Woman's Heart*, 1985, Hilary Spurling, Hodder & Stoughton, London.

CONS, EMMA 1837–1912. Social reformer and theatre manager. Native Londoner, lived in **London [Westminster]**; active in **London [Lambeth]**, the stage where her own full life was acted out; died in **Edenbridge**.

COOKSON, CATHERINE; née MCMULLEN b. 1906. Novelist. Born and raised in **Jarrow**, lived in **Hastings**. *Our Kate*, Catherine Cookson, Macdonald, London, 1969; *Catherine Cookson Country: Her Pictorial Memoir*, Catherine Cookson, Heinemann, London, 1986.

COOPER, EDITH EMMA; 'MICHAEL FIELD' 1862–1913. Writer and poet. Native of **Kenilworth**.

COOPER, GLADYS CONSTANCE 1888–1971. Actress and theatre manager. Born in **London [Lewisham]**; career in the West End; buried in **London**

[Camden]. *Gladys Cooper: a Biography*, Sheridan Morley, Heinemann, London, 1979.

COOPER, SELINA JANE; née COOBE 1864–1946. Suffragist and campaigner. Born in Cornwall, grew up in **Nelson**, where she was politically active; supported the **Cradley Heath** chainmakers. *The Life and Times of a Respectable Rebel*, Jill Liddington, Virago, London, 1984.

COOPER, SUSIE b. 1902. Pottery designer and manufacturer. Working life in **Stoke-on-Trent**. *Elegance and Utility: Susie Cooper*, A. Woodhouse, Wedgewood, Stoke-on-Trent.

CORELLI, MARIE; MARY MACKAY 1855–1924. Novelist. Wrote in **London [Kensington and Chelsea]**; last colourful years in **Stratford-upon-Avon**, where she was buried. *Now Barabbas Was a Rotter: the Extraordinary Life of Marie Corelli*, Brian Masters, Hamish Hamilton, London; *Marie Corelli: the Woman and the Legend*, Eileen Bigland, Jarrolds, Norwich, 1953.

COUTTS, ANGELA BURDETT-. See BURDETT-COUTTS, ANGELA.

CRAIG, EDITH 1869–1947. Actress, theatre manager, costume designer. Daughter of ELLEN TERRY, lived in **Smallhythe**. *Ellen and Edy : A Biography of Ellen Terry and Her Daughter, Edith Craig 1847–1947*, Joy Melville, Pandora Press, London, 1988.

CRAIGIE, PEARL MARY TERESA; 'JOHN OLIVER HOBBES' 1867–1906. American playwright and novelist. Lived, wrote and died at **Ventnor**.

CRAIK, MRS; née DIANA MARIA MULOCK 1826–87. Writer. Born and educated in **Stoke-on-Trent** area; lived in **London [Bromley]**, where she was buried.

CROMPTON, RICHMAL; RICHMAL CROMPTON LAMBOURN 1890–1969. Children's writer. School days in **Darley Dale**; taught in **London [Bromley]**. *Just Richmal: the Life and Work of Richmal Crompton Lambourn*, Kay Williams, Genesis, Guildford, 1986.

CULLICK, HANNAH; MRS MUNBY 1833–1909. Diarist. Born in **Shifnal** and died there. *The Diaries of Hannah Cullick: Victorian Maidservant*, Liz Stanley [ed.], Virago, London, 1984.

'CUTPURSE MOLL'. See FRITH, MARY.

D d

DAMER, ANNE SEYMOUR; née CONWAY 1749–1828. Artist, sculptor. Studio in **London [Richmond]**; sculpture and parental home at **Henley**; died in **London [Westminster]**; buried in **London [Bromley]**.

DARLING, GRACE 1815–42. Heroine. Born in **Bamburgh**; lived on the **Farne Islands**, scene of her heroic rescue; last illness and death in **Bamburgh**, where she was also buried. *Grace Darling: Maid and Myth*, Richard Armstrong, Dent, London, 1965.

DAVIES, GWENDOLIN ELIZABETH 1882–1951. Patron of the arts. Childhood home in **Llandinam**; built arts centre at **Newtown**; donated collection to **Cardiff**. *The Ladies of Gregynog*, Eirene White, University of Wales Press, 1985.

DAVIES, MARGARET LLEWELYN 1861–1943. Organiser of the Co-operative Women's Guild, pacifist. Londoner, educated in **London [Westminster]** and **Cambridge**; lived and worked in **Manchester** and **Kirkby Lonsdale**. *Caring and Sharing: the Centenary History of the Co-operative Women's Guild*, Jean Gaffin and David Thomas, Co-operative Union, Manchester, 1983.

DAVIES, MARGARET SIDNEY 1884–1963. Patron of the arts. Childhood home in **Llandinam**; established arts centre at **Newtown**; donated collection to **Cardiff**. *The Ladies of Gregynog*, Eirene White, University of Wales Press, 1985.

DAVIES, SARAH EMILY 1830–1921. Educational pioneer. Born in **Southampton**, childhood there and **Gateshead**; moved to **London [Westminster]**; educated women in **Hitchin** and **Cambridge**; died in **London [Westminster]**. *Significant Sisters*, Margaret Forster, Secker & Warburg, London, 1984; *Emily Davies and Girton College*, Barbara Stephen, Constable, London, 1927.

DAVIS, CHRISTIAN; née CHRISTOPHER WELSH CAVANAGH 1677–1739. Soldier. Born in Dublin, after active service, ran a public house and retired in **London [Kensington and Chelsea]**, where buried.

DAVISON, EMILY WILDING 1872–1913. Suffragette. Born in London, educated there and at **Oxford**; imprisoned in **London [Camden]** and

Manchester; sacrifice at **Epsom**; funeral in **London [City]**; buried at **Morpeth**.

DAWSON, MARGARET MARY DAMER 1875–1920. Policewoman. Founded the women's police service in **London [Kensington and Chelsea]**; died and buried in **Lympne**. *The British Policewoman – Her Story*, Joan Lock, Hale, London, 1979.

'DELAFIELD, E. M.'; EDMEE ELIZABETH MONICA DASHWOOD; née DE LA PASTURE 1890–1943. Writer. Born in Monmouthshire; lived, wrote and died in **Collompton**.

DELANEY, MRS; née MARY GRANVILLE 1700–88. Writer and flower artist. Born in **Coulston**; lived in **Buckland**; first marriage spent at **Penryn**; second happier marriage mostly passed in Ireland; widowhood brought her to **London [Westminster]**, and **Windsor**. Her art work is housed in the British Museum. *Mrs Delaney: Her Life and Her Flowers*, Ruth Hayden, British Museum publications, London, 1980.

DERVORGUILLA 1213–90. Educational reformer, religious benefactress. Supported **Oxford** college, built bridge in **Dumfries**, died and was buried in **New Abbey**.

DESPARD, CHARLOTTE; née FRENCH 1844–1939. Suffragette, socialist, Sinn Feiner. Born in Kent; welfare work in **London [Wandsworth and Kingston upon Thames]**; last active years spent fighting for Irish causes in Ireland; died in Northern Ireland. *An Unhusbanded Life: Charlotte Despard, Suffragette, Socialist and Sinn Feiner*, Andro Linklater, Heinemann, London, 1980.

DEVLIN, MARGARET. See ASHFORD, DAISY.

DISRAELI, MARY ANNE; née EVANS 1792–1872. Political partner. Born in **Exeter**; second marriage spent at **Hughenden**, where she died and was buried. *Mrs Dizzy: the Life of Mary Anne Disraeli, Viscountess Beaconsfield*, M. Hardwick, Cassell, London, 1972.

DIXIE, LADY FLORENCE CAROLINE; née DOUGLAS 1857–1905. Journalist, suffragist. Born in Scotland; married life based in **Market Bosworth**, buried in **Kinmount**.

DOOLITTLE, HILDA; H.D. 1886–1961. Poet. Born in the USA; literary life in **London [Kensington and Chelsea]**. *Herself Defined*, Barbara Guest, Collins, London, 1984; *H.D. and Her London*, Diana Collecott [forthcoming].

DORA, SISTER DORA OF WALSALL; DOROTHY WYNDLOW PATTINSON 1832–78. Nursing pioneer. Born at **Hauxwell**; nursed at **Walsall**. *Sister Dora: a Biography*, M. Lonsdale, Kegan Paul, Trench and Co., London, 1888; *Sister Dora: the Life of Dorothy Pattinson*, Jo Manton, Methuen, 1971.

'DOUGLAS, O'. See BUCHAN, ANNA.

DOUGLASS, DOROTHEA KATHERINE; MRS CHAMBERS 1878–1960. Tennis player. Champion in **London [Merton]**.

DRUMMOND, ANNABELLA *c.* 1350–1401. Ruler of Scotland. Died at **Scone**; buried at **Dunfermline**.

DUNBAR, AGNES; COUNTESS OF MARCH AND DUNBAR; 'BLACK AGNES' *c.* 1300–69. Military leader and Scottish heroine; defended her family home in **Dunbar**.

DUNCAN, GEILLIS d. *c.* 1590. Healer, 'witch'. Lived and died at **North Berwick**.

DYSART, ELIZABETH, DUCHESS OF LAUDERDALE; née MURRAY *c.* 1627–97. Second marriage spent at **London [Richmond]**, where she was buried.

E E

EARDLEY, JOAN KATHLEEN HARDY 1921–63. Artist. Trained and painted in **Glasgow**; had studios at **Catterline**, where her ashes were scattered. *Joan Eardley*, William Buchanan, Edinburgh University Press, Edinburgh, 1976.

EARHART, AMELIA 1898–1937. American pioneer aviator. Transatlantic crossing lands at **Burrey Port**. *Amelia Earhart*, B. Davis, 1977; *Letters from Amelia Earhart 1901–1937*, Jean L. Backus [ed.], Beacon Press, Boston, 1982; *Soaring Wings: a Biography of Amelia Earhart*, George Palmer Putnam, Harrap, London, 1940.

EDGEWORTH, MARIA 1768–1849. Writer for adults and children. Born at **Black Bourton**; grew up at **Hare Hatch** and **Northchurch**; educated in **Derby**; adult life mostly spent in Ireland but visited **London [Westminster]**. *Maria Edgeworth: a Literary Biography*, Marilyn Butler, Clarendon Press, Oxford, 1972.

EDWARDS, AMELIA ANNE BLANDFORD 1831–92. Egyptologist, writer and patron. A native of London she died in **Weston-super-Mare**; buried in **Bristol**; supported Egyptology in **London [Camden]**. *Amelia Blandford Edwards*, K. Macquoid, 1897.

EISNER, LISBETH d. 1949. German poet and political activist. Major part of her life spent in Germany; retirement and death in **Mere**.

ELA, SAINT d. 1261. Saint; born in **Canford**; built cathedral at **Salisbury**.

ELEANOR OF CASTILE, 'ST ELEANOR' 1240–90. Saintly ruler. Brought up in Spain, came to England as Queen. Stays in **Caernarfon** and **Conwy**; died at **Harby**; buried in **Lincoln** and **London [Westminster]**; crosses at **Geddinton, Northampton, Waltham Cross, London [Westminster]**. *The Court and Household of Eleanor of Castile in 1290*, J. C. Parsons [ed.], 1977.

ELFRIDA *fl.* 978. Saxon Queen. Dynastic manoeuvres at **Corfe Castle**.

'ELIOT, GEORGE'; MARY ANNE CROSS; née EVANS; MARIAN EVANS 1819–80. Born and grew up near **Nuneaton**; educated in **Attleborough**; later lived in **Coventry** and **London [Westminster, Merton]**; visitor to the **Scilly Isles** and **Gainsborough**; died in **London [Kensington and Chelsea]**; buried in **London [Haringey]**. *George Eliot: a Biography*, Gordon S. Haight, Clarendon Press, Oxford, 1968; *George Eliot and Her*

World, Marghanita Laski, Thames & Hudson, London, 1973; *George Eliot: The Emergent Self*, Ruby Virginia Redinger, Bodley Head, London, 1976.

ELIZABETH I, QUEEN. Ruler of England 1533–1603. Born in **London [Greenwich]**; childhood home at **Hatfield**; once Queen she had several royal homes, and travelled her kingdom, visiting among other places **Kenilworth**; fiery speech at **Tilbury**; college foundation at **Oxford**; died at **London [Richmond]**; buried at **London [Westminster]**. *The First Elizabeth*, Carolly Erickson, Macmillan, London, 1984; *Elizabeth the Great*, Elizabeth Jenkins, Gollancz, London, 1985 [original publication 1958].

ELIZABETH OF BOHEMIA; ELIZABETH STUART; 'THE WINTER QUEEN' 1596–1662. Born in Scotland, lived abroad after marriage; returned to Britain in 1661; died and buried in **London [Westminster]**; house built for her at **Lambourn**. *Elizabeth the Winter Queen*, Jessica Gorst-Williams, Abelard, London, 1977; *The Winter Queen: the Story of Elizabeth Stuart*, Josephine Ross, Weidenfeld & Nicolson, London 1979.

ELIZABETH, QUEEN MOTHER b. 1900. Born at **Glamis**, saved historic building at **Mey**. *Elizabeth of Glamis*, David Duff, Muller, London, 1973; *Queen Elizabeth: a Life of the Queen Mother*, Penelope Mortimer, Viking, Harmondsworth, 1986.

ETHELBURGA, SAINT d. *c.* 678. Abbess at **London [Barking]**.

ETHELDREDA, SAINT *c.* 630–79. Religious leader, saintly medical woman; born near **Newmarket**; married in Northumbria; led a religious life in **Ely**, where she is buried. *Saint Etheldreda, Queen and Abbess*, C. J. Stranks, Ely Cathedral, Ely, n.d.

EUGENIE, EMPRESS 1826–1920. Empress of France. Born in Spain; early married life in France; exile in **London [Bromley]** and **Farnborough**, where she was buried. *Napoleon and Eugénie*, Jasper Ridley, Constable, London, 1979.

EVANS, DAME EDITH MARY 1888–1976. Actress. Native Londoner. Lived in **London [Westminster]** where much of her acting career was spent; died in Kent. *Edith Evans, a Personal Memoir*, J. Batters, Hart Davis MacGibbon, London, 1977; *Dame Edith Evans: Ned's Girl*, Bryan Forbes, Little, Brown, London, 1978.

EVANS, MARIAN. See 'ELIOT, GEORGE'.

EVANS, MARY ANNE. See DISRAELI, MRS.

EVANS, MARY ANNE. See 'ELIOT, GEORGE'.

EWING, MRS JULIANA HORATIA; née GATTY 1841–85. Children's writer. Born in **Ecclesfield**; married life in Canada and **Aldershot**; died in **Bath**, buried in **Trull**. *Mrs Gatty and Mrs Ewing*, Christabel Maxwell, Constable, London, 1949; *Mrs Ewing, Mrs Moleworth and Mrs Hodgson Burnett*, Marghanita Laski, Arthur Barker, London, 1950.

F F

FAIRFIELD, CICELY. See WEST, REBECCA.

'FAIRLESS, MICHAEL'; MARGARET FAIRLESS BARBER 1869–1901. Writer of novels and short stories. Lived in **London [Kensington and Chelsea]**; buried near **Steyning**. 'A Biographical Note', M. E. Duncan, in *The Complete Works of Michael Fairless*, Duckworth, London, 1931.

FAITHFULL, EMILY 1835–95. Feminist printer and worker for women's rights. Born in **Headley**; worked and lived in **London [City, Kensington and Chelsea** and **Camden]**. 'Emily Faithfull and the Victoria Press', William E. Fredeman, in *The Library* [fifth series], XXIX [2], 1974.

'FAUCIT, HELEN'; HELENA SAVILE, LADY MARTIN 1820–98. Actress. Career in **London [Westminster]**; last years in **Llangollen**; burial place in **London [Kensington and Chelsea]**.

FAWCETT, DAME MILLICENT GARRETT; née GARRETT 1847–1929. Leading suffragist, writer. Born in **Aldeburgh**; married life in **Cambridge**, **Brighton**, **Bath** and **London [Camden]**, where she campaigned and later died; commemorated in **London [Westminster]**. *Millicent Garrett Fawcett*, Ray Strachey, John Murray, London, 1931.

FAWCETT, PHILIPPA GARRETT 1868–1948. Suffragist. Studied at **Cambridge**; campaigned in **London [Camden]**.

FELL, MARGARET; MARGARET FELL FOX; née ASKEW 1614–1702. Leader of the Quaker movement; active life at **Ulverston**; buried near there. *Margaret Fell: Mother of Quakerism*, Isabel Ross, William Sessions Book Trust, York, 1984 [new edition].

FERRIER, KATHLEEN 1912–53. Singer. Born in Lancashire; worked in **Preston**; lived in **London [Camden]**; buried in **London [Barnet]**. *Kathleen Ferrier, Her Life*, Winifred Ferrier, Hamish Hamilton, London, 1955.

FIELDS, GRACIE; MAY STANSFIELD 1898–1979. Singer, comedienne. Born in **Rochdale**; stage life spent mostly on tour; retired to Italy, where she died. *Sing As We Go*, Gracie Fields, Muller, London, 1960.

FIENNES, CELIA 1662–1741. Traveller and writer. Lived at **Newton Toney**, where she was later buried, and possibly **London [Barnet]**, when not travelling; visitor to **Broughton, Bath, Canterbury, Knares-**

borough, among many other places; died in **London [Hackney]**. *The Illustrated Journeys of Celia Fiennes, c. 1682–1712*, Christopher Morris [ed.], MacDonald, London, 1982.

FINCH, ANNE, COUNTESS OF WINCHILSEA; née KINGSMILL *c.* 1661–1720. Poet. Born in **Sydmonton**; lived in **Canterbury**; died in **Eastwell**.

FITTON, MARY *c.* 1578–1647. Muse; possible 'Dark Lady of the Sonnets'. Born at **Gawsworth**; court life in **London [Richmond]**; stayed near **Nuneaton**.

FITZHERBERT, MRS; MARIA ANNE WELD; née SMYTHE 1756–1837. Unacknowledged wife of George IV. Born in **Tong**; educated in France; residences in **London [Ealing, Richmond and Westminster]**; lived in **Brighton**, where she was later buried. *Three Wedding Rings for Mrs Fitzherbert of Brighton*, Robert Bogan, Bernardette's, Brighton, n.d.; *The Uncrowned Queen*, Geraldine Sampson, 1971; *Mrs Fitzherbert*, Anita Leslie, Hutchinson, London, 1960.

FLEMING, MARJORY 1803–11. Child writer. Lived and died in **Kirkcaldy**. *Marjorie Fleming*, Arundell Esdaile, 1934.

FLETCHER, CHRISTIAN; MRS GRAINGER *fl.* 1650. Scottish patriot and heroine; heroism in **Dunnottar** and **Old Kinneff**.

FOUNTAINE, MARGARET 1862–1940. Naturalist. Birthplace and childhood home at **South Acre**; early adulthood in **Norwich**, where collection is housed; died in the West Indies. *Love Among the Butterflies*, W. F. Carter [ed.], Collins, London, 1980.

FOWLER, KATHERINE. See PHILIPS, KATHERINE.

FOX, MARGARET FELL. See FELL, MARGARET.

FREUD, ANNA 1895–1982. Psychoanalyst. Born in Austria, emigrated to Britain, settling in **London [Camden]**; cremated in **London [Barnet]**. *Anna Freud, a Life Dedicated to Children*, Uwe Hendrick Peters, Weidenfeld & Nicolson, London, 1985.

FRITH, MARY; 'MOLL CUTPURSE' *c.* 1584–1659. Folk heroine; highwaywoman. Wild life in **London [City]**, where she was buried. *Moll Cutpurse: Her True Story*, Ellen Galford, Stramullion, Edinburgh, 1984 [fictional account].

FRY, ELIZABETH; née GURNEY 1780–1845. Prison reformer, health worker, religious leader. Birth and youth in **Norwich** area; social work in **London [City]**; lived at **London [Newham]**; buried in **London [Barking]**. *Elizabeth Fry*, June Rose, Macmillan, London, 1980.

G G

GANDHI, INDIRA; née NEHRU 1917–84. Politician. Born in India, educated there and in England; studied at **Oxford**; political leadership in India. *Indira Gandhi's Emergence and Style*, N. P. Saghal, 1978; *Letters to a Friend, 1950–1984*, Indira Gandhi, Weidenfeld & Nicolson, London, 1986.

GASKELL, MRS ELIZABETH CLEGHORN; née ELIZABETH CLEGHORN STEVENSON 1810–65. Writer of novels and biography. Born in **London [Kensington and Chelsea]**; grew up in **Knutsford**; educated in **Stratford-upon-Avon**; married life in **Manchester**; visitor to **Haworth** and **Whitby**; died in **Holybourne**; buried in **Knutsford**. *Mrs Gaskell*, Winifred Gerin, Oxford University Press, Oxford, 1980. The Gaskell Society, Secretary, Far Yew Tree Cottage, Over Tabley, Knutsford, Cheshire, WA16 0HN.

GATTY, MARGARET 1809–73. Children's writer and publisher. Married life and burial in **Ecclesfield**. *Mrs Gatty and Mrs Ewing*, Christabel Maxwell, Constable, London, 1949.

GEDDES, JANET; 'JENNIE' *fl*. 1637. Scottish folk heroine. Defied church authorities in **Edinburgh**.

GENEE, DAME ADELINE; née ANITA JENSEN 1878–1970. Dancer and dance teacher. Born in Denmark; dancing career centred on **London [Westminster]**; commemorated in **East Grinstead**. *Adeline Genée: a Lifetime of Ballet Under Six Reigns*, Ivor Guest, Black, London, 1958.

GERE, MARGARET 1878–1965. Artist. Trained in **Birmingham** and **London [Camden]**; latterly lived and painted at **Painswick**.

GLOVER, CATRIONA; 'THE FAIR MAID OF PERTH'. Fourteenth-century folk heroine. Lived in **Perth**.

GLUCK; née HANNAH GLUCKSTEIN 1895–1978. Artist. Native Londoner, studied art in **London [Westminster]**; painted at **Lamorna**; last years at **Steyning**. *Gluck: Exhibition of Paintings*, Martin Battersby [ed.], Fine Art Society, London, 1973 [exhibited catalogue].

GLYN, ELINOR; née SUTHERLAND 1864–1943. Writer of novels. Born in **Jersey**; lived in **Sheering** and **London [Westminster]**; buried in London. *Elinor Glyn*, A. Glyn, 1955; *The 'It' Girls*, Meredith Etherington-Smith and Jeremy Pilcher, Hamish Hamilton, London, 1986.

GODIVA, LADY; GODGIFU *fl.* 1040–80. Folk heroine and benefactor. Lived in **Coventry**, where she was buried.

GORDON, LADY JANE, COUNTESS OF SUTHERLAND d. 1628. Businesswoman and entrepreneur. Started industry in **Brora**, probably lived at **Golspie** and buried in **Dornoch**.

GORDON, JANE; DUCHESS OF GORDON; née MAXWELL 1748–1812. Political hostess and beauty. Born in **Edinburgh**, political life in both Scottish and English capitals; died in **London [Westminster]**; buried near **Kincraig**.

GORE-BOOTH, EVA SELINA 1870–1926. Poet, suffrage campaigner, writer. Born in Ireland, childhood homes there and in **London [Westminster]**; adult life in **Manchester**. *Biographical Introduction to the Poems of Eva Gore-Booth*, Esther Roper, Longmans Green, London, 1929.

'GRAND, SARAH'; FRANCES ELIZABETH BELLENDEN MCFALL; née CLARKE 1845–1943. Suffragist, writer, feminist. Born in Ireland; life of travel abroad and in Britain; lived at **Norwich**, **Warrington**, **Tunbridge Wells** and **Bath**. *Darling Madame: Sarah Grand and Devoted Friend*, Gillian Kersley, Virago, London, 1983.

GRANT, MRS ANNE 1755–1838. Writer; poet. Born in Scotland; adolescence in Albany, New York; lived at **Fort Augustus** and **Laggan Bridge**; died and buried in **Edinburgh**.

GRANT, ELIZABETH; MRS SMITH 1797–1885. Writer. Born in **Edinburgh**; lived in **Rothiemurchus** then India. *Memoirs of a Highland Lady 1797–1827*, Lady Strachey [ed.], John Murray, London, 1960.

GRANT, DR ISOBEL 1887–1983. Historian, collector. Born in **Edinburgh**; opened museum on **Iona**; moved it to **Kingussie**. 'Dr I. F. Grant [1887–1983]: the Highland Folk Museum and a Bibliography of Her Written Works', Hugh Cheap, in *Review of Scottish Culture*, 2, 1986.

GRANT, JANE. See STRACHEY, LADY JANE.

GRAY, EFFIE. See MILLAIS, EUPHEMIA.

GRAY, EILEEN 1878–1976. Architect; designer of furniture and interiors. Began career in **London [Camden]**; mainly worked in France. *Eileen Gray*, J. Steward Johnson, Museum of Modern Art, New York, 1979.

GREENAWAY, KATE 1846–1901. Illustrator and writer of children's books. Born in **London [Hackney]**; lived and studied in **London [Camden]**, also buried there.

GREY, LADY JANE; née DUDLEY; 'THE NINE DAYS QUEEN' 1537–54. Political figure. Born near **Leicester**; grew up in various family homes, including **Astley**, and **London [Kensington and Chelsea]** and **Winchcombe**; declared Queen in **Ware**; beheaded in **London [City]**. *Lady Jane*

Grey and the House of Suffolk, Alison Plowden, Sidgwick & Jackson, London, 1985; *Lady Jane Grey*, Hester W. Chapman, Grafton, London, 1985.

GRIFFITHS, ANN; née THOMAS 1776–1805. Welsh hymn writer. Born and raised near **Llanfihangel-yng-ngwyfa**, where she was also buried.

GUBBAY, MRS DAVID d. 1968. Collector. Collection on show near **Guildford**.

GUEST, LADY CHARLOTTE; née BERTIE; later LADY CHARLOTTE SCHREIBER 1812–95. Welsh scholar, translator, writer, businesswoman, collector. Born at **Uffington**; first marriage spent at **Dowlais**; died and buried in **Canford**; collection in **London [Kensington and Chelsea]**. *The Diaries of Lady Charlotte Schreiber*, Montagu Guest [ed.], Bodley Head, London, 1911.

GUNN, MARTHA; 'THE BATHING WOMAN OF BRIGHTON' 1727–1815. Health worker. Spent all her life in **Brighton**.

GWYN, NELL 1650–87. Actress. Born in **Hereford**; acting career in **London [Westminster]**; accompanied the king on his travels, including **Newmarket**; homes in **London [Hammersmith]**; buried in **London [Westminster]**. *Nell Gwyn*, Bryan Bevan, Hale, London, 1969.

GWYNNE-VAUGHAN, HELEN; née FRASER 1879–1967. Administrator and feminist publisher. War service in **Guildford**, publishing in **London [City]**. *A Heroine in her Time*, Molly Izzard, Macmillan, London.

H H

HAINAULT, PHILIPPA DE. See PHILIPPA OF HAINAULT.

HALKETT, LADY ANNE; née MURRAY 1623–99. Scholar, writer, romantic. Born at **Eton**; adult life mainly in Scotland; latterly lived in **Dunfermline**, where she died. *The Memoirs of Anne, Lady Halkett*, J. Loftis [ed.], 1979.

HALL, MARGUERITE RADCLYFFE; known as 'JOHN' 1883–1943. Writer, novelist, poet. Born in **Bournemouth**; lived in **London [Kensington and Chelsea]**; also lived in Sussex and Paris; buried in **London [Haringey]**. *Radclyffe Hall at the Well of Loneliness*, Lovatt Dickson, Collins, London, 1975; *Radclyffe Hall: a Case of Obscenity?*, Vera Brittain, A. S. Barnes, New York, 1969; *Our Three Selves: a Life of Radclyffe Hall*, Michael Baker, Hamish Hamilton, London, 1985.

HAMILTON, ELIZABETH 1758–1816. Writer. Lived in **Edinburgh**; died in **Harrogate**.

HAMILTON, LADY EMMA; née AMY LYON; also known as EMMA HART 1765–1815. Romantic folk heroine. Born at **Great Norton**; lived near **Petersfield**, then **London [Westminster]**; marriage took her abroad, where she met Horatio Nelson; shared home with him in **London [Merton]**; died in France; commemorated in **Milford Haven**; memorabilia in **Monmouth**. *Emma Hamilton*, Nora Lofts, Coward, McCann & Geoghegan, New York, 1978.

HANFF, HELENE b. 1917. Writer. Has lived all her life in the United States, but long association with **London [Westminster]**. *84 Charing Cross Road*, Helene Hanff, Penguin, Harmondsworth, 1971.

'HARDWICK, BESS OF'. See TALBOT, ELIZABETH.

HARGREAVES, ALICE. See LIDDELL, ALICE.

HARLEY, LADY BRILLIANA; née CONWAY 1598–1643. Heroine of the Civil War. Born abroad at Brill in the Netherlands; childhood and youth in Warwickshire; married life at **Brampton Bryan**, which she defended.

HARRISON, JANE ELLEN 1850–1928. Scholar, classicist, anthropologist, archaeologist. Born in Yorkshire; educated at **Cheltenham** and **Cam-**

bridge where she later taught. *Jane Ellen Harrison: a Portrait from Letters*, Jessie G. Stewart, Merlin Press, London, 1959.

HARTLEY, MARIE Historian, writer and collector. Collection in **Hawes**.

HARVIE ANDERSON, BETTY 1914–79. Politician. Educated in **St Andrews**; served in **London [Westminster]**.

HASSALL, PHOEBE 1713–1821. Soldier. Born in **London [Tower Hamlets]**; served with regiment abroad; buried in **Brighton**.

HASTINGS, SELINA, COUNTESS OF HUNTINGDON; née SHIRLEY 1707–91. Religious reformer; philanthropist. Brought up at **Staunton Harold**; established chapels including those in **Brighton** and **Bath**; and training college at **Trefecca**; as a widow lived in **London [Tower Hamlets]**, and **Ashby-de-la-Zouch**, where she was buried. *The Coronet and the Cross: or Memorials of the Right Honourable Selina, Countess of Hastings*, Alfred H. New [ed.], Partridge & Co., London, 1857; *The Countess of Huntingdon and her Circle*, H. Keddie, 1907.

HATHAWAY, ANNE *c.* 1556–1623. Literary wife. Her home until her marriage to William Shakespeare was near **Stratford-upon-Avon**.

HATHAWAY, DAME SYBIL; DAME OF SARK d. 1974. Community leader and diplomat. Life on **Sark**, where she was buried. *Sybil, Dame of Sark*, Barbara Stoney, Hodder & Stoughton, London, 1978.

HAYS, MARY 1760–1843. Feminist writer. Brought up in **London [Southwark]**.

HEELIS, MRS BEATRIX. See POTTER, BEATRIX.

HELENA, SAINT *fl.* 306–30. Saintly religious pioneer. Born in **Colchester**; widowed in **York**; buried in Istanbul.

HEMANS, MRS; née FELICIA DOROTHEA BROWNE 1793–1835. Poet, writer. Birth and early years in **Liverpool**; married life began in **St Asaph**; on separation returned to **Liverpool**; then moved to Dublin, where she died. *Mrs Hemans*, Peter W. Trinder, University of Wales Press, Cardiff, 1985.

HENDERSON, ELSIE; BARONESS DE COUDENHOVE 1880–1967. Artist and printmaker. Childhood and married life on **Guernsey**, trained in **London [Camden]**.

HEPWORTH, BARBARA 1903–75. Artist, sculptor. Born and educated in **Wakefield**; studied in **Leeds**; worked in **London [Camden]**; and **St Ives**, where she died. *A Pictorial Autobiography*, Barbara Hepworth, Adams & Dart, Bath, 1970.

HERBERT, MARY. See SIDNEY, MARY.

HERSCHEL, CAROLINE LUCRETIA 1750–1848. Astronomer. Born in Hanover, came to England, living first at **Bath** and **Windsor**; then settled in **Slough**; retired to Hanover, where she died. *Stars in Her Heart*, E. M. Robinson, Review & Herald Publishers, Washington, DC, 1971 [fictional biography].

HEYER, GEORGETTE; MRS RONALD ROUGIER 1902–74. Historical novelist. Born in **London [Merton]**; lived in **London [Westminster]**. *The Private World of Georgette Heyer*, Jane Aiken Hodge, Bodley Head, London, 1984.

HILDA, SAINT; HILDA OF WHITBY 614–80. Saintly religious leader; abbess. Born in the North of England; baptised in **York**, **Hartlepool** and finally **Whitby**, where she died.

HILL, OCTAVIA 1838–1912. Social reformer, philanthropist; conservationist. Born in **Wisbech**; lived and worked in **London [Westminster, Camden, Kensington and Chelsea]**; preserved building in Alfriston; buried at **Brockham**; commemorated at **Brasted** and **London [City]**. *Josephine Butler, Octavia Hill and Florence Nightingale: Three Victorian Women Who Changed their World*, Nancy Boyd, Macmillan, London, 1982.

HODGKIN, DOROTHY CROWFOOT b. 1910. Scientist. Born in Egypt, studied at **Oxford** and **Cambridge**.

HODGKINS, FRANCES 1869–1947. Artist. Born in New Zealand, much travelled in the Old World, living mainly in England and France. Last years spent in **Corfe Castle**; died in **Dorchester**.

HOLDEN, EDITH BLACKWELL 1871–1920. Artist. Born, raised and studied art in **Birmingham**; died in **London [Richmond]**. *The Edwardian Lady: the Story of Edith Holden*, Ina Taylor [ed.], Michael Joseph, London, 1980.

HOLTBY, WINIFRED 1898–1935. Journalist, writer, novelist. Born and brought up in **Rudston**; educated at **Scarborough** and **Oxford**; worked in **London [Westminster]**; buried in **Rudston**. *Testament of Friendship*, Vera Brittain, 1940, republished by Virago, London, 1978.

DE HORSEY, ADELINE HORSEY DE HORSEY; COUNTESS OF CARDIGAN AND DE LANCASTRE 1824–1915. Socialite. Brought up in **London [Westminster]**; estates included property near **Leeds**; married life mainly at **Deene Park**, where she is buried. *My Recollections*, Countess of Cardigan and Lancastre, Evelyn Nash, London, 1915.

HOWARD, CATHERINE *c.* 1521–42. Political pawn; Queen of England. Fifth of Henry VIII's wives; brought up in Norfolk; married at **Oatlands**; began her royal marriage in **Ewelme**; visited **Buckden**; died in **London [City]**. *A Tudor Tragedy: the Life and Times of Catherine Howard*, Lacy Baldwin Smith, Jonathan Cape, London, 1961.

HUNT, DAME AGNES GWENDOLINE 1866–1948. Pioneer nurse of physically handicapped. Born and nursed in **Baschurch**. *This is My Life*, Agnes G. Hunt, Blackie, London, 1938.

HUNT, ISOBEL VIOLET 1866–1942. Novelist. Lived in **London [Kensington and Chelsea]**.

HUNTINGDON, COUNTESS OF. See HASTINGS, SELINA.

HUTCHINSON, ANNE 1591–1643. Religious reformer in America. Born in Lincolnshire; emigrated from **Boston**; killed in American colony. *Unafraid – a Life of Anne Hutchinson*, W. F. Rugg.

HUTCHINSON, LUCY; née APSLEY 1620–?. Biographer. Born in **London [City]**; civil war spent in **Nottingham**. *Memoirs of the Life of Colonel Hutchinson*, James Sutherland [ed.], Oxford University Press, London, 1973.

I

INCHBALD, ELIZABETH; née SIMPSON 1753–1821. Actress, writer. Born near **Bury St Edmunds**; acting in **Bristol**, and **London [Westminster, Kensington and Chelsea]**.

INGELOW, JEAN 1820–97. Poet and children's writer. Born in **Boston**; adolescence in **Ipswich**. *Jean Ingelow: Victorian Poetess*, Maureen Peters, Boydell Press, Ipswich, 1972.

INGILBY, JOAN. Yorkshire historian and collector. Collection of local folklife at **Hawes**.

INGLIS, ELSIE MAUD 1864–1917. Doctor, suffragist, military medical officer. Born in India, childhood abroad, educated and early medical studies in **Edinburgh**; further study in **Glasgow**; worked in **London [Westminster]** and **Edinburgh**; war service abroad, died *en route* home. *Shadow of Swords, a Biography of Elsie Inglis*, Margot Lawrence, Michael Joseph, London, 1971.

'IRON, RALPH'. See SCHREINER, OLIVE.

J J

JAMESON, ANNA BROWNELL; née MURPHY 1794–1860. Writer, art critic. Born in Dublin; adolescence in **London [Ealing** and **Westminster]**, where she wrote; worked for women's recognition; died in **Ealing**, buried in **London [Brent]**. *Love and Work Enough: the Life of Anna Jameson*, Clara Thomas, MacDonald, London, 1967.

JAMESON, STORM 1891–1986. Novelist, traveller, academic. Born and raised in **Whitby**; last years in Cambridgeshire. *Journey from the North*, Storm Jameson, Virago, London, 1982.

JEKYLL, GERTRUDE 1843–1932. Gardener, writer, collector. A Londoner by birth, she grew up in Surrey; studied art in London; designed many gardens including those at **Guildford**, **Hambledon**, **Hestercombe**, **Ilminster**, **Knebworth**, **Lindisfarne**, **Renishaw**, **Robertsbridge** and **Rolveden**; buried at **Busbridge**; commemorated in **London [Lambeth]**. Some gardens are occasionally open to the public on single days in aid of charities under the various national gardens scheme. *Gardens of a Golden Afternoon*, Jane Brown, Allen Lane, Harmondsworth, 1982; *Miss Jekyll: Portrait of a Great Gardener*, Bernard Massingham, Country Life, London, 1966; *The Gardens of Gertrude Jekyll in the North of England*, Michael and Rosanna Tooley, Michaelmas Books, Witton le Wear, 1983.

JESSUP, PHYLLIS ANNE *fl.* 1793. Artist. Painted in **Norwich**.

JEWSBURY, GERALDINE 1812–80. Writer of novels. Born in **Measham**; lived in **Manchester** and **London [Westminster]**; buried in **London [Kensington and Chelsea]**. *Geraldine Jewsbury: Her Life and Errors*, Susanne Howe, 1935.

JEX-BLAKE, SOPHIA 1840–1912. Medical practitioner. Born in **Hastings**; educated in **London [Westminster]**; studied medicine abroad and in **Edinburgh**; taught and practised medicine in the Scottish and English capitals; retired to **Tunbridge Wells**; buried at **Rotherfield**. *The Life of Sophia Jex-Blake*, Margaret G. Todd, Macmillan, London, 1918.

JOHN, GWEN 1876–1939. Artist. Born in **Haverfordwest**; grew up there and in **Tenby**; studied in **London [Camden]**, then spent most of her life in France. *Gwen John: an Interior Life*, C. Langdale and D. F. Jenkins, Phaidon, London, 1985; *Gwen John*, Mary Taubman, Scolar Press, 1985.

JOHNSON, AMY; MRS MOLLISON 1904–41. Aviator. Birth and youth in **Kingston upon Hull**; student in **Sheffield**; learnt to fly in **London [Brent]**; long-distance flight from **London [Croydon]** and **Pendine**; memorabilia at **Bridlington**. *Amy Johnson*, Constance Babington Smith, 1967; *Silvered Wings*, published by Kingston upon Hull City Council for the Amy Johnson Festival, 1980.

JONES, MARY 1784–1872. Bible student. Born and lived at **Llanfihangel-y-Pennant**; buried at **Bryncrug**.

JOURDAIN, ELEANOR 1863–1924. Educational pioneer. Born in **Ashbourne**; educated at **Oxford**; taught in **London [Haringey]**; college principal at **Oxford**.

JULIANA OF NORWICH; MOTHER JULIAN *c*. 1343–1423. Religious mystic, writer. Simple religious life spent in **Norwich**.

K k

KAUFFMANN, ANGELICA 1741–1807. Artist. Born in Switzerland; painted there and in Austria and Italy, came to **London [Westminster]**; murals in **Barnsley**; returned to Europe on second marriage; died in Rome.

KAY-SHUTTLEWORTH, RACHEL 1886–1967. Collector and textile historian. Collection displayed at **Padiham**. *Rachel Kay-Shuttleworth: a Memoir*, Canon G. A. Williams, Padiham, 1980.

KAYE-SMITH, SHEILA 1887–1956. Writer. Born in **Hastings**; childhood in **St Leonards**; lived in **Hastings** until her marriage; then lived at **Northiam**, where she died. *Three Ways Home*, Sheila Kaye-Smith, Cassell, London, 1937.

KEILLER, MRS *fl*. 1797. Conserve maker. Started famous industry in **Dundee**.

KEMBLE, FANNY; FRANCES ANNE KEMBLE 1809–93. Actress and writer. Educated in **London [Kensington and Chelsea]** where she also lived towards the end of her life; acting debut in **London [Westminster]**; acted in Britain and America; buried in **London [Brent]**. *The Terrific Kemble*, Eleanor Ransome [ed.], Hamish Hamilton, London, 1978; *Fanny Kemble*, Dorothy Marshall, Weidenfeld & Nicolson, London, 1977.

KEMPE, MARGERY; née BURNHAM *fl*. 1373–1438. Religious mystic, writer, healer. Born and lived in **King's Lynn**; visits **Norwich**, **London [Lambeth]**, and the Holy Land. *The Boke of Margery Kempe*, B. A. Windeatt [trans.], Penguin, Harmondsworth, 1985.

KENNEDY, MARGARET 1896–1967. Writer. Educated at **Cheltenham** and **Oxford**; lived in **London [Hounslow]**. *The Constant Novelist*, Violet Powell, Heinemann, London, 1983.

KENNEY, ANNIE 1879–1953. Suffragette, trade unionist. Born outside **Manchester**; worked in mills, moved to **London** with the Pankhursts; demonstrated in **Manchester**, **London [Lambeth]** and other centres; frequent visitor to **Bath**; retired to **Letchworth**; died in **Hitchin**. *Memoirs of a Militant*, Annie Kenney, Arnold, London, 1924.

'KENT, HOLY MAID OF'. See BARTON, ELIZABETH.

KILHAM, HANNAH; née SPURR 1774–1832. Missionary; linguist. Born in

Sheffield, educated there and in Derbyshire; philanthropic work in **Sheffield**; missionary activity in Africa; died at sea. *The Powerful Bond: Hannah Kilham 1774–1832*, Mora Dickson, Dennis Dobson, London, 1980.

KING, ADA AUGUSTA; COUNTESS OF LOVELACE; née BYRON 1815–52. Mathematician. A Londoner by birth; brought up at **Kirkby Mallory**, where she is commemorated; homes in **London [Westminster]** and **Esher**; visitor to **Exmouth**; buried in **Hucknall**. *Ada Countess of Lovelace: Byron's Legitimate Daughter*, Doris Langley Moore, John Murray, London, 1977; *Ada: a Life and a Legacy*, Dorothy Stein, MIT Press, Cambridge, 1986.

KING, JESSIE MARION 1876–1949. Artist, book illustrator. Grew up in **Kirkcudbright**; studied art in **Glasgow**; worked in Paris; settled in **Kirkcudbright**.

KINGSLEY, MARY 1862–1900. Traveller, writer, anthropologist, biologist. Grew up in **London [Haringey]**; lived in **Cambridge**; left from **Liverpool** to travel to West Africa, died in South Africa. *Eminent Victorian Women*, Elizabeth Longford, Weidenfeld & Nicolson, London, 1981; *Western Women in Colonial Africa*, C. Oliver, Greenwood Press, London, Connecticut, 1982; *A Voyager Out: The Life of Mary Kingsley*, Katherine Frank, Hamish Hamilton, London, 1986.

KNIGHT, DAME LAURA; née JOHNSON 1877–1970. Artist. Born in **Long Eaton** and brought up in **Nottingham**, where she also studied art; lived and painted in **Staithes**, **Newlyn** and **London [Westminster]**, where she died. *Laura Knight*, Janet Dunbar, Collins, London, 1975.

L L

LADIES OF LLANGOLLEN. See LADY ELEANOR BUTLER and SARAH PONSONBY.

LAMB, LADY CAROLINE; née PONSONBY 1785–1828. Writer. Early years in Italy; then educated in **London [Kensington and Chelsea]**; married to Lord Melbourne, homes at **Melbourne, Lemsford** and **London [Westminster]**, where she died; buried in **Hatfield**. *Lady Caroline Lamb*, Elizabeth Jenkins, Penguin, Harmondsworth, 1974.

LAMB, MARY ANN 1764–1847. Writer. Most of her life spent in the English capital; baptised in **London [City]**; lived in **London [Islington]**; buried in **London [Enfield]**.

LAMBURN, RICHMAL CROMPTON. See CROMPTON, RICHMAL.

LANDON, LETITIA ELIZABETH; MRS MACLEAN 1802–38. Writer. Lived in **London [Kensington and Chelsea]**; died in West Africa.

LANGHAM PLACE GROUP or CIRCLE. See **London [Westminster]**.

LANGTRY, LILLIE; LILLIE DE BATHE; née EMILIE CHARLOTTE LE BRETON; 'THE JERSEY LILY'. 1853–1929. Actress. Born in **Jersey**; lived in **London [Kensington and Chelsea]**; raced at **Newmarket**; home in **Bournemouth**; last years in Monaco; buried in **Jersey**. *The Gilded Lily*, E. Dudley, 1958.

LANIER, EMILIA; née BASSANO *c.* 1569–1645. Poet. A candidate for William Shakespeare's 'Dark Lady', wrote poetry at **Cookham**; lived and buried in **London [Tower Hamlets]**. *Poems of Shakespeare's Dark Lady*, A. L. Rowse [ed.], 1978.

LAUDERDALE AND RICHMOND; DUCHESS OF. See MURRAY, ELIZABETH.

LAURIE, ANNIE 1682–1764. Romantic folk heroine. Spent all her life near **Moniaive**. *The Lauries of Maxwelton*, I. O. J. Gladstone, Research Publishing Company, London, 1972.

LEE, ANN; MOTHER ANN LEE 1736–84. Religious leader. Born in **Manchester**, whence she led her followers, the Shakers, to America in 1774. *The American Shakers from Neo-Christianity to Presocialism*, H. Desroches, 1971.

LEE, JENNIE; BARONESS LEE OF ASHRIDGE b. 1904. Politician. Born in **Lochgelly**; studied in **Edinburgh**; Member of Parliament for **Lanark**; active in Parliament, **London [Westminster]**; educational founder at **Milton Keynes**. *My life with Nye*, Jennie Lee, Penguin, Harmondsworth, 1980.

LEHMANN, ROSAMUND b. 1901. Writer. Born and brought up at **Bourne End**, with sister, the actress Beatrix Lehmann. *Rosamund Lehmann: an Appreciation*, Gillian Tindall, Chatto & Windus, London, 1985.

LEIGH, VIVIEN; VIVIEN MARY HARTLEY 1913–67. After a successful acting career, retired to **Tickerage**. *Vivien Leigh*, Anne Edwards, W. H. Allen, London, 1977.

LIDDELL, ALICE PLEASANCE; MRS REGINALD HARGREAVES 1852–1934. Model for fictional character. Childhood in **Oxford** and **Llandudno**; buried in **Lyndhurst**.

LILLIARD d. 1545. Military heroine. Fought at battle of **Ancrum**.

LIND, JENNY; JOHANNA MARIA LIND; MRS GOLDSCHMIDT; 'THE SWEDISH NIGHTINGALE' 1820–87. Singer. Born and grew up in Sweden; British debut 1847; touring career took her throughout Europe and, via **Liverpool**, North America; home in **London [Kensington and Chelsea]**; retired to **Malvern** where she died and is buried. *Jenny Lind*, Joan Bulman, Barrie, London, 1956.

LINWOOD, MARY 1755–1845. Artist. Lived in **Leicester**, where she was buried; exhibited in **London [Westminster]**.

'LLANGOLLEN, THE LADIES OF'. See BUTLER, LADY ELEANOR and PONSONBY, SARAH.

LLEWELYN DAVIES, MARGARET. See DAVIES, MARGARET LLEWELYN.

LLOYD, MARIE; née MATILDA ALICE VICTORIA WOOD 1870–1922. Music-hall singer. Born in **London [Hackney]**; stage career in **London [Westminster]** and around the then English-speaking world; buried in **London [Camden]**. *Marie Lloyd and Music Hall*, Daniel Farson, Tom Stacey, London, 1972.

LONSDALE, DAME KATHLEEN; née YARDLEY 1903–71. Scientist and pacifist. Born in Ireland; studied and taught in **London [Camden]** and **Leeds**; held research and posts in **London [Camden]**. 'Kathleen Lonsdale' in *Biographical Memoirs of Fellows of the Royal Society*, Dorothy M. C. Hodgkin, Royal Society, London.

LOUDON, JANE; née WEBB 1807–58. Novelist and garden designer. Native of **Birmingham**; garden designs in **London [Westminster]**; buried in **London [Brent]**. *Lady with Green Fingers: the Life of Jane Loudon*, Bea Howe, Country Life, London, 1961.

LOUGHLIN, DAME ANNE 1894–1979. Trade unionist. Born in **Leeds**; led strike in **Hebden Bridge**. *Women and Trade Unions*, Sarah Lewenhak, Ernest Benn, London, 1977.

LOVELACE, ADA. See KING, ADA.

LUMSDEN, LOUISA INNES 1840–1935. Educational pioneer. Born in Scotland; studied in **Hitchin**; taught in **Cheltenham** and **St Andrews**; graduated from **Cambridge**. *Yellow Leaves*, Louisa Lumsden, William Blackwell, Edinburgh, 1933.

'LYALL, EDNA'. See BAYLEY, ADA ELLEN.

LYTTON, LADY CONSTANCE GEORGINA; 'JANE WHARTON' 1869–1923. Suffragette. Born in Austria, childhood and education abroad; adult home at **Knebworth**; imprisoned in **London [Islington]** and **Liverpool**. *Prisons and Prisoners, Some Personal Experiences by Constance Lytton and Jane Wharton*, Heinemann, London, 1914.

M M

MACARTHUR, MARY REID; MRS ANDERSON 1880–1921. Trade union activist. Born and educated in **Glasgow**; early union involvement in **Ayr**; moved to **London [Camden]**; led **Cradley Heath** strikers. 'Mary Macarthur, a biographical sketch', M. A. Hamilton in *Women in the Labour Movement*, Linda Middleton [ed.], Croom Helm, London, 1977; *Mary Macarthur*, Mary Agnes Hamilton Leonard Parsons, London, 1925.

MACAULAY, CATHERINE; MRS GRAHAM; née SAWBRIDGE 1731–91. Historian, writer, pamphleteer. Born in **Wye**; first marriage spent in the English capital; widowhood and second marriage in **Bath**; travelled in France and North America; died and buried in **Binfield**. 'Mrs Macaulay: historian and controversialist', D. L. Hobman in *Fortnightly*, 171, 1952.

MACAULAY, DAME EMILY ROSE 1881–1958. Writer of novels, essays, poetry and accounts of travels. Born in **Rugby**; childhood in Italy; educated at **Oxford**; literary life in **London [Westminster]**. *Rose Macaulay: a Biography*, Constance Babington Smith, Collins, London, 1972; *Rose Macaulay*, A. R. Benson, 1969.

MACCHETTA, BLANCHE ROOSEVELDT; MARQUESA D'ALLEGRI 1858–98. Writer. Born in USA; married in France; wrote and died in **London [Kensington and Chelsea]**.

MACDONALD, FLORA 1722–90. Jacobite heroine. Born in **South Uist**; grew up at **Monkstadt**; educated in **Edinburgh**; heroism in **Benbecula**, **Kingsburgh** and **Portree**; resulting imprisonment in **London [City]**; emigrated to North America; died at **Kingsburgh**; buried at **Kilmuir**. *Flora the Highland Heroine*, Jarrold Publications, Norwich; *Flora MacDonald, Her Life in the Highlands and America*, E. G. Vining, 1967.

MACDONALD, MARGARET ETHEL; née GLADSTONE 1870–1911. Socialist and activist in women's issues. Lived and worked for the Labour Party in **London [City]**; commemorated there and in **Leicester**; cremated in **London [Brent]**; ashes buried near **Lossiemouth**. *Women in the Labour Movement*, Linda Middleton [ed.], Croom Helm, London, 1977.

MACKINTOSH, MARGARET MACDONALD; née MACDONALD 1865–1933. Artist and designer. Trained and practised in **Glasgow**.

MCLAUGHAN, MARGARET d. 1685. Covenanter, martyr. Martyred at **Wigtown**.

MACMILLAN, CHRYSTAL 1882–1937. Suffrage campaigner and advocate. Born and studied in **Edinburgh**, after school education in **St Andrews**, campaigned in **London [Westminster]**.

MCMILLAN, MARGARET 1860–1931. Social and educational reformer. Childhood in **Inverness**; major work in **London [Lewisham]**. *Margaret McMillan: the Children's Champion*, G. A. N. Lowndes, Museum Press, London, 1960.

MCMILLAN, RACHEL 1859–1917. Social and educational reformer. Childhood in **Inverness**; opened school in **London [Lewisham]**. *The Life of Rachel McMillan*, Margaret MacMillan, Dent, London, 1927.

MAITLAND, LADY. Collector. 1890–1982. Her collection is on view in **Glamis**.

MANLEY, DELARIVIER; MRS MANLEY *c.* 1663–1724. Writer. Born in **Jersey**; adolescence in **Landguard Fort**; plays performed in London; after an unconventional life she died and was buried in **London [City]**. *A Woman of no Character: an Autobiography of Mrs Manley*, Fidelis Morgan [ed.], Faber & Faber, London, 1986.

'MANSFIELD, KATHERINE'; KATHERINE MANSFIELD BEAUCHAMP; MRS MURRY 1888–1923. Writer. Born in New Zealand; educated in **London [Westminster]**; had a home in **London [Camden]**, which was to be her British base, though she did spend time at **Mylor**, and was frequently at **Garsington**; ill health took her to the continent, and she died young in France. *The Life of Katherine Mansfield*, Antony Alpers, 1980; *Katherine Mansfield: a Biography*, J. Mayers, 1978.

MAPP, MRS SARAH; née WALLIN *fl.* 1736. Medical practitioner, bonesetter. Born at **Hindon**; practised in **Epsom** and **London [Westminster]**.

MARCET, JANE; née HALDIMAND 1769–1858. Educational writer. Born in Switzerland but childhood in Britain; wrote and died in **London [Westminster]**.

MARGARET, SAINT, QUEEN OF SCOTLAND *c.* 1040–1093. Ruler, religious leader, diplomat. Brought up in Hungary, adolescence at English court; married life mainly in **Dunfermline**, where she was initially buried; relics abroad; had chapel built in **Edinburgh**; refounded abbey on **Iona**. *Mediaeval Women*, Derek Baker [ed.], Blackwell, Oxford, 1979.

MARGARET CLITHEROE, SAINT. See CLITHEROE, SAINT MARGARET.

MARION, MAID; MATILDA HOOD mythic folk heroine. Supposedly born in **Wakefield** and married in **Edwinstowe** or **Wakefield**; associated with **Nottingham**. *Marion's Christmas Rose . . . The Story of Maid Marion*, Barbara Green, Merlin Books, Braunton, 1984.

MARKHAM, BERYL; née CLUTTERBUCK 1902–86. Aviator and writer. Born in **Melton Mowbray**; most of her life spent in Africa; pioneering flight from **Abingdon**. *West with the Night*, Beryl Markham, Virago, London, 1984; *Straight on 'til Morning*, Mary S. Lovell, Hutchinson, London, 1987.

'MARKHAM, MRS'; ELIZABETH PENROSE 1780–1837. Writer for young people. Wrote and died in **Lincoln**.

MARKIEVICZ, COUNTESS CONSTANCE; née GORE-BOOTH 1868–1926. Politician; campaigner for Irish Nationalism and women's suffrage; born in **London [Westminster]**; lived and campaigned in Ireland; imprisoned in **London [Islington]**. *The Rebel Countess*, A. Marreco, 1967.

MARSDEN, KATE 1859–1931. Nurse and traveller. Lived in **London [Haringey]**. *Travelling Ladies, Victorian Adventuresses*, Alexandra Allen, Jupiter, London, 1980.

MARTIN, MARIA d. 1827. Victim. **Polstead** was the scene of her tragic death.

MARTIN, SARAH 1791–1843. Prison reformer. Born in **Caistor**; worked for improvements in **Great Yarmouth**, where she is commemorated. *Miss Sarah Martin*, Dorothy Skippings, Great Yarmouth, 1969.

MARTINEAU, HARRIET 1802–76. Journalist, novelist, abolitionist. Born in **Norwich**, educated there and in **Bristol**; worked as a writer in **London [Westminster]**, convalesced in **Tynemouth**; settled in **Ambleside**, where she later died; buried in **Birmingham**. *Autobiography*, Harriet Martineau, originally 1877, republished by Virago, London, 1980; *Harriet Martineau, the Woman and Her Work*, Valerie Kossew Pichaniack, University of Michigan Press, Ann Arbor, 1980; *The Life and Work of Harriet Martineau*, Vera Wheatley, Secker & Warburg, London, 1957.

MARX, JENNY JULIA ELEANOR; ELEANOR MARX-AVELING 1855–98. Political writer and activist. Born in **London [Westminster]**, where she grew up and later worked; taught in **Brighton** briefly; visitor to **Ventnor**; latterly lived in **London [Lewisham]**, where she died; ashes buried in **London [Haringey]**. *Eleanor Marx: Family Life 1855–1883* and *Eleanor Marx: the Crowded Years*, Yvonne Kapp, Lawrence & Wishart, 1972, 1976.

MARY I, QUEEN OF ENGLAND, MARY TUDOR, 'BLOODY MARY' 1516–58. Ruler, first English queen to rule in her own right. Born in **London [Greenwich]**; adolescence in **Ludlow**; adult life spent in various royal households; buried in **London [Westminster]**. *The Reign of Mary Tudor*, David Loades, Benn, London, 1979; *The Life and Times of Mary Tudor*, Jasper Ridley, Weidenfeld & Nicolson, London, 1973.

MARY II, QUEEN OF ENGLAND 1662–94. Ruler. The Mary of William and Mary. Moved to Holland on marriage; returned as queen; various royal homes including **London [Kensington]**; buried in **London [Westminster]**. *William's Mary*, Elizabeth Hamilton, Hamish Hamilton, London,

1972; *Mary II, Queen of England*, Hester W. Chapman, Cape, London, 1953.

MARY QUEEN OF SCOTS; MARY STUART 1542–87. Ruler, romantic heroine and tragic queen. Born in **Linlithgow**; educated in France, where she married and became Queen of France; returned to Scotland as queen; eventful reign with various incidents in **Edinburgh**; personal retreat on **Inchmaholme**; imprisonment in **Loch Leven**, **Ashby de la Zouch** and later **Sheffield**; several other places of imprisonment in England, ultimately **Fotheringhay**, where she died; initially buried at **Peterborough**; final resting place **London [Westminster]**. *Mary Queen of Scots*, Antonia Fraser, Weidenfeld & Nicolson, London, 1969; *Queen of Scots*, Rosalind Marshall, HMSO, London, 1987; *A Queen's Progress*, David Breeze and Gordon Donaldson, HMSO, London, 1987 [locates many more buildings associated with Mary Queen of Scots].

MARY DE GUISE 1515–60. Ruler, Regent of Scotland. Born in France; came to Scotland as queen through marriage; spent time in **Edinburgh**; became mother of MARY QUEEN OF SCOTS at **Linlithgow**. *Mary of Guise*, Rosaline Marshall, Collins, London, 1977.

MARY OF GUELDRES *c.* 1433–63. Ruler, Regent of Scotland. Came to Scotland on marriage. Founded hospital in **Edinburgh**, built **Ravenscraig** castle; won victory at **Roxburgh**. *The Stuart Kingdom of Scotland 1371–1603*, Caroline Bingham, Weidenfeld & Nicolson, London, 1974.

MATILDA, QUEEN OF ENGLAND 1080–1118. Ruler, benefactor. Born in Scotland. Benefactor in **London [Barking, Newham]**; buried in **London [Westminster]**.

MATILDA 1102–67. Claimant to the English throne. Born in England, daughter of MATILDA and Henry I; lived in Germany, where marriage made her Holy Roman Empress; widowed, returned to England; pursuit of her claims to the English throne brought battles in **Lincoln**; imprisonment in **Oxford**, and escape to **Wallingford**, she finally withdrew to Normandy where she died.

DU MAURIER, DAPHNE 1907– . Writer. Settled in Cornwall; one of her novels set at **Bodmin**. *The Rebecca Notebooks and Other Memories*, Daphne du Maurier, Gollancz, London, 1981.

MAXWELL, MRS. See BRADDON, MARY.

MAYNARD, CONSTANCE 1849–1935. Educational pioneer. Student in **Hitchin**; taught in **St Andrews**, before founding London College. *Between College Terms*, Constance Maynard, James Nisbet, London, 1910.

MAYOR, F[LORA] M. 1872–1932. Writer. Born and brought up in **London [Kingston upon Thames]**; studied at **Cambridge**; last years and burial in **London [Camden]**. *Spinsters of This Parish*, Sybil Oldfield, Virago, London, 1984.

MELLON, HARRIOT; MRS COUTTS; DUCHESS OF ST ALBANS 1777–1837. Actress. Lived in **London [Haringey]**; acted in **Skipton**; eventual married life in **London [Westminster]**; latterly lived in **Brighton**.

MEW, CHARLOTTE MARY 1869–1928. Writer; poet. Born in **London [City]**; lived for a short time in France; wrote in **London [Camden]**. *Charlotte Mew and Her Friends*, Penelope Fitzgerald, Collins, London, 1984.

MEYNELL, ALICE CHRISTIANA GERTRUDE; née THOMPSON 1847–1922. Writer. Childhood in Europe; married and writing life based in **London [Westminster]**; buried in **London [Brent]**. *Alice Meynell: A Memoir*, V. Meynell, 1929; *Meynell, Her Life and Work*, K. Michalik, 1934.

MICHEL, LOUISE 1830–96. French political activist, communard and socialist. Born in France, political involvement followed by imprisonment in New Caledonia; further action in France followed by exile in **London [Southwark, Camden]**; died in her native country. *Louise Michel*, Edith Thomas, Black Rose Books, Canada, 1971.

MILLAIS, EFFIE [EUPHEMIA]; EFFIE RUSKIN; née GRAY 1828–1897. Muse, artist's model. Born near **Perth**, brief marriage to John Ruskin, happy second marriage spent near **Perth** and in **London [Kensington and Chelsea]**; visitor to **London [Bexley]**; buried near **Perth**. *Pre-Raphaelite Sisterhood*, Jan Marsh, Quartet Books, London, 1985.

MILLAR, LADY ANNA; née RIGGS 1741–81. Literary hostess. Lived, entertained and died in **Bath**, where she is also buried.

MITFORD, MARY RUSSELL 1787–1855. Writer. Birth and early life in **New Alresford**; educated in **London [Kensington and Chelsea]** and **Reading**; her home town till 1820; visited **Lyme Regis** and **Bristol**; lived and wrote for thirty years at **Three Mile Cross**; last years and burial in **Swallowfield**. *Life in a Country Town: Reading and Mary Russell Mitford*, Pamela Horn [ed.], Beacon Press, Abingdon, 1984.

MITFORD, NANCY FREEMAN 1904–73. Writer. Born in **London [Kensington and Chelsea]** and brought up at **Swinbrook**, where she was later buried, having spent most of her adult life in France; had a home in **London [Hounslow]**. *Nancy Mitford: a Memoir*, Harold Acton, Hamish Hamilton, London, 1975; *Nancy Mitford*, Selina Hastings, Hamish Hamilton, London, 1985; *The House of Mitford*, Jonathan Guinness with Catherine Guinness, Hutchinson, London, 1985.

MOBERLEY, CHARLOTTE ANNE ELIZABETH; ANNIE MOBERLEY 1843–1937. Educational pioneer. Born in **Winchester**; lived in **Salisbury**, then **Oxford**, where she led a women's college.

MONTAGU, MRS ELIZABETH; née ROBINSON 1720–1800. Blue Stocking, intellectual, writer. Born in **York**; brought up in **Cambridge**; lived in **London [Westminster]**, where she held literary salons, also in **Bath**; buried in **Winchester**. *Mrs Montagu, 'Queen of the Blues': Her Letters and*

Friendships, 1762–1800, R. Blunt [ed.], 1923; *Sisters of the Quill*, Alice A. Hufstader, Dodd Mead, New York, 1978.

MONTAGU, LADY MARY WORTLEY; née PIERREPONT 1689–1762. Writer, traveller, medical practitioner, feminist. Childhood at **Perlethorpe** and **Tong**; childhood holidays at **West Dean**, early married life in Yorkshire, then in Turkey; several homes in **London [Westminster]**; other residences abroad and **Newcastle upon Tyne**; died and buried in **London [Westminster]**; memorials in **Lichfield** and **Barnsley**. *The Life of Lady Mary Wortley Montagu*, Robert Halsband, Clarendon Press, Oxford, 1956.

'MONTEZ, LOLA'; née MARIE DOLORES ELIZA ROSANNA GILBERT 1818–61. Dancer. Born in Ireland; educated in **Montrose** and France; stage career abroad and in England: **London [Westminster]** and **Bath**; died in USA. *Lola Montez*. Amanda Darling, Stein & Day, New York, 1972.

MOORE, DORIS LANGLEY. Dress historian and collector. Collection on display in **Bath**.

MORE, HANNAH 1745–1833. Writer of religious tracts; educational and moral reformer. Born in **Bristol** where she was educated and later taught; briefly in the English capital but returned to the West Country to teach at **Cheddar** and **Blagdon**; lived in **Bath** and **Wrington**; died in **Bristol**; buried in **Wrington**. *Hannah More*, Mary G. Jones, Cambridge University Press, 1952.

MORGAN, LADY; SYDNEY OWENSON 1782–1859. Born on board ship in the Irish Sea; much of her life in Ireland; lived in **London [Kensington and Chelsea]**, where she was later buried. *Lady Morgan: the Life and Times of Sydney Owenson*, Mary Campbell, Pandora Press, London, 1988.

MORRELL, LADY OTTOLINE ANNE VIOLET née CAVENDISH-BENTINCK 1873–1938. Literary hostess, patron, pacifist. Studied briefly at **Oxford**, literary hostess in **London [Camden]** and **Garsington**; died in **Tunbridge Wells**; buried at **Holbeck**. *'Ottoline', the Life of Lady Ottoline Morrell*, Sandra J. Darrough, Chatto & Windus, 1976.

MORRIS, JANE; née BURDEN 1839–1914. Embroiderer, designer and artist's model. Early married life in **London [Bexley]**, and last years in **Kelmscott** in her native Oxfordshire. *Jane and May Morris*, Jan Marsh, Pandora Press, London, 1986.

MORRIS, MAY 1862–1938. Embroiderer, design-teacher, socialist. Born in **London [Bexley]**, active life in **London [Hammersmith]** and **Kelmscott**. *Jane and May Morris*, Jan Marsh, Pandora Press, London, 1986.

MOTT, LUCRETIA COFFIN 1793–1880. Feminist, abolitionist, campaigner, founder of the American Women's Rights Movement. Began her campaigning for women after **London [Westminster]** meeting; most of her life spent in her native USA. *Lucretia Mott*, O. Cromwell, Harvard

University Press, Cambridge, 1958; *Valiant Friend: the Life of Lucretia Mott*, M. H. Bacon, Walker, New York, 1980.

MULOCK, DIANA MARIA. See CRAIK, MRS.

MURDOCH, IRIS JEAN b. 1919. Philosopher and novelist. Born in Ireland; studied at **Oxford** and **Cambridge**.

MURRAY, ELIZABETH. See DYSART, ELIZABETH, DUCHESS OF LAUDERDALE.

MURRAY, FLORA 1869–1923. Military doctor. Active in **London [Westminster]**; buried in **Penn**.

MUSGRAVE, THEA b. 1938. Composer. Born in Scotland; studied in **Edinburgh**; career in Britain and USA.

N n

NAIRNE, LADY CAROLINA, BARONESS NAIRNE; née OLIPHANT 1766–1845. Writer of Scottish ballads. Born at **Gask**, where she was later buried.

'NEILSON, ADELAIDE'; née ELIZABETH ANN BROWN 1846–80. Actress. Born in **Leeds**; grew up in **Skipton**; acting career begins in the English capital; toured Britain and USA; died in France; memorabilia at **Smallhythe**.

NESBIT, E[DITH] 1858–1924. Writer of books for children. Born in **London [Lambeth]**; educated abroad; married life in **London [Greenwich]**; buried near **Dymchurch**. *E. Nesbit: a Biography*, Doris Langley Moore, Ernest Benn, London, 1967.

NICHOLAS, JEMIMA *fl*. 1797. Welsh wartime heroine. Significant action in **Fishguard**.

NICHOLSON, WINIFRED; née ROBERTS 1893–1981. Artist. Lived and painted near **Brampton**.

NIGHTINGALE, FLORENCE 1820–1910. Nursing pioneer, health reformer. Born in Italy; family homes at **Lea Hurst** and **Embley**; initial nursing abroad and **London [Westminster]**; led nurses in the Crimean War; lived in **London [Westminster]**; visited **Middle Claydon**; buried at **East Wellow**. *Florence Nightingale 1820–1910*, Cecil Woodham-Smith, Constable, London, 1950; *Significant Sisters*, Margaret Forster, Secker & Warburg, London, 1984.

NORTH, MARIANNE 1830–90. Botanical artist. Born and grew up in **Hastings** and Norfolk; educated in Norwich; travelled extensively abroad, based in **Hastings** and **London [Westminster]**; her work is shown at **London [Richmond]**; buried at **Alderley**. *A Vision of Eden: The Life and Work of Marianne North*, J. P. M. Brennan [ed.], Webb & Bower, London, 1980; *Recollections of a Happy Life*, 1892 and *Further Recollections of a Happy Life*, 1893, Marianne North.

NORTON, CAROLINE ELIZABETH SARAH; née SHERIDAN 1808–77. Poet, novelist, campaigner on women's issues. Early childhood in Scotland, then **London [Richmond]**; married in **London [Westminster]**, where she eventually died. *Caroline Norton*, Alice Acland, Constable, London, 1948; *Significant Sisters*, Margaret Forster, Secker & Warburg, London, 1984.

O o

OLDFIELD, ANNE 1683–1730. Actress. Acting career in **London [Westminster]**, where she was buried.

OLIPHANT, CAROLINE. See LADY NAIRNE.

OLIPHANT, MRS MARGARET; née WILSON 1828–97. Writer. Born in **Wallyford**; adolescence in **Liverpool**; married life in London; widowhood near **Eton**, where she was buried; commemorated in **Edinburgh**. *Autobiography and Letters of Mrs Margaret Oliphant*, Harry Coghill [ed.], Leicester University Press, Leicester, 1974.

OLIVIER, EDITH 1879–1948. Writer. Lived at **Wilton**, **Teffont Magna** and **Quidhampton**.

OPIE, AMELIA; née ALDERSON 1769–1853. Writer. Born in **Norwich**; marriage in **London [Westminster]**; widowhood in **Norwich**, where she was buried.

ORCZY, BARONESS EMMUSKA; MRS MONTAGU BARSTOW 1865–1947. Novelist. Born in Hungary; studied in Europe and Britain; lived at **Acol** and France; died in London; *The Scarlet Pimpernel Looks at the World*, Emmuska Orczy, 1934.

'ORINDA'. See PHILIPS, KATHERINE.

OSBORNE, DOROTHY; LADY TEMPLE 1627–95. Letter writer. Childhood at **Chicksands**; met husband at **Carisbrooke**; exile abroad; married in **London [City]**; honeymoon at **Rickmansworth**; official residence abroad; retirement in **Farnham**; buried in **London [Westminster]**. *The Letters of Dorothy Osborne to William Temple*, G. C. Moore Smith [ed.], 1947; *Two Quiet Lives*, David Cecil, 1948.

'OUIDA'. See RAMEE, MARIE LOUISE DE LA.

OWEN, ANNE; 'LUCASIA' *fl.* 1650–60. Writer. Corresponded at **Cardigan** with KATHERINE PHILIPS.

OWENSON, SYDNEY. See MORGAN, LADY.

P p

PANKHURST, ADELA CONSTANTIA; ADELA WALSH 1885–1961. Socialist and feminist. Born in **Manchester**; brought up there and **London [Camden]**; campaigned in **Sheffield**, emigrated to Australia.

PANKHURST, DAME CHRISTABEL HARRIETTE 1880–1958. Suffragette. Grew up in **London [Camden]** and **Manchester**; campaigned in both cities and many others; exiled in Paris; parliamentary candidate in **Birmingham**; visitor to **Bath**; settled in USA, where she died; commemorated in **London [Westminster]**. *Queen Christabel*, David Mitchell, MacDonald and Jane, London, 1977; *Unshackled*, Christabel Pankhurst, Hutchinson, London, 1959.

PANKHURST, MRS EMMELINE; née GOULDEN 1858–1928. Suffra-gette. Born in **Manchester**; lived and campaigned in **London [Camden]** and **Manchester** and throughout Britain; visitor to **Bath**; moved to Canada and France; last years in Britain; buried in **London [Kensington and Chelsea]**; commemorated in **London [Westminster]**. *The Suffragette Movement*, E. Sylvia Pankhurst, 1931, republished by Virago, London, 1977; *Rise up, Women!*, Andrew Rosen, Routledge & Kegan Paul, London, 1974; *My Own Story*, Emmeline Pankhurst, 1914, republished by Virago, London, 1979.

PANKHURST, ESTELLE SYLVIA 1882–1960. Suffragette, artist. Born in **Manchester**, educated there and in **London [Camden]**; suffrage activity in **London [Hackney, Tower Hamlets]**; painted in **Stoke-on-Trent**; later life in **London [Redbridge]** and then Ethiopia, where she died. *The Suffragette Movement*, E. Sylvia Pankhurst, 1935, republished by Virago, London, 1977; *Sylvia Pankhurst, Artist and Crusader: an Intimate Portrait*, Richard Pankhurst, Paddington Press, London, 1979; *E. Sylvia Pankhurst*, Patricia W. Romero, Yale University Press, Newhaven, 1987.

PARKES, BESSIE RAYNER; MRS BELLOC 1829–1925. Editor, publisher, journalist, suffragist. Ran journal in **London [Westminster]**; married life in France; retired to Sussex. *I, Too, Have Lived in Arcadia: a Record of Love and Childhood*, Mrs Belloc Lowndes, Macmillan, London, 1941.

PARMINTER, JANE d. 1811. Architect and interior designer. Built several properties at **Exmouth**, where she died and was buried.

PARMINTER, MARY d. 1841. Architect and interior designer. Built several properties at **Exmouth** with her cousin JANE PARMINTER; buried there.

PARR, CATHERINE 1512–48. Ruler, scholar, last queen of Henry VIII. Born in **Kendal**; royal marriage brought her to **London [Richmond** and **Kensington and Chelsea]**; last marriage and burial near **Winchcombe**. *Queen Katherine Parr*, A. Martinssen, Secker & Warburg, London, 1973.

PASSFIELD, BARONESS. See BEATRICE WEBB.

PASTON, MARGARET; née MAUTBY *c.* 1423–*c.* 1482. Writer of letters. Born at **Mautby**; married life at **Caistor**; widowhood at **Norwich** and **Mautby**. *The Paston Letters*, N. Davis [ed.], Part I, 1971.

PATERSON, EMMA ANNE 1848–86. Trade unionist. Born in **London [Westminster]**, where she worked for women's union representation; attended conference in **Glasgow**; buried in **London [Brent]**; commemorated in **London [Camden]**. *Emma Paterson: She Led Women Into a Man's World*, Harold Goldman, Lawrence & Wishart, London, 1974.

PATTI, DAME ADELINA 1843–1919. Singer. Born in Spain; much travelled youth; career success in **London [Westminster]**; married in **Brecon**; settled in **Craig-y-Nos**, where she died; commemorated in **Swansea**.

PATTISON, DOROTHY. See SISTER DORA OF WALSALL.

PAUL, ALICE 1885–1977. Suffragette, feminist, pacifist. Born in USA; studied in **Birmingham** and **London [Westminster]**, where she campaigned; returned to USA, continuing struggle for women's rights.

PAVLOVA, ANNA 1882–1931. Ballet dancer. Born in Russia, where she trained, toured throughout Europe, settled and died in **London [Barnet]**. *Anna Pavlova*, Oleg Kerensky, Hamish Hamilton, London, 1973; *Pavlova: Impressions*, Margot Fonteyn, Weidenfeld & Nicolson, London, 1985.

PEMBROKE, COUNTESS OF. See SIDNEY, MARY.

PENROSE, ELIZABETH. See 'MARKHAM, MRS'.

'PERDITA'. See ROBINSON, MARY.

PETHICK-LAWRENCE, EMMELINE; née PETHICK 1867–1954. Suffragette. Born in **Bristol**; worked in **London [Westminster]**; campaigned there, stood for election in **Manchester**; visitor to **Bath**. *Pethick-Lawrence: a Portrait*, Vera Brittain, Allen & Unwin, London, 1963; *The Suffragette Movement*, E. Sylvia Pankhurst, 1931, republished by Virago, London, 1977; *My Part in a Changing World*, Emmeline Pethick-Lawrence, Gollancz, London, 1938.

PHILIPPA OF HAINAULT *c.* 1315–69. Ruler, Queen of England, wife of Edward III. Born and brought up in the Netherlands. As queen, supported significant industries in **Newcastle upon Tyne** and **Norwich**; military campaign in **Durham**; buried in **London [Westminster]**; commemorated by **Oxford** college.

PHILIPS, KATHERINE; née FOWLER; 'MATCHLESS ORINDA' 1632–64. Writer, translator. Born in **London [City]**; educated in **London [Hackney]**; adolescence and marriage in **Cardigan**, centre of her literary circle; died in **London [City]**. *The Matchless Orinda*, P. W. Souers, 1931.

PHILPOT, ELIZABETH 1780–1857. Geologist. Lived and studied in **Lyme Regis**. 'The Fossil Collection of the Misses Philpot of Lyme Regis', J. M. Edmonds, in *Proceedings of the Dorset Natural History and Archaeological Society*, 98, 1976.

PHILPOT, MARGARET d. 1845. Geologist. Lived and studied in **Lyme Regis**.

PHILPOT, MARY 1777–1838. Geologist. Lived and studied in **Lyme Regis**.

PIOZZI, HESTER. See THRALE, MRS.

PLATH, SYLVIA 1932–63. Writer. Born in Boston, USA; studied at **Cambridge**; briefly taught in USA; returned to Britain; buried at **Heptonstall**. *Letters Home*, Sylvia Plath, Faber & Faber, London, 1975.

POCAHONTAS; MRS JOHN ROLFE 1596–1617. Folk heroine, diplomat. Grew up in Virginia, USA; after marriage came to England, buried at **Gravesend**. *Pochahontas*, G. S. Ward, 1970; *The Double Life of Pocahontas*, Jean Fritz, Putnam, New York, 1983.

PONSONBY, CAROLINE. See LAMB, LADY CAROLINE.

PONSONBY, SARAH 1755–1831. Diarist. Born in Ireland; eloped to **Denbigh**; settled in **Llangollen**, where she is buried. *The Ladies of Llangollen*, Elizabeth Mavor, Penguin, Harmondsworth, 1973; *A Year with the Ladies of Llangollen*, Elizabeth Mavor [ed.], Viking, London, 1984.

POTTER, BEATRIX; MRS HEELIS 1866–1943. Writer and illustrator of children's books, sheep breeder. Born and brought up in **London [Kensington and Chelsea]**; childhood summers near **Dunkeld**; visitor to **Long Melford**, **Gloucester** and **Lyme Regis**; settled at **Near Sawrey**, where she died. *The Tale of Beatrix Potter*, Margaret Lane, Penguin, Harmondsworth, 1972; *The Magic Years of Beatrix Potter*, Margaret Lane, Frederick Warne, London, 1978; *Cousin Beattie: a Memory of Beatrix Potter*, Ulla Hyde Parker, Frederick Warne, London, 1981.

PREECE, PATRICIA b. 1900. Artist. Lived and painted at **Cookham**.

PROCTER, ADELAIDE ANNE 1825–64. Poet and feminist. Born in London; lived and worked in **London [Westminster]**; buried in **London [Brent]**.

PROCTOR, DOD. See SHAW, DOD.

PUDDICOMBE, ANN ADALISA; 'ALLEN RAINE' 1836–1908. Novelist. Spent most of her life in her native Wales; educated at **Cheltenham**.

Q q

Queens have been listed under their first name – i.e., ELIZABETH; PHILIPPA OF HAINAULT; VICTORIA – unless they have a surname in general use, in which case their entry appears by surname: BOLEYN, ANNE; HOWARD, CATHERINE.

R R

RADCLIFFE, ANN; née WARD 1764–1823. Writer of novels. Born in **London [City]**; educated in **Bath**; married life mainly in the capital; died and buried in **London [Westminster]**. *Anne Radcliffe: a Biography*, Aline Grant, Allen Swallow, Denver, 1951.

'RAINE, ALLEN'. See PUDDICOMBE, ANN.

RALPHSON, MARY; TROOPER MARY *fl*. 1698–1746. Soldier. Born in west of Scotland, active at **Culloden**.

RAMBERT, DAME MARIE 1888–1982. Ballet dancer, choreographer, teacher and company manager. Born in Poland; studied in France and **London [Kensington and Chelsea]**; commemorated in **London [Westminster]**. *Quicksilver: an Autobiography*, Marie Rambert, Macmillan, London, 1972.

RAMEE, MARIE LOUISE DE LA; 'OUIDA' 1839–1908. Writer of novels. Born and educated at **Bury St Edmunds**; lived in France, **London [Hammersmith and Westminster]**, and latterly in Italy. *Ouida: the Passionate Victorian*, Ellen Bigland, Jarrolds, Norwich, 1950.

RATHBONE, ELEANOR FLORENCE 1872–1946. Suffragist, politician, social reformer. Native Londoner; grew up in **Liverpool**; studied at **Oxford**; political and social work in **Liverpool** and **London [Westminster]**. *Eleanor Rathbone*, Mary Stocks, Gollancz, London, 1949.

READ, MARY *c*. 1690–1721. Soldier, pirate. Possibly born in **Plymouth**; military and pirate careers abroad.

REDPATH, ANNE 1895–1965. Artist. Born in **Galashiels**; educated at **Hawick**, studied art in **Edinburgh** and abroad; lived in **Hawick** and **Edinburgh**. *Anne Redpath*, George Bruce, Edinburgh University Press, Edinburgh, 1974.

REEVE, CLARA 1729–93. Novelist. Born and died in **Ipswich**.

RHEAD, CHARLOTTE 1885–1947. Pottery designer. Active working life in **Stoke-on-Trent**, her native town.

RHONDDA, VISCOUNTESS; MARGARET HAIG THOMAS 1883–1958. Suffragette, editor and publisher. Educated in **St Andrews**; studied at **Oxford**; published *Time and Tide* in **London [City]**; campaigned in

London [Westminster]; buried at **Llanwern**. *This Was My World*, M.H. Thomas, Macmillan, London, 1933.

RICHARDSON, DOROTHY MILLER; MRS ODLE 1873–1957. Novelist. Born and educated in **Abingdon**; lived in **London [Camden]**; married and writing lives spent there and in Cornwall: **Trevone**; buried in **London [Lambeth]**. *Dorothy Richardson: the Genius they Forgot*, John Rosenberg, Duckworth, London, 1973; *Dorothy Richardson: a Biography*, Gloria G. Fromme, University of Illinois Press, Evanston, 1977.

RICHARDSON, HENRY HANDEL; ETHEL FLORENCE LINDESEY RICHARDSON; MRS J. G. ROBERTSON 1870–1946. Writer of novels. Born and brought up in Australia; studied in Germany; married in Ireland; married life in Strasbourg and **London [Westminster]**; widowhood spent in **Hastings**. *Myself When Young*, Henry Handel Richardson, 1948; *Ulysses Bound: Richardson and Her Fiction*, D. Green, 1973; *Henry Handel Richardson*, Kirsty McLeod, Cambridge University Press, Cambridge, 1985.

RICHMOND AND LENNOX, FRANCES DUCHESS OF 1647–1702. Muse, model, beauty. Married life near **Haddington**; buried in **London [Westminster]**.

ROBINS, ELIZABETH; 'C. E. RAYMOND' 1862–1952. Actress, feminist, suffragist, playwright, novelist. Born and raised in the USA, active in **London [City]**. *Both Sides of the Curtain*, Elizabeth Robins, Heinemann, London, 1940.

ROBINSON, MARY; née DARBY; 'PERDITA' 1758–1800. Actress and writer. Born at **Bury St Edmunds**; brought up in **Bristol**; lived in **London [Westminster]**; died in **Egham**; buried in **Windsor**.

ROBSON, DAME FLORA 1902–1984. Actress. Born in **South Shields**; childhood in **London [Enfield]**; active career touring Britain and abroad; last years in **Brighton**; memorial in **London [Westminster]**. *Flora Robson*, Janet Dunbar, Harrap, London, 1960.

ROPER, ESTHER 1870–1938. Suffrage campaigner. Born in Cheshire; educated in **Manchester**; active there and throughout north-west England.

'ROSAMUND, FAIR'. See DE CLIFFORD, ROSAMUND.

ROSSETTI, CHRISTINA GEORGINA; 'ELLEN ALLEYNE' 1830–94. Writer of poetry. Born and mostly lived in **London [Camden]**, taught in **Frome**; visitor to **Old Dailly**, **Wallington** and **London [Bexley]**; died and buried in **London [Haringey]**. *Christina Rossetti*, Georgina Battiscombe, Constable, 1981; *Christina Rossetti*, Margaret Sawtell, Mowbrays, London, 1955.

RUSSELL, DORA WINIFRED; née BLACK 1894–1986. Feminist writer and activist. School education in **London [Sutton]**; studied at **Cambridge**; ran school in **Petersfield**; last years at **Porthcurno**. *The Tamarisk Tree*, Dora Russell, Elek Pemberton, London, 1975.

RUTHERFORD, ALISON *fl.* Eighteenth century. Writer, salon hostess. Held salons in **Edinburgh**.

RUTHERFORD, DAME MARGARET TAYLOR 1892–1972. Actress. Londoner, born in **London [Wandsworth]**; educated in **London [Merton]**; acting career mainly in the south of England; last years and burial in **Gerrard's Cross**.

RYDER, SUE, BARONESS RYDER OF WARSAW IN POLAND AND CAVENDISH IN SUFFOLK b. 1923. Social worker, philanthropist. Centre of her work is at **Cavendish**.

RYE, MARIA SUSAN 1829–1903. Social worker, feminist. Born and worked in **London [Southwark]**, where she campaigned and supported women; visited Australia, New Zealand, Canada, via **Liverpool**; retired to **Hemel Hempstead**, where she is buried. *Emigrant Gentlewomen*, A. J. Hammerton, 1979.

RYLAND, BERTHA *fl.* 1914. Suffragette. Active in **Birmingham**.

S s

SACKVILLE-WEST, VICTORIA; MRS HAROLD NICOLSON 1892–1962. Writer of poetry, novels, gardening journalist and designer. Born and grew up at **Knole**; married life in **London [Kensington and Chelsea]** and **Sissinghurst**; buried at **Withyham**. *Vita*, Victoria Glendinning, Weidenfeld & Nicolson, London, 1983.

SAINT POLE, MARIE DE, COUNTESS OF PEMBROKE *c*. 1304–77. Patron of scholarship and religious institutions. Founded college in **Cambridge**.

SAMPSON, AGNES d. 1592. Lay healer; 'witch'. Originally from **Haddington**; tried for witchcraft at **North Berwick**.

SANDS, ETHEL 1873–1962. Artist. Born in USA; studied in France; settled in England at **Garsington** and **London [Kensington and Chelsea]**. *Miss Ethel Sands and Her Circle*, Wendy Baron, Peter Owen, London, 1977.

SAVAGE, WENDY b. 1935. Medical practitioner. Educated in **London [Croydon]**; studied at **Cambridge**, practised medicine in Britain and overseas; currently in **London [Tower Hamlets]**.

SAYERS, DOROTHY LEIGH 1893–1957. Writer. Born in **Oxford**; grew up at **Bluntisham** and **Christchurch**; educated in **Salisbury**; studied at **Oxford**; working life and worship in **London [Westminster]**; settled in **Witham**; buried in **London [Westminster]**; **Kirkcudbright** was setting for a novel. *Dorothy L. Sayers: the Life of a Courageous Woman*, J. Brabazon, Gollancz, London, 1981; *Such a Strange Lady*, Janet Hitchman, New English Library, London, 1975. The Dorothy L. Sayers Historical and Literary Society: Secretary, Rose Cottage, Malthouse Lane, Hurstpierpoint, Sussex, BN6 9JY.

SCHREIBER, LADY CHARLOTTE. See GUEST, LADY CHARLOTTE.

SCHREINER, OLIVE EMILIE ALBERTINA; OLIVE CRONWRIGHT-SCHREINER; 'RALPH IRON' 1855–1920. Writer of novels, socialist, anti-racist. Born and brought up in South Africa; ten years in England in **London [Camden** and **Westminster]**, **Hastings**, **Bournemouth**; married life in South Africa, travelled there; died in England; buried in South Africa. *Olive Schreiner*, Ruth First and Ann Scott, Andre Deutsch, London, 1980; *Olive Schreiner: Feminism on the Frontier*, Joyce Aurech Berkman, Eden Press, Vermont, 1979.

SCOTT, ELISABETH WHITWORTH; MRS RICHARDS 1898–1972. Architect. Born and educated in **Bournemouth**; studied in **London [Camden]**; examples of her work in **Stratford-upon-Avon**, **Cheltenham** and **Cambridge**.

SEACOLE, MARY; née MARY GRANT 1805–81. Nursing pioneer. Born in Jamaica, nursed and supplied food and accommodation there, in Panama and the Crimea. Retired to **London [Westminster]**, where she died; buried in **London [Brent]**. *Wonderful Adventures of Mrs Seacole in Many Lands*, Ziggy Alexander and Audrey Dewjee [eds], Falling Wall Press, Bristol, 1984.

SEWARD, ANNA; 'THE SWAN OF LICHFIELD' 1749–1809. Writer of poetry and letters. Born in **Eyam**; majority of her life spent in **Lichfield**, where she died; visitor to **Bath**. *The Singing Swan*, Margaret Ashmun, Greenwood Press, London, Connecticut, 1960.

SEWELL, ANNA 1820–78. Writer of works for children. Born in **Great Yarmouth**; lived in **Brighton** and **Norwich**; buried in **Lamas**. *Anna Sewell and Black Beauty*, M. J. Baker, 1956.

SEWELL, MARY 1797–1884. Writer of works for children. Lived in **Great Yarmouth**, **Brighton** and **Norwich**; buried in **Lamas**.

SEYMOUR, JANE *c.* 1509–37. Queen to Henry VIII. Attended court in **London [Richmond]** before her short marriage to the king; buried at **Windsor**. *Jane Seymour*, Francis B. Clarke, Sphere, London, 1972.

SHAW, DOD; DOD PROCTOR 1892–1972. Artist. Active at **Lamorna** and **Newlyn**.

SHEEPSHANKS, MARY RYOTT 1872–1958. Social and political reformer, pacifist. Born in **Liverpool**; family moved to **Norwich**; student at **Cambridge**; worked in **London [Lambeth]** and died in **London [Camden]**. *Spinsters of this Parish: the Life and Times of F. M. Mayor and Mary Sheepshanks*, Sybil Oldfield, Virago, London, 1984.

SHELLEY, MARY WOLLSTONECRAFT; née GODWIN 1797–1851. Writer of novels. Born in **London [Islington]**; youth in Europe and **Dundee**; elopement abroad; short residences at **Bath** and **Marlow**; widowed in Italy; buried in **Bournemouth**. *Mary Shelley*, Eileen Bigland, Cassell, London, 1959.

SHEPPARD, KATHERINE WILSON; née MALCOLM 1848–1934. Campaigner for women's rights in New Zealand. Born in **Islay**; emigrated to New Zealand where she fought successfully for women's votes and other rights.

SHERIDAN, CLARE CONSUELO; née FREWEN 1885–1970. Sculptor; journalist. Londoner by birth, she led a much travelled life. Studio in **London [Westminster]**; last years at and near **Brede** where she is buried.

Cousin Clare: the Tempestuous Life of Clare Sheridan, Anita Leslie, Hutchinson, London, 1976; *Clare Sheridan [1885–1970]*, Betty Taylor, Hastings, 1984.

SHERWOOD, MARY MARTHA; née BUTT 1775–1851. Writer of novels, especially for children. Born at **Stanford on Teme**; educated at **Reading**; visited **Bath**; married life in India; returned to **Worcester**, where she died.

SHIPTON, MOTHER *c.* 1488–1561. Prophet. Born and prophesied in **Knaresborough**.

SIDDONS, SARAH; née KEMBLE 1755–1831. Actress. Born in **Brecon**; travelling childhood; own acting career toured provinces, acted in **Manchester, Bath, Bristol**, and finally **London [Camden** and **Westminster]**; buried in **London [Westminster]**; memorabilia in **Smallhythe**. *Sarah Siddons, Portrait of an Artist*, Roger Manvell, Heinemann, London, 1977; *The Great Sarah, the Life of Mrs Siddons*, Kathleen Mackenzie, Evans Brothers, London, 1968.

SIDNEY, LADY FRANCES, COUNTESS OF SUSSEX d. 1589. Benefactor. Founder of **Cambridge** college; buried in **London [Westminster]**.

SIDNEY, MARY; MARY HERBERT, COUNTESS OF PEMBROKE 1561–1621. Poet, patron, translator. Born in **Bewdley**; childhood in **Ludlow** and **Penshurst Place**; homes in **Wilton, London [City** and **Kensingston and Chelsea]** and **Ampthill Park**; buried in **Salisbury**.

SINCLAIR, CATHERINE 1800–64. Writer of books for children; welfare worker. Born in **Edinburgh**, where she did much social work; youth in **London [Richmond]**; died in London.

SINCLAIR, MAY 1870–1946. Writer of novels and poetry. Born in Merseyside; educated in **Cheltenham**; died in Buckinghamshire; buried in **London [Camden]**. *Miss May Sinclair: Novelist*, Theophilus E. Boll, Associated Universities, 1973.

SITWELL, DAME EDITH LOUISA 1887–1964. Writer of poetry, literary criticism and biography. Born in **Scarborough**; grew up there and **Renishaw**; lived in **London [Kensington and Chelsea]**; buried at **Weedon Lois**. *Edith Sitwell: a Unicorn Among the Lions*, Victoria Glendinning, Oxford University Press, Oxford, 1983.

SLESSOR, MARY MITCHELL 1848–1915. Missionary. Born in **Aberdeen**; adolescence and early working life in **Dundee**; missionary activity in West Africa, died there. *The Expendable Mary Slessor*, James Buchan, St Andrews Press, Edinburgh, 1980; *Western Women in Colonial Africa*, C. Oliver, Greenwood Press, London, Connecticut, 1982.

SMITH, BARBARA LEIGH. See BODICHON, BARBARA.

SMITH, CHARLOTTE; née TURNER 1749–1806. Novelist, poet, translator. Born in **London [Westminster]**; lived and wrote in **Woolbeding**; buried near **Guildford**.

SMITH, MARY ELLEN; née SPEAR 1862–1933. Politician in Canada. Born in **Tavistock**; emigrated in 1891 to Canada, where she had a significant political career.

SMITH, STEVIE; née FLORENCE MARGARET SMITH 1902–71. Writer of poetry and novels. Born in **Kingston upon Hull**; most of her life spent in **London [Enfield]**; cremated in **Torquay**. *Ivy and Stevie: Ivy Compton-Burnett and Stevie Smith: Conversations and Reflections*, K. Dick, 1971; *Stevie. a Biography of Stevie Smith*, Jack Barbera and William McBrien, Heinemann, London, 1985.

SMYTH, DAME ETHEL MARY 1858–1944. Composer and suffragette. Brought up in **London [Wandsworth]**; music training abroad; campaigned for women's votes in **London [Islington]**; died in **Woking**. *Ethel Smyth: a Biography*, Christopher St John, Longmans, London, 1959; *Impetuous Heart: the story of Ethel Smyth*, Louise Collis, William Kimber, London, 1985.

SNELL, HANNAH 1723–92. Soldier. Born in **Worcester**; joined army in **Coventry**, served abroad and at **Culloden**; last years and burial in **London [Kensington and Chelsea]**. *The Female Soldier: or the Surprising Adventures of Hannah Snell*, 1750.

SOMERVILLE, MARY; née FAIRFAX 1780–1872. Astronomer, mathematician. Born at **Jedburgh**, grew up in **Burntisland**; moved to **London [Westminster]** after second marriage; died in Italy, associations with **Oxford** and **Cambridge**; memorabilia in **Kirkcaldy**. *Mary Somerville 1780–1872*, Elizabeth Chambers Patterson, 1979; *Mary Somerville and the Cultivation of Science, 1815–1840*, Elizabeth Chambers Patterson, Martinus Nijhoff Publishers, Dordrecht, 1983.

SOUTHCOTT, JOANNA 1750–1814. Prophet, religious leader. Moved from her native Devon to **London [Westminster]** where she died. *A Woman to Deliver Her People: Joanna Southcott and English Millenarianism in an Era of Revolution*, James K. Hopkins, University of Texas Press, Austin, 1982.

SPAIN, NANCY 1917–64. Journalist, broadcaster, detective fiction writer. Born in **Newcastle upon Tyne**; educated near **Brighton**; died in plane crash. *Why I'm not a Millionaire*, Nancy Spain, Hutchinson, London, 1956.

SPENCER, GEORGIANA. See CAVENDISH, GEORGIANA.

SPENCER, HILDA. See CARLINE, HILDA.

SPRY, CONSTANCE; née FLETCHER 1886–1960. Writer and practitioner of flower arranging and cookery. Born in **Derby**; worked in Ireland; career success while living near **Windsor**. *Constance Spry: a Biography*, Elizabeth Coxhead, William Luscombe, London, 1975.

DE STAEL, MADAME; née ANNE LOUISE GERMAIN NECKER 1766–1817. Writer of novels and political criticism. French woman whose exiles in England were spent near **Mickleham** and **London [Westminster]**; also exiled in Switzerland. *Madame de Stael*, Renee Winegarten, Berg, London, 1985.

STANHOPE, LADY HESTER LUCY 1776–1839. Traveller. Born in **Chevening**; lived in **London [Westminster]** and resident in **Walmer**; visitor to **Builth Wells**; travelled in the Middle East; settled in Lebanon, where she died. *Lady Hester Stanhope*, Joan Haslip, Cassell, 1987; *Lady Hester Stanhope*, James Hogg, Longwood, London, 1986.

STANLEY, VENETIA 1600–33. Society beauty. Lived at **Tong** all her life.

STANTON, ELIZABETH CADY 1815–1902. Campaigner of American women's rights. Born and lived in the USA; crucial meeting in **London [Westminster]**. *Eighty Years and More*, Elizabeth C. Stanton, 1898; *Elizabeth Cady Stanton: a Radical for Women's Rights*, Lois W. Banner, Little, New York, 1980.

STOPES, MARIE CHARLOTTE CARMICHAEL 1881–1958. Birth control campaigner, social reformer, palaeontologist. Born and educated in **Edinburgh**; studied in **London [Camden]**, where she later taught, and Germany; taught at **Manchester**; country homes at **Dorking** and **Portland Bill**; birth control clinics in **London [Islington** and **Camden]**, and **Leeds**; died at **Dorking**; cremated in **London [Barnet]**. *Marie Stopes*, Ruth Hall, Andre Deutsch, London, 1975.

STOWE, HARRIET BEECHER 1811–96. Writer and abolitionist. Spent most of her life in the United States, but visits to Britain included **Liverpool** and **Manchester**.

STRACHEY, LADY JANE; née JANE MARIA GRANT d. 1928. Suffragist. Born and brought up in **Rothiemurchus**; married life in **London [Camden]**. *Remarkable Relations*, Barbara Strachey, Gollancz, London, 1980.

STRACHEY, PHILIPPA 1872–1968. Campaigner for women's rights. Brought up in **London [Camden]**, field for her campaign activity. *Remarkable Relations*, Barbara Strachey, Gollancz, London, 1980.

STRACHEY, RAY RACHEL CONN; née COSTELLOE 1887–1940. Journalist and novelist. Educated in **London [Kensington and Chelsea]**; studied in **Cambridge** and USA; campaigned and published in **London [Camden]**. *Remarkable Relations*, Barbara Strachey, Gollancz, London, 1980.

STRICKLAND, AGNES 1796–1874. Historian, writer of biography, poetry and works for children. Native Londoner, lived in **London [Camden]**; retired to **Southwold** where she is buried. *Agnes Strickland, Biographer of the*

Queens of England, 1976–1874, Una Pope-Hennessy [U. C. Birch], Chatto & Windus, London, 1940.

STUART, LADY ARABELLA 1575–1615. Political pawn. Long imprisonment at **Hardwick**, followed by later imprisonment and death in **London [City]**. *Arabella Stuart*, David N. Durant, Weidenfeld & Nicolson, London, 1978.

STUART, FRANCES. See RICHMOND AND LENNOX, FRANCES DUCHESS OF.

STUART, MARY. See MARY QUEEN OF SCOTS.

SUTHERLAND, MILLICENT DUCHESS OF; née ST CLAIR-ERSKINE 1867–1955. Philanthropist. Born in Fife; married life at **Stoke-on-Trent**, **Golspie** and **London [Westminster]**; retired to France, died there but buried at **Golspie** and commemorated in **Dornoch**. *Millicent, Duchess of Sutherland*, Denis Stuart, Gollancz, London, 1982.

'SWAN OF LICHFIELD'. See ANNA SEWARD.

SWANWICK, HELENA M.; née HELENA SICKERT 1864–1939. Suffragette, pacifist, journalist. Born in Germany, educated in England and France and **Cambridge**; married life in **Manchester** and **Knutsford**. *I Have Been Young*, Helena Swanwick, Gollancz, London, 1935.

SZABO, VIOLETTE 1921–45. Wartime heroine. Born in France; grew up in **London [Lambeth]**; married in **Aldershot**; active in France, where she died. *Carve Her Name with Pride*, R. J. Minney, George Newnes, London, 1956.

T T

TALBOT, ELIZABETH, COUNTESS OF SHREWSBURY; 'BESS OF HARDWICK'; née ELIZABETH HARDWICK 1518–1608. Businesswoman, political intriguer, powerful landowner. Born at **Hardwick**; four marriages; properties include **Chatsworth** and Bolsover, as well as **Hardwick**; brief imprisonment in **London [City]**; buried in **Derby**. *Bess of Hardwick*, Ethel Carleton Williams, Chivers, Bath, 1977; *Bess of Hardwick*, David Durant, Weidenfeld & Nicolson, London, 1977.

TANQUERAY, ANNE; née WILLAUME *fl.* 1717–34. Silversmith. Worked in **London [City]**.

TAYLOR, ANN; MRS GILBERT 1782–1866. Children's writer. Native Londoner; youth in **Colchester** and **Lavenham**.

TAYLOR, JANE 1783–1824. Children's writer. Native Londoner; youth in **Colchester** and **Lavenham**; died and was buried in **Chipping Ongar**.

TEERLINC, LIEVINA or TERLING, LAVINIA; née BENNINCK *c*. 1515–76. Born in Bruges, Flanders, worked in English courts, such as **London [Richmond]**; died in **London [Tower Hamlets]**.

TEMPEST, DAME MARIE; née SUSAN MARY ETHERINGTON 1864–1942. Actress. Career based in **London [Westminster]**.

TEMPLE, LADY. See OSBORNE, DOROTHY.

TERRY, DAME ALICE ELLEN 1847–1928. Actress. Born in **Coventry**; travelling childhood; acting career based in **London [Kensington and Chelsea]**; country home and collection of memorabilia at **Smallhythe**; visitor to **Freshwater**; buried in **London [Westminster]**. *Ellen Terry*, Roger Manvel, Heinemann, London, 1968; *Ellen and Edy: A Biography of Ellen Terry and Her Daughter, Edith Craig, 1847–1947*, Joy Melville, Pandora Press, London, 1988.

THATCHER, MARGARET HILDA; née ROBERTS b. 1925. Politician. Born and educated in **Grantham**; studied at **Oxford**; political career based in **London [Westminster and Barnet]**.

THOMAS, MARGARET HAIG. See VISCOUNTESS RHONDDA.

THOMPSON, FLORA JUNE; née TIMMS 1876–1947. Writer of auto-biographical novels. Born in **Juniper Hill**; educated in **Cottisford**; worked in **Fringford**; wrote in **Dartmouth** and **Brixham**; buried in **Dartmouth**. *Flora Thompson*, Margaret Lane, John Murray, London, 1976.

THORNDIKE, DAME SYBIL CASSON 1882–1976. Actress. Born in Gainsborough; childhood in **Rochester**; acting career in **Manchester** and **London [Lambeth]**; died in **London [Kensington and Chelsea]**; commemorated in **London [Westminster]**. *Sybil Casson Thorndike*, Elizabeth Sprigge, Gollancz, London, 1971.

THRALE, MRS HESTER LYNCH; née SALUSBURY; later MRS PIOZZI 1741–1821. Writer of diaries and letters. Born in **Pwllheli**; grew up at **Tremeirchion**; married in **London [Westminster]** and lived in **London [Southwark]**; often on tour; visitor to **Brighton, Bath, Denbigh**; had a country home at **Treimeirchion**, where she is buried; last winter in **Penzance**; died in **Bristol**. *Hester Lynch Piozzi [Mrs Thrale]*, James L. Clifford, Oxford University Press, Oxford, 1951.

TILLEY, VESTA; née MATILDA ALICE POWLES; later LADY DE FRECE 1864–1952. Actress. Debut in **Gloucester**; career in **London [Westminster]**; died in Monaco. *Recollections of Vesta*, Vesta Tilley, 1934; *Vesta Tilley*, Sarah Maitland, Virago, London, 1986.

TOWARD, AGNES d. 1975. Hoarder. Home in **Glasgow**. *Miss Toward of the Tenement House*, W. K. Ritchie, Scottish National Trust, Edinburgh, 1986.

TREVELYAN, LADY PAULINE; née JERMYN 1816–66. Artist and patron of artists and writers. Home at **Wallington**; died in Switzerland.

TROLLOPE, MRS FRANCES; FANNY TROLLOPE; née MILTON 1780–1863. Writer of novels and travel books. Born near **Bristol**; childhood at **Heckfield**; married life in **London [Camden** and **Harrow]**; travelled extensively latterly, last years in Italy where she was buried. *The Life, Manners and Travels of Fanny Trollope*, Joanna Johnston, Constable, London, 1979.

TUCKWELL, GERTRUDE MARY 1861–1951. Trade unionist and worker for women's rights. Born in **Oxford**; last years in **Godalming**; memorial collection in **London [Camden]**.

TUDOR, MARY. See MARY, QUEEN OF ENGLAND.

TUSSAUD, MADAME ANNE MARIE; née GRASHOLTZ 1760–1850. Wax-artist. Early life and career in France, exhibited her work in **London [Westminster]**, eventual permanent home. *Madame Tussaud: Waxworker Extraordinary*, Anita Leslie and Pauline Chapman, Hutchinson, London, 1978.

TWINING, LOUISA 1820–1912. Social reformer, philanthropist. Born and worked in **London [Westminster]**; active retirement in **Tunbridge**

Wells; buried in **London [Brent]**. *Recollections of Life and Work, Being the Autobiography of Louisa Twining*, Louisa Twining, Edward Arnold, London, 1895.

U u

UTTLEY, ALISON; née TAYLOR 1884–1976. Writer for children and adults. Born near **Cromford**; studied at **Manchester**; taught in **London [Kensington and Chelsea]**; lived, wrote and died in **Penn**. *The World of Alison Uttley*, Elizabeth Saintsbury, Howard Baker Press, London, 1980; *Alison Uttley: the Life of a Country Child*, Dennis Judd, Michael Joseph, London, 1986.

V v

DE VALERIE, MAUD *fl.* Twelfth century. Welsh heroine. Born at **Hay-on-Wye**; died in **Corfe Castle**,

VAUGHAN, BRIDGET; later BRIDGET BEVAN 1698–1779. Educational pioneer. Her home was at **Laugharne**, before her marriage.

VAUGHAN, HILDA b. 1892. Writer of novels. Born at **Builth Wells**.

VESTRIS, LUCIA ELIZABETH; MADAME VESTRIS; née BARTHOLEZZI 1797–1856. Actress and theatre manager. Career based in the English capital; she lived and worked in **London [Westminster]**; buried in **London [Brent]**.

VEZELAY, PAULE; née MARGERY WATSON-WILLIAMS 1892–1984. Artist. Born in **Bristol**; studied in **London [Camden]**; painted mostly in France. *Women of Our Century*, Leonie Caldecott, Ariel Books, London, 1984.

VICTORIA, QUEEN 1819–1901. Ruler of the British Empire. Born in **London [Kensington and Chelsea]**; childhood spent there and near **Esher**; holidayed at **Ardverikie** before making her Scottish home at **Balmoral**; died at her home at **East Cowes**; buried at **Windsor**. *Victoria R.I.*, Elizabeth Longford, Weidenfeld & Nicolson, London, 1964; *Victoria*, Stanley Weintraub, Unwin Hyman, London, 1987; *Queen Victoria in her Letters and Journal*, Christopher Hibbert [ed.], John Murray, London, 1984.

VILLIERS, BARBARA, COUNTESS OF CASTLEMAINE and DUCHESS OF CLEVELAND 1640–1709. Influential royal mistress. Adult life at court; homes in **London [Hounslow]** and **Cliveden**; buried in **London [Hounslow]**. *The Illustrious Lady, a Biography of Barbara Villiers*, Elizabeth Hamilton, Hamish Hamilton, London, 1980.

W w

WADDELL, HELEN 1895–1965. Medievalist, translator, novelist. Born in Japan; studied in Ulster and **Oxford**; taught there and in **London [Camden]**; died in Ireland. *Helen Waddell: a Biography*, D. Felicitas Corrigan, Gollancz, London, 1986.

WALKER, DAME ETHEL 1861–1951. Artist. Born in **Edinburgh**; studied in **London [Camden]**; studios at **Robin Hood's Bay** and **London [Kensington and Chelsea]**.

WALLACE, NELLIE; MRS ELEANOR JANE LIDDIE 1870–1948. Music-hall comic. Born in **Glasgow**; touring career in Britain and USA; death in **London [Barnet]**.

WALTERS, CATHERINE; 'SKITTLES'; 'MRS BAILEY' 1839–1920. Courtesan. Born in **Liverpool**; social life took her abroad, but based in **London [Westminster]**; buried in **Crawley**. *The Girl with the Swansdown Seat*, Cyril Pearl, Robin Miller, 1980.

WARD, BARBARA MARY; BARONESS JACKSON OF LODSWORTH 1914–1981. Economist, reformer. Brought up in **York**; studied at **Oxford**; active in **London [Westminster]**.

WARD, MRS HUMPHREY; MARY AUGUSTA WARD; née ARNOLD 1851–1920. Novelist and social reformer. Born in Australia; educated at **Ambleside**; lived and worked in **Oxford**; married life there and **London [Camden** and **Westminster]** and **Aldbury**; visitor to **Levens Hall** and **Long Sleddale**; buried at **Aldbury**. *Mrs Humphrey Ward*, Enid Huwy Jones, Heinemann, London, 1973.

WARNER, SYLVIA TOWNSEND 1893–1978. Novelist, poet and prose writer. Lived in Dorset; museum in **Dorchester**. *This Narrow Place*, Wendy Mulford, Pandora Press, London, 1988.

WASTE, JOAN 1534–56. Martyr. Lived and died in **Derby**.

WATERFORD, LOUISA MARCHIONESS OF; née STUART 1818–91. Artist. Childhood at **Christchurch**; widowhood spent at **Ford**, where she was buried. *The Lady Waterford Hall and its Murals*, Michael Joicey, The Trustees, Ford, 1983.

WATT, CHRISTIAN 1833–1923. Diarist. Adult life spent mostly in

Aberdeen. *The Christian Watt Papers*, David Fraser [ed.], Paul Harrison Publishing, Edinburgh, 1983.

WATTS, MARY; née MARY FRASER-TYTLER 1850–1937. Artist, architect and designer. Ran a school in **Compton**.

WEBB, GLADYS MARY 1881–1927. Writer of novels. Born at **Leighton**; childhood at **Shrewsbury** and **Much Wenlock**; married life in **Weston-super-Mare**, **Lyth Hill** and **London [Camden]**; died in **St Leonards**; buried in **Shrewsbury**. *The Flower of Light*, Gladys Mary Coles, Duckworth, London, 1978.

WEBB, MARTHA BEATRICE; née POTTER 1858–1943. Social reformer. Born near **Gloucester**; social work in Lancashire and London; married life **London [Camden]**; buried in **London [Westminster]**. *The Diaries of Beatrce Webb*, Norman and Jean MacKenzie [ed.], vol. 1, 1982, vol. 2, 1985; *The Apprenticeship of Beatrice Webb*, Deborah E. Nord, Macmillan, London, 1985.

WESLEY, SUSANNAH; née ANNESLEY 1669–1742. Educator. Youth in **London [Tower Hamlets]**; raised and educated her family at **Epworth**; buried in **London [City]**.

WEST, REBECCA; née CICELY ISABEL FAIRFIELD 1892–1983. Journ-alist, novelist, critic. Born in London; educated in **Edinburgh**; literary life based in **London [City]**; latterly lived in Buckinghamshire. *Rebecca West*, Fay Weldon, Viking, London, 1985; *Rebecca West*, Victoria Glendinning, Weidenfeld & Nicolson, 1987.

WESTON, AGNES ELIZABETH 1840–1918. Welfare reformer. Londoner by birth; brought up in **Bath**; welfare work in **Devonport** and **Portsmouth**; buried in **Devonport**.

WHISTLER, ANNE MATHILDA; née MCNEILL; 'WHISTLER'S MOTHER' 1807–81. Artist's model and mother. Lived in **London [Kensington and Chelsea]** and **Hastings**, where she died.

WHITE, ANTONIA; EIRENE ADELINE BOTTING 1899–1980. Writer of novels, translator, actress. Lived in **London [Kensington and Chelsea]**.

WILBRAHAM, LADY ELIZABETH; née MYTTON d. 1705. Builder. Lived at **Shifnal**.

WILKINSON, CECILY ELLEN 1891–1947. Reformer, feminist, politician. Born in **Manchester**, studied there; parliamentary representative for **Middlesbrough** then **Jarrow**. *Ellen Wilkinson*, Betty D. Vernon, Croom Helm, London, 1982.

WILLIAMS, IVY 1877–1966. Lawyer and academic. Born and studied in **Oxford**, later taught there; studied law in **London [City]**.

WILLMOTT, ELLEN ANN 1858–1934. Musician, gardener, photographer.

Family home at **Great Warley**; worked at **Stratford-upon-Avon**; buried at **Brentwood**. *Miss Willmott of Warley Place: Her Life and Her Gardens*, Audrey le Lievre, Faber & Faber, London, 1980.

WILSON, MARGARET d. 1685. Covenanter, martyr. Martyred at **Wigtown**.

WINIFRIDE, SAINT d. *c.* 650. Saint. Religious life at **Holywell**; relics in **Shrewsbury**.

WOLLSTONECRAFT, MARY; MRS GODWIN 1759–97. Feminist reformer and writer. Born in **London [Hackney]**; educated in Yorkshire; worked in **Bath**, and **London [Islington, Camden]**; originally buried in **London [Camden]**, where she died; then buried in **Bournemouth**. *The Life and Death of Mary Wollstonecraft*, Clare Tomalin, Penguin, Harmondsworth, 1977; *Mary Wollstonecraft: Her Life and Times*, Edna Nixon, Dent, London, 1971; *Mary Wollstonecraft: a Social Pioneer*, Margaret Tims, Millington, London, 1976.

WOOD, MRS HENRY; née ELLEN PRICE 1814–87. Writer of novels. Born and brought up in **Worcester**; married life mostly in France; last years in **London [Westminster]**; buried in **London [Haringey]**.

WOODHULL, VICTORIA; née CLAFLIN 1838–1927. American feminist and British suffragette. Born and active in politics and business in USA; lived in **London [Kensington and Chelsea]**; retired to **Bredon's Norton**; commemorated in **Tewkesbury**. *Mrs Satan: the Incredible Saga of Victoria Woodhull*, Joanna Johnston, Macmillan, London, 1967.

WOOLF, ADELINE VIRGINIA; née STEPHEN 1882–1941. Writer of novels. Born in **London [Kensington and Chelsea]**; childhood there and **St Ives**; later homes in **London [Camden]**; country homes in **Lewes** and **Rodmell**, where she was buried; visitor to **Firle**; inspiration for *Orlando* at **Knole**; press at **London [Richmond]**, **Letchworth** and now at **Sissinghurst**. *Virginia Woolf: a Biography*, Quentin Bell, Hogarth Press, London, 1972 [2 vols]; *Virginia Woolf and Her World*, John Lehmann, Thames & Hudson, London, 1975; *Woman of Letters: a Life of Virginia Woolf*, Phyllis Rose, Pandora, London, 1986; *Virginia Woolf: a Writer's Life*, Lyndall Gordon, Oxford University Press, Oxford, 1985.

WORDSWORTH, DOROTHY 1771–1855. Writer of diaries. Born in **Cockermouth**; grew up in **Halifax**; briefly lived in **Penrith**, then Norfolk, then near **Bettiscombe**; settled in the Lake District at **Grasmere** and near **Ambleside**; buried at **Grasmere**. *A Passion for the Particular: Dorothy Wordsworth: a Portrait*, Elizabeth Gunn, Gollancz, London, 1981; *Dorothy Wordsworth*, Robert Gittings and Jo Manton, Oxford University Press, Oxford, 1985.

WRIGHT, FRANCES; FANNY WRIGHT; FRANCES D'ARUSMONT 1795–1852. Social reformer; utopianist. Born in **Dundee**, brought up in London;

visits to the USA led to her radical work there; frequently overseas, died in USA. *Frances Wright and the 'Great Experiment'*, Margaret Lane, Manchester University Press, Manchester, 1972; *Fanny Wright: Rebel in America*, C. M. Eckhardt, Harvard University Press, Cambridge, 1984.

WRIGHT, PATIENCE 1725–86. Spy; artist; salon hostess. Most of her life spent in her native USA. Held her salons at **Lonson [Westminster]**; died in EEngland. *Patience Wright: American Artist and Spy in George III's London*, C. C. Sellers, Middletown [Conn.], 1976.

Y y

YONGE, CHARLOTTE MARY 1823–1901. Writer of novels and works for children. Lived all her life at **Otterbourne**, where she is buried. *Charlotte M. Yonge*, Georgina Battiscombe, Constable, London, 1943; *A Chaplet for Charlotte Yonge*, Georgina Battiscombe and Marghanita Laski [eds], Cresset Press, London, 1965.

YOUNG, E[MILY] H[ILDA]; MRS DANIEL 1880–1949. Writer of novels. Born in Northumberland, educated in **Gateshead**; married life in **Bristol**; last years in **Bradford on Avon**.

How to find out more

Readers may wish to find out more about women's history. Clearly different aspects will appeal to different people. What follows are some starting points which may be helpful.

BOOKS

If you want to learn more about the women mentioned by name in the Gazetteer, you will find references in the **Biographical Index** to published works, where these have been traced. These will be either biographies or sometimes autobiographies. Some of their own works also feature in the place entries, mainly novels and other literary writings.

There is a growing literature in the field of women's history, ranging from the general and informative to the highly specialist and academic, often interpreted by feminist theory. A useful starting point for those beginning to explore the past experience of women is: *Discovering Women's History – a practical manual*, Deirdre Beddoe, Pandora Press, London, 1983. It suggests several topics deserving attention and gives guidance on ways to tackle them, with plenty of useful addresses and pointers for further reading, all presented in a way which shows the writer's infectious enthusiasm for her subject.

General books on women in specific periods include:

Eighteenth Century Women: an Anthology, Bridget Hill, Allen & Unwin, London, 1984.

Feminism in Eighteenth Century England, K. M. Rogers, University of Illinois Press, Evanston, 1984.

The Fourth Estate – a History of Women in the Middle Ages, S. Shulamith, Methuen, London, 1983.

Mediaeval Women, Derek Baker [ed.], Blackwell, Oxford, 1979.

Only Halfway to Paradise: Women in Postwar Britain 1945–1968, E. Wilson, Tavistock Press, London, 1980.

Ordinary Lives – a Hundred Years Ago, Carol Adams, Virago Press, London, 1982.

Strong-minded Women and Other Lost Voices from Nineteenth-Century England, Janet H. Murray, Penguin, Harmondsworth, 1984.

Tudor Women: Queens and Commoners, Alison Plowden, Weidenfeld & Nicolson, London, 1979.

The Weaker Vessel: Women's Lot in the Seventeenth Century, Antonia Fraser, Weidenfeld & Nicolson, London, 1984.

Women in Anglo-Saxon England and the Impact of 1066, Christine Fell, British Museum Publications, London, 1984.

Women in England 1870–1950. Jane Lewis, Wheatsheaf Press, Brighton, 1984.

Women in English Society 1500–1800, M. Prior [ed.], Methuen, London, 1985.

Women in Stuart England and America – a Comparative Study, R. Thompson, Routledge & Kegan Paul, London, 1978.

Working Life of Women in the Seventeenth Century, Alice Clark, Routledge & Kegan Paul, London, 1982 [first published in 1919].

Women with a Past. A Brief Account of Some Aspects of Women's History in the Nineteenth and Twentieth Centuries, Annmarie Turnball *et al.,* The Feminist Library, London, 1984.

There are also works which survey women's contributions in particular spheres, be these types of work, social experience, class, age, etc. The following titles cover some of the areas of achievement represented by the women in this Gazetteer:

Architecture
Women Architects: Their Work, Lynne Walker [ed.], Sorella Press, London, 1984.

Art
Angels in the Studio: Women in the Arts and Crafts Movement 1870–1914, Anthea Callen, Astragal Books, London, 1979.

The Obstacle Race: the Fortunes of Women Painters and Their Work, Germaine Greer, Secker & Warburg, London, 1979.

Old Mistresses: Women, Art and Ideology, Rozsika Parker and Griselda Pollock, Routledge & Kegan Paul, London, 1981.

Pre-Raphaelite Sisterhood, Janet Marsh, Quartet, London, 1985.

The Subversive Stitch, Rozsika Parker, Women's Press, London, 1984.

Women Artists: Recognition and Reappraisal from the Early Middle Ages to the Twentieth Century, Karen Petersen and J. J. Wilson, Women's Press, London, 1978.

Design
A Woman's Touch: Women in Design From 1860 to the Present Day, Isabelle Anscombe, Virago Press, London, 1984.

Entertainment
The Joke's on Us, Morwenna Banks and Amanda Swift, Pandora Press, London, 1987.

Health and Welfare
Caring and Sharing: the Centenary History of the Co-operative Women's Guild, Jean Gaffin and David Thomas, Co-operative Union, Manchester, 1983.

A Pictorial History of Nursing, M. Masson, Hamlyn, London, 1985.

Rewriting Nursing History, C. Davies [ed.], Croom Helm, London, 1980.

Literature and Journalism
A Dictionary of Women Writers 1660–1800, Janet Todd [ed.], Methuen, London, 1985.

First Feminists: British Writers 1578–1799, Moira Ferguson, Feminist Press and Indiana University Press, Bloomington, 1985.

Mediaeval Women Writers, Katharina M. Wilson [ed.], Manchester University Press, Manchester, 1985.

Mothers of the Novel: One Hundred Women Novelists Before Jane Austen, Dale Spender, Pandora Press, London, 1986.

Time and Tide Wait for No Man, Dale Spender [ed.], Pandora Press, London, 1984.

Women of Ideas and What Men Have Done to Them, Dale Spender, Ark Paperbacks, London, 1983.

Politics
Biographical Dictionary of British Feminists: Volume 1, 1800–1930, Olive Banks, Harvester Press, Brighton, 1985.

The Cause: a Short History of the Women's Movement in Great Britain, Ray Strachey, Virago Press, London, 1978 [first published 1928].

One Hand Tied Behind Us: the Rise of the Women's Suffrage Movement, Jill Liddington and Jill Norris, Virago Press, London, 1978.

The Suffragette Movement: an Intimate Account of Persons and Ideals, E. Sylvia Pankhurst, Virago Press, London, 1978 [first published 1931].

Sweet Freedom: the Struggle for Women's Liberation, Anna Coote and Beatrix Campbell, Picador, London, 1982.

Women and Popular Struggles: a History of English and Scottish Working-Class Women, James D. Young, Mainstream Publications, 1985.

Women in Protest 1800–1850, M. Thomas and J. Grimmett, Croom Helm, London, 1982.

Religion
Women of Grace: a Biographical Dictionary of British Women Saints, Martyrs and Reformers, Kathleen Parbury, Oriel Press, Stocksfield, 1984.

Science, Technology and Medicine
Hypatia's Heritage: a History of Women in Science From Antiquity to the Late Nineteenth Century, Margaret Alic, Women's Press, London, 1986.

Trade Unionism
Women in the Labour Movement, Linda Middleton [ed.], Croom Helm, London, 1977.

Women in Trade Unions, Barbara Drake, Virago Press, London, 1984.

Women Workers and the Trades Union Movement, Sarah Boston, Davis-Poynter, London, 1980.

Travel
The Blessings of a Good Tweed Skirt, Mary Russell, Collins, London, 1986.

Britannia's Daughters: Women of the British Empire, Joanna Trollope, Hutchinson, London, 1983.

Travelling Ladies, Victorian Adventuresses, Alexandra Allen, Jupiter, London, 1980.

Victorian Lady Travellers, Dorothy Middleton, Chicago, 1982.

In addition there are many general works, often focusing on how women's history has remained unwritten for so long; a few titles are:

Hidden from History, Sheila Rowbotham, Pluto Press, London, 1983.

Not in God's Image: Women in History, J. O'Faolain and L. Martines, Virago Press, 1973.

Virgins and Viragos: a History of Women in Scotland from 1660–1970, Rosaline K. Marshall, Collins, London, 1983.

Women, Katharine Moore, Batsford, London, 1970.

Several bibliographies of women's studies literature have also been published; many include sections on history.

Biographical dictionaries are the place to begin tracking down individual women, although the amount of detail given will vary. In addition to the many volumned *Dictionary of National Biography*, these titles can be helpful:

The Dinner Party: a Symbol of our Heritage, Judy Chicago, Anchor Press/Doubleday, Garden City, New York, 1979.

The Europa Biographical Dictionary of British Women, Anne Crawford *et al.* [ed.], Europa Publications, London, 1983.

The Macmillan Dictionary of Women's Biography, Jennifer Uglow [ed.], Macmillan Press, London, 1982.

As far as possible, these are recent works which should be available through local libraries. If they are not held in the local stock, then they can be ordered through the national network known as the Inter-library Loan Scheme. The library staff will be able to help with this. Staff at your local library may be members of Women in Libraries, an organisation of women working in libraries to improve services to women, to ensure that works by and about women are available in library collections and to support and encourage women library staff. They will also help in tracking down articles in journals, magazines, newspapers and other periodical literature.

There are several British publishers which specialise in books by, about or of interest to women. These include Pandora Press, Virago Press, The Women's Press, Sheba Feminist Publishers, Stramullion, and others. Most large publishing houses now include women's studies books in their lists. These publications are for sale at most bookshops and, if not in stock, can be ordered through the bookshops. There are some bookshops which sell only books of interest to women, and these will also undertake searches for out of print books. These include:

Edinburgh
Womanzone, 119 Buccleugh Street, Edinburgh

Liverpool
Carol Maginn, 58 Grosvenor Street, Wallasey, Merseyside.

London
Sisterwrite, 190 Upper Street, London N1

Silver Moon, 68 Charing Cross Road, London WC2

There is also The Women's Press Bookclub, 34 Great Sutton Street, London EC1V 0DX, which is a mail order bookclub with a quarterly list covering a wide range of women's interests and issues, and women's fiction.

There are also some specialist libraries which will be of interest:

Bath
The Feminist Archive, University of Bath, Claverton Down, Bath BA2 7AY

London
Fawcett Library, City of London Polytechnic, Old Castle Street, London, E1

The Feminist Library, First Floor, Hungerford House, Victoria Embankment, London WC2

Hall-Carpenter Archives, 67/69 Cawrocs Street, London, EC1N 6DP

Manchester
Lesbian Archive Collective, Lesbian Link, 61A Bloom Street, Manchester

COURSES

Most sizeable communities will provide adult education courses in a wide variety of subjects during the day or in the evenings. These may be organised through local community colleges, the Workers' Educational Association [WEA], university continuing education or extra-mural departments. Your local library should have a current list of what is available locally. Many offer crèche facilities. Subjects of interest to women are often offered, looking at women's history or literature or art, or contemporary issues. If nothing is offered on the programme, contact the organisers and tell them your interest. They will respond to local demands, and can usually find tutors or class leaders quite easily.

Full-time courses in women's studies are being offered by universities and colleges at a variety of levels. The Open University, based at Milton Keynes, also has courses which can be followed at home, using directed reading, television and radio programmes in its distance learning scheme, with regional tutors. The Feminist Library in London [address above] keeps up-to-date lists of current women's studies courses, many of which are inter-disciplinary.

WOMEN'S HISTORY GROUPS

Some women have organised themselves into small local history groups to explore the women's history of their community. Sometimes members have their own individual interests and projects, but they get together for mutual support and to try out ideas. Other groups may all be working on one research venture.

Some are well established by now. These include:

Birmingham Feminist History Group,
c/o Bleak House, 137 Newton Road, Birmingham 11

Liverpool Feminist History Group,
c/o 12 Devonshire Road, Liverpool 8

London Feminist History Group,
c/o The Feminist Library, Hungerford House, Victoria Embankment, London, WC2

Manchester Women's History Group,
c/o Manchester Area Resource Centre, Bloom Street, Manchester

Sheffield Women's History Group,
78 Walkley Road, Sheffield 6

Welsh Feminist History Group,
c/o Department of Arts and Languages, Polytechnic of Wales, Pontypridd, Mid Glamorgan

Your local women's centre may be able to put you in touch with other women in your area who are researching women's history nearby. Equally the museum, library, record office or oral history archive may know of people who share your interests. They should certainly be able to give you the contact person for general local history societies, some of whose members may be able to help and encourage you.

MUSEUMS AND ART GALLERIES

Women, Heritage and Museums [WHAM] is a new group which aims to give women's heritage and history more gallery space in museums. Its members are museum users and museum workers. They seek to present a more balanced view of the heritage by giving fairer coverage of women's creative work and their contribution to all aspects of history and the material heritage and to promote positive images of women in all museum activities. WHAM also aims to draw attention to the potential of museums and art galleries as research resources for women's history. Most museums are able to display only a proportion of their collections at any one time, but their reserve collections, associated documentation, small specialist libraries and research files can generally be consulted by appointment. WHAM is organised into regional networks. The national contact is:

Margaret Brooks
Department of Sound Records, Imperial War Museum, Lambeth Road, London, SE1 6HZ

Museums with collections of special relevance to women's heritage include:

Glasgow
The People's Palace, Glasgow Green, Glasgow

London
Museum of London, 150 London Wall, London EC2

Imperial War Museum,
Lambeth Road, London SE1

Science Museum,
Exhibition Road, South Kensington, London SW7

All museums and galleries hold material of interest to women, and staff are keen to respond to local interests. Your local museum's resources may surprise you.

RECORD OFFICES AND ARCHIVES

County Record Offices and the Public Record Offices hold collections of original documents which may be useful in many fields of women's history: parish registers; wills; marriage settlements; letters; diaries; inventories; official records of towns, schools, institutions, churches and chapels; building plans; family papers; court records; guild records; manorial records, etc. Most are open to the public on a regular basis and all are staffed by knowlegable people who are willing to help and encourage newcomers to history research.

'Tracing your Matrilineal Ancestry', an article by Julia Carley published in *History Workshop Journal* 16, 1983, highlights the problems of doing family history research into the lives of female forebears, and offers some solutions.

There are other specialist archives associated with businesses, public institutions, professional bodies etc. These may require special appointments for consultations. Local record offices will have details of them.

HOLIDAYS

There are many small guest houses, hotels and other establishments offering accommodation and catering by and for women and their children and friends. Some of these are named in a series of booklets covering England and Wales. These are entitled: *A Feminist Local History and Holiday Guide*, all written and published by Susan Evesdaughter c/o 49 St George's Road, London E7. She has produced guides to the North, Central England, Wales and the Border Country, the Home Counties, the West Country and London.

PUBLIC MONUMENTS

You may also on your travels have noticed that women feature in much public sculpture and statuary. Although these are sometimes memorials to specific women, they are more often allegorical female figures representing peace or victory or motherhood or art or industry etc. *Monuments and Maidens: the Allegory of the Female Form*, Marina Warner, Weidenfeld & Nicolson, London, 1985, is enlightening reading which may make you look with new eyes at these monuments.

WHICHEVER LINE OF WOMEN'S HISTORY YOU PURSUE, ENJOY IT.

Pandora Press is a feminist press, an imprint of Unwin Hyman. Our list is varied: we publish new fiction, reprint fiction, women crime writers, history, biography and autobiography, social issues, health and humour written by women and celebrating the lives and achievements of women the world over. For further information about Pandora Press books, please write to the Mailing List Dept. at Pandora Press, Unwin Hyman Ltd, 15/17 Broadwick Street, London W1V 1FP; George Allen & Unwin Australia pty Ltd., PO Box 794, 8 Napier St, North Sydney, NSW 2060, Australia; or, Allen & Unwin, Inc, 8 Winchester Place, Winchester, MA 01890, USA.

Some Pandora titles you will enjoy:

Discovering Women's History

A Practical Manual

Deirdre Beddoe

This is a practical handbook for people who are prepared to venture into attics, art galleries, cinemas, libraries, museums and record offices in pursuit of the history of British women. It is also for those who prefer to sit in an armchair and read old novels and women's magazines, or watch old films on television.

Discovering Women's History offers down-to-earth and constructive advice on how to locate and use all these sources to find out about the lives of ordinary women in Britain from 1880 to 1945. There are useful sections on publicizing your findings and a helpful address list.

Discovering Women's History is an enjoyable and informative read for anyone interested in British Women's history, from sixth formers to women's groups and local history societies or interested individuals. It transforms historical research into an exciting, practical activity available to us all.

'An invaluable and fascinating guide to the raw material for anyone approaching this underexplored territory.'
Sean French, *The Sunday Times*

'Deirdre Beddoe's book does exactly what it sets out to: it offers a clear, detailed and well-conceived guide to anyone who is interested, or thinks they could be interested, in digging into the past . . . She encourages us to begin from where we are now, to find out about our own family or school or street or workplace; to reappropriate our past as a way of understanding what we are and what we could be.'
Margaret Walters, *City Limits*

'A long-overdue guide to historical source material many people genuinely believe does not exist . . . (it) deserves a place in every history department.' Sallie Purkis, *Teaching History*

'Deirde Beddoe's book is more than simply a practical manual; it is a feminist history, a researcher's bible and a fascinating glimpse into the lives of our forebears.'
Katie Campbell, *Spare Rib*

'It's thrilling and rewarding and jolly good fun.'
Ann Jones, *South Wales Argus*

ISBN 0-86358-008-4

Price £4.95 net

Half The Earth

Women's Experiences of Travel Worldwide

Half The Earth is a travellers' handbook written by and for women. It addresses crucial issues and experiences ignored by most guidebooks, issues concerning safety and harassment, the assumptions that are made about us in other countries and the particular contacts we, as women, are able to make.

Compiled with the contributions of over 300 women – and covering some 70 countries worldwide – these personal accounts span every kind of travel. There are pieces on life in Tokyo and on working in the

Arab world, on trekking alone in Nepal, contacts with the feminist movement in Colombia and, not least, holidaying closer to home – in Mediterranean Europe and in the United States. Supported with detailed listings, informed country by country introductions and with constant updatings in mind, this is a book that prepares and inspires.

ISBN 0-86358-092-0

Price £4.95 net

Jane and May Morris
A Biographical Story 1839–1938
Jan Marsh

'Why should there be any special record of me when I have never done any special work?' *Jane Morris.*

'I'm a remarkable woman – always was, though none of you seemed to think so.' *May Morris.*

As the wife of William Morris and icon of the Pre-Raphaelites, Jane Morris's fame is reflected against that of a famous Brotherhood. Her daughter May has also been allotted a walk-on part in all that has been written about those men – William Morris, Dante Gabriel Rossetti, George Bernard Shaw notably – who feature in Jan Marsh's story. This time, however, it is the women who take centre-stage. This story of the lives of celebrated mother and daughter spans a century. It is a fascinating tale, told with narrative zest, illuminating the relationships of both with the women around them. It reveals them as women of their times and, scrupulously researched, gives us new insights into the artistic movement and the society in which they lived. Carefully chosen illustrations complete the picture of Jane and May Morris.

ISBN 0-86358-026-2

Price £4.95 net

Woman of Letters
A Life of Virginia Woolf
Phyllis Rose

'I view Woolf's feminism as the crux of her emotional as well as her
intellectual life' says Phyllis Rose in this compelling interpretative
biography.

In presenting Woolf as a 'woman of letters', Rose stimulates a new
way of viewing this important writer and the shape of her career,
striving to overcome the usual emphasis on Woolf's illness and suicide
by showing the extent to which she directed her own life. She tells the
story of Virginia Woolf's life as Woolf herself might have perceived it,
with a point of view that is feminist. She revises the image of Woolf as
an isolated technician unconcerned with social reality, giving us
instead the picture of a woman immersed in issues that have become,
if anything, more pressing since her death.

'Phyllis Rose writes with considerable insight and feeling of Woolf's
attitude to herself as a woman and of the possibility of being a woman
writer'
Margaret Drabble, New Statesman

'An admirable book'
Frank Kermode, New York Review

ISBN-86358-066-1

Price £3.95 net

Ellen and Edy
A biography of Ellen Terry and her daughter,
Edith Craig, 1847–1947
Joy Melville

Ellen Terry lived during the reign of Queen Victoria when women
were required to live according to the strictest of moral codes. She
broke the rules of that code, marrying three times, living with her
lover, Edward Godwin by whom she had two illegitimate children.
Yet, paradoxically, she demonstrates in her life and in her beliefs the
concerns of her age and, despite her huge public fame – modern

equivalents might be Madonna or Meryl Streep – she has remained an enigmatic figure. Her daughter, Edith Craig, was a talented theatre producer and costume designer, a suffragette who founded the Pioneer Players and who lived for most of her life with another woman, Christopher St John. Joy Melville focuses on the everyday lives, and the loves, of Ellen and Edy. Whilst she follows Ellen's adventures in England and America and her relations with, among others, Edward Godwin, Henry Irving and George Bernard Shaw, this is above all the story of the stormy, mutually possessive, but ultimately strong and loving bond between a remarkable mother and daughter. Edith Craig emerges for the first time as a person worthy of attention in her own right, and the biography is enhanced by carefully chosen and illuminating illustration.

ISBN 0-86358-078-5

Price £6.95 net

This Narrow Place

Sylvia Townsend Warner and Valentine Ackland:
Life, Letters and Politics, 1930–1951

Wendy Mulford

'Sylvia kept hearing of a young woman in the village who lived alone. . . She wore trousers, which were not commonly found on young women at that period. Not in Dorset, anyway. And she wrote poetry.'
William Maxwell, editor of Sylvia Townsend Warner's *Letters*.

'I had shown her some poems of mine; very weakly and bad ones, and she had seen good in them, or perhaps seen good in me, and become friendly to me.'
Valentine Ackland, For Sylvia: An Honest Account

Sylvia Townsend Warner and Valentine Ackland were remarkable and unorthodox women. They met in Dorset in 1926, shortly after the publication of Sylvia's first novel, *Lolly Willowes*, whilst Valentine was recuperating from an abortion and an unhappy marriage. Both women became politically committed writers, Communist Party activists and peace campaigners; together they embarked upon literary and radical careers that would lead to the collaborative volume of poetry, *Whether a Dove or a Seagull* [1934], and take them to Spain during the Civil War and to the USA. They lived together for nearly 40 years, until Valentine's death. It was a relationship that spanned the heady period of left-wing cultural activity during the 1930s and 1940s, and survived the strains of Sylvia's increasing fame as a novelist and short story writer as well as Valentine's search for consolation through drinking and other relationships.

This Narrow Place celebrates a poignant and unique partnership – personal, literary and political – and for the fist time throws light on Sylvia's mysterious lover, the less well known poet, Valentine Ackland. Focusing on the most politically active years of their relationship, Wendy Mulford sets the scene of their lives together and their important, but hitherto overlooked, contribution to the radical politics and culture of that era. In these contexts, she examines the literary works of those years, reclaiming for Sylvia Townsend Warner her rightful status as a powerful novelist and polemicist, uncovering the richness of Valentine Ackland's poetry, and drawing on unpublished letters, journals and photographs to bring us a vivid and moving picture of their lives together.

ISBN 0-86358-056-4

Price £14.95 net cloth

ISBN 0-86358-262-1

Price £5.95 net pbk

Lady Morgan
The Life and Times of Sydney Owenson
Mary Campbell

Lady Morgan was born Sydney Owenson in 1776. She was the daughter of an itinerant actor, Robert Owenson, a native Irishman and proudly nationalistic, and the strictly Methodist, very English Jane Hill of Shrewsbury. Brought up in Dublin, she was forced by fluctuations in her father's fortune to become a governess at the start of her career, but nevertheless acquired a title on her wedding day and established one of the most influential literary and social salons in Dublin, which she later transferred to London. She also created an eager and large readership in both Ireland and England for her novels, like the spectacularly successful *The Wild Irish Girl*, and was the first woman writer to be granted a pension – £300 per annum – for her service to the 'world of letters'.

Sydney Owenson was believed by some, including Thackeray's own daughter, to be the model for Becky Sharpe. Whether she was or not, like Becky, she rose by her wits and talents to shine in London and Paris society. But she was so much more than that. Dublin was her native city but she was also admired in France and Italy for her determination to assert her independence as a woman writer in an age of discrimination; for her radical and democratic opinions, and for her pioneering form of nationalism.

Mary Campbell's biography of this fascinating woman takes us through one of the most evocative periods in Ireland's history: between the Act of the Union in 1800, which ended the elegant heyday of the Georgian Ascendancy, and the Great Famine which finally finished off what was left of the old Gaelic culture. Against this background of social and political upheaval, Lady Morgan emerges as a brave and resilient woman whose 'national tales' – 'tissues of woven air' as she called them – were serious enough to influence politics and policies, and to contribute to the ideas upon which modern Ireland was founded. In one of her Prefaces, Lady Morgan reminded her readers that she wrote in an age 'when to be a woman was to be without defence, and to be a patriot was to be a criminal.' She was proud to be both, and spent her life fighting vigorously and successfully to improve the status of her sex and country.

ISBN 0-86358-203-6

Price £5.95 net pbk